# WE THE MINERS

# WE THE MINERS

## Self-Government

## in the

## California Gold Rush

ANDREA G. MCDOWELL

Harvard University Press

*Cambridge, Massachusetts* · *London, England*

2022

Second printing

Publication of this book has been supported through the generous provisions of the
Maurice and Lula Bradley Smith Memorial Fund.

Library of Congress Cataloging-in-Publication Data
Names: McDowell, A. G., author.
Title: We the miners : self-government in the California gold rush / Andrea
G. McDowell.
Description: Cambridge, Massachusetts : Harvard University Press, 2022. |
Includes bibliographical references and index.
Identifiers: LCCN 2021045373 | ISBN 9780674248113 (cloth)
Subjects: LCSH: Gold miners—Legal status, laws,
etc. —California—History—19th century. |
Democracy—California—History—19th century. | Emigration and
immigration law—California—History—19th century. | Indians, Treatment
of—California. | California—Gold discoveries. | California—Race
relations—History—19th century. | California—History—1846–1850.
Classification: LCC F865 .M154 2022 | DDC 979.4/04—dc23/eng/20211018
LC record available at https://lccn.loc.gov/2021045373

# CONTENTS

# WE THE MINERS

# Introduction

Two gold mining partners, Price and Easterbrook, shared a tent at Oak Bottom in Northern California in 1851. They spent the evening of March 15 drinking and playing cards with their neighbors, whose tent also served as a store. Price left first and went home to sleep. Easterbrook ordered more alcohol but was refused, so he asked for his bill. As he was paying, Price called out to him from his bed, saying, "Don't be paying out other people's money." According to the record of Easterbrook's subsequent trial, "he said he was not paying out other people's money and would shoot Price," and went over to their tent. The neighbors, whose names were Isaac Roop and Mr. Short, then heard Easterbrook say, "Prepare yourself, for G-d d—n you, I intend to shoot you," to which Price calmly replied, "Don't talk so, but lay down and go to sleep." Easterbrook made some further threats, and then there was the report of a gun.[1]

Roop and Short rushed over to find Price bleeding and unable to speak and Easterbrook running away. He stopped and came back when they called him. Told that he had killed Price, Easterbrook said, "Have I shot him?" When Roop and Short replied that "he most undoubtedly had," he said, "Do what you please with me, it was an accident and I was drunk." Price died about an hour later without having said another word.

The next day, the people of the neighborhood brought Easterbrook to Shasta City, ten miles away, to be tried by a "a meeting of the citizens," also known in California as "Judge Lynch." Modern readers brace themselves for a quick and unruly hanging, but what follows was very

1

formal. Enos Dutton took the chair, while R. W. Crenshaw, Esq., served as secretary and subsequently sent the official account of the meeting to the *Sacramento Transcript*, from which these facts are taken. "A motion was made and seconded, to appoint a committee of three to select a jury of twelve men, to try the cause before the people, which was carried unanimously: Whereupon, Messrs. Welsh, Weber, and Daniel Hine, were appointed said committee." The committee accordingly elected twelve jurors, all of whom are named in the report. Further motions were made and seconded that the prisoner should have a fair and impartial trial; that the jury call witnesses; that A. M. Herron be appointed to carry out the verdict of the jury; and that the chairman swear the jury and the witnesses. All of these motions were adopted.

The witnesses were the neighbors, Isaac Roop and Mr. Short. When they finished testifying, Easterbrook was asked if he had anything to say in his defense. He answered, "Gentlemen of the Jury: I stand before you as a criminal, as a man on the verge of another world, and as true as I believe there is a God in Heaven, I feel in my mind guiltless of any premeditated intention to kill Mr. Price." He told the jury that he had a wife and three young children. "Taking my life would not bring to life Mr. Price," he added. "It would only make one more widow, and three more orphans; and on their account only do I plead for mercy."

Having heard the evidence, the jury retired, elected a foreman and a secretary from among themselves, debated, and reached a verdict, which they all signed. Their secretary read it out to the prisoner and the assembly: "The Jury are of the unanimous opinion that Pearson G. G. Easterbrook is guilty of murder in the first degree, and that he be punished immediately by hanging by the neck, until he is dead." Easterbrook was executed an hour later, between five and six o'clock in the evening.

This trial was run by a meeting of the whole population following parliamentary procedure. The assembled crowd elected a chairman, made motions and voted upon them, chose attorneys, and adopted an elaborate procedure for choosing jurors. The record reads like minutes: it uses formal language, is largely in the passive voice, and focuses on decisions rather than debate, if indeed there was any debate. For all we know, the throng was drinking and shouting and breaking into fist-fights, but that behavior would never appear in the transcript.

As this book shows, miners held meetings to run all their trials and also to adopt law codes in the absence of any government presence in the mining region, which lasted for years after gold was discovered. When America took California in 1848 at the end of the Mexican War, it was a remote, sparsely inhabited, largely unproductive territory for which the United States had no particular plans. The journey to San Francisco from the nearest states, Texas and Iowa, was some 1,500 miles overland. San Francisco's population in 1847 was only around eight hundred souls, and that included two companies of New York Volunteers stationed there during the war with Mexico.[2] Kimball Dimmick, a captain in the Volunteers, repeated a fellow officer's remark that San Francisco was so boring that "he gets no real satisfaction here except when he can catch a flea and kill it or get drunk."[3]

The interior was barely settled, and the Sacramento Valley, four hundred miles long and an average of forty miles wide, was, as Bancroft put it, "practically undisturbed by civilization."[4] Fifty or so Americans and Europeans held enormous Mexican land grants in the northern half of the valley, and some of them reached as far east as the foothills, but none extended into the mountains where gold would later be discovered.[5] The social and trading hub of the Sacramento Valley was John Sutter's adobe fort, which also served as inn, warehouse, and retail store.[6] A Swiss who had taken Mexican citizenship, Sutter held fifty thousand acres. He granted farms to American pioneers and frontiersmen and employed hundreds of Indians and some Hawaiians to farm and tend his cattle.[7]

With the gold discovery, hundreds of thousands of people poured in, but Congress failed to provide for the territory because it was paralyzed by the question of whether California would join the union as slave or a free state.[8] The military governors of California—General Kearney, Colonel (later General) Mason, and General Riley—governed the civilian population without explicit authority. Riley said that "the law of necessity" allowed him to exercise this role, but he did not go so far as to make laws.[9] The citizens could not even continue to use the Mexican laws because, in the words of California's first governor, Peter Burnett, they "knew nothing of the laws of Mexico and had no means of learning" since they were "in a language we did not understand and we had no translations and for some time could have none."[10] California was therefore in a legal limbo until its population went ahead and adopted a constitution without congressional approval in December 1849.[11] It was not until the summer of 1850, more than two years after the discovery of gold, that the new state courts were finally organized and ready to hear cases. By then, the mining camps had become accustomed to managing on their own.

The circumstances of the early gold rush hardly seemed conducive to orderly meetings. The population was made up almost entirely of relatively young men from around the globe who were constantly on the move, chasing rumors of rich diggings elsewhere. None of them planned to stay; they had come to California to get rich and go home to the family and friends they had left behind. They lived in temporary "round tents, square tents, plank hovels, log cabins" and even shelters "formed of pine boughs and covered with old calico shirts."[12] Hardly any married women lived in the American camps, that is, wives who might induce men to put down roots.[13] The first historian of the gold rush, Hubert Howe Bancroft, wrote that order and respectability would only come about in the mining towns "by the presence of woman, when she came, as well as of churches, schools, lyceums and piano-fortes."[14] Families and voluntary associations would transform the camps into communities.

In communities, people know one another and care about their reputations, but the inhabitants of new mining camps were strangers to one another and, in a sense, to their communities at home. A well-known frontier rhyme went like this:

> *What was your name in the States?*
> *Was it Thompson, or Johnson or Bates?*
> *Did you murder your wife and fly for your life?*
> *Say what was your name in the States?*[15]

This suggests that criminals came West to escape their pasts, but the California records suggest almost the opposite: respectable young men shed their principles and inhibitions in the anonymity of the mining camps. Temperance men drank; religious men did not keep the Sabbath; and heads of families gambled. And why not? As one observer wrote, it was hard to see the evil in that when "in truth, the whole mining system in California is one great gambling or, better perhaps, lottery transaction."[16] Miner Daniel Woods met an old, drunken sailor who said (and others confirmed) that while staggering drunk, he had kicked over a stone, and under it found a lump of gold worth $500.[17] This made a mockery of the values instilled at home.

The absence of any authority or institutions in the mines, the floating population of young men, and the effect of instant riches and terrible disappointments all made an unlikely setting for community meetings and parliamentary procedure. But while the diggings were lawless, in the formal sense, they were not chaotic. The miners' habit of using meetings for all joint projects from criminal trials to engineering projects to organizing Fourth of July celebrations imposed a degree of order and even surprising formality on the mining camps. The accounts of these meetings show that the miners knew basic rules of order. They understood the vocabulary and the process of meetings, could propose resolutions, and in many cases could assume the role of chairman or secretary. Most importantly, all accepted the decision of the majority. In other words, the miners in the California gold rush shared a culture of meetings with which they performed some of the functions of government at a time when California had minimal government and essentially no law.

This book is about the miners' use of parliamentary procedure as a form of governance, both in matters that are ordinarily the province of the legislature or the courts and for the organization and day-to-day management of large mining undertakings. In the absence of government in California, the miners used meetings to enact mining codes, resolve private disputes, hold criminal trials, and eject foreigners from the mines. And finally, this book examines their failure to organize to stop groups that massacred Indians and to speak out against those that expelled Spanish-speaking miners from the diggings, although at least some Americans deplored these outrages.

The miners' organizational skills and taste for procedure was shared by nineteenth-century Americans everywhere. As Alexis de Tocqueville wrote in an oft-quoted passage, "Americans of all ages, all conditions, and all dispositions, constantly form associations. . . . The Americans make associations to give entertainments, to found establishments for education, to build inns, to construct churches, to diffuse books, to send missionaries to the antipodes; and [to] found hospitals, prisons, and schools."[18] In short, for all the good works that the state did not do and for fellowship and entertainment.

De Tocqueville's observation that Americans had a particular knowledge of "how to combine" has been a jumping-off point for much scholarship about civil associations in American history. In *Bowling Alone*, the now classic account of the late-twentieth-century decline of America's long tradition of associations, Robert Putnam provides evidence for de Tocqueville's observation about the American habit of forming associations. He demonstrates that in the nineteenth and early twentieth centuries, Americans participated in an astonishing number and diversity of organizations and voluntary associations, such as churches, bridge clubs, and Veterans of Foreign Wars posts. Putnam is most interested the benefits to the participants of belonging to multiple groups and regularly interacting with fellow members. He argues that the members built social capital to advance their careers and to provide support in times of need, and that the resulting network of connections created community out of what might otherwise have been just thousands of individuals living in the same area.[19]

De Tocqueville himself, on the other hand, was interested in associations not so much as wellsprings of community as in their usefulness in getting things done. Associations as such were not uniquely American; there were an astounding number and variety of clubs and associations in Britain and its colonies in the eighteenth and nineteenth centuries.[20] What struck de Tocqueville about America's associations was their ability to undertake new initiatives, big and small. In England, he wrote, it was men of rank who took the lead in projects like founding hospitals and schools, whereas in France, it was the government. In America, associations "stand in lieu of those powerful private individuals whom the equality of condition has swept away."[21]

All American citizens had learned how to get many men to work together toward a common goal, which de Tocqueville called "an art," "a science," and "a general theory." Their participation in political associations, which served as "large free schools" of association, taught them "how order is maintained among a large number of men, and by what contrivance they are made to advance, harmoniously, and methodically, to the same object."[22] The "science" de Tocqueville had in mind was almost certainly the rules of parliamentary procedure that evolved in the British House of Commons and that were adopted by the American colonial bodies and, later, the United States Congress and state assemblies.[23] These are now widely used as a tool for facilitating any kind of group decision-making in corporations, voluntary associations, faculty meetings, and an endless list of other bodies. A recent edition of *Robert's Rules of Order* called it "the best method yet devised to enable assemblies of any size . . . to arrive at the general will on the maximum number of questions of varying complexity in a minimum amount of time" no matter how divided opinions may have been at the outset.[24]

As Thomas Jefferson noted, however, it is "really not of so great importance" that the rules were the *best* of their kind: "It is much more material that there should be a rule to go by, than what the rule is."[25] Without clear rules, it is difficult to get things done, as Jefferson observed when he attended the lower house of the Maryland assembly in 1766. He was surprised to see three, four, and five of the legislators speaking at once; when a motion was made, "the speaker instead of putting the question in the usual form only asked the gentlemen whether they chose that such or such a thing should be done, and was answered by a yes sir, or no sir; and tho' the voices appeared frequently to be divided, they never would go to the trouble of dividing the house, but the clerk entered the resolution, I supposed, as he thought proper."[26] In short, the members did not know what they had voted for and did not know the final tally. Jefferson, who studied parliamentary procedure throughout his life, later published the first American handbook on the subject, *Manual of Parliamentary Practice for the Use of the Senate of the United States* (1801).

Parliamentary practice also includes steps for organizing a mass meeting or a new association from scratch—and this is what was so useful in the gold rush. The first step for transforming a crowd into a body is that some person comes forward and says, "The meeting will please come to order; I move that Mr. A. act as chairman of this meeting." Someone else seconds the motion, and the first speaker asks those present to vote. If the majority says aye, the motion is carried and Mr. A takes the chair. A secretary is then elected by the same means. From here, someone may offer a series of resolutions prepared in advance, which are then seconded and put to a vote. Alternatively, someone can move the appointment of a committee to prepare resolutions, and in this case, the chair nominates a committee or takes nominations from the floor. The committee retires to draft the resolutions and reports back. Its proposed resolutions may be adopted at once or debated, modified, and, finally, voted upon.[27]

America was not just a nation of joiners, but also a nation of organizers. Citizens in the Eastern states often used parliamentary procedure to organize themselves to achieve an end. For instance, in a particularly early case, the citizens of New York met at the City Hotel on February 17, 1817, to raise funds "for the relief of the Poor, then suffering from the extreme inclemency of the weather, and other causes." They elected a general committee, which directed the chairman, secretary, and treasurer to report their findings to the public . . . and they were on their way.[28]

In 1842, citizens of Greenwood, South Carolina, met to found a lyceum "to promote the advancement of Science and Literature" and for "procuring the services of able lecturers."[29] At a meeting of the people of Greenwood, "the Rev. William P. Hill was called to the Chair, and Geo. W. Curtiss appointed Secretary." A preamble and constitution for the new lyceum had been prepared in advance and were presented to the assembly.

Several states to the north in 1842, the citizens living north of the river in Nashua, New Hampshire, held a meeting in response to a town meeting south of the river in Nashua regarding the erection of a town house. They chose a chairman and a secretary, and after several gentleman set forth their regret and surprise "that they should be excluded from all share in the management of town affairs in which they were deeply interested," the meeting appointed a committee of five to prepare a set of suitable resolutions and report back in two days. Said report and resolutions were unanimously adopted and one thousand copies printed.[30]

In all three cases, individuals united to form a brand-new body for the purpose of carrying out a project, founding an organization, or expressing the feelings of the population. Thanks to widespread participation in meetings, Americans of all classes and professions were versed in the forms and language of parliamentary procedure. In 1845, Luther Stearns Cushing published *Manual of Parliamentary Practice* for ordinary citizens.[31] The *Law Reporter*, in endorsing the book, stated that "the necessity of such a work as this has been very generally felt in our country, where almost every citizen is occasionally called upon to exercise the duties of a presiding officer."[32]

The miners brought this knowledge with them from their homes in the States or on the frontier and put it to use in California, where they used it to organize mining operations and, most importantly for present purposes, to make and enforce laws. Joseph Warren Wood's journal includes a wry description of "a meeting of the citizens to revise the laws" in Jacksonville on Sunday, January 20, 1850. "Here was democracy in its simplicity," he wrote, "as simple as in the case supposed by Paine in his work entitled 'Common Sense.'" He thought the actual proceedings were amateurish, however. "The People had curious Ideas & curious understandings or rather misunderstandings," Wood said. "I left the assembly while they were adopting a criminal code & an Englishman was telling how many of the States of the World he had been in."[33] By June 25, 1852, however, Wood remembered only good things about this and similar assemblies, writing that "[t]he laws were wise and adapted to the circumstances of the case. The meetings were organized and effective, and the miners enacted laws that were both wise and practical."[34]

J. D. Borthwick, a Scot who published an account of his three years in California for readers in Great Britain, included a very similar description of a miners' meeting "for legislative purposes." The proceedings again took place in front of a store; the chairman used an empty pork barrel as his platform, and the secretary placed his writing materials on a pile of empty boxes. "The chairman . . . told [the crowd] the object for which the meeting had been called, and said he would be happy to hear any gentleman who had any remarks to offer; whereupon some one proposed an amendment of the law relating to a certain description of claim, arguing the point in a very neat speech." Following some discussion, the matter was put to a vote, and the ayes carried the motion. Several other rules were enacted in the same manner. "The meeting was then declared to be dissolved, and accordingly dribbled into the store, where the legislators, in small detachments, pledged each other in cocktails as fast as the storekeeper could mix them."[35] Though the setting was casual, the proceedings themselves were strictly formal.

Borthwick, like de Tocqueville, considered this organizational skill to be unique to Americans, noting that they were "of all the people in the world the most prompt to organize and combine to carry out a common object." It was in their blood, he said.

> They are trained to it from their youth in their innumerable, and to a foreigner unintelligible, caucus-meetings, commit-tees, conventions, and so forth, by means of which they bring about the election of every officer in the State, from the President down to the policeman; while the fact of every man belonging to a fire company, a militia company, or something of that sort . . . accustoms them also to the duty of choosing their own leaders, and to the necessity of afterwards recognizing them as such by implicit obedience.[36]

Frank Marryat, an Englishman who had come to write about California hunting and racing, of all things, also remarked on the Americans' success as legislatures. "The mining population have been allowed to constitute their own laws relative to the appointment of 'claims,'" he observed, "and it is astonishing how well this system works."[37]

French observers themselves remarked on the Americans' skill at self-organization. Albert Bernard de Roushaile did not have a particularly high opinion of Americans generally. He described them as a "savage and primitive race . . . They always carry revolvers and draw them at the least provocation. . . . As a race, they laugh at honor and decency whenever it is to their advantage to do so," and much more of the same. But Roushaile did praise political meetings in California: "[T]hey are always orderly, quite unlike our meetings in France. If ten Frenchmen come together, they will be quarreling and insulting one another within five minutes. Whenever government at home sees a crowd gathering on the street, the troops are at once called in to break it up."[38] The French *Journal des Débats,* quoted in the California *Placer Times* of December 1, 1849, had fulsome praise for the skill with which Americans colonized California, in contrast to the French difficulties in Algeria. It provided a useful lesson for the French, the paper said, "that laborious but timid population— enemies of anarchy, but who do not know how to unite and organize themselves—which forms the immense majority of the French Society."[39]

The Scot Borthwick also thought that the French lacked the "cohesiveness and mutual confidence necessary for the successful prosecution of a joint undertaking." They never carried out the kind of operations that required the cooperation of fifteen to twenty men, he said.[40] It is only fair to point out, however, that between 1855 and 1860, a French company built a water company in Nevada County at a cost of $950,000, so they were evidently not hopeless.[41]

The mining codes offered the ultimate opportunity for the miners to apply their republican skills. Miner Joseph Warren Wood wrote, "Every man was a legislator yes! more than a congress man for he had a vote & what was better made more than 8 dol[lars] a day."[42] There were five hundred mining districts in California before 1860, and all of these enacted mining laws, some 175 of which are preserved.[43] In a few cases, the drafters made the most of the occasion, adding wildly ambitions preambles that echoed America's founding documents. The most audacious of all—evoking the constitution—was that of the laws of Warren Hill:

> We the miners and citizens of Warren Hill, in order to form
> a more perfect and correct understanding among ourselves
> and all others that may come among us, respecting our rules
> of mineing [*sic*] our claims of ground, the condition of be-
> coming peaceable and permanent possession therein, to es-
> tablish Justice and secure harmony, do enact and draft the
> Laws as follows.[44]

The epilogue of the Mariposa Mining Code, enacted June 25, 1851, recalls the Declaration of Independence: "That for the full and faithful maintenance of these rules and regulations in our County of Mariposa, we sacredly pledge our honors and our lives."[45] On a less lofty plane, the miners of Dry Creek said they enacted their laws in part because they believed "that it is the duty as well as the right of the miners of every mining section to hold their meetings, organize their district and to pass such laws as they may deem best to govern their own local interest"[46]; while the quartz miners of the Drytown Mining District said that they adopted their rules "for the security peace and harmony of the miners."[47]

The actual "laws" were skeletal and dry. They concerned mainly the practical details about mining claims (maximum claim size, work requirements, notice requirements, and the number of claims a miner could hold) and sometimes established a forum for dispute resolution, procedures for calling future meetings, and other details. In a sense, they were dry because they were successfully lawlike. The drama, if any, was bleached away, and only facts of the meeting and the resolutions are reported in legal language.

The miners most dramatic assumption of government's function was in holding criminal trials. Again, it was the miners' meeting, following parliamentary procedure, that ran the trials, in effect serving as the judge. There was always a jury, and it decided the question of guilt or innocence. If the jury acquitted, that was the end of the story. But if the jury found the defendant guilty, then the crowd debated the sentence and the decision was by majority vote. When the chairman of the meeting asked what the sentence should be, it seems that there was always someone in the crowd who shouted, "Hang him!" This was where the rules of order were most important: reasonable men did not have to be heroes to make a motion for a lesser punishment, and, indeed, there was often "some opposition to taking his life." In the end, some thieves were hanged, but most were sentenced to whipping, cropping their ears, shaving their heads, and/or banishment. In a few instances, decorum was abandoned, and the members of the crowd fought over the fate of the convicted man.[48] This kind of lynch trial was held everywhere on the American frontier, although it has not heretofore been distinguished from racist lynchings.

Far from being defensive about lynch law, the miners were proud of the formality and orderliness of the trials. There were hundreds of these trials in California, and they were well documented in letters, diaries, and newspaper accounts. The miners justified lynch law on the grounds that sovereignty derived from the people and that they had a natural right to self-defense. Two mining codes included criminal law provisions—further evidence that the miners believed that criminal law fell under the general heading of self-government.[49]

Early lynch trials were surprisingly restrained. Then they grew wilder. At their worst, they descended to the level of mob violence, except that the mob paused for a quick vote on the guilt of the accused before hanging him. As the new State of California began to reclaim the power to punish crime after 1850, lynch trials were speeded up because the miners believed—not without reason—that corrupt sheriffs, shoddy jails, and long delays would allow the prisoners to escape. "The Officers have got a way of letting Criminals off," wrote a miner by the name of William Binur, "and the people wont [sic] stand it so they take them from the Shireff [sic] choose a Jury[,] try them and have them strung up in an hour or two which is the only wae [sic] to do it in these parts."[50]

Clearly a culture of meetings is not the only way to create order in mining camps. Indeed, the mining claim system—property rights based on continuous use—is roughly the same the world over, and other ethnicities experience no more disorder than the Americans. The meetings were unique to Americans, however, and this had its advantages and disadvantages. The main advantage of a shared knowledge of how to "do" meetings was an ability to enable large groups of strangers to act together on very short notice. The miners formed joint-stock mining companies to carry out large projects like diverting rivers from their beds to get at the gold beneath and building canals and flumes to deliver water to distant diggings. French miners in California were unable to do the same, wrote the French vice-consul on October 7, 1850. The main reason that they had less success at mining than the Americans was, he said, "the difficulties, the impossibilities of their working in company." All of their associations for mining projects broke up within twenty-four hours, "whereas magnificent profits crown the collective efforts of the American population."[51] This really was an American strong suit.

The main danger of government-by-meetings was hubris. American miners were convinced that majority rule was best and, therefore, that they did not need to defer to any other authority. The miners were so comfortable with lynch law that they never felt called upon to invest in the state judicial system or in social order generally. The philosopher Josiah Royce made this point in his book on mining camp society

published in 1886.[52] Californians complained that the state courts were
not fit for purpose and that months passed between sessions of the district courts, giving the prisoner ample time to escape from flimsy jails—
often with the help of the guards—while witnesses scattered to other
diggings. But instead of voting for better sheriffs or contributing funds
for better jails, they speeded up their lynch trials and even kidnapped
suspects from the authorities for a quick trial and hanging.

The miners also made "rules" giving themselves the authority to eject
foreigners from the diggings and, of course, to appropriate their claims.
The first article of the earliest preserved code, adopted at Iowa Log Cabins
on December 9, 1849, reads "[t]hat no foreigners shall be permitted to
work at these mines after the tenth day of December, 1849."[53] A number
of miners report specifically that they attended meetings "to exclude
foreigners," an issue that evidently generated enough zeal for men to
interrupt their work and vote for a law code.[54] These evictions violated
federal law, specifically treaties with France and Mexico, and more generally a norm of welcoming immigrants to the United States on equal
terms with current citizens. Here the miners used their meeting to bully
outsiders, and since "the people" were the source of all law, they saw no
reason why they should not.

One of the great things about the many, many eyewitness accounts
of the gold rush, however, is that one need not speak just about "the
miners" or Americans—as I have just done—because there are accounts
of differences and debates among the participants. For instance, many
people opposed the expulsion of foreign miners, and the topic generated
passionate debate, resolutions, and counterresolutions. Similarly, the
miners who were present at lynch trials sometimes disagreed about the
proper sentence for a convicted thief, leading to debates, arguments, and
even fights in the crowd. There is even quite a lot of information about
how juries were selected, who sat on various juries, and retrials when
the jury could not reach a verdict. The infliction of the punishment—
whether hanging, whipping, or cutting off the ears—is described in
great detail, from which we learn that many miners participated in
hangings, but there was great reluctance to administer the lash, and
a sentence of branding was sometimes commuted at the last minute
because no one was willing to carry it out.

What we learn from the gold rush material, therefore, is not just how Americans organized themselves in the absence of government, but how moderates, gamblers, natural leaders, and excitable Americans behaved at meetings. Letters and diaries illustrate what a good man could do to try to prevent the execution of a thief, an expedition to destroy an Indian village, or efforts to throw foreigners off their claims. Often, the good men were outnumbered, but parliamentary procedure gave them an opportunity to argue their case and sometimes to bring a majority over to their side.

The centrality of parliamentary procedure to the miners' self-government has not received any attention in part because it is not immediately obvious. Nineteenth-century writers took the formalities for granted and often barely mentioned them, sometimes referring only to a vote or a resolution. Modern readers may overlook the language of meetings because it is so familiar to us and so boring. Records of meetings lack excitement because, by definition, they follow certain formal rules, reporting only the procedurally relevant portions of the meeting and skipping the content and conflicts of the debate. Observers' accounts in their journals, letters home, and reminiscences are so much more entertaining that we have failed to notice and take seriously the references to resolutions and votes. But once one starts to pay attention, one sees orderly formal procedures everywhere.

In fact, there is evidence that similar meetings and trials were an equally omnipresent and equally overlooked part of frontier life beyond California. Most obviously, claim clubs were created and run by meetings using parliamentary procedure. The settlers united to protect their claims against speculators when the government made the land available for sale, and they did so by holding a meeting, choosing a chairman and a secretary, asking a committee to draft a constitution, debating that document, and making changes through resolutions and votes—in short, by following all of the proper steps.[55]

Trials by Judge Lynch also took place across the frontier. John Phillip Reid presents an engrossing study of trials on the Overland Trail.[56] The emigrants' trials were more conscientious and formal than the miners'—more like trials and less like meetings. Trials in other Western settlements, however, were strikingly similar to those in California, and indeed the practice was probably introduced to California by frontiersmen from Oregon.

The detailed description in this book of meetings, codes, dispute resolution, and criminal trials in California is therefore a step toward reconstructing the law of the frontier as a whole. It is a different picture from that of sheriffs, posses, and vigilantes of popular literature. Instead, the story is one of chairmen and committees, motions and resolutions, elections and joint-stock companies. Until now, the outlaws and vigilantes of the frontier have had the lion's share of attention; the time has come to focus on the meetings through which the frontiersmen managed their internal affairs.

## The Sources

Thousands of miners recorded their experiences because they knew that they were participating in one of the great events of American history: they kept diaries, wrote letters to their families at home, or published their memoirs when they got back. Many families kept these letters and diaries through the generations and eventually donated or sold them to historical societies or universities or published them. In addition, half-a-dozen California newspapers included almost daily reports "from the mines." Then there are the mining codes, court records, debates in the US Congress and the California legislature, and local histories written in the 1880s. These were purchased by the forty-niners, among others, thirty years after they had dug for gold, portraits of their middle-aged selves appearing opposite accounts of the great events of their youths. In short, there is a wonderful quantity and variety of firsthand accounts of life and law in the gold rush.

No source is entirely trustworthy, however.[57] The young letter writers did not want to distress their parents and sweethearts; and the diary keepers, who also expected to be read by their families, were similarly constrained. Some writers exaggerated their successes or drew a curtain on their moral lapses. C. C. Mobley, a miner in 1850 and 1851, confessed to his diary, "I took 1 glass or two of wine this evening," but did so in code so that no one else would know (the code is a simple straight substitution, so that even I could decipher it).[58] Considering what others were doing in the way of gambling, fighting, and whoring, this guilty secret seems almost endearing. Edward Austin was another young man who did not want his mother to know everything he was up to in California. He was outfitting a saloon and asked his brother, George, to "[s]end out a few, say four or six, chaste pictures of naked women in good frames," adding, "I put this in a separate letter so that you can keep it 'shady.' Don't let the folks know any of this—not even Lucy." One can only imagine how George—himself presumably a respectable young man—would get his hands on large paintings of naked women and then ship them to California, with frames, without anyone knowing.[59] A son would presumably be even less willing to disclose his part in massacring Native Americans or in hanging a convicted thief.

More importantly, the letters and diaries were all written by one subset of men in the mines: literate men with homes and families to which they expected to return. There are almost no letters and diaries by frontiersmen, and gamblers and thieves left no accounts at all. The portrayal of any society based on the letters of dutiful sons to their mothers is bound to be distorted.

Newspapers had their own agendas—to please their readers and to encourage immigration to California. The editors probably took an overly positive view of lynch trials, for instance, because the miners preferred not to hear criticism of an institution in which they had all taken part. The *Alta California* sometimes condemned lynching and but also defended it by explaining away the worst outrages as deviations from authentic lynch law. Judge Lynch "has done some things badly in his day," the editors said, "but suffers more from his counterfeit rival Mob Law, than from any act of his own."[60] The *Placer Times* (later the *Sacramento Transcript*) dared to call a lynch trial's sentence of mutilation "a mockery of law and an outrage of humanity," but like the *Times*, as an old and well-established newspaper, it could afford to be blunt occasionally.[61] The Sacramento *Index*, however, which was first published on December 23, 1850, was forced to fold because of its unpopular condemnations of lynch law.[62]

Individuals also sent reports on events of interest in the mines to the California papers, which these printed without further investigation. Some writers sang the praises of their diggings, describing them as rich and orderly; they may have been merchants who aimed to attract miners to the area or claim holders who hoped to inflate the value of their claims. Others, like the man who submitted the minutes of the trial of Easterbrook, wanted to legitimize the miners' use of lynch law through transparency as well as by documenting the care that they took to get everything right.

Memoirs written years after the events they describe are all suspect. The gold rush was literally a legend in its own time; by 1850, the men of 1849 were already admired and envied. Narratives written forty or fifty years later are often more thrilling but, sadly, unreliable; most significantly, they describe fighting over claims that is not documented in any of the contemporary accounts.[63] Memories had faded, and authors were bound to embellish the facts, particularly when, like Francis A. Hammond, they were writing for such sensationalist publications as the *Juvenile Instructor* (1894).

Only so much can be done to counteract such distortions and biases. I have relied mainly on contemporary eyewitness accounts rather than memoirs and on descriptions of specific events rather than generalizations. In the end, however, the picture of American law in the mining camps will inevitably be rosier than the reality.

# CHAPTER 1

# Before Property

I n 1848, California was America's furthest frontier, without government or land; and with the discovery of gold, even basic norms of property disintegrated. Eventually, a new form of property—the mining claim—would emerge, but even that was unknown in the initial months after James Marshall's discovery. Because of the extent of the gold region and the amount of gold near the surface, miners were always on the move, barely scraping the ground in their search for gold. A few lucky men managed to find seams and lumps of pure gold almost without digging; most had to work much harder, shoveling gold-rich dirt and washing it in a pan or a cradle, but even they did not dig down very far.[1] If the gold lay more than a few feet below the topsoil, they went looking for a better spot. The miners were more like hunter-gatherers than property holders.

The economy was turned upside down too. It was commonly believed that average earnings in the mines were one to two ounces a day, worth sixteen to thirty-two dollars, so farmhands, shopkeepers, and newspapermen alike abandoned their jobs. The few who remained at their posts demanded double or triple pay, raising the price of everything. The absence of roads, bridges, or any kind of infrastructure added to the cost of goods in the mines. Miners *had* to make a small fortune just to support themselves. Regular rumors of tremendous success elsewhere convinced them that they were digging in the wrong place, and off they would go, losing valuable time in the process.

These circumstances were typical of surface gold mining ever after. Random success and failure, sudden fortunes based on chance, the disappearance of traditional forms of property to be replaced by use rights, inflation and the readiness to spend exorbitant sums on "sprees"—all of these are characteristic of gold rushes since days of '49 in California and presumably before. It took Californians some months to adjust to this new world. Tracing the events of those months will acclimatize the reader to the sometimes surreal conditions of gold mining.

## Setting the Scene

In 1847, John Sutter began to build his lumber mill in the Coloma Valley on the American River, forty-five miles from his fort. He chose the site because the South Fork of the American River provided a steady flow of water and a good drop to turn the mill wheel. It was also relatively accessible, between hills but not in the hills, and had a good supply of timber for building the mill and for sawing.[2] This turned out to be one of the easiest parts of the mining region to reach. The miners who penetrated further into the wilderness found it very heavy going indeed, with no paths to guide them and almost every route cross-cut by ravines and rivers. The number of early miners who drowned is quite astonishing. But this is getting ahead of the story.

The race of Sutter's Mill and the water flowing through it happened to work like the mining apparatus that would later be called a sluice. The race as first constructed was too narrow, so James Marshall, "to save labor, let the water directly into the race, with a strong current, so as to wash it wider and deeper."[3] As in the riverbeds and the miners' sluices, the ordinary dirt was washed away while the gold in the soil was left behind, trapped behind rocks and in crevices. On January 24, 1848, a sparkle caught the eyes of Sutter's workmen. It was gold. Although Marshall and his men were wildly excited, they did not appreciate the enormity of their discovery for some time, having no idea how much gold there was. At Marshall's request, his men did not quit their day jobs for several weeks, though they did manage to dig for gold in their free time. When they finally finished their engagement to Marshall and Sutter, they took up gold mining in earnest. Many of these earliest miners were Mormons.

They and their compatriots gave their name to the first major diggings, Mormon Island.

In the beginning, conventions of property and contract unraveled very slowly. The men who were present when gold was discovered at Sutter's sawmill in January 1848 knew nothing about gold, or gold mining, or mineral law. The group subjected Marshall's nugget to various inventive tests—boiling it, hammering it—to determine whether it was in fact the precious metal; and when they had convinced themselves that it was the real thing, and that there was more of it in the stream along which they were building their mill, they were uncertain what to do next. There was no precedent for a gold mine on the "public lands." (These were actually Indian lands, but they were treated as public from day one.)[4] Even an expert could not have told them whether Mexican or American law applied; certainly Sutter and his men knew nothing about the law of gold mines in either legal system. Indeed, there was no American law of gold mining even in the States; and the governor, Colonel Richard B. Mason, abolished the "Mexican laws and customs now prevailing in California, relative to the denouncement of mines" on February 12, 1848.[5] Sutter and his companions were in a legal vacuum.

Mason was not thinking of gold when he revoked the Mexican mining laws: quicksilver, or mercury, was the exciting new business venture in the winter of 1847 to 1848. Rich deposits of mercury-bearing ore had been discovered near San Jose, and since mercury was necessary to the gold mining in progress in South America, mining it looked like an excellent investment. The Mexican law of denouncement provided that if there was mineral deposit on private land, and if the owner was not exploiting it, any other person could "denounce" the deposit and so acquire the right to work it. "The old laws require that every person denouncing should within a specified time have a 'pozo' or hole 30 feet deep and obtain judicial possession of it."[6] It was to stop such denouncements on private land that Mason made his proclamation of February 12, 1848.[7] By annulling the Mexican law, Mason secured "to each private owner of land all he may have on it, by which means a purchaser of mineral land will obtain a fair compensation."[8]

The Mexican law of denouncements was irrelevant to the gold miners because the gold was on public land, not private land, and it was not anywhere near thirty feet down. This particular rule was not a model for gold mining claims. Mason's abolition of the law does, however, show Americans rejecting a rule that promoted use for one that protected the interests of landowners.

Meanwhile, Sutter and Marshall were thinking in terms of land grants and land claims, not mineral rights. They decided to use every possible means to create a legal interest in the land near Sutter's Mill at Coloma. When Sutter reached Coloma, he and Marshall contracted a twenty-year lease on the surrounding land and the right to build a sawmill with one of the nearby Indian tribes.[9]

On February 8, 1848, Sutter sent a sawmill worker to Colonel Mason at Monterey asking him to recognize preemption rights in the quarter section around the mill.[10] Mason refused their request on the mistaken grounds that California was at that time a Mexican province occupied by the United States (the treaty of Guadalupe Hidalgo had in fact been signed a few days before). Moreover, preemption claims could not be recognized before a public survey had been made.[11] So that did not work. As to Sutter's contract with the Indians, Mason said that "[t]he United States do not recognize the right of Indians to sell or lease the lands on which they reside . . . to private individuals."[12] Mason later made this very important point: "This is public land, and the gold is the property of the United States; all of you here are trespassers, but, as the Government is benefited by your getting out the gold, I do not intend to interfere."[13] This meant that as far as mining was concerned, they were outside the law and in a state of nature. Marshall's and Sutter's next best option was now to keep the gold discovery secret for as long as possible.[14]

Since California's internal gold rush did not begin until May, there were few people who could have contested Marshall, Sutter, and Brannan's claims except their own men. The Mormon workers thought their employers were well within their rights to privatize a few hundred acres. Henry Bigler wrote, "The mill hands . . . respected [Sutter's and Marshall's] claims, knowing they at least were in possession of settlers' rights and had commenced improvements months before the gold was discovered."[15] In other words, they recognized the usual preemption rights of the frontier rather than any gold-specific rules: the word *claim* is used here in its colloquial sense, not to signify a mining claim of the kind that would soon emerge.

## Mormons

From the gold discovery in January 1848 to Brannan's electrifying broadcast of the news in May that year, the gold rush was primarily a Mormon affair. About 350 Mormon men and 155 Mormon women and children were in California in 1848. They had come in two groups. The colony led by Samuel Brannan had arrived in 1846. It consisted of 220 Mormons known as the *Brooklyn* Mormons because they traveled on the ship *Brooklyn*.[16] The second, much larger group of Mormons was the Mormon Battalion, or the "Battalion Boys," of about 350 men, reduced to at most 290 in 1848.[17] The Battalion was formed in 1846 to fight in the Mexican War and was discharged in Los Angeles in July 1847.[18]

Mormon accounts are the most complete records of the first months of the gold rush. Several of the men present at Sutter's Mill kept diaries, most notably Henry Bigler, Azariah Smith, and John Borrowman, and these are very valuable.[19] Fortunately, they have all been subjected to serious scholarship, most notably by Will Bagley and Kenneth N. Owens, who not only provide full collections of primary sources, including unpublished texts, but also put them through rigorous analysis and source criticism.[20] Thanks to them, a great deal is known about Mormons in the gold rush.

After the gold discovery, the old world order continued for several months while—the Mormons continued to work on Sutter's mills and hunted for gold in their free time. Sutter's main concern was not gold mining but getting his lumber mill up and running. He allowed his workers to collect gold from the mill race on Sundays and even supplied them with pocket knives for the purpose, at least in part so that they would not leave his construction unfinished.[21] His employees, meanwhile, were not ready to give up their day jobs for the uncertainties of gold mining, especially since they had no idea how much gold there might be.[22] Their gold hunting was haphazard and literally superficial; they did not pan for gold or even dig for it, but picked out gold nuggets with their knives.[23] Bigler was the only one who even went beyond the mill race, and the others did not learn until February 22 that there was gold beyond Sutter's land.

Another reason for staying on at the mill was that the men needed provisions and tools to start mining, let alone to survive for some time in the mountains, and Sutter was the only source of supplies; there were no other traders within a hundred miles. Sutter also owed his workers about $150 each for four months labor, which they did not want to abandon.[24] Marshall offered them a reasonable deal: if they worked out their contracts, he would give them tools and supplies and let them work "their" (his and Sutter's) gold claims.[25] In effect, he would "stake" them, that is, furnish the capital in return for a portion of their profits. Marshall and Sutter's exclusive access to provisions was more important at this point than his self-proclaimed rights in the land.

It is not clear how long this staking arrangement lasted or whether the Mormons actually paid Marshall his share. A certain Captain Phelps whose whole ship's crew wanted to go to the gold mines in May 1848 made a similar deal with them that he would continue to pay their ship's wages and rations, and supply their tools, in return for two-thirds of the gold they found.[26] Thomas O. Larkin also staked some of his employees and provided them with Indian laborers.[27] We do not know how much, if anything, these sleeping partners collected. Later emigrants from the United States would be "staked" by acquaintances back home, but it is unlikely that they ever saw a return on their investments because average earnings barely covered the cost of provisions.

Some of the Mormon hands working on Sutter's *other* mill, the flour mill, did quit in early March without finishing their job.[28] Two of them, Sidney Willis and Wilford Hudson, struck gold almost immediately, on March 2, 1848, at the place later called Mormon Island. It proved to be one of the richest areas in the whole of California, and yet there were only seven Battalion men there in mid-April, making one hundred dollars a day.[29]

Willis and Hudson, the discoverers of Mormon Island, at first tried to control it as their own property. They charged other miners working there a fee for the privilege; and the Mormon leader, Samuel Brannan, quickly associated himself with them. Like Marshall and Sutter, Brannan's first thought was to put in a preemption claim to a large tract of land. On his ride to San Francisco to publicize the gold discovery, he stopped at the home of a Stephen Cooper in Benicia to change horses. Cooper's daughter, Susan, told a newspaper in 1900 that Brannan told them that he was going to "locate all the land he could and return to Monterey and file on it."[30] One of those present, a certain John Wolfskill, informed Brannan that "it was placer mining and that they could not hold it all."[31] As we now know, Brannan could not legally hold *any* of it since there were no land rights of any kind. Nevertheless, news of his intention, or perhaps false reports of his success, reached the ears of Thomas O. Larkin in San Jose. Larkin wrote to Colonel Mason on May 26, 1848, that "Mr. Brannan the Mormon I understand claimed some two or three miles by some right of discovery or preemption."[32] Mason, of course, knew this was not true; Sutter had tried that trick, and Mason turned him down. If Brannan did in fact file his claim for the land, he was refused.

Nevertheless, the miners at Mormon Island paid a toll, "which was thirty dollars out of a hundred, which goes to Hudson and Willis, that discovered the mine, and Brannan who is securing it for them."[33] Translation: Hudson and Willis took Brannan into partnership, in return for which he would somehow "secure" or obtain a legal interest in the land for the three of them. We know that he could not secure legal title, and he must have known it himself by mid-May; but he evidently forgot to tell his partners.

This handful of Mormons had the diggings almost to themselves for almost four months because it was only on May 10, 1848, that Brannan's dramatic announcement in San Francisco touched off the internal gold rush. The *Californian* did publish a short article on an inside page on March 15: "Gold Mine Found—in the newly made raceway of the saw mill." On March 25, Brannan's own newspaper, the *California Star*, informed its readers laconically that "gold has become an article of trade" in the area surrounding the new mines. The *Star* provided a few more details on April 1 in a booster edition intended to promote California generally. Local residents might reasonably have taken its report of "gold collected at random and without any trouble" with a grain of salt, sandwiched as it was between paragraphs on the superiority of California's peaches and its healthful climate.[34] Despite his arrangement with Willis and Hudson. Brannan himself did not visit the mines and realize their potential until May.

Few men followed up these early reports and those who did found very little. The gold was invisible to the naked eye; but for Marshall's mill race, it might have gone undiscovered for years. People who were not entirely convinced that there was any gold did not work very hard to find it. On Sunday, April 23, Bigler and his fellow Mormons looked on complacently while newcomers poked around near their tents. Bigler noted self-righteously, "Like Christians we kept the Sabbath day while a lot of Gentiles came into our camp to look for gold but found none"—as though he himself had not spent every Sunday looking for gold while he was working for Sutter.[35] The Mormons may well have rested on this Sunday so that the visitors would not know that they dug for gold in little gulches at some distance from their camp.

When Brannan visited his partners at Mormon Island personally, he finally grasped the scale of the thing.[36] On May 10, 1848, Brannan returned to San Francisco, shouting "Gold! Gold! Gold from the American River!" Two days later, on May 12, the *Californian* confirmed the discovery of gold. That touched off an internal gold rush; the entire male population of Northern California dropped what it was doing to go to the mines, leaving towns, farms, and ships virtually deserted.[37] Reports on the "complete revolution in the ordinary state of affairs," to use Thomas O. Larkin's words, are almost incoherent with excitement. "Every blacksmith, carpenter, and lawyer are leaving; brick yards, saw mills and ranches are left perfectly alone," Larkin reported to Buchanan.[38] A stable keeper in San Jose received a letter from his brothers in the mines telling him to come and to burn the stable if he couldn't sell it.[39] First California and then the whole world was whipped into a frenzy that cannot be described except by pages and pages of detail.

Now, for the first time, there was some crowding at the existent diggings in the neighborhood of Sutter's Mill and at Mormon Island, raising the question of who would have access, the issue at the core of the later mining codes. The little gulches of the men near Sutter's Mill "were soon lined from end to end by gold diggers, who already began to dispute Marshall's claims to the land and commenced mining wherever they pleased."[40] Not only did they reject Marshall's alleged property rights, they appear not to have held claims of their own and worked wherever they could elbow in.

At Mormon Island, at least some of the new arrivals were fellow Mormons. These newcomers resented Brannan's fee but paid it anyway because of their uncertainty about their rights and their willingness to do the decent thing. John Borrowman's diary entry for May 19 said, "[M]ade $22 but as Brannan & Co. requires thirty percent my share only came to $8 as Brother Wood and I are in company."[41] At least half of Borrowman's eight dollars would have gone for provisions and supplies. But on May 30, he spoke out against paying "rent," which he considered "an imposition."[42] Borrowman did not continue to dig at Mormon Island without paying; instead, he went prospecting for new diggings, presumably someplace not claimed by "Brannan & Co.," as he called them. Brannan collect shares from other miners until July 1848, when Colonel Mason visited the site. Some Mormons asked Mason whether Brannan was in fact entitled to collect a percentage of their profits, and Mason reply was supposedly, "Brannan has a perfect right to collect the tax, if you Mormons are fools enough to pay it."[43] Whether or not the anecdote is true, the miners stopped their payments at about this time. That they had been sharing their earnings on the basis of supposed "discovery or preemption" suggests that it took them some time to shake off their old ideas about large preemption rights.[44]

In short, the ranchers and businessmen of California initially hoped to profit from the gold discovery in traditional ways, by acquiring the mines or employing the miners, but they were disappointed. Within three or four months, it was clear that it was not only impossible for individuals to hold land as private property, but it was equally impracticable for one person to hire another. Capitalists quickly learned that they got greater and safer returns for their investments in real estate, trade, and other businesses incidental to the gold rush than by sponsoring mining expeditions directly.

Thus, traditional forms of property—indeed, all real property—failed. The mining claim system that everyone associates with the gold rush did not appear until at least six months after Brannan announced the discovery of gold; and the first codes, which standardized the size and requirements of holding mining claims, appeared only in 1849. In the interim, there were only use rights, at least in part because early mining techniques were very primitive and the miners went after only the most accessible gold. A few men who had a special knack went off on their own looking for pockets of gold. Some found thousands of dollars' worth under rocks and just below ground in dry gullies. Chester Lyman and his partner Douglass discovered that "the Gold here is found most abundantly in the side ravines or gulches; the excavations are generally from 1 to 3 feet deep & about the same width following the bottom of the gulch."[45] These two started about a rod apart and, digging toward each other, picked out a tidy seven ounces *each* from such a gulch in one day.[46] A few men even "mined" by pulling up clumps of grass and shaking out the gold-rich earth from the roots.[47] These foragers had no need for mining claims; if they found a rich or convenient site, they kept it secret for as long as possible.

Most miners, however, packed into diggings known to be rich, such as Mormon Island. They might work shoulder to shoulder or, where the gold was deeper, control the hole where they were actively at work. Governor Colonel Mason was not quite right when he wrote that "conflicting claims to particular spots of ground may cause collisions, but they will be rare, as the extent of the country is so great and the gold so abundant, that at present there is room enough for all."[48] The richest locations, which attracted both beginners and experienced miners, were very crowded.[49]

After Brannan's dramatic announcement, everyone then in California abandoned his trade and headed for the mines. Emigrants from abroad started arriving midsummer. Native and white Hawaiians arrived beginning in July. "People in great numbers are daily arriving here from the Sandwich Islands and other places," Kimball Dimmick wrote his wife on September 3, 1848, and "some vessels are compelled to remain here their men having deserted until there are not enough left to work ship or raise an anchor."[50] American pioneers from Oregon arrived in August,[51] and Mexicans, Chileans, and Peruvians in October, November, and December.[52] (The Mexicans came with mining experience that was at first welcome and then seen as a threat.) Pioneers who had set out on the Overland Trail to California in the spring heard the electrifying news of gold from the Mormons headed east. Though they could not travel any faster than they were going already, they became even more eager to complete their journey. The great influx of gold seekers from the United States began much later, in the summer of 1849.[53]

The most common interests in land were first, none at all, and second, the miner's right to the hole in which he was working. "No interest" means the miner had no power to exclude others from his hole even while he was digging it. Walter Colton's journal entry for October 17, 1848, contains an account of how this worked:

> A German this morning, picking a hole in the ground . . . for a tent-pole, struck a piece of gold, weighing about three ounces. As soon as it was known, some forty picks were flying into the earth all around the spot. You would have thought the ground had suddenly caved over some human being, who must be instantly disenhumed or die.[54]

The original discoverer was not pushed out; he was entitled to the space his body occupied and the ground on which he was standing, but that was it. A miner had a right not to be shoved aside. One of the early gold seekers told Charles Shinn that in those days, "there was not even a custom, so that a man hardly objected to your digging close beside him so long as you gave him room to swing a pick."[55] (Ordinarily, a recollection of this kind does not bear much weight; but in this case, the source was "a graduate of Yale.") Non-Americans might be crowded out altogether. A Mexican miner took out two points of gold in small pieces. "As soon as this was known, four of the New York volunteers struck in each side of the Sonorian, and dug him out; and the old man very quietly retired." Their greed availed the Volunteers not, however. They dug all day, found no gold, and gave up. The next morning, the Mexican came back to the same site and "before night he struck another pocket, and took out a pound and a half of gold."[56]

These were descriptions of exceptional diggings, where the gold was found in "pieces" and "pockets." Few miners had the luck to find such deposits of solid gold; instead, they used pans to wash gold-rich dirt and separate out smaller particles of gold, that is, gold dust or gold scales. Bigler mentioned that he and his fellow Mormon miners had one tin pan between them on April 13, 1848.[57] With pans in such short supply, some miners used tightly woven Indian baskets.

By May, some miners were already using the rocker or cradle.[58] The cradle used the same mechanism as that which originally deposited the gold in the riverbeds, where the running water had pushed and carried dirt downstream while the gold, being heaver, sank to the bottom or got lodged in cracks and crevices. In the case of the cradle, an eight-to-ten-foot-long wooden box formed the water channel, while slates or cleats attached to the bottom played the part of the rocks and holes in the riverbed. A miner poured water through a grille at the head of the cradle, and the water flowed down and out the end, carrying with it the dirt and small pebbles but leaving the gold trapped behind the slats. The cradle was not very efficient, but it was much better than the pan. Larkin estimated that the "[a]verage white man using only spade, pickaxe and pan" found one ounce of gold, worth sixteen dollars, per day, while "there are many men with the tin pan and machine who are obtaining 30$ to 60$ daily."[59] Over the years, the cradle would be replaced by the "long tom" and then the "sluice," but the basic idea was the same. The new technology just had a longer and longer box, and the miner directed running water into the head instead of pouring bucketfuls in by hand. In a letter to Buchanan dated June 28, 1848, Larkin estimated that there were about two thousand men in the mines making one ounce per day with a pan alone and two ounces per day with a cradle.[60]

To get rich dirt for the cradle, miners had to dig. According to Buffum, who observed the miners at work at Foster's Bar on the Yuba shortly after, in November 1848, "The manner of procuring and washing the golden earth was this." He wrote, "The loose stones and surface earth being removed from any portion of the bar, a hole from four to six feet square was opened, and the dirt extracted there from was thrown upon a raw hide placed at the side of the machine."[61] Note how very small these openings were, the smallest being about the size of a dining table, and they were up to twelve feet deep. Miners were taking one hundred dollars a day from these holes, and one hundred miners completely filled the bar. Buffum and his partners could not get a place.

In fact, Buffum said that "all the bars upon which men were then engaged in labour were 'claimed,' a claim at that time being considered good when the claimant had cleared off the top soil from any portion of the bar."[62] Buffum put quotation marks around the word *claimed,* as one might for a word used in a new sense. Now, this was around the same time that the German made a lucky strike and was helpless to keep out the dozens of other men who started digging there. The difference at Foster's Bar was that those miners had to invest in their holes. If they found gold on the bedrock, as was often the case, it is almost unthinkable that another miner would jump in to grab a share because that would be as bad as stealing, and in any case, a four-feet-wide, twelve-feet-deep hole would not accommodate more than one miner at a time. In other words, the accessibility or otherwise of the gold, rather than the passage of time, might account for the appearance of exclusive rights.

The holes that Buffum described, packed together in crowded diggings, were a species of claim; their holders enjoyed certain fairly specific rights that were respected by the other miners. Although Buffum called them claims, others just called them holes. "There was no mining laws and no mining claims" in the first year of the gold rush, a former miner by the name of Peckham recollected. "If a man left his tools where he had been working, this was title to the hole in which they were found; outside of this any man dug where he pleased."[63] Peckham perhaps felt that the right to a hole was merely convention, whereas mining claims were created by miners' meetings.

It is a reasonable guess that a miner's right in his hole was the model for the mining codes because the basic principles were the same. Felix Paul Wierzbicki wrote of 1848–1849, "As a general rule, it [wa]s a practice among the miners to leave each digger a sufficient space for a hole, upon which nobody has a right to encroach; from four to ten feet they allow among themselves to be sufficient for each, according as they may be more or less numerous and as digging may be more or less rich." As for notice, Wierzbicki said, "a tool left in the hole in which a miner is working is a sign that it is not abandoned yet, and that nobody has a right to intrude there." This system is said to have been "adopted by silent consent of all [and] generally complied with"—evidently, without meeting, debate, or vote.[64] If he is to be believed, then the rules of mining sometimes evolved without organization, that is, miners' meetings were not absolutely necessary to the property regime: even individuals in the wilderness staked out claims and expected miners who arrived after them to respect their property.[65]

After the claim system was well established, the hole-with-tools continued as a default rule in areas not covered by a mining code. Bayard Taylor wrote of 1849 that "[a] man might dig a hole in the dry ravines, and so long as he left a shovel, pick, or crowbar to show that he still intended working it, he was safe from trespass," adding that "[h]is tools might remain there for months without being disturbed."[66] Even in established diggings, a tool in the hole was still respected as a sign that someone was coming back. At Mormon Island in April 1850, when there had long been a mining code, a party of men only recently arrived in the mines looked around for an old hole that had no tools in it and began to dig.[67]

The transition from an informal consensus to "rules and regulations" did not happen all at once. At the end of 1848, formal claims were known in some places but not in others. Oregon pioneer P. H. Burnett and his associates purchased a claim on Long's Bar on the Yuba River, twenty feet along the river and reaching back fifty feet.[68] The size and shape of this river claim correspond to the norm established in later mining codes; and it was also recognized as a form of property that could be bought and sold. But some very sparsely occupied areas still had no claims. At Weaver's Creek in December, for instance, Buffum and nine companions went out on their own every day, hunting for nuggets and pockets of pure gold. Buffum called this technique "dry digging" as opposed to "wet digging," that is, washing dirt with a pan or a cradle. It did not require cooperation, as using a cradle had done. "Our partnership did not extend to a community of labour in gold-digging," he wrote, "but only to a sharing of the expenses . . . and labours of our winter life."[69] There were only about a dozen huts on Weaver's Creek at this time, December 1848, and every man wandered off on his own to search for gold. Buffum said that he searched in a different area almost every day. It is fair to say that he had no use for a claim because he did not intend to return to any particular spot.

Some people made a fortune in 1848. Chester Lyman's method of literally cleaning up is described above. Edward Gould Buffum, who had phenomenal luck himself,[70] also had good stories about other incredible finds in 1848. A Frenchman and his son working in a riverbed took out $3,000 with no tools except a hoe and a spade. Two men at Kelsy's Bar gathered fifty pounds of gold, or nearly $10,000, in two days. Buffum also talked to reliable, honest men who said that for several days they had reaped $500 a day.[71] James Carson, who was *not* necessarily reliable, claimed that he himself and a small party took out an average of 180 ounces ($2,880) *each* in a ten-day stretch at Carson's Creek.[72]

News of such rich strikes induced the miners making average wages to abandon their claims and head off to the new diggings. The working assumption in 1848 was that average earnings in the mines were one ounce (sixteen dollars) or more per day,[73] but mining was already described as a lottery. Some miners made more, and others much less. Several observers did their best to gauge earnings over the whole season while struggling to define "average" in a summer when some people made thousands of dollars and others succumbed to hunger and exposure. Is there an average between rich and dead? An industrious man could wash ten to twenty dollars of the fine gold each day, Kimball Dimmick wrote in a letter to his wife, Sarah, on August 2, 1848. But some men had found $800 of the coarse gold in a day, he said, and one man picked up $1,100 in three hours, "[w]hile others have worked on the same ground for a month and fund not more than five hundred and many not so much."[74]

Even the miners who reported making an ounce per day meant an ounce per *working* day. Time spent prospecting, moving, or getting supplies reduced the average income. Colton's description of this phenomenon in October 1848 cannot be bettered. "I have taken some pains to ascertain the average per man that is got out; it must be less than half an ounce per day," he wrote. Half an ounce would be eight dollars per day:

> It might be more were there any stability among the diggers; but half their time is consumed in what they call prospecting; that is, looking up new deposits. An idle rumor, or mere surmise, will carry them off in this direction or that, when perhaps they gathered nothing for their weariness and toil. A locality where an ounce a day can be obtained by

patient labor is constantly left for another, which rumor has enriched with more generous deposits.[75]

No one was immune to the temptation to rush to the site of the latest big strike. Even those who knew better "yield[ed] at last to the same phrensied fickleness." Chester Lyman and his partner moved on to a new location as soon as things got slow, but in at least one instance they returned from such an excursion five days later, sadder but wiser. "We had the pleasure of the trip," Lyman recorded in his diary, "but were *minus* the amount of gold we *might* have dug had we remained behind, many of our friends having made from 300 to 1000 dollars during our absence."[76]

These miners took their tools with them, of course, and the hole they left behind was deemed to be abandoned and could be jumped by anyone who wanted it. In this sense, tools were an excellent signal of occupation. In later years, when miners posted notices on their claims instead of leaving their tools, it was less clear when a claim had been abandoned or was "jumpable," in the miners' vocabulary. A Belgian miner's recollection of his first sight of a claim notice shows how meaningless a claim was without a community consensus about acceptable forms of property rights. "I only half understood what it meant," he said. "I saw very clearly, according to the notices, that the right of working the claims belonged to those who had signed them, but I wondered on what they based the right to make these their territories, and what would happen if another came to work there."[77] This was where the mining codes came in, the form of notice and how long one could leave it unworked before it could be jumped.

The mining claim system emerged spontaneously before the first miners' meetings and, as will be seen in Chapter 4, similar rules appear in gold rushes the world over. What distinguished Americans was not the property regime but the meetings at which they self-consciously exercised the functions of government, namely adopting laws and holding trials.

# CHAPTER 2

# Powerless Judges and Discharged Soldiers

The most audacious act of self-government by meetings was criminal trials run by the local population, called lynch trials. The miners argued that the law of necessity justified these measures, the necessity being the absence of law enforcement or courts. There was an alternative route not taken, however. At the end of the Mexican War, California had no civil government, but there were two institutions there that, in theory, could have provided law and order: the military government, with the few soldiers who were left at the end of the war, and the Mexican office of *alcalde*, a low-level judge.

In principle, with different leadership, either of these might have helped keep the peace and avert lynch law. Legally, however, the army could be used to protect towns against attack but not to enforce the criminal law; and in any case, there were hardly any troops in California and the government in Washington ignored pleas for more. With better use of the office of alcalde for criminal trials, however, the miners might not have gone as far down the path of lynch law as they did, to the point where—when there were jails—they kidnapped defendants from the authorities and gave them a hasty trial before executing them. The early miners did recognize the institution of the alcalde in the sense that they elected alcaldes to hold trials, but they then regularly pushed these officers aside in favor of arbitration and miners' meetings. All of these developments were as characteristically American as the miners' meetings themselves; the government in Washington had no commitment to imposing order from above, while the miners were reluctant to submit themselves to an elected official.

The military governors—first Colonel R. B. Mason and then General Benet Riley—governed by default. Since Congress had not confirmed the military governors as head of a civilian government, they had no constitutional authority to do much of anything; or, worse, they were not sure of the limits of their authority. Gary Lawson and Guy Seidman have studied the extraordinary justifications put forward for their government, which they aptly characterize as the Hobbesian Constitution.[1] On October 7, 1848, Secretary of State James Buchanan wrote that Mason headed a "government de facto . . . with the presumed consent of the people, until Congress shall provide for them a territorial government." How could this be? "The great law of necessity justifies this conclusion."[2]

But Governor Mason was painfully aware that he was in uncharted waters. His boldest step was ordering the collection of import duties at San Francisco harbor, a move that was challenged all the way to the United States Supreme Court. Mason was found to have acted legally, but the Supreme Court had to stretch beyond the normal bounds of constitutional analysis to justify even this small initiative.

## Alcaldes in the Towns

The only sense in which the governors were involved in the government of towns and mining camps was that they recognized and in some small ways supported the authority of the alcaldes. The office of alcalde was a holdover from the Mexican period that had no counterpart in American government in that the chief alcalde of a district was a judge in civil and criminal matters, presided over the town council, and executed local and provincial decrees.[3] At the time of the gold discovery, many towns had an American alcalde who may or may not have applied Mexican law. Walter Colton, alcalde of Monterey, wrote on July 22, 1848, that "[t]he laws by which an *alcade* here is governed, in the administration of justice, are the

Mexican code as compiled in Frebrero and Alverez—works of remarkable comprehensiveness, clearness, and facility of application. They embody all the leading principles of the civil law, derived from the institutes of Justinian."[4] Under the American military government, the extent of the alcaldes' jurisdiction was left vague, though Mason eventually tolerated the trial and execution of murderers by juries in the towns.[5] That was a model that could have been used in the mining camps; but the miners never embraced the institution of alcalde and instead used trial by Judge Lynch, the criminal law of the frontier.

At first, Colonel Mason hoped that his remaining soldiers could protect the towns from depredations. Colonel Stevenson and his New York Volunteers were being discharged in August 1848, but Mason begged them to stay in Los Angeles "in the name of humanity because its citizens had surrendered their arms and were utterly unprotected."[6] William Tecumseh Sherman, who was on administrative duty in California, also wrote to Stevenson at this time, saying, "Colonel Mason is in a tight place. In San Francisco is great disorder and loud calls for assistance. In Los Angeles the same. Two companies to meet all these contingencies and no civil organization in the country."[7]

Mason's worst fears were not realized, but at least four horrible crimes were committed against civilian communities in December 1848. Soldiers hunted down the murderers and turned them over to the citizens for trial and punishment. In the response to these crimes, we see the cautious first steps toward lynch law and Mason's equally guarded endorsement thereof.

A certain Peter Raymond, by himself or with partners, was responsible for three murders.[8] Raymond killed miner John R. von Pfister at Sutter's Mill for no reason except that Raymond was drunk and yelling in the middle of the night and Von Pfister got out of bed to calm him down. The miners put Raymond's fate to a vote: Should they hang him on the spot or send him to Sutter's Fort for trial? They sent Raymond to Sutter's Fort, and he escaped. He then fell in with a German, Joseph Lynch, and together they murdered two miners en route to San Francisco and took from them $2,000 worth of gold.[9] Then Raymond, Lynch, and three other outlaws who joined them along the way carried out the most sensational crime of the gold rush (except, of course, the massacre of the Indians). They murdered thirteen men, women, and children at the Mission of San Miguel, which lies about halfway between Monterey and Santa Barbara.[10]

Both the murder of Pfister and the massacre were reported to Colonel Mason at Monterey, some four hundred miles from Sutter's Fort. On October 21, 1848, even before the massacre at San Miguel, Mason had announced a $500 reward "for the apprehension of Peter Raymond, the murderer of John R. von Pfister, or for his head, in case he cannot be taken prisoner."[11] A license to kill like this was highly unusual, if not unique, in the California gold rush. Mason also wrote to John Sinclair, now alcalde of the Sacramento district, authorizing him to summon a jury and try Raymond if he was caught.[12] Alcaldes did not have the authority to hold trials in capital cases, so Mason was sanctioning a citizen trial, or what frontiersmen called a lynch trial.

The mass murder of William Reed, his family, servants, and guests galvanized the coastal population. Mason ordered Sherman to send Lieutenant Ord and a party of soldiers from Monterey to hunt down the murderers. Raymond and his gang had headed south, however, actually passing through Santa Barbara on the way, so it was the citizen posse of Santa Barbara that first reached the outlaws. In a brief gunfight, they killed Raymond and another man and captured the three others alive.

So now the people of Santa Barbara asked themselves what to do with the prisoners in the absence of courts or jails and bearing in mind how easily Raymond had escaped from Sutter's Fort. Apparently, someone wrote to Mason for instructions; at any rate, Mason did instruct the alcalde to try the men suspected of the murders at the mission and hang them if the jury sentenced them to death.[13] After a short break for Christmas, the jury found all three defendants guilty and sentenced them to be shot. They were executed by firing squad two days later, on December 28.[14]

Colonel Mason gave the proceedings his imprimatur. A written copy of the verdict in the Santa Barbara Mission archives carries this notation: "The foregoing findings and sentences in the cases of Peter Remer, Peter Quin and Joseph Lynch are approved by authority of Col. R. B. Mason, Gov. of California. E.O.C. Ord, 1st Lt. U.S. Artillery."[15] This colophon claims to legitimize the trial and execution, although, technically, Mason did not have the authority to sentence civilians to death.

Mason justified the proceedings to General Roger Jones in Washington, DC, in a letter dated December 27, 1848, the day between the trial and the execution. "There are no civil courts here and strictly speaking no legal power to execute the death sentence," he acknowledged, "but the country is full of lawless men and it is necessary for good citizens to take the law into their own hands."[16] Secretary of State Henry W. Halleck said in a letter to Kimball Dimmick, alcalde of San Jose in May 1849, "It is believed that under the existing laws of California, the first *alcalde* of each district has jurisdiction in criminal cases." But whether they did or not, they had to hold such trials because "there can be no doubt that, under existing circumstances, cases will sometimes arise where the exercise of such power is absolutely necessary for the security of life and property."[17]

Mason also tacitly endorsed an alcalde's trials in at least two other instances. In December 1848, two miners carrying twenty-three pounds of gold were assaulted and robbed on the road between the San Joaquin River and San Jose. The victims reported the crime to Kimball Dimmick, the San Jose alcalde. Dimmick had served as alcalde in the mines and had tried several thieves there before moving to San Jose. The suspects were given a regular jury trial, found guilty, and sentenced to death by hanging.[18]

Dimmick sent Colonel Mason a bill for the jurors' fees. Mason's reply did not sanction the proceedings in so many words, but he expressed his sympathy with citizens of San Jose and said that he understood why they had to take the law into their own hands. Again, Mason made the moral argument for extralegal trials. He wrote, "The country affording no means—jails or prisons—by which the persons of these lawless men could have been secured and society protected, it is not much to be wondered that . . . the strict bounds of legal proceedings should have been a little overstepped." But Mason refused to pay the jurors' fees. "It is not within the scope of my power or authority to order the disbursement of the public moneys in paying the costs of trials not strictly legal," he told Dimmick.[19] Mason's authority to pay for any institutions of civil government was tenuous; and here he also recognized that trials outside the courts were "not strictly legal" and tolerated only through necessity.

In short, the military government gave tacit approval—or more—to alcalde courts in 1848 and 1849, using the same arguments the miners would make in later years. Like the miners, the inhabitants of the coastal towns were careful to do everything as correctly as possible, providing a judge, a jury, and a decent interval before sentence was carried out. There is no reason to believe that the miners who held citizen trials in 1848 and 1849 knew about Mason's correspondence with the coastal towns, but all of the parties were drawing on the same frontier customs, and all, including Mason, believed that extralegal criminal trials were necessary.

## Alcaldes in the Mines

The alcaldes with whom Mason corresponded were based in the towns and were, in his own words, "civil magistrates of California" and subject to removal by the governor.[20] In the mining camps, the miners elected alcaldes on their own authority and allowed them to hold trials, even criminal trials. One of these was Kimball Dimmick, later of San Jose. A captain in Stevenson's Volunteers and a member of the New York bar, Dimmick claimed to have been the "first Judge in the mines"—he did not use the word *alcalde*—and was also one of the few to write about his experience. After he arrived on September 25, 1848, a committee waited on him to say that he was appointed judge in order to try an alleged thief. "The Court was soon organized," Dimmick said, "and the man who stole the money arraigned and after a fair trial conducted on common law principles was found guilty." He was banished from the gold region, and his property was transferred to the victim in compensation. The next day, Dimmick again presided over a "fair trial." Two men were found guilty: one was sentenced to fifty lashes of a rawhide whip and the other to twenty-five. From then on, he "ruled these 'diggins,' meeting out Justice and making the laws."[21]

First Lieutenant Edwards C. Williams, also of Stevenson's Volunteers, was at Jamestown in autumn of 1848. The miners made him alcalde on the basis of a spectacular feat of horsemanship that he performed earlier. He later said that he wielded the power of life and death in the mines, although the only sentence he pronounced was whipping a Mexican thief.[22]

Both Dimmick and Williams were officers, chosen perhaps by their own soldiers to be alcalde. But men of Dimmick's caliber did not stay in the mines for long; they had better opportunities in California than serving as an alcalde in a mining camp. Dimmick was alcalde of San Jose by March 1849, and Williams, too, resigned after two weeks on the job.

After 1848, alcaldes seemed to fall into one of two groups: outrageous crooks or steady storekeepers who did some judging on the side. The latter, part-time alcaldes, appear to have been unremarkable; at least, the miners say little about them in their letters and diaries. John Scollan, who played a part in the Chilean War in December 1849, was the proprietor of a trading post on the South Fork of the Calaveras River.[23] Mr. Sears, the alcalde on the big bar of the Mokelumne River in 1849, kept a store.[24] The first justice of the peace of Tuttletown, elected in November 1851, was "a worthy carpenter of good education"; Marryat included a sketch of this "Judge Brown" deciding a dispute with the tools of his trade by his side.[25] And a young man at Goodyear's Bar wrote to his father in 1850 that "[o]ur *Alcalde* or he who deals out justice keeps a gambling house, whether he is a gambler by profession or not I cannot say."[26]

Men who kept a store or other establishment were a good fit for alcalde because they were known to all and sundry, they were likely to be in the diggings for a longer time than most, and hearing cases did not interfere with their daily business. In fact, dispute resolution could also promote trade, as in the case of Judge White of Sonoma, "who also kept a store, by-the-by, and gave his ball with an eye to business."[27]

A storekeeper also had a less obvious incentive for serving as alcalde, namely, that a reputation for order was thought to be good for a mining camp. Tradesmen, eager to attract customers, were no doubt behind the many letters to the editors of the California papers praising the riches of individual diggings. The *Alta California*, for instance, reprinted a letter from a miner at Wood's Creek on August 31, 1849. "The people here seem all very quiet, orderly and peaceably disposed," it said. "Some times there are cases of disputed rights as to mines, boundaries, water privileges, encroachments and so forth; but they are either settled amicably by reference and arbitration, or else adjudicated upon by the Alcade, Mr. Fallon, who is a very excellent and efficient magistrate." The discoverer of a new diggings gave his name to the new mining camp, set up a store, or became a judge—or all three—in the interest of attracting miners. For example, Mr. Shaw was elected alcalde of Shaw's diggings at the miners' first meeting there, and Jamestown was "named in honor of Mr. James, who is an *Alcalde* 'as is an *Alcalde*,' and who dispenses grub and justice to the satisfaction of all."[28] The letters to the *Alta* boosting Wood's Creek and Jamestown were typically positive and vague about the actual duties of the alcaldes. There are few actual descriptions of cases adjudicated by the worthies, perhaps because they were not memorable or perhaps because they were uncommon.

Then there was the other group: preposterous alcaldes. Why judges seemed to cluster at either end of the spectrum is a bit of a mystery; it may have been that if the storekeeper would not take the job as a service to his customers, then it went to someone who thought he could make some money out of it. The position was in fact meant to be a sideline, not a profession. Secretary of State Henry W. Halleck, answering an inquiry from an alcalde, said that the job did not come with a salary: alcaldes in Northern California were sufficiently remunerated by fees, he wrote, especially since official duties did not interfere with their private business.[29]

In contrast to meetings, which were intensely earnest no matter how trivial the issue under consideration, elections of any sort seemed to bring out the miners' most juvenile behavior. Texan miner James H. Cutler described the election of a constable at Mississippi Bar in the fall of 1850. The Texans voted in a "close fisted, hard hearted miser" as a practical joke, "much to the annoyance (and that was the object) of a certain very pompous, and rather ambitious Yankee, who was elected justice of the Peace at the same time." Hilarity ensued.[30] Similar silliness characterized the election for members of the new California state government at Lower Bar on the Mokelumne. In November 1849, Bayard Taylor described the proceedings, which were held in the largest tent in the neighborhood, a saloon that did good business supplying the voters with drinks. "The choosing of candidates from lists, nearly all of whom were entirely unknown, was very amusing," Taylor reported. He continued:

> Some went no further than to vote for those they actually knew. One who took the opposite extreme, justified himself in this wise: — "When I left home," said he, "I was determined to go blind. I went it blind in coming to California, and I'm

not going to stop now. I voted for the Constitution, and I've never seen the Constitution. I voted for all the candidates, and I don't know a damned one of them. I'm going it blind all through, I am."[31]

In a new community, people did not know one another, and men chose candidates the way that they might place bets at the racetrack. "Names, in many instances, were made to stand for principles; accordingly, a Mr. Fair got many votes," Taylor wrote. Stephen Field, the first alcalde of Marysville, was elected to the bench only three days after he arrived in that fledgling town. He joked that he did not get the office without a struggle; his opponent, who had been in Marysville for six days, used Field's newcomer status against him. And to add to the madness, a certain William H. Parks—someone who had never met Field—swung the election in his favor. Parks was transporting goods to the mines and reached Marysville while the voting for alcalde was in progress. He and a friend made a bet on the outcome; the winner would treat the other to dinner. Parks then got his eleven teamsters to vote for Field and won the prize.[32] Field had only a nine-vote majority—hence, Parks's claim that Field owed the office to him. Thus began the career of one of California's greatest jurists: a future chief justice of the California Supreme Court and associate justice of the United States Supreme Court. For once, random selection turned up a competent man.

Stories about the alcaldes' outlandish judgments were popular. Not coincidentally, the outrageous stories about the worst alcaldes always seemed to involve their judgments against foreigners. Americans could afford to laugh because they could ignore the alcalde if they liked by settling their differences through arbitration or by appeal to the miners' meeting. It may have taken Spanish speakers a little longer to realize that the so-called judge was a sham.

Historian Theodore Hittell reported that Alcalde Major Sullivan of Columbia "was charged with a regular system of swindling everybody with whom he had dealings; and though this charge may not have been entirely true, it seems certain that he always managed to get large fees and not always from the proper parties."[33] His first case was brought by an American who accused a Spanish speaker of stealing leggings.

The defendant was fined three ounces for the theft and the plaintiff one ounce "for complaining of him."[34]

James Carson said that he was a juror in a trial at Rich Gulch in the spring of 1849 when "two Spaniards who were known to have had great luck in digging gold" submitted "a dispute about the ownership of an old mule, worth about twenty dollars." They deposited three ounces in gold as the alcalde's fee, but as this officer could not understand a word of their testimony, he recommended a jury trial. That entailed another two ounces for the sheriff, and one each for the twelve jurors, and three ounces for the jury's liquor. Unable to reach a verdict, the jury advised the litigants to draw straws. The total cost for the proceedings was twenty-three ounces, or $368. "This the Spaniards cheerfully paid, drew *straws* and went on their way rejoicing."[35]

These particular stories may not be reliable. Everything seems wrong about the Spaniards and the mule: the reference to the Spaniards deep pockets must be intended to make the account funnier, and the assertion that they happily paid $368 for a nonjudgment about a twenty-dollar animal adds insult to injury by suggesting they were imbeciles. Moreover, the same story, almost word for word, appears in Frank Marryat's *Mountains and Molehills*, except that the ending was slightly changed: Marryat said that when the whole trial was over, the litigants were informed that another Spanish speaker "had taken the opportunity to steal the mule, and had departed to parts unknown."[36] Were it not for Carson's claim that he was on the jury, one might conclude that it was a tall tale.[37]

However, Spanish language writers—who were familiar with actual, professional alcaldes—confirmed that some of the Americans who held that title were crooked, especially in their treatment of foreigners. Chilean miner Vicente Pérez Rosales's description of the alcalde of San Francisco is almost a summary of the Americans' anecdotes:

> The supreme authority in San Francisco is not an *alcalde* as many say he is. He is only a Yankee, more or less drunk, whom they call *alcalde*. His only function, if two Yankees are quarreling, is to smooth things over; if the quarrel is between a Yankee and someone who speaks Spanish, his job is to declare the Spaniard guilty and make him pay the court costs;

if the dispute is between two Spaniards, he sees to it that the
decision goes against the one who has money enough to pay
the costs and the interpreter.[38]

Rosales also noted this further distinction between American and
Spanish-speaking alcaldes: their duties were the same, but the orders of
the Spanish officers were always carried out, "while those of the California
or San Francisco *alcalde* were carried out only if convenient."[39] This was
no doubt the key to why Americans put up with incompetent judges. It
was said that when Thomas D. Bonner of Plumas, who always favored
the party best able to pay his fees, made a ruling even more absurd than
usual, a meeting was called and a committee appointed to order him to
adjourn his court. Bonner refused, and the committee said, "If this court
chooses to place itself in contempt of the people, it must take the consequences."[40] "The people" then adjourned Judge Bonner's court. The story
may be apocryphal, but it illustrated what everyone believed: the alcalde
held his office on sufferance, and the population was the ultimate judge.

The alcalde could be ignored in civil matters, and he was usually
pushed aside entirely in criminal cases. A criminal trial always involved a
chairman or president, but instead of letting the previously elected official take this role, the miners regularly elected a new man on the spot to
conduct that day's trial. This was despite the fact that the regular alcalde
did hear criminal cases, as we know from the accounts of Dimmick and
Field. Moreover, the only mining code that includes a section on criminal
law—that of Jacksonville—provided for the alcalde to preside at criminal
trials, assisted by the sheriff. The trier of fact was a jury, of course.[41]

Even Stephen J. Field, as alcalde, felt that he had to make concessions to the popular desire for harsh punishments. Field naturally
followed proper criminal procedure. When two men were accused of
stealing gold dust, he issued a warrant for their arrest; and, finding the
gold dust on one of them, he called a grand jury, which indicted the
man. Field "then called a petit jury and assigned counsel for the prisoner." The trial took place at once, and the accused was convicted, the
whole process taking less than a day.[42]

"Curiously enough," Field wrote, "my real trouble did not commence
until after the conviction." There was no jail, and sending the man to

San Francisco would have cost fifty dollars plus the expense of an escort and a ball and chain. There was no budget for that. Meanwhile, the large crowd was excited, and there was "some talk of lynching." Field feared that if he let the thief off too lightly, the crowd might take matters into its own hands. To save the man's life, and though he found it "repugnant," he ordered the man to be given fifty lashes and banished from Marysville. But he "privately ordered a physician to be present" to be sure that the lashes were not harsher than necessary.[43] Field says in so many words what one suspects from the many lynch trials in which the crowd determined the sentence; some number of lashes was the minimum penalty that was acceptable to the more violent members of the crowd, and moderate men knew that it was no use proposing anything less. Even Field, future justice of the US Supreme Court, felt compelled to yield to popular sentiment.

Dimmick and Field were exceptionally respected and were allowed, as it were, to preside over criminal trials. Generally, however, the population of the diggings managed trials on their own, beginning with the election of a president for the purpose. J. H. Carson's memoir of the gold old times, written in 1852, wrote that the miners submitted "trifling disputes" to their alcaldes, "[b]ut if theft, robbery or murder were committed, we threw down our mining tools, shouldered our rifles, and the offending parties were soon on a trial before a jury; if he was found guilty, he then and there paid the penalty."[44] As far as the participants in a lynch trial were concerned, it was their choice whether to go with the officeholder or to try him themselves at a meeting of the miners—just as they did in later years, when the office of alcalde had been abolished. The experience of alcaldes in the mines demonstrates that Americans did not take officeholders seriously. They did not even take the *election* of such officeholders seriously and regarded themselves not only as the source of authority but the actual authority when it came to criminal trials.

## Soldiers

The military could have been another force for order, but, to make a long story short, it was not. Sent to California during the war with Mexico, long before the discovery of gold, it consisted of two groups: regular soldiers and Stevenson's Volunteers. The two army companies were small before the gold rush, totaling only 195 troops, and they almost all deserted to the mines. Company C of the First Dragoons, which was stationed in Los Angeles, behaved even more badly. It had about sixty troops when gold was discovered and only five in October.[45] Company F was almost as bad. Its commander, Lieutenant Edward O. C. Ord, later General Ord, was beside himself with anger about the desertions. He fumed to his brother Pacificus on October 21, 1848: "Of the 102 men of this co who landed here, one half of whom were Americans, not more than thirty are left, and nearly all those are Irish & Germans."[46] No one counted the sailors who deserted their ships of war upon arrival in Monterey Bay.[47] By December 1848, the month when the news of the gold rush reached the East Coast, there were only thirty-five regular soldiers in California.[48]

Washington sent some six hundred troops in the spring of 1849, a portion of whom were intended to keep the peace between the miners and the Indians whose lands were being overrun.[49] This was certainly where military force was most needed, but it is unclear whether the United States forces were able to stop any aggression against the native populations. Many of the soldiers deserted, and those who stayed were poorly supplied, poorly housed, and often sick. Captain Hannibal Day, who commanded Camp Far West near Bear Creek, a tributary of the Sacramento River, wrote that his depleted forces could offer only "the merest pretense of protection or aid of any kind to the inhabitants." He suggested that Indian agents be sent to the native population to warn them "of their probable fate unless they discontinue their thieving and submit with a better grace to being shot down."[50]

The miners were on their own at least partly because the United States government left them on their own. Neglect hardly seems like a political philosophy, but as David Goodman shows in his outstanding book comparing the Australian and California gold rushes, it was a manifestation of an American view of government. Australians had greater faith in institutions as a stabilizing force than in the character of the population, while Californians believed that the character of its citizens was the surest guarantee of harmony in society.

Australia did have a civilian government—unlike California—and its government's prime concern with respect to the gold rush was the maintenance of order. The source of order was institutions. "Order in Victoria," Goodman writes, "was widely understood . . . to involve respect for law and established institutions, among them the hierarchical nature of society."[51] The miners were governed by a body of gold field commissioners, "young men of good family," whose jobs included verifying that each miner had a license, regulating public houses, ensuring that Sundays were properly observed, and arbitrating disputes. The government invested heavily in police: Australia aimed to get two thousand police in the diggings, and it was prepared to raise police salaries to do so.[52] This large force was not sufficient to suppress crime in the mines—indeed, crime flourished—but it provided a display of order and hierarchy.

The Californian political philosophy, Goodman shows, was rather that the intelligence and virtue of the individual was the source of good government and good order.[53] With Goodman's theory in mind, it is easy to find statements, both public and private, expressing such faith in the ability of Americans to govern themselves that institutions were almost unnecessary. Senator Thomas Hart Benton said this in almost so many words in his famous, or infamous, letter to the people of California published in the *Alta California* on January 11, 1849 (written, admittedly, before Benton knew of the gold rush). "Having no lawful government," he wrote, "nor lawful officers, you can have none that can have authority over you except by your own consent." Benton positively discouraged Californians from enacting a constitution on their own authority, not only because that would be unconstitutional, but also because they could do without.

Visitors to the mines, as well as the miners themselves, were impressed by how well the diggings got on without laws or formal institutions. Some of this was, of course, for the consumption of worried wives and mothers back home, but the miners at least managed to fool Governor Riley during his tour of the diggings in 1849. He had heard rumors of irregularities and crimes but was agreeably surprised to find that order and regularity prevailed throughout. "In each little settlement or tented town the miners have elected their local *Alcaldes* and

Constables, whose judicial decisions and official acts are sustained by the people, and enforced with much regularity and energy."[54] We know that alcaldes were not, in fact, generally respected; and when the governor spoke with individual miners, butter would not melt in mouths. ("What's going on in this classroom?" "Nothing, Sir!") Nevertheless, the idea of peaceful assembly and orderly self-government was one that Americans loved as much as Australians distrusted, and leaving the miners to their own devices in the diggings was, if not official policy, at least not a source of concern to the federal government.

# CHAPTER 3

# Indian Miners

Private property in mining claims disintegrated in 1848, as did the judiciary and the army. Judges and soldiers went to the mines; *everyone* went to the mines. San Francisco was left empty, all work abandoned, everyone believing that he would make his fortune in gold in a matter of weeks. At first, it seemed that one foundation of California society—the exploitation of Indian labor—was secure. Ranchers, most of whom had been in California for some three to seven years before the gold discovery, owned huge tracts of land in the Sacramento Valley that were worked by Indians.[1] They planned to use their hundreds of laborers for mining on a grand scale, counting on their readiness to work for a little food and cheap trade goods, as well as their ignorance of gold and its value. Within six months, however, most ranchers had given up working with Indians and shifted to trade or other ventures.

Employers failed to make money because using hired labor, no matter how cheap, was not profitable. This was one reason why direct capital investment in gold mining had to wait until the surface gold was mined out. When miners rejoiced that labor had the upper hand of capital, they did not mean that labor was able to exclude capital, but that there were no opportunities for capital investment. There was no profit there. In fact, it would become clear that placer gold mining itself—mining on individual, surface claims—was almost always less profitable than wage labor. Miners of European and American descent never fully accepted this because of the magic of gold.

Trying to see the 1848 gold rush through Indian eyes gives a realistic view of the economics of 1848. Persons of European descent described the Indians as naive and easily manipulated, whereas, in fact, their lack of preconceptions was an advantage. It was the immigrants whose judgment was clouded by their knowledge of the value of gold in the developed world. The following discussion in no way challenges the evidence that the Indians generally were exploited, cheated, enslaved, and, beginning in the fall of 1848, slaughtered or that they were eventually driven from their land altogether.[2] Ultimately, the Americans killed or expelled all of the native population. These atrocities are the big story—and the fact that a few Indians managed not to get cheated in 1848 does not change that.

In pre–gold rush days, whites classified Indians as "tame" or "wild," like animals.[3] The former were those who worked for white ranchers while the latter followed their traditional way of life in their own villages.[4] The Indians whom the ranchers first brought to the mines were ranch hands, whereas those who mined for themselves lived locally.

Early successes by miners working on the Feather River attracted "all the settlers in the upper end of the [Sacramento] valley, each one accompanied by a score or more of Indians, who did the mining under direction of their employers, their wages being plenty of meat to eat, and trinkets of little value."[5] Colonel Richard B. Mason himself wrote that Antonio María Suñol and his partners employed thirty Indians whom they paid with merchandise.[6]

Ranchers working with Indians are prominent in the accounts of jaw-dropping sums earned in the summer of 1848. Richard B. Mason provided the following financial crawler in a letter dated August 17, 1848: William Daly (Daylor) and Perry McCoon made $17,000 gross in one week with four whites and one hundred Indians; John Sinclair made $16,000 net in five weeks with fifty Indians; Job F. Dye made 273 pounds (about $70,000) in seven weeks and two days with fifty Indians.[7] Major Pierson B. Reading was reported to have made $80,000 in mining with a crew of Indians in the region of the Trinity River.[8] In a letter to James Buchanan, Thomas Larkin reported that "[o]ne man told for this number he expected from 40 Indians $1 a minute, 10 hours in a day, $600."[9] This calculation was absurd; nothing about mining was predictable.

All these figures are implausibly well-rounded to pounds of gold and multiples of $1,000; and, at best, they represent the companies' balance sheet at the height of their success: the phrase "in one week" meant in their best week. The correspondence between the rancher Thomas O. Larkin and his partners in the mines, Charles Sterling and three brothers of the Williams family, documents how much their fortunes fluctuated. Sterling reported to Larkin on August 15 that after a shaky start, their Indians were averaging $200 to $500 per day and they had "about 20 lbs. of gold nearly clean and about 150 or 200 lbs. not clean."[10] Twenty pounds would be worth about $5,000. Shortly after this letter, however, nearly all of the whites in camp became sick and the work came to an abrupt halt.[11] On September 4, after a sad interval in which Squire Williams died and his brother James was near death but recovered,[12] the third brother, John, took up the pen to Larkin:

> You express in one of your letters that we have on hand some 18 or 20 thousand dollars. This is over-estimated. We worked but eighteen days previous to our sickness, which so disarranged our plans that I found it necessary to send the greater part of the Indians back.[13]

On October 18, John Williams wrote to say he was very much surprised by reports that Larkin had told people that the company had made even *more*—namely, $30,000.[14] The rumor mill had inflated the $5,000 or $10,000 total gross earnings for the season to $20,000 and then $30,000. What Larkin's company really had left at the end of the summer may have been a couple of thousand dollars. It is probable that other reports of fortunes made with Indian labor also reflected short-lived bonanzas and that even these were wildly exaggerated.

Even the alleged fortunes made with Indian labor suggest low returns per Indian. *Supposing* that Thomas O. Larkin's report to Buchanan that a few men with forty Indians were making $2,000 per week was correct, even though that is a suspiciously round sum, then each Indian generated less than ten dollars per day, or about half as much as a miner working for himself. The Indians had no incentive to exert themselves, after all. Larkin's partners in the mines found that it was impossible to force them to work hard at this uncongenial labor. Little more than a week after they began mining, about June 29, "the Indians became discontented and complained that they wanted their squaws, and became quite saucy & John was under the necessity of thrashing one of them and that night every one of them *ran* away and long before this are on the Rancho." The partners had to dig for themselves and "worked like *horses*" at "the hardest labour that God ever willed that white men should perform."[15]

Further, employers discovered that their Indian workers consumed more in provisions than they produced in gold. The cost of food was a serious concern. Writing in November 1848, William Tecumseh Sherman gave his opinion that Indian wage labor was a losing proposition. "I have not yet seen one of those parties do well," he said, "when the Master provides all the grub, cooks it, tends to horses, cures the sick &c &c and depend upon the proceeds of this labor for his profits." Sherman claimed also to know that Indian laborers pocketed some of the gold that they found, adding that "Californians or Yankees or foreigners are not too good to do the same."[16]

And then there was the problem of blankets, which in itself could represent the economy of 1848. After Larkin's Indians quit, partner John Williams went to Sutter's Fort to "buy what he would need to get the Indians to come back,"[17] while Sterling went to San Francisco for wares, particularly blankets. "I do not know what I will do for blankets," Sterling wrote Larkin on July 14. "We need them for our Indians on their arrival." Samuel Brannan had bought up everything that resembled a blanket, including double-width carpeting.[18] Clearly, the Indians could not be forced to work; they had to be lured, and they were not willing to work for just anything; they demanded blankets, serapes, and other goods that were very now hard to get.

By December 1848, very few whites were still working with large teams of Indians, although there were some still doing so into 1849.[19] One reading of this development is that Native Americans stopped working for wages when they realized they could do better on their own and that ranchers, in turn, adapted by going into trade. That was the impression of Englishman William Thurston, who observed in 1849 that "[e]ven the poor Indian, when you talk of hiring him, shakes his bag of gold in your eyes." According to Thurston, when Indians started mining for themselves, the last source of wage labor had dried up. "The consequence is, we have no hired labourers—no servants; every man must black his own boots. . . . This is a practical democracy—no theory—no talking about equality."[20] In other words, the claim that it was impossible for capital to oppress labor in the gold rush, once labor knew its strength, extended to Indians. Meanwhile, Americans realized that they could make more money by trade than by supervising Indian workers.

## Trading with Indians

From the beginning, Indians collected gold on their own and traded it with individual miners—literally for the shirts off their backs—or with traders. Some observers in 1848 described trade as just another way to exploit the natives, in this case by taking advantage of their ignorance about the value of gold or by outright cheating.[21] "The Indians had learned what the gold was and how to collect it, but knew nothing of its real value," wrote an ex-miner thirty years later. "[A] dollar's worth of gold with them was the weight of a silver dollar."[22] The evidence for this, however, is mixed.

Some merchants claim simply to have charged Indians higher prices than they did whites. Larkin's man Schallenberger reported matter-of-factly, "Sell vary high to Indians . . . shirts 16$, to whites 5$."[23] More often, sellers boasted of tricking Indian customers. Chester Lyman, who was himself a trader, wrote in his diary on October 25, 1848, "From the Indians all sorts of prices are taken and much deception is practiced. A common practice is to use a two oz weight for an oz &c."[24]

Edward Gould Buffum, a New York Volunteer who was in the mines in 1848, was disgusted that traders would take advantage of an Indian buyer who was "ready to part with his gold, of the value of which he had no idea, on the most accommodating terms . . . purchasing raisins and almonds at sixteen dollars a pound."[25] But Buffum went further and suggested that the traders literally, as well as metaphorically, robbed their customers. The Indians eventually made a practice of visiting a trader in groups of ten or twelve, he wrote. They would sit in a circle around the shop and approach the counter one by one. Each in turn would offer a teaspoonful of gold dust and indicate the article he wanted to buy. If the dealer refused, the bidder would go back to his place and bring back a little more dust until, eventually, he reached an amount that was acceptable to the seller. Further, if the Native American wanted to buy several of an item, he would buy each one separately, bringing the required quantity of dust from his place in the circle each time. "The only conceivable object of this mode of proceeding," Buffum thought, was that "the poor creatures have been frequently plundered, and are afraid to trust themselves alone with a white man with too much gold upon their persons."[26] Buffum implies that the trader might otherwise have confiscated the gold without handing over the desired goods, but also that the Indians knew this and adapted.

Since Americans murdered Indians on a whim, it is entirely plausible that they also robbed them, but it was not necessarily true that traders charged them more than they did whites. Writers were astounded that Indians were willing to pay sixteen dollars for a shirt and the same amount for a pound of raisins, but whites in fact paid the same prices. If Larkin's employee Schallenberger sold shirts to whites for five dollars when Indians were willing to pay sixteen dollars, he was a chump because other traders were charging sixteen dollars across the board. Buffum himself recounted, "As my clothing was all dirty and wet, I concluded to indulge in the luxury of a new shirt, and going down to the river found a shrewd Yankee in a tent surrounded by a party of naked Indians . . . and for a coarse striped shirt which I picked up with the intention of purchasing, he coolly asked me the moderate price of sixteen dollars!"[27] Of course. Why would a trader sell a white man a shirt for less than he could get from an Indian?

As for raisins, Theodore Johnson reported that at the Stanislaus diggings "a box of raisins sold also *weight for weight,* or about four thousand dollars in gold dust."[28] The reason: "[R]aisins were eaten for the cure of scurvy, prevailing without remedy." Buffum estimated that at least half the miners suffered from scurvy in 1848, himself included.

He asked someone to buy him a dose of salts and to "pay for it any price that should be asked." The messenger returned empty-handed, having "found only two persons who had brought the article with them, and they refused to sell it at any price."[29] In a case of life or death, men would pay whatever it cost.

One white man, the Mexican Californian Antonio Franco Coronel, set an even higher value on his clothing than the Indians were willing to offer. On the day that Coronel and his partners arrived at Stanislaus camp, as he later reminisced, they were visited by "seven tame Indians, each one with little sacks of gold shaped like sausages, of an average length of ten to twelve inches."[30] One of these Indians wanted to buy a dirty old blanket and showed how much of his gold sausage he was prepared to pay. Coronel refused because he would not be able to replace the blanket. The Indian increased his offer; Coronel again refused. When the Indian raised his offer yet again, Coronel's servant advised him to sell, adding that he could make Coronel a new saddle blanket out of grass. The deal was done, and the gold turned out to weigh 7.25 ounces, worth $116 at the time. Another Indians immediately offered to buy Coronel's other blanket for the same price; the latter again refused, but eventually sold the second blanket for nine ounces. Then the Indians tried to buy his se-rape, his main protection from the elements. They pooled their resources to bid *three and one-half pounds of gold* (italics in the original)—almost $900—and he still refused.[31] When Coronel dictated his reminiscences thirty years later, the offer still amazed him, but his own refusal of $900 was just as amazing. He valued the serape more than the Indians did.

The whites who made money from trade with Indians were the ones who were fair in their dealings. John Murphy first traded with Indians at Weber's Creek, "taking in gold very fast, selling glass beads for their weight in gold."[32] But Murphy later moved his tent to be near "a small tribe of wild Indians who gather gold for him, and receive in return provisions and blankets," according to Walter Colton, who added, "Though never before within the wake of civilization, they respect his person and property,"[33] a reminder that a lone white man was there at the sufferance of the local population.

The most complete description of trade with Indians was by Alonzo Delano, who had a store near a village of Oleepa Indians for three

months in 1850.[34] Delano's memoirs include detailed observations of
the Indians and accounts of his relations with them. It is true that the
economy of the mining region in 1850 was vastly different from what
it was in 1848; but where native communities remained intact, the inhabitants cannot have changed completely, and Delano's portrait of the
Oleepa suggests very little Westernization.

Delano "took every occasion which offered to conciliate them." Some
of Delano's friendly gestures were calculated, such as his statement to
group of Indians that "I was a physician, (Heaven help me for the de-
ceit!) and if they got sick I would cure them." He gave each of them a
small pill of opium as a sample, which they swallowed at once. Not surprisingly, "they seemed delighted" when he said that he would make his
camp near them and that they would be very good friends. Although he
said he only pretended to be a doctor, Delano knew a good deal about
medicine, and this helped to earn him the friendship of the Oleepa. It
did not earn him any money directly, however, as the idea of paying for
medical care was foreign to his patients.[35]

Delano may have set out to ingratiate himself with the Oleepa villagers,
but over time, a genuine friendship developed between them. The Oleepa
impressed Delano as affectionate and kind, gentle, generous, honest in
their dealings with one another, and "probably less likely to break the
laws which they recognize as right, than are the whites to break theirs."[36]
Delano claims to have been strictly honest in his business dealings with
the natives. "My confidence was never abused," he wrote. "I never abused
theirs."[37] From his accounts, it seems that the Indians liked and respected
him as much as he did them. One incident in particular demonstrates
the mutual affection. Delano went down to the river with a bevy of little
boys to watch a steamboat go by in the dusk. As it passed, its smokestack
emitted a burst of sparks. The terrified little boys threw themselves into
Delano's arms and clung to his legs and coat. "[T]heir affectionate confidence thrilled my heart," he wrote, "and I am not ashamed to confess,
betrayed me into unusual emotion."[38]

Delano did not get rich from his trading days and eventually sold out
his stock and returned to mining for himself.[39] Others who cultivated
the goodwill of Indian communities made enormous profits, however.
"A little short fat Dutchman named Smidt" was said to be "one of the

few who obtained a considerable quantity of gold dust, by employing Indians to dig." "Employing" here means trading with them for gold. Smidt "acquired his influence with the Indians chiefly by kindnesses and a knowledge of their language."[40] It seems that Indians knew little of the value of gold, but they knew enough to prefer honest and friendly traders to those who prided themselves on their ability to dupe them.

## Indians as Gold Miners

Indians are not known to have risked their health for gold, but apart from that, groups and individuals reacted differently to the new source of income. Some Indians adopted gold digging as another form of foraging. According to Edward Gould Buffum, Indian mining differed little from basket weaving or gathering berries. He wrote that "[a] portion of the tribe go daily to the Yuba River, and wash out a sufficient amount of gold to purchase a few pounds of flour, or some sweetmeats, and return to the rancheria at night to share it with their neighbours; who in their turn go the next day, while the others are chasing hare and deer over the hills."[41] These Indians were digging not to get rich, but to augment their dinners.

Other Indians enjoyed drinking. As one miner said in a letter to his wife dated May 1851, "I have seen some of the squaws digging gold all day with a child on their Back slung in a Basket what gold they dig does not amount to much for they generally lay it out in Brandy and men woman and children gets drunk together."[42] Drinking, and indeed "frivolous squandering" generally, is typical of gold rush culture the world over. Miners in Africa, Brazil, Papua New Guinea, and, of course, California repeatedly spent all of their earnings on a "spree," after which they went back to digging. Indians who dug all day to get drunk in the evening were no different from gold miners everywhere.[43]

For their part, white miners were largely blind to the Indian economy and missed opportunities both to make money and to make their own lives in the mines more comfortable. Few knew what products the Indians desired most; fewer still stopped to consider that they could learn from Indians about survival in the foothills of the Sierra Nevada. One could say that the whites *overvalued* gold in that they mined it and used it to buy necessities that they could have gotten more easily in other ways.

Whites understood, or were made to understand, the value of blankets in the mines; but they continued to regard beads as mere trinkets and thought it was a good joke that Indians paid such high prices for them. The "outrageous prices" that the "poor Indians" paid for beads were in fact the norm.[44] The Indian Chief Antonio had "more than a bushel and a half of beads," which "had cost the chief their weight in gold—that being the price of beads when the bulk of them were purchased."[45] At his death in the spring of 1850, the beads, along with his serapes and blankets, were burned on his funeral pyre. Beads and blankets were as good as currency among the Native Americans. Alonzo Delano wrote of his neighbors, the Oleepa, that "[t]hey are most inveterate gamblers, and frequently play away every article of value they possess; but beads are their staple gambling currency."[46] Insofar as beads were the Indian's currency, it seems almost fitting that they should trade for their weight in the white man's currency, namely, the equally decorative and useless gold.

If only the forty-niners had known to bring beads across the plains with them, they would have spared themselves a great deal of misery. A miner by the name of Ananisas Pond and his companions arrived at the Feather River in October 1849 and wished to buy a salmon from an Indian who came to their camp:

> I offered Gold he showed me he wished Beads by taking some & showing[. O]f this kind of Merchandise we were not possessed[.] I tried Silver No A Hunters knife Still No, again he showed the beads A Calico shirt. Nothing would do but Beads. We were not bad furnished with money Arms provisions & clothing with all we could not purchase the Naked Indians Fish.[47]

A Native American who wanted only beads was a rarity; but it was not by chance that Pond had none of that article. Americans did not take beads seriously. John Swan sceptically added a pound of glass beads to 240 pounds of provisions and trade goods when he set out for the mines in late July 1848. "Some people told me glass beads sold to the Indians for their weight in gold in the mines," he wrote in his memoir, "but though I did not believe it, I took them with me as they were of not much weight and took up but little room."[48] Swan eventually sold his beads to Indians for seven ounces and was happy with that.[49] He thought prices had dropped, but one wonders whether he bargained hard enough. As to what Swan might have paid for those beads, it was later reported that one of the earliest traders at Wood's Crossing, in the southern mines, "actually obtained $6,000 worth of gold, for a small lot of beads, that cost $2.50 in San Francisco."[50]

One trader exploited the gap between the value that newly arrived immigrants attached to beads and the price that Native Americans were prepared to pay. Smidt, the "little short, fat Dutchman" mentioned above, "sold common glass beads all last winter, whenever he could obtain them from Kanakas, or newly-arrived emigrants, to the Indians for gold, weight for weight."[51] There is a wonderful parallel universe here. Migrants who had no conception of the value of beads sold them to Smidt for much less than they were worth; and when he and others sold those beads to the Indians for their weight in gold, the Americans thought the *Indians* were the dupes. One wonders whether the Dutch who bought Manhattan Island for trade goods including beads in fact overpaid for that bit of real estate, given the local economy.

Resentment against Indians eventually put an end both to trade and employment. James Savage's Indians were harassed, and passing Oregonians broke up Reading's workforce on the Trinity River.[52] General violence against Indians also drove many from the mines. There was a share of the white population that simply hated all Indians, gold diggers or not, and killed them for no reason.[53] Mr. Smidt related a terrible story. A white man, "in looking for a lost horse, called an Indian boy to go and aid him: the poor boy not understanding him ran away in fright, but was instantly shot dead by the rifle of his pursuer."[54]

Nevertheless, despite the opposition to Indian labor, some Indians continued to work for whites at least into 1850. Some employers did well, but others found that working with Indians was not profitable. "Indians are said to be willing to provide their services to anyone who will provide beef, bread and blankets," wrote Thomas Butler King in his report on the mines published in March 1850, "but even at this rate it hardly pays to employ them since they won't work."[55] Batchelder made a similar observation in his journal; the Indians "are not to be depended on as laborers, being unused to and too lazy to work and will leave it whenever they take a fancy to do so."[56] The exploitation of the Indians would come in the much worse form of massacring them and driving them from their land.

The general observation that "labor rules the diggings" and that employers could find no opportunity in the mines held true even for those with native Californian workers. In one of the greatest gold rushes in history, the vast majority of miners—Indian or white—barely produced enough to survive and definitely not enough to generate wealth for their employers. These economic paradoxes cap the list of fundamental institutions missing from the gold region: there was no government, no laws, no judges and no police. And there was no community and no family: the miners of any mining camp were strangers to one another and elected a stranger to the post of alcalde.

Meetings took the place of government and social institutions, that organized the mining companies and ran the criminal trials. Most famously, it was meetings that adopted the mining codes, the laws of the gold rush.

# CHAPTER 4

# The Mining Codes

The first mining codes were probably enacted in early 1849 as the final step in the transition from no property rights to an agreed upon set of rules governing mining claims. The study of gold rush law has long focused on these mining codes because they are so impressively *legal*. The opening words of several codes, "We the Miners," echoed the "We the People" of the US Constitution; and the form of a preamble followed by numbered rules, or "laws," is instantly identifiable as a law code. The miners themselves considered the codes to be among their main legal accomplishments, criminal trials being the other; and their mining rules were recognized and applied by the California courts when those began to take mining cases. The first scholarly work on the miners' own laws was a thirty-page section in Gregory Yale, *Legal Titles to Mining Claims and Water Rights in California,* published in 1867 when miners were still adopting codes.[1] In 1884, Charles Howard Shinn published *Land Laws of the Mining Districts,* the first book on gold rush "law"; and Clarence King's *The United States Mining Laws,* a massive collection of mining codes from California and other Western states commissioned by the Department of the Interior, appeared the following year as part of the US Serial Set.[2] In short, the miners themselves made big claims for their codes, and the imprimatur of the courts and Department of the Interior, together with modern scholarship, have created the impression that code making was the miners' greatest legal accomplishment.

And yet, the fundamentals of the California claim system turn out to have been nothing special. There have been many gold rushes around the world, and although the miners elsewhere did not enact codes, the mining rules were much the same in Australia, Canada, Brazil, West Africa, and Papua New Guinea. In every case, a miner was entitled to a certain small area that he forfeited if he left for more than a few days. The universality of the claim system therefore appears not to be a choice, but an inevitability dictated by the presence of gold near the surface, on the one hand, and a surplus of would-be miners, on the other. The claim system was not invented and did not reflect particularly American values.

The fact that the miners adopted mining codes at miners' meetings, however, *was* distinctively American. The population of a diggings agreed on detailed rules very efficiently, and in doing so, they were making laws, since the rules would apply to everyone present and also to those who might arrive in the future. In Australia and Canada, the governments made a point of controlling the mining rules, while in other gold rushes, norms appear to have emerged spontaneously.[3]

In Canada, a small population of miners was active in the Yukon region before the gold rush in the Klondike (1897–1899). These miners were mostly Americans or Americanized, and they organized themselves in the American manner; that is, each community governed itself through miners' meetings that also served as a criminal court and as a forum for civil disputes.[4]

This democratic system was foreign to the Canadian tradition of centralized government now known as metropolitanism, but for a time, Ottawa left the miners to themselves.[5] Ottawa's policy changed in 1894 when it decided to send a force of Mounted Police to the Yukon, in part as a statement of Canadian sovereignty over the region and also in response to calls from local traders for government supervision. One of the Mounties' first moves was to suppress the miners' meetings, at least in their capacity of legal decision makers. The land agent, Charles Constantine, achieved this in the summer of 1896 by voiding the ruling of a miners' meeting over a claim dispute and substituting a decision in line with formal Canadian law. As he told the miners, their private lawmaking "was not legal and must not occur again."[6] The miners, faced with ten Mounties and their officer, submitted. Thus, at the time of the subsequent great gold strike, 1986, Canada had an active and visible police force in place and had ensured that the property regime in the mines would be determined in Ottawa.

The California gold rush, of course, did not have the benefit of a government; and for American miners, written codes had advantages over informal norms. First, bright-line written rules regarding claim size and work requirements reduced conflict; and when disputes did arise, they were easier to resolve. In enacting a code, miners also decided emotionally charged questions, including most importantly, whether each miner was entitled to only one claim or whether successful miners could, instead, accumulate claims and hire others to work them. And finally, meetings served as a mechanism for changing the rules, such as, for instance, reducing claim size when there was an influx of miners or increasing claim size when the area was worked out.

Although American miners did not invent the idea of temporary-use rights in auriferous land, they celebrated this naturally occurring instance of what we might call "worker control of the means of production." Their letters and diaries disclose a deep well of resentment against men of money and power at home, men who employed them, profited from their labor, were believed to look down on them, and, most of all, who enjoyed money and independence beyond their reach. They had come to California to get rich and to be able to buy the farm or the workshop that represented independence. That was the reason that some miners gave for supporting a one-claim-per-miner rule: allowing successful miners to buy up multiple claims would allegedly reduce others to the status of wages laborers, precisely what they had come to California to escape. The fear of "capital" and "monopoly," however unreasonable, manifested a kind of us-versus-them populism that, in later years, justified taking an accused criminal from jail and hanging him after a speedy trial. All power derived from the people, and they could reclaim it at will.

This chapter describes the mining code system and claim jumping as an integral part of that system. It discusses modern attempts to explain the miners' choice to have limited use rights in land rather than ownership and shows that the system was *not*, in fact, a choice, but an inevitability given the distribution of gold. There were decisions to be made regarding details, however, and here the miners' meeting did do real work.

## The Mining Claim System

Early mining claims were very small—ten feet by ten feet was common—and if the claim holder was gone for more than a few days—three, five, or ten days depending on the code—anyone else could jump in and take the claim for himself. In other words, the claim holder had a use right to a standard-size plot; if he did not use it, he lost it. This is a very limited kind of property, like a student's right to a cubical in a crowded library. No one owns a particular spot, but someone who is currently occupying it will be left in peace.

The claim system provided an agreed upon signal that a claim was occupied and the claim holder was coming back. Unlike the student and his cubicle, which is a clearly defined space, the miners also needed consensus on the maximum dimensions of a claim and whether a person could hold more than one claim at a time. Also, unlike students, the miners held meetings to enact rules that would apply to everyone in the diggings. The first of these were drafted in the winter of 1848–1849. The rules, as miner John Borthwick wrote, "were generally very few and simple":

> They defined how many feet of ground one man was enti- tled to hold in a ravine—how much in the bank, and in the bed of the creek; how many such claims he could hold at a time; and how long he could absent himself from his claim without forfeiting it. They declared what was necessary to be done in taking up and securing a claim which, for want of water, or from any other cause, could not be worked at the time.[7]

Miners were constantly abandoning claims because they proved disap- pointing or because of rumors of fabulous new diggings elsewhere. It was a cliché in the mines that mining was a lottery, and, as with all lotteries, success was unrelated to deserts. Some diggings were rich, and every claim yielded lots of gold; while others yielded a small but steady income. But most miners worked in diggings where the gold seemed to be distributed almost randomly. As Bayard Taylor wrote, "In holes dug side by side, I noticed that the clay would be reached eighteen inches below the surface in one, and perhaps eight feet in the other. This makes the digging something of a lottery, those who find a deposit always finding a rich one, and those who find none making nothing at all."[8] A hundred parties could be at work on a bar, all digging from dawn to dusk, and one would hit upon a fortune in gold while the others barely made their keep. Even a single claim could yield very different amounts from one day to the next, so that future earnings could not be predicted from the history of the claim. "Cases are very frequent of persons making $100 in a day, and sometimes in a single hour, and the whole week following making nothing," a gold seeker reported.[9]

Miners played this lottery because they were addicted to the thrill of the chase and the dream of fabulous wealth. "Some fifty thousand persons are drifting up and down these slopes of the great Sierra," Walter Colton wrote in the spring of 1849, "tumultuous and confused as a flock of wild geese taking flight at the crack of a gun. . . . All are in quest of gold; and, with eyes dilated to the circle of the moon, rush this way and that, as some new discovery or fictitious tale of success may suggest."[10] They *knew*—or soon learned—that they would have been better off working steadily in one place; the rumors were always exaggerated, and time was too valuable to lose in chasing after them. Simon Doyle, a miner on the Feather River in 1851, lamented that "had we stayed at this place from the time we first came here and worked along the River for what we could have made we mite now have had $300,00 a pecis [*sic*] but like nearly every body else I wanted to make my pile in a few weeks and go—and instead of making spent what we had made."[11]

Claim jumping was the essence of a system of use rights: an unused claim was free for the taking. L. M. Schaeffer, describing the longed for return of the rainy season in September 1851, said, "Now the absent miners return; now our village presents a more cheerful appearance; claims that were deserted are being 'jumped' by new comers, and claims which yielded well and were watched over by the miners during the summer months, are being restaked, and active preparations going on for the ensuing winter."[12] Abandoned claims were jumped when miners saw value in them, and that was a sign that the diggings were promising.

Americans naturally held a meeting to adopt rules. "It was customary for the few miners who chanced to be at work in any particular vicinity to meet together under some tree, and after organizing in town meeting form to pass a system of law which should have force in the particular diggings," wrote miner Joseph Warren Wood. The phrase "town meeting form" itself evoking the habits of home, and "system of law" suggests, again, that this was not only an agreement among the miners who were present, but a set of rules that would apply to everyone who might come to the diggings.[13]

Any change in the rules entailed a follow-up meeting. "Of course, like other laws they required constant revision and amendment, to suit the progress of the times," as J. D. Borthwick noted.[14] When disputes over claims were appealed to the miners' meeting, its decision might, in effect, create a new rule. The large body of subsidiary rules that would be necessary in any camp was probably created entirely through such individual judgments, which may or may not have been remembered when a similar dispute arose at a later date.[15]

The meetings took the usual form. The code of the Warren Hill Mining District, one that begins "We the Miners," was the end product of a process that began at seven o'clock in the evening, October 21, 1853, with the election of J. H. Kilbourn as chairman. Having chosen a chairman, the miners then elected a committee to draft laws, which the assembled miners would discuss either immediately or at a second meeting. Even these preliminary measures adhered strictly to parliamentary procedure:

> On motion of Mr. Haymond the chairman appointed the following gentleman [sic] as a committee to draft a constitution and Bye Laws viz: W.H. Lester C.M. Bosworth C. Bordwell C.F. Jackson Geo. McKelvey
>
> On motion of W.H. Lester, the chairman was added to the committee and Creed Haymond appointed Secretary.
>
> On motion of Mr. R.B. Sigafoose, the meeting proceeded to elect a recorder

On motion of Mr. Hall, the vote was taken by ballot, Geo. H. Stockwell and J.S. Hayden acting as Tellers.

59 votes were given of which J.H. Kilbourn received 37, C.F. Jackson 14, scattering 8.

On motion the meeting adjourned.[16]

This was quite an undertaking just to appoint a chairman, secretary, and committee and to elect a recorder. At least 118 persons were present, since that is the number who cast votes. Five motions were made by at least four different people, not counting the election of the chairman; and at least nine men were candidates or served as committee members or tellers. It was all in a day's work for Americans, even ones who did not know one another. At four o'clock the next day, the drafters presented their proposed constitution, as they called it. "It was taken up article by article" and adopted unanimously.

Attendance at meetings was open to all Americans, that is, to anglophone American citizens and others who intended to become citizens. Voters included miners who had just arrived, who had no claim, and who had no immediate prospect of a claim.[17] Transaction costs do not appear to have been a problem: the immigrants were experienced in the routine of self-organization and could base their own code on customary law and the codes of other districts so that the meetings need not have taken much time. Those who did not have claims had little else to do, in any case. Meetings and elections were also frequently scheduled in the evenings or on a Sunday, a day many miners set aside for business and chores.

The codes were a natural place for the miners to apply their republican skills. In a few cases, the drafters made the most of the occasion, adding wildly ambitious preambles that echoed America's founding documents, like that of the laws of Warren Hill.[18] The rules themselves, however, hardly represented a new social contract. With one exception, the codes applied only to mining law.[19] They generally included provisions on maximum claim sizes, the number of claims one miner could hold, a standard form of notice, and a work requirement. If there were various forms of mining in the district—dry diggings, river turning, quartz mining, coyote holes, etc.—then the specifications for each could run to twenty-three articles or more.[20] Many codes also provided mechanisms for resolving claim disputes and for future revisions of the laws; many, also, excluded non-Americans from the mines. The common law sufficed for all other areas, most notably contract law, and criminal law was almost never codified.

Claim size was naturally a fundamental building block of any code; there had to be a limit on how much one man could hold by location— that is, by jumping an old claim or staking out a new one on virgin ground, as opposed to buying a claim from its current holder—because otherwise one man could "claim" an entire diggings. If a miner located more than the maximum, the excess could be jumped. In 1849, claims were usually ten feet by ten feet in dry diggings and fifteen feet by twenty feet along a river.[21] Smaller claims would have been impracticable; a claim ten feet square was hardly big enough to contain both the hole and the pile of dirt that came out of it, and one was not allowed to throw dirt on one's neighbor's claim. At the phenomenally rich Mokelumne Hill, which was divided into ten-foot claims, one miner would have to put off digging until his neighbor had cleared his claim.[22] At this point, the diggings were effectively packed. At Rich Bar in the spring of 1851, only one in twenty newcomers could secure a vacant claim; the rest had to move on.[23] The maximum claim size grew over the years as the diggings were exhausted and mining methods advanced to allow processing larger volumes of dirt.[24] By the mid-1850s, claims were one hundred feet square, that is, ten thousand square feet; they produced a small but steady income, and the chances of striking it rich had disappeared.

Every mining code specified the form of notice required to hold a claim and the maximum time that the claim holder could be away. The specifics varied: miners might have to post notices bearing the signature of the claimant and the date of the claim; to drive a two-foot-long, three-and-one-half-inch-wide stake into the center of the claim; or to drive a stake into each corner and one in the middle bearing the number of the claim.[25] Some requirements suggest earlier abuses; for instance, the rule that the claimant sign his notice indicates that some miners had been reserving claims for friends who had not yet arrived. Almost all early mining codes required miners to work their claims at least once in every five, seven, or ten days to retain them, unless the claim holder was sick or disabled.[26] Notice requirements and use requirements overlapped in that regular use was itself a kind of notice, as suggested in rules of Big Oak Flat: "[E]very claimant shall, from time to time, give reasonable evidence that he has not abandoned his claim, by leaving effective tools, or doing such work as will sustain the fact."[27]

It was in the claim holder's interest to provide notice of his claim to keep off others; but the notice and work *requirements* served newcomers by letting them know which claims were jumpable, or free for the taking. They might otherwise put a lot of work into a spot that turned out to be occupied, as when a party of novices who had only been in the mines ten days found an old hole without tools in it and began to dig. (This was at Mormon Island in April 1850.) They dug all day, but at night the "owner" came back and claimed it. The inadvertent jumpers surrendered the claim, though they kept the ten dollars they had made from it.[28]

All diggings allowed a miner only one claim by location, that is, by taking unoccupied ground. Diggings differed, however, on whether they allowed a miner to hold more than one claim by purchase: some codes allowed miners to locate one claim and to buy as many others as they liked; while according to others, a miner could not hold more than one claim of any description at a time.[29] This made an enormous difference—the difference between a group being able to buy up a significant share of the diggings, on the one hand, and every man having only as much as he was actually using, on the other. The argument for allowing unlimited purchase was, as the California Supreme Court held much later, in 1861, that mining claims were property and, like all property, could be transferred.[30] This rather begged the question, of course. The argument against allowing individuals to hold multiple claims, as miner Pringle Shaw explained, was that "miners and mining laws are in most instances in radical opposition to all monopoly."[31] The effect of the one-claim rule in camps that adopted it was that a miner could hold only as much as he was working, while he was actively at work. He could locate or buy another claim only if he gave up the first.

There is some scanty evidence that the default rule was one claim per person. One of these is "The Miner's Ten Commandments" of 1853, a witty and extremely popular variation on the rules revealed to Moses in the Bible.[32] Most of the "commandments" are elaborate caricatures of miners' bad habits. The injunction against getting drunk is particularly amusing because it captures the miners' incongruous taste for fancy cocktails: "Neither shalt thou destroy thyself by getting 'tight' . . . drinking smoothly down—'brandy slings,' 'gin cocktails,' 'whiskey punches,' 'rum toddies,' nor 'egg-noggs.' Neither shalt thou suck 'mint juleps,' nor 'sherry-cobblers' through a straw." But the first commandment, corresponding to "Thou shalt have no other gods before me," was simply, "Thou shalt have no other claim than one." The echo of the real first commandment was a joke, but the joke worked because one claim was the norm.

In diggings with a one-claim rule, the analogy between a miner's rights in his claim and a library reader's rights in his cubicle is particularly strong. Both are the kind of use rights that Blackstone imagined existed at the beginning of human society. "The ground was in common, and no part of it was the permanent property of any man in particular," Blackstone wrote, "yet whoever was in the occupation of any determined spot of it, for rest, for shade, or the like, acquired for the time a sort of ownership from which it would have been unjust, and contrary to the law of nature, to have driven him by force: but the instant that he quitted the use or occupation of it, another might seize it, without injustice."[33] Many diggings, however, allowed a miner to hold one claim by location and as many as he wished by purchase, providing that someone was working each claim. As Edmund Booth told his sister, "My partner at Yankee Hill has shares in four claims. He works one and puts hired men on the rest."[34]

The mining claim, a use right in mineral land, was fundamentally different from other property rights in land that Americans had known. Although it had striking similarities to the earlier claim clubs on the frontier, the latter were formed to provide settlors a path to ownership, which the mining codes did not. Claim clubs were organized by pioneers who arrived in a territory before the land was officially available for settlement because they had no legal right to their claims and because settlers or speculators could in principle outbid them for the land—in which case they would lose not only their homes, but also the value of their improvements. The club members therefore agreed to recognize and defend one another's claims and to support one another when the land was eventually auctioned off by, for instance, "discouraging" other bidders.[35]

Few, if any, California miners had had any experience of use rights like the mining claim, and their choice to hold such limited rights in their claims has intrigued social scientists for at least forty years. Economist John Umbeck was the first modern scholar to do a full-scale study of the mining codes, and his work is still influential.[36] Umbeck argued that violence was the basis of all property rights in the mines; he noted that although very little violence was reported in the early years, the threat of violence was always present because many miners carried guns. Since they were indifferent whether they spent their energy in working their land or in fighting for more land, he said, claim sizes stabilized at the point where the cost of acquiring more land through violence was greater than the benefit of putting more effort into mining what they had already. Umbeck saw the codes as contracts by which the miners skipped the process of actually fighting and bound themselves by the rules that would have evolved in any case.

This theory that the rules of mining were shaped by violence or the threat of violence is not literally true; we know enough about the first mining claims to be sure of that. Many further weaknesses of Umbeck's theory are listed by Richard Zerbe and C. Leigh Anderson, who note that it failed to take account of the deference to majority rule in the mines, for the miners' own accounts of their motivations, and for the almost complete absence of violence among Americans in the early gold rush as opposed to the many examples of violence between Americans and other equally well-armed ethnic groups.[37]

Zerbe and Anderson themselves stressed the importance of cultural focal points in overcoming coordination problems.[38] In the mines, they argue, the miners' shared culture enabled them quickly to agree on governing institutions and rules and also promoted order once the rules were in place. They note that the American tradition—almost a habit— of democratic self-government, including respect for the decision of the majority, meant that a random assembly of miners at a new diggings could draft and pass a mining code for themselves in a matter of hours. In this sense, cultural norms facilitated the creation of institutions and presented a manageable number of options for the rules themselves.

Zerbe and Anderson further suggest that miners willingly abided by and enforced these particularly because they were "fair" by some standard that the miners brought with them from America or even in some absolute sense. They characterize this fairness as "Lockean" combined with Jacksonian ideas about "the labor theory of value," or "producerism." Specifically, Zerbe and Anderson mention equality, treating people according to their just deserts, the right to have what one worked for, a preference for self-employment, and a reluctance to be hired. They predict that a mining system based on these values would award claims on a first-come-first-serve basis, that all claims would be of equal size, that this size would be no more than they could work themselves, and that a miner's rights would last only as long as he was actually at work. And this is, of course, what emerged in the California gold fields.

Karen Clay and Gavin Wright stress that the most striking feature of the California mining claim system was that it struck a balance between the rights of claim holders and of others who might want the claim. The rules limited the size of claims and required claim holders to work the claim regularly; if the claim holder failed on either of these counts, any other miner could take the claim by jumping it. The right to jump an underused or oversized claim had the effect of enforcing the use and size requirements, and the rules, generally, established order. But Clay and Wright also suggest that they tied claim holders to their claims and generated litigation. On the positive side one had peace and order; on the negative side, small claims and strict work requirements generated their own inefficiencies, as evidenced by the low average earnings of around two dollars per day.[39]

In my early work on the origins of mining claims, I agreed with Zerbe and Anderson's argument that the American commitment to majority rule enabled the miners to reach consensus and also that the forty-niners shared the Jacksonian identification with artisans and farmers and hostility to corporation. I still do agree with them on these points. I added that, in the unique circumstances of the gold rush where every miner expected shortly to leave a current claim and find a new one, everyone was both an insider and an outsider, and the rules balanced the interests of both. Like Zerbe and Anderson, I saw this as a rejection of capital itself in the context of gold mining—because that was what the miners said themselves.

Antimonopoly, antispeculator, and anticapital sentiment was strong in America generally and in the mines in particular, even if it did not determine the system of property rights. The miners did not distinguish between these terms: they used them all to refer to men who were not themselves laborers but who controlled so much that ordinary men were obliged to do wage labor for them and thus had no chance of striking it rich. Forty-niner William McCollum, in one of the first published descriptions of the gold rush, argued that the US government should not sell off parts of the gold region: "The direct effect of its sale would be monopoly; the giving of CAPITAL an advantage over LABOR."[40]

Many of the miners had come to California specifically to liberate themselves from the control of richer men by collecting enough gold to set up in business for themselves or by paying off the mortgage on the family farm. On being asked why he had come to California, one gold seeker answered, "I find that in this world the standard by which men are estimated is wealth, and only wealth." Before arriving at the mines, he said, "I used to pass men who would bend upon me such looks of *patronizing tolerance* . . . simply because their fathers were rich or had bestowed upon them the fruits of their ill gotten gains, only because I was clad in a laborer's garb or engaged in honest labor."[41] A miner in 1851 reported similarly that thousands of Americans had come to the mines to "extricate themselves from the iron grasp of *land sharks*, that are scattered throughout the length and breadth of our country."[42] Another complained that it was difficult for a wage laborer in the East to save enough to become independent. "I can hardly make a living here," wrote one miner, explaining his decision to leave for California although the trip would cost everything he had and then some. "We have no capital to carry on business with and it will be a long time before we can get a start." In California, it did not take money to make money: "Labor is *capital* out there."[43]

This last assertion—that labor was the only source of wealth in the diggings and that there were no opportunities for capitalists—was a recurrent theme in gold rush literature, and it was a good thing too, according to the writers. Some, at any rate, believed enthusiastically that the conditions in the gold mines neutralized the artificial inequalities of a complex society. "Working side by side in all these gulches are the sons of toil and those reared in the lap of ease. . . . Here the wielder of the pick is as proud as a lord, and bends the knee to no man."[44] If anyone had an advantage, it was those who had previously been at the bottom of the social ladder, the manual laborers and, especially, sailors.[45]

If outright ownership of gold-mining claims was allowed, some miners argued, it would enable speculators to monopolize the good diggings and to subordinate the laborer. The Carson's Creek mining code of 1851 states that it was passed to protect the individual miners:

> Resolved, That monopolies are anti-republican, and should not be insisted upon by capitalists, nor permitted by the operatives of a free country.

> Resolved, That in all mining operations in this State, equal and exact justice to all should be the motto, and to encourage industrious and skillful miners, such extent of ground be allowed as to make it generally profitable to work the same.[46]

Although the rules that followed applied to quartz mining rather than the square claims in the dry diggings, they were enacted by the same population as drafted the other codes. The actual provisions are unremarkable, but the introductory resolutions link limited claim size with anticapitalist sentiment promoting the interests of "industrious and skillful miners."

Henry George, though not a contemporary, was a Californian; and the gold rush directly inspired his hugely influential book, *Progress and Poverty*. George said that the miners had a blank slate on which to draw up their property regime and that "the essential idea" of the system they chose "was to prevent monopoly."[47] He added that mining laws of Mexico and the diamond fields of South Africa were based on the same principles.[48]

At the California constitutional convention of October 1849, a select committee considered the question of whether the new state should sell the mineral lands. The committee submitted two separate reports on February 9, 1850. The majority report recommended a policy of granting leases or permits for working small tracts to American citizens and prospective American citizens only, but it rejected the idea of sales or grants of title on the basis that a market in property would open the door to monopoly. That, they argued, would be bad for labor and for the community because monopolists would seek out cheap labor without considering the character of their workforce.[49]

The minority report of the committee objected not only to sales and grants, but also to leasing mineral lands. Any of these systems, the minority argued, would result in a monopoly of the valuable placers by a few claim holders "whose interests would thereby become immediately adverse to those of the masses, that from necessity are compelled to labor."[50] Like the majority report, that of the minority uses the language of republicanism; "the true policy of the Government is that which tends to secure to every citizen a competency; and the best wealth that a nation can boast of, is that every citizen has a comfortable home that he can claim his own."[51]

The California convention did not, in the end, pass any laws intended to supersede the laws and customs of the miners, but the talk about selling mineral land, at both the federal and the state level, alarmed some miners. Samuel McNeil, for instance, who was in the mines in 1849, said, "I shall blame Uncle Sam . . . if he is too hasty in selling the California gold lands in lots to speculators—to rich speculators, who are too wealthy already, that they may place it beyond the reach of our poorer classes."[52]

That the miners associated fee simple ownership with monopoly and capital ownership of the mineral region, which they loathed, originally led me to believe that they chose the mining claim system to give everyone an equal chance in accordance with the Jacksonian, republican sentiment of the day. I saw it as a rejection of capitalism and suggested that, given the chance to invent a new world, Americans would reject private property.

In 2003, however, at a conference on gold rushes around the world, I learned that the mining claim system is widespread across cultures, if not universal; it is not chosen by the miners but rather emerges naturally when gold is easily accessible.[53] In California, as in gold rushes around the world, capital is not a threat; it has no choice but to let individual miners take the surface gold before it can invest in mining operations. The custom of temporary-use rights and the inability even of property owners to control mining on their own land, let alone to monopolize it, are universal.[54] It follows that the California system was neither designed nor based on American values.

Whether a gold rush is spectacular or humble, whether it is in Africa, Asia, South America, or North America, it will almost certainly have mining claims. The nineteenth-century gold rushes in Australia and Canada were only slightly later than California's, drew on the American experience, and included miners who had previously worked in California, so it is not surprising that those countries adopted the same form of property.[55] It is remarkable, however, that similar mining claims have emerged in modern gold rushes whose population was completely unaware of the California mining claim system, including Brazil, Papua New Guinea, Indonesia, and Burkina Faso. Those places have no links with the California gold rush or with each other; the only thing they have in common is placer gold. It seems, therefore, that the distribution of gold—the very fact of a gold rush—rather than social norms or political movements determines the kind of property regime.

In all of these gold rushes, the discovery of surface gold, whether on private or public land, attracts hordes of gold seekers who could not be stopped except by twenty-four-hour armed guards. Each gold rush featured small, individual claims that belonged to the claim holders only while they were using them. As in California, custom in the Brazilian gold rush of the 1980s gave special privileges to the miner who discovered new diggings, but he could not keep out other miners or even stake out an extra-large claim for himself. For a time, the discoverer was allowed to mark out and allocate claims to newcomers, in return for which he received approximately 10 percent of their earnings; but as more and more miners arrived and took claims further from the original strike, the discoverer's authority became attenuated and eventually collapsed. The latest arrivals refused to make contributions to the discoverer, and soon everyone stopped paying.[56] In short, even the discoverer of new diggings could not monopolize them.

Even the owner of private property cannot stave off the crowd that pours in when gold is discovered on his or her land. The California gold rush happened in a legal vacuum, and the miners did not have to confront property owners, but in Brazil, Papua New Guinea, and Indonesia, gold rushes swept away private property rights. Some landowners in remote parts of Brazil tried to run private, or "closed," diggings, where workers had to sell their gold to the landowner and were searched when they left the diggings to prevent them from smuggling. An owner who discovered gold on his land had to act quickly to seal the area and had to have enough gunmen to exclude independent miners. "If the attempt to restrict access is contested," David Cleary writes, "and the landowner loses, then he loses all legitimacy in the eyes of the [miners] and may even be killed by them."[57]

Landowners in Indonesia also found it impossible to exclude independent miners from their concessions. According to a 2001 article in the *Wall Street Journal,* the government found it difficult to bar miners from land in which Aurora Gold Ltd. held mining rights. In 1988, the Indonesian government evicted illegal miners from private land with military and police forces and then kept them out by staging "night raids on their camps and posting police in the mines full time."[58] Years later, however, the trespassers were back, and the new, democratic government was no longer willing to crack down on them. In January 2001, Aurora Gold pulled out of Indonesia, taking a $42 million loss.

In Papua New Guinea, it was CRA, a mining company, that discovered fabulously rich placer gold at Mount Kare. News of the find leaked out in early 1988, and within five months, eight thousand to ten thousand individuals were working at the site.[59] The mining company and the two local tribes engaged in years of litigation, but in the short term, CRA was unable to exclude individual miners and had to write off hundreds of millions of dollars' worth of surface gold.[60]

Tilo Grätz's study of the Benin gold rush found that the government of Benin also tried to force illegal miners from the field and confiscated their property, but this did not stop the miners. "At first a cohort of the *gendarmerie* deployed at the site were corrupted," writes Grätz, permitting further mining in return for bribes. (Governor Richard B. Mason in California also feared that his soldiers would desert and mine for themselves if they were stationed near the mines.) Then, when the guards were withdrawn from the gold regions, many miners simply returned to work. Eventually, the government changed its policy to partial legalization.[61]

In all of these rushes, investors stayed out of a gold region until individual, surface mining was no longer profitable. At that point, capital could take advantage of superior technology, economies of scale, and lower wages. Clearly, the mining claim system and the inability of capital to get a foothold in the mines has nothing to do with culture.

The unrealistically high wages during the gold rush would have been an insurmountable barrier to capital in California even if it had been allowed to buy land because mining was not profitable. The great majority of men who went to California made so little money that they would have been better off staying home. Daniel Woods put a lot of effort into calculating the earnings of his company of 141 men and produced the following breakdown:

| | |
|---|---|
| 2 men made | $15,000 and $7,000 by trade |
| 2 men made | $6,000 each by mining and manufacture respectively |
| 3 men made | $2,000 by mining, trading, and teaming |
| 2 men made | $1,500 and $1,000 respectively |
| 70 men made | a mere living |
| Rest [62] | died.[62] |

That is, the very few men who made a profit, nine out of the 141, were engaged in trade or a combination of mining and trade. The remainder, including all of those who mined full time, were not able to save anything. Other Californians offered similar estimates: one in twenty would break even; or one in forty; or, according to one optimistic miner, one in three.[63]

In fact, the average wage laborer earned more than the independent miners. Writing in 1849, the richest year, Felix Wierzbicki explained that "in hiring a man to drive a team, one must pay him from two to three hundred dollars per month, as every one expects that in whatever business he engages, his chances to make money should be as good as those of the miner."[64] Since the miners had unrealistically high expectations of success, wage laborers actually earned more than they did. Thomas van Doorn, who employed workers himself, said in 1850 that "men can obtain 150 to 200$ per month + found as readily as they can that rate per year in the States. . . . This is what we pay our hands + is the current rate."[65] This was good money, and it was pure profit since it was "and found," that is, including room and board. And it was risk free.

As Dame Shirley explained, "[T]he person who is willing to be hired generally prefers to receive the six dollars per diem, of which he is sure in any case, to running the risk of a claim not proving valuable."[66] Let the employer take that risk.

Since wage laborers earned more, on average, than claim holders, reasonable men would work for wages. Gold mining was nothing but a gamble; it was "nature's great lottery scheme," as Dame Shirley said, and "almost all with whom we are acquainted seem to have lost."[67] But the great majority of miners were gambling addicts or were sucked into addiction. Peter H. Burnett, an early arrival in the mines and California's first governor, put it this way:

> The people of California, in proportion to numbers, have been, and are yet, the most speculative in America, if not in the world. At least one half of the men who came to this country were full of the most eager desire to make fortunes. A good, reasonable competency would not satisfy their magnificent expectations.[68]

Borthwick opined that only "cold-blooded philosophers . . . who had not sufficient inventive energy to direct their own labour" would work for hire.[69] This explains why Kimball Webster and his partners gave up a job sawing wood for the Vezie Company at twelve to fifteen dollars per day, or $240 to $300 per month, to go for the elusive pile.

Meanwhile, the employer, who put workers on multiple claims, was doubling down on the risks for the chance of a bonanza. In 1851, George McKinley Murrell bought several claims at enormous expense and had many men working them. Although he and his partner got at least $11,000 from their claims, this did not cover their expenses. He wrote charitably, "Upon the whole I have made little or nothing over & above what I commenced with in the Spring. But I have the consolation that . . . I have given employement [sic] to [a] good many hands at fair wages, paid them up punctualy [sic] & owe no man a cent."[70] At the very least, one can say that Murrell was no better off than his workers.

Where it did make sense to hire labor was when miners held claims that they knew or believed to be rich. River turning operations, for instance, had just a short window in which to mine the riverbed before the autumn rains destroyed their dams, so they took on many workers in September and October to get the job done. Placer miners, too, might hold several rich claims and put workers on each. In those cases, everyone came out ahead.

Outside investors were perfectly aware that there was no scope for investment while the gold rush raged, that "[w]hile gold can be found lying within a few inches of the earth's surface, and the only capital required to extract it consists in the capability to purchase a pick and a shovel, there is no need of combination," in the words of Edward Gould Buffum.[71] Unlike the miners, however, Buffum and others who contemplated California's future thought this leveling was not necessarily a good thing, on the ground that capital and wage labor were necessary for progress, that is, for effective gold mining, road building, and the growth of industry; but even these agreed that this would not happen until the placers were exhausted. "When this gold mania ceases to rage, individuals will abandon the mines; and then there will be a good opportunity for companies with heavy capital to step in," said Wierbicki as early as 1849, "and it is then that the country will enter on a career of real progress."[72] Senator Thomas Hart Benton strongly opposed the sale of mineral lands on the grounds that this would inevitably result in monopoly, but he, too, thought that the sooner the gold rush was over, the better it would be for California. "Then the sober industry will begin which enriches and ennobles a nation."[73]

On reexamination, many of the observations about labor's advantages over capital in the diggings can be read not as evidence of an agenda that shaped the mining rules, but as an acknowledgment about the realities of gold mining. When writers gloated that "labor has . . . the upper hand of capital" in California, "or rather has become capital itself," they were talking about the reality of placer gold mining: "[N]either business nor capital [could] oppress labor in California."[74] There were simply no opportunities for capital at the height of the gold rush because the only known labor-saving devices were the long tom and the flume. The San Francisco *Californian* made this point as early as August 1848: "From the fact that no capital is necessary . . . men who were only able to procure one month's provisions, have now thousands of dollars of the precious

metal." In this sense, "[t]he laboring class have now become the capitalists of the country."[75] Labor was the only means to generate wealth.

The leveling effect of the gold mines that was so striking in 1848
continued to a lesser degree in 1849 and even 1850, but by 1851, the
placers were yielding only a fraction of their former riches. Edward
Gould Buffum, writing in 1851, noted that capital had had few opportunities thus far because individual gold washing had been so profitable,
but good times were coming. "The era which follows . . . will be one,
when, by a union of capital, manual labour, and machinery, joint-stock
companies will perform what individuals now do."[76] In the late 1850s,
quartz mining and hydraulic mining indeed became profitable investments mainly because of technological innovations. The few individual
claim holders who were left made a steady but modest income. But by
then, the men of the gold rush had taken their earnings—or accepted
their losses—and moved on.

In sum, there was no danger—indeed, no possibility—of capitalist
monopoly at the height of the gold rush. The United States senators
who proposed selling mineral land did not understand placer mining,
and their suggestions went nowhere. It follows that the mining claim
system was not part of a plan for preserving the gold rush for laborers
and excluding capitalists. No such plan was needed because capitalists
had no desire to invest in mining at the time. The mining codes therefore did not represent the choice of one property regime over another,
but were simply agreements among those present about the basic requirements for claim holders in their diggings.

As we have seen, the gold rush phenomenon is precultural or acultural:
the same mining claim system has recurred around the world. In describing the California gold rush, Americans naturally used their own
language, speaking in terms of the labor theory of value and a Jacksonian hostility to capitalists and speculators, but this was descriptive
rather than normative. The mining claim system, as a whole, was not
*designed* to maintain labor's advantage over capital. In the first place,
it was not designed at all; and in the second place, labor's position was
never threatened. It did, however, prompt at least some miners to think

about the roles of capital and labor. The new world where "labor has the upper hand of capital" led some to see the economics of the East in a new light; while others who already adhered to the labor theory of value recognized the "natural" order of the mining camps as a manifestation of the workingmen's ideals.

# CHAPTER 5

## Resolving Disputes

The mining claim system appears to have been inevitable: wherever gold lies near the service, a similar form of property will emerge. One could also say that private property fails, or rather, that an attempt to treat mining claims like traditional property is generally unsuccessful. In Brazil, Papua New Guinea, Burkina Faso, and Indonesia, even bona fide landowners find that they are unable—or barely able—to exclude gold miners from their land. Gold rushes around the world are also relatively stable; there is little or no fighting over claims. Good order in the mining region was therefore not a particularly American phenomenon.

Still, there will be disagreements among claim holders about things like the boundaries of their claims or whether a claim has been abandoned, and every country has its own means of dispute resolution. In California, the method was quintessentially American: if the problem could not be solved by arbitration, the litigants took their case to a meeting of the miners. On the one hand, it made sense to ask a miners' meeting to decide issues for which the mining code did not provide a clear answer because the decision maker in such cases had to invent a new rule and the meeting was the maker of rules. On the other hand, it meant that the whole population spent part of every Sunday deciding claim disputes.

Disputes did not arise as often as one might expect from a use-based system of property, especially in places like California where there were no judges, police, or jails and the population included many rough frontiersmen, uneducated and impatient of authority, as well as gamblers and troublemakers. It would hardly have been surprising if claim holders and jumpers alike often had to use their guns. Instead, the diggings enjoyed a kind of "spontaneous order," that is, order without official law enforcement. This was not because miners were so well behaved. The California gold rush had plenty of debauchery and fighting, but that was largely confined to the "towns" that sprang up near the diggings (if a store, a gambling house, a hotel, and a few tents constitute a town). The town was where the ne'er-do-wells wasted their days and where serious miners let themselves go on a Sunday, their day off.

The diggings were a different matter entirely; the good order there impressed the forty-niners themselves, as did the sober industry of the claim holders. Mining was unbelievably hard work. "[U]p at daylight at work before sunrise, continue it till sunset, with only two hours rest in the heat of the day and this for every day in the week except Sundays," as miner James Cutler explained to a correspondent at home.[1] In the diggings, a German visitor said, "[n]o one spoke a word, only the rattling of the machines interrupted the silence."[2] Of course, some of the claims of perfect order in the diggings may be exaggerated since they were made in the letters that miners wrote home to their wives and mothers. James Canfield was no doubt sincere when he told his wife that "[t]he mines are the most quiet places I ever saw"; but surely he was carried away when he added that a "man is as safe here as he would be locked up in a room at home."[3] Nevertheless, the bars and flats where the mining was done were the opposite of rowdy.

With a little reflection, it seems obvious that lawless types would not want to steal claims, given how much work they demanded. For someone criminally inclined, it was much easier to steal gold from a miners' tent or saddlebag than to dig for it; indeed, robberies and burglaries were common, whereas fights over claims were not.

In fact, taking land by force is probably rare in any settled area. A modern homeowner may be cheated out of the property by scam artists, but not robbed of it at gunpoint. Robbery would end in farce since the perpetrator is more or less rooted to the scene of the crime and surrounded by witnesses. It is not strangers who instigate property disputes, but neighbors quarreling over a fence on the wrong side of the line, an overhanging tree, a nuisance, an interference with ancient lights, a trespass, or a misunderstanding.[4] Such infractions might lead to long-running quarrels or private lawsuits, which sometimes escalate into physical fights, but those are different from attempts to take someone's house by force.

To add to the perils of taking a claim at gunpoint, an assailant who happened to kill the claim holder would be guilty of a crime and punished by lynch law. There happens to be an example of this occurrence. In 1854, William Lipsey and James Logan were executed before a crowd of six thousand people for killing their opponents in two separate disputes over mining claims. Logan gave a long and rambling address from the gallows presenting his version of events, which we are, of course, free to doubt. He said he had acted in self-defense. The claim in question—at Coon Hollow—was his claim, and he went there on the fatal day to take it back from a man named Fennel. Logan claimed that "[i]n answer to propositions to settle the difficulty by law or arbitration, he had rashly replied that there was a shorter and better way— but he did not mean it." He showed Fennel his pistol—"merely showed it," he insisted. Fennel then went off, got a revolver, and was about to shoot Logan, when the latter—at the last possible moment and in self-defense—shot Fennel instead. Logan admitted he could have run from Fennel instead of shooting him, but he "had a principle of courage in his composition that prevented him from running away." And for that, "[t]he court, jury and district attorney had treated him as a murderer." Clearly Logan's story did not win over the crowd. The case demonstrates what one would have expected in any case: killing a claim holder to take his claim would backfire.[5]

Deliberate assaults like Logan's were very, very unusual. There were some fights about claims, but they arose from arguments that spun out of control rather than unprovoked attacks. Both parties in such cases usually had a plausible claim to the property in dispute. The correct course of action in such circumstances, as Logan's victim Fennel had proposed, was to seek litigation; but these fights were not really about settling a claim—they were about frustration and anger. For example, two men argued about ownership of a lodging house: "[T]he excitement went so far that one seized a mining pick that stood by the side of the door and the other endeavored to find something to defend himself with."[6] A lodger, Perry Gee, intervened, and, in the end, one of the disputants gave up his claim to the house, probably in return for a payment. Rival claimants sometimes came to blows, just as men fought about cards or women or nothing at all, but this was very different from throwing a man off his claim.

There were two exceptions to the general rule that miners did not take claims at gunpoint. First, some individual Americans did take the claims of foreigners by force. Multiple accounts describe Americans robbing Mexicans in particular. A "Yankee would invade the claim of a Sonoran with his revolver in hand," according to Chilean miner Ramón Gil Navarro. He added, "He would watch the Mexican panning for gold for a while until he was sure it was a good claim. Then he would go up to the poor Mexican, put his pistol to his head and order him off."[7]

Second, clashes between *groups* could escalate. As the miner Frank Marryat observed, while most claim disputes were "submitted to a jury of the resident miners," this was not always true "where twenty men or so are met by twenty men, and in these cases there is first a grand demonstration with fire arms, and eventually an appeal to the district court."[8] Groups confronted each other in various situations: where companies of miners clashed with other companies; where Americans confronted foreigners; and where the discoverers of new diggings tried to keep out later arrivals.

This last problem, where the miners on the spot tried to keep out newcomers, was usually solved by a miners' meeting, but it could also result in violence. In 1850, at an unnamed—and therefore probably new—diggings on the Feather River, five miles south of Nelson's Creek, a company of three men held "a larger claim than they were entitled to by the law of the mines." An interesting phrase, this last, since claim size differed from diggings to diggings; the author presumably meant an unreasonably large claim. A second group happened upon the same promising spot, "measured off what the law allowed them, and then jumped the balance." The original claimants did not take this philosophically: "[T]hey commenced stoning, and the result was, that a man by name Clayton Bell, was actually stoned to death."[9] That was murder, just as Logan's shooting of Fennell was murder. The three perpetrators fled. Meanwhile, some forty miners came over from another diggings, held a meeting, elected a justice of the peace pro tem, and investigated the matter "as far as possible." So even in an uninhabited area, one could not get away with murder.

One could not even get away with the lesser offense of breaking the rules of the local mining code: compliance was enforced by neighbors and those seeking a new claim. Newcomers were quick to note when one had been abandoned because they were on the lookout for claims to jump, especially in rich diggings. As Gregory Yale wrote in his 1867 study of California Mining Law, "any individual who is satisfied that the rules have been violated, and that the claimant has worked a forfeiture may proceed to enter the claim according to the rules, and take possession of the claim."[10] It was therefore the would-be jumpers who policed the claim holders, and vice versa, or as Yale charmingly put it, the code was enforced by "an irresponsible, but eager and vigilant public."[11]

If a claim holder had actually abandoned his claim, he was powerless when someone else jumped it, even if that person struck it rich. Miner Richard Cowley narrowly missed making his fortune several times, in the sense that we all would be rich if we had bought the right stock at the right time. Once, after Cowley had abandoned a claim, it yielded the next owners fourteen pounds of gold, worth $224. "Before these men struck in this place," Cowley wrote in his journal, "Pickering, Sanderson, and myself worked there a day and a half, but did not happen to strike the right place, [and] finally gave it up when this party of six jumped in, dammed it off, and took out the above mentioned weight."[12] Cowley was not even resentful; the jumpers' success stimulated his own company to get working on a wing dam on the river.

A miner named Clark had a similar experience. He had bought an interest in a claim for ninety dollars, but had to leave to get provisions. A storm delayed his return, the partners who were supposed to be holding the claim left for some reason, and then "others set in + refused to give up so all of us lost a fortune together."[13] As Clark knew, that was what happened when a man did not work his claim regularly.[14]

These and the hundreds of other disputes that arose could come before any of three fora. The parties could take their case to an alcalde, with or without a jury. Or they could submit to arbitration by three to five miners chosen by themselves. Or they could request a full miners' meeting to decide the issue, of the type that enacted the codes. A few mining codes included a prescribed method for dispute resolution; Karen Clay and Gavin Wright count twenty-four codes with such a provision.[15] But the miners seemed to ignore them and did whatever suited them—with a preference for miners' meeting when the issues were novel or the claims particularly valuable.

The title *alcalde* was borrowed from the Mexicans, but the Americans had little or no idea of this officer's duties in pre–gold rush days. They elected alcaldes mainly to hold civil and criminal trials.[16] However, as we have seen, American miners invested little or no effort in electing a man worthy of this office and did not respect his decisions— except in rare cases where the alcalde *was* competent, like Stephen Field, the future Supreme Court justice, but this is the exception that proves the rule. Men of Stephen Field's caliber did not often accept the job of alcalde.

More commonly, the parties agreed to arbitration, sometimes in the form prescribed by the local code and sometimes not.[17] The code of Big Oak Flat of September 1851, for instance, required that "all disputes concerning claims shall be decided by arbitration—the number of arbitrators being five—each party choosing two disinterested persons, and the four thus chosen selecting a fifth." Up until this point, the provision was typical, but the next requirement suggests that arbitration was compulsory: "[W]hen one of the parties refuses to choose two arbitrators, the two chosen by the other parry shall select a third individual, and the three so chosen shall decide the dispute."[18] This sounds like a recipe for disaster. Miners who refused arbitration in the first place, and then learned that three men chosen by their opponents had found against them, were unlikely to accept the verdict and might very well appeal to the full miners' meeting. Better, then, to bypass the arbitration and go straight to the meeting, as many disputants did.

Miners' letters and diaries do report actual disputes submitted to arbitration. In June 1850, two miners, Lippard and Oats, submitted their dispute to two other men, J. R. Rogers and Decker. The latter wrote in his diary, "We heard the evidence[,] decided in Mr. Lippard's favor &

both parties seemed satisfied having agreed to abide our decision."[19] The miners' choice of forum could be ad hoc. Daniel Woods, for instance, tells a story about two miners who disputed a narrow strip of land between their two claims. "As they could not amicably settle the dispute," Woods wrote, they agreed to leave it to a newcomer "who happened by who had not yet done an hour's work in the mines." This passerby measured out ten-foot squares of the two claims and took the strip left over as compensation for himself. According to the story, that little strip yielded $7,435, while the larger claims turned out to be worthless.[20]

Frank Marryat also described another kind of impromptu dispute resolution. "I have had my claim in the digging more than once, of ten feet square," he wrote. "[I]f a man 'jumped' it, and encroached on my boundaries, and I didn't knock him on the head with a pickax, being a Christian, I appealed to the 'crowd,' and my claim being carefully measured from my stake and found to be correct, the 'jumper' would be ordered to confine himself to his own territory, which of course he would do with many oaths." This was not actually arbitration, since Marryat's antagonist had not agreed to accept the crowd's decision; it seems rather that he called in the surrounding miners to confirm his rights.[21]

Marryat's case turned on a question of fact, namely, the dimensions of his claim. But many disputes turned on matters of law or, rather, asked the decision maker to declare new rules. The codes left many gray areas, such as whether the work requirement was waived while the claimant was sick; whether procuring machinery for the claim counted as "working" it; and whether a claim was forfeited if a notice was blown away or torn down by someone else. In such a case, the claim holder naturally argued that he had not abandoned the claim, while the newcomer might reasonably believe that he had forfeited his rights.[22] Perhaps it was the legal issue at the heart of many disputes that induced many miners to bypass the alcalde or committee of neighbors and take their case directly to a meeting of the miners.

So we are back to meetings. For example, miner Perry Gee wrote that "a dispute arose today between our company and another company of miners about some dirt that we had thrown up on their claim."[23] The question was whether the dirt belonged to those who had thrown it up or to those on whose claim it now was. This was one of the convoluted legal questions that no mining code had foreseen. "[A] miners meeting was called to settle the dispute," wrote Gee, "and they desided that we take the dirt on one side of the raven [ravine] and they the dirt on the other side." The parties were to divide the dirt between them. Three weeks later, at the same diggings, Gee participated in a miners' court—another term for a meeting sitting as a court. The issue was whether a miner (the defendant) could allow the tailing, or runoff, from his mining operation to run across the claim of another miner (the plaintiff), and the court found that he could.[24] Both cases, but especially the second one, required the meeting to make new rules; it was, in effect, filling in the gaps left in its mining code.[25]

Meetings as a forum for dispute resolution rarely feature in diaries and letters, but according to newspaper articles and other reliable observers, they were very common indeed. In effect, the meeting served as a civil trial, and its decision created a precedent for the diggings—a new rule. A correspondent of the *Sacramento Daily Union* offers a detailed description of this method "of dealing out justice without the aid of Judge or jury" at Piko Flat in Grass Valley. The parties settle a time for submitting their case to a meeting and then the canvassing begins: "From that time until the hour appointed, the disputants are on the alert, among their friends and neighbor miners for electioneering purposes, and not unfrequently carry a bottle of fourth proof in their pockets to enable the hombres to fully understand their side of the question." At the appointed time, the meeting proceeds like any other. The assembled miners elect a chairman, and the litigants make their cases directly to the whole assembly. When all the evidence has been submitted, "a neutral line is now drawn, and the chairman requests those favorable to Mr. A's holding the claim, to form in a line on one side, and the opposition party on the other, where they stand until their noses are counted and the decision stated from the chair." Those who supported the winning side cheer wildly; the losers grumble and curse, "and all is over."[26]

In some diggings, the miners held meetings weekly to settle claim disputes. In 1852, Dame Shirley wrote from Indian Bar that there were "innumerable arbitrations" and that "nearly every Sunday there is a miners' meeting connected with this subject."[27] Perry Gee also recorded in his journal, "I was under the necessity of calling a miners meeting

today to recover water that was taken away from me out of spite and
through selfishness[. S]uch difficulties are of almost every day occurrence."[28] The date of this journal entry was also a Sunday.

What kept all of this litigation from being impossibly burdensome
was that the miners rather enjoyed it. Sunday was the miners' day off,
and the trials took place "in and around some trader's cabin, or the most
commodious saloon in the camp," which was where the crowds would
be in any case.[29] The correspondent to the *Sacramento Daily Union*,
quoted above, said that the miners of the neighborhood were not the
only ones who participated: "[S]ometimes, when the claim is uncom-
monly rich and the excitement runs high, they are seen pouring down
the ravines and hill-sides, for a mile around and take their stations on
the disputed territory."[30] They wanted to hear the case for each side and
to influence the outcome. True, one miner suggested that attendance
was required: Jonathan Wheeler Bryant wrote to his brother, "I have
been summoned to a meeting of this kind yesterday," and if he was not
there, "folks will jump my claims and thare will be nobody [to] help me
out of it."[31] But Bryant may have meant this figuratively—that he needed
to be a good citizen and maintain the goodwill of his fellow miners in
case he himself needed help in the future.

Little is known about these civil trials before the miners' meetings beyond the fact that they existed, so one can only speculate about whether
they created precedents that effectively modified the local mining code.
A man styling himself "Tuolumne" published two letters in the *Sonora
Herald* of 1852 arguing that the mining claim system was unworkable
and should be replaced with fee simple property rights claims. Tuolumne
claimed that it "is well known that mining laws are often made to suit
particular instances—are, in fact, ex post facto and often go into disuse
as soon as the emergency expires."[32] If this means anything, which is not
a given with this opinionated author, it may be a reference to rules decided at the Sunday meetings to hear claim disputes. The idea of creating a fee simple in mineral land would go nowhere since the miners
had zero interest in owning their claims; but the problem of underdevel-
oped codes was real.

When a miners' meeting decided a dispute about mining claims, the
meeting functioned as a civil court, just as in lynch trials the meeting

acted as the judge in a criminal trial. The system had its advantages and disadvantages. The advantage to the litigants included the finality of the verdict: "[F]rom the decision of the meeting there was no appeal."[33] A miners' meeting was naturally able to enforce its decisions since it was the community itself organized for business. At Shaw's Flat in 1852, two men jumped the claim of two other miners named Courrier and Barker. "The miners met on the ground in dispute, A.M. . . . and having read the laws of Shaw's Flat" decided against the jumpers. At noon, Courrier reported to the miners that the jumpers refused to surrender the claim; and they held another meeting with president and secretary. "It was then moved that a committee of three . . . be appointed to notify the said [jumpers] to leave the ground in fifteen minutes after being notified, and if they did not leave within the specified time the miners of Shaw's Flat would carry them and their tools below Stevens' store and put them on foot, and if they returned again they would be dealt with in a different way. Carried." The committee duly read the notice to the jumpers. "The miners then waited fifteen minutes and started for the ground," and, finding that the jumpers had disappeared, the meeting adjourned.[34] So noncompliance with the meeting's decision meant, in this case, that the parties would be thrown out of the diggings. If this was the general understanding, then the meeting would rarely have to take action against the losing party.

In 1856—admittedly a very late date—the local recorder, Pringle Shaw, had to call a meeting to deal with a blatant violation of local rules. An American had sold a claim to a company of fifty Chinese miners; "a bill of sale was given, and the whole formula of the laws rigidly complied with." Nevertheless, the next day, three Arkansans, "gaunt long-haired fellows, each with a pistol in his belt," turfed them out with the words "*Vamos!* Clear!" and occupied the claim. There was no legal issue here; the Arkansans did not even allege that they had any right to the claim besides a supposed right to take what they wanted from Chinese men. But the recorder could not eject the jumpers himself: the frontiersmen told him, "We'll skin you like a 'possum, and fat our har with your taller, ef you don't clar in a bee line whar you b'long."[35]

The next step was to call a meeting of "the whole white population" (even in pursuit of racial justice, equality only went so far), which

passed a resolution ordering the jumpers to withdraw. The latter refused, and in twenty minutes, "upwards of a hundred men were armed
and equipped, and proceeded in regular military array to the scene of
conflict." The chairman of the committee informed the three that any
of them who was still on the claim in five minutes' time would be shot.
He called out the minutes while the Arkansans stood their ground in
silence. Shaw was terrified, "for I knew as surely as that powder would
blaze—they were dead men at the conclusion of the call, if they still
retained their stubborn position." With less than a minute to go, the
jumpers' spokesman said to his fellows that they could not emerge with
honor from a fight of one hundred against three; they shouldered their
tools and left the claim to its Chinese owners.[36]

This was an unusual case; ordinarily, it was quite safe to take a claim
from Chinese miners. The intervention would not have happened
if Shaw had not pursued it, and, even then, the miners could have
voted that the claim belonged to the Arkansans. Once the meeting had
reached a decision, however, it was very effective at forcing the losers to
accept it.

These miners' meetings as trial courts also had serious disadvantages, however. First, they demanded huge amounts of time and energy.
As the correspondent at Piko Flat said of the booming diggings there,
"They must be rich indeed, to pay the miners interested for the time
they consume in attending miners meetings, for the purpose of settling
claim difficulties."[37] And second, the decisions were not noted down, so
there were of limited precedential value. The record was the memory of
those present at the meeting, which was not helpful to people who arrived at the diggings later. The problems this could cause were reflected
in the preamble to the Magalia Mining District Code, which stated
that the new code was necessary because "the Old laws of this district
have long since been lost and abrogated by the custom and usage of the
miners."[38] This uncertainty was not necessarily so bad, but it was a cost
of the flexibility of the system.

The amount of litigation was to be expected, given crowding and
the value of the disputed property; but the miners would have saved
themselves a lot of effort if they had created a court with the power to
hear cases and set precedents for the future. They were too reluctant to

delegate their authority, however. And then, the Californians could not even be bothered to elect decent alcaldes.

## Bending the Rules

The main challenges to the integrity of the rules came not from claim jumping but from the same abuses that also plague settled societies: rule bending and insider arrangements. There must have been innumerable tricky methods for cheating—and the best ones, perhaps, were never detected or recorded—but most of the known examples fall under three headings. The first men to discover new diggings could adopt a code that allowed them to hold very large claims or very many claims. Or they could control the whole area by taking one claim each by location, and then through a series of sham sales among themselves end up with large portfolios. And finally, in existing diggings, individuals might take claims in the names of fictitious partners. Work on one partner's claim held all of the others, so the only real partner controlled all of these claims. The main reason for this kind of trick was speculation: the hope that the area would turn out to be rich, the value of claims would increase, and the early bird could sell his excess claims to newcomers.

If the mining claim system was really inevitable, these efforts should have failed; and, in fact, they did fail where the diggings were rich enough to attract a critical mass of outsiders who wanted to change the rules. Rule bending compromised the system; it did not undermine it altogether.

In 1852, James H. Carson described the first tactic, by which the first arrivals at a new diggings adopted rules that allowed them to hold very large claims. Carson wrote that "if there is a new discovery made at present, the few who make it call in their relations and friends; then measure the best of the ground off, and divide it into claims of such size as will cover it, let it be five or five hundred feet, and then proclaim that the rule of those diggings."[39] The first miners to discover gold at French Bar, in February 1850, used this trick. In fact, their claims occupied the entire diggings, as Daniel B. Woods and his companions discovered when they arrived.[40] The newcomers start to dig at an untouched and unmarked spot, but the older miners drove them off. Asked "why they had not left their pick or spade there, according to the custom" to mark their claims, they replied, essentially, that they had divided the diggings up among themselves and were prepared to defend them. "All the miners there were bound to stand by each other in maintaining their claims, which were known to each other," they said. Woods and his partners found that "most of the ground is held in this way, without being marked off or designated." Their alcalde was as bad as the rest and was reported to hold thirty claims. This was absurd, of course; neither custom nor any known code allowed unmarked claims known only to the interested parties. It took Woods and his partners some time to get the message that "comparatively a few persons have undertaken to monopolize most of the gold soil in the gulch," and they were ejected from five places before they finally moved on.[41]

If the diggings attracted a crowd of newcomers, however, these could call a new meeting. Voters included miners who had claims and those who had no immediate prospect of a claim; in short, the haves and the have-nots, although at least one digging required a six-day residency period for citizenship.[42] If newcomers outnumbered existing claim holders, they could change the rules, even to the point of depriving the earlier miners of some of their ground. The *Illustrated History of Plumas, Lassen and Sierra Counties, California*, published in 1882, tells the story of a thousand miners returning from a failed expedition, who poured in upon the newly discovered diggings on the Feather River and took up every inch of ground. The *Illustrated History* relates that "[i]n many cases where the first workers had measured off generous-sized claims, the newcomers called a meeting, made laws reducing the size of claims, and proceeded to stake out their locations."[43]

Danish miner Peter Justesen and his partners experienced this from the receiving end. They had found a gold-rich area from which they estimated they could make $12,000–$15,000 and "immediately marked off three large 'claims' right up the hillside—but almost instantly came Adams, who kept a public house in Wood's Creek, and after him several others, and all took up claims on the same ground."[44] Justesen's party was disappointed, but they did manage to make $1,500 from the location, "and that without working very long." Crowds similarly overwhelmed the discoverers of Stewart's Diggings at Yreka. There five men managed to take out 120 pounds of gold before they were disturbed, but a month after news of their discovery leaked out, there were one thousand men on the spot.[45]

The second shady arrangement was for a group of miners to locate and sell claims among themselves. We owe all of our knowledge about this to critics—because the practitioners did not write about their deals. A man using the pseudonym "Peregrine Pilgrim" wrote several "Letters from the Mountains" for the *Alta California* explaining the problems raised by the concentration of claims in a few hands. In his "Letter from the Mountains at Montezuma City" dated January 10, 1853, he said that Montezuma City was rich: "I judge they are generally doing better than at any other camp in the country." But a few men could "monopolize whole acres of ground to the exclusion of others" by locating claims themselves and "selling" them to each other:

> Jones, Smith, Muggins, and Pritchard . . . [each] lays off a claim and puts on the necessary labor in order to hold it. Now Smith sells his claim to Jones and takes up another: so does Muggins and so does Pritchard. Then again Jones sells to Smith and he takes up another, then Muggins sells his new claim to Pritchard, and Pritchard to Muggins.[46]

These transactions were permitted under the local code so that the only way to break up their vast holdings, Pilgrim implied, was to change the rules. But new miners arrived at Montezuma City in groups of three or four; they could never outvote the Smiths and Joneses who were on site. They saw how the ground lay and moved on. Had even a quarter of miners who passed through remained, Pilgrim said, "they would ere this have been in such a majority that all these greedy claims would have been put out of existence." That is, the miners who were shut out would have called a miners' meeting and limited the number of claims that one miner could hold.

The miners of Warren Hill addressed exactly this problem of sham sales. The Warren Hill code included a rule that a purchaser had to "take a bill of sale, showing . . . the cost thereof attested by one or more witnesses" and that payment for the claim had to be "given in good faith and without collusion between the parties."[47] Such a rule would have stopped the abuses at Montezuma City.

The most drastic measure for preventing or even reversing excessive holdings was for the majority—if one could be assembled—to hold a meeting and institute a one-claim rule that would dispossess miners of their excess claims. In the summer of 1850, the miners at Murphy's Diggings voted "that from and after this date no person shall hold more than one claim."[48] Miners who held claims there under the old rules would be dispossessed; the *Sonora Herald* advised them to get back there if they did not want their claims to be jumped. Similarly, the first resolution of the June 19, 1850, code passed at Weaver Creek was that "[e]ach and every miner shall be entitled to hold one claim at a time and no more, either by purchase or otherwise from this time forth."[49]

Such a change in the rules could amount to a "taking" of property, especially if a miner had purchased multiple claims, which he then had to surrender and especially if the vote was close. The same Peregrine Pilgrim who objected to the monopolization of diggings was also troubled that a relatively small number of miners could contrive to take some of their neighbors' property by "taking advantage of circumstances, get together a miners' meeting, with a majority favorable to their views," and cut down the size of claims.[50] There are even a few accounts of bizarre rival meetings. The preamble to the Mining Laws of Jamestown District, dated November 23, 1853, stated, "Whereas a number of persons who were not inhabitants of this district assembled together and assumed to make rules and regulations for our government, which rules and regulations were in a manner inapplicable to us; therefore for our own government, we do hereby enact the following."[51] In this case, the miners in situ managed to fend off a takeover, but they could not have done so if they were greatly outnumbered.

In the one case where the newcomers did not pass resolutions but simply marked off reasonably sized claims, the original claim holders reacted violently. They ordered the newcomers off and, when the latter refused to obey, commenced stoning, and the result was that a man by the name Clayton Bell was actually stoned to death.[52]

In short, a group could not hold an outsized portion of mineral land against a flood of new miners coming into the area, just as landowners in Brazil could not keep out gold seekers without security guards.[53] And the first discoverers knew that their shenanigans would not work once the outside world knew that they held rich diggings. These attempts to control land are therefore the exceptions that prove the rule; they worked only until the world learned about the gold, and then the original claim holders could not keep out the multitude that was attracted to the spot.

The final ruse was holding claims in the name of nonexistent partners. The practice of working in partnership made it difficult to tell who owned what. Placer mining was done most efficiently by three or four men working together—one to dig, one to carry dirt, one to work the mining "cradle," and another to pour in water.[54] Partners shared all expenses, labor, and profits; they usually lived together, took turns doing the cooking, and cared for one another in sickness while the partnership lasted.[55] Although they held one claim each, the codes explicitly or tacitly allowed their joint labor on one of their claims to hold the rest.[56] Some groups took advantage of the confusion and held claims for partners who were absent or simply invented for this purpose.[57] For example, four men could hold eight claims, and if they were challenged, they could always claim that the extra members were off running errands.

The very fact that a number of codes prohibited taking claims in the names of nonexistent partners indicates that it was fairly common. The most explicit rule was that of Carson's Creek, passed on June 1, 1851, which applied to quartz claims; the same games were played in this context as in placer diggings.[58] The first resolution carries a hint of exasperation: "That monopolies are anti-republican, and should not be insisted upon by capitalists, nor permitted by the operatives of a free country." Among the provisions to effect that end were:

Resolved, That any person using fictitious names representing claims, upon due proof thereof before a jury shall forfeit his right to his claim.

Resolved, That the president of each company shall be required to have for exhibition to any persons interested, a list of the names, number, and residence of each member of his company.

Similarly, the code of Warren Hill provided that when a miner wished to record claims for himself and the other members of his company, the recorder was allowed to "record the claim for the party present but shall refuse to record the claim of the absent party, unless the party present make affidavit of the existence of said partnership, which affidavit shall be taken by the recorder and made a matter of record."[59] Such provisions signaled past problems and also demonstrated the solution: change the rules to make the subversions illegal.

Where miners were limited to one claim each, miners could not accumulate claims and work them with hired help. Here, would-be employers used a little subterfuge; they got their laborers to locate claims in their own names. The workers got their wages, and their boss got the gold they found. Again, rules prohibiting the practice are the best evidence that it was widespread. A proposed model code for the diggings, probably drafted by Peregrine Pilgrim, included a rule limiting miners to one claim each and provided that "if any person shall attempt to evade the law restricting people to one mining claim, by inducing others to locate claims in their own names, the profits of which shall, in whole or in part, accrue to the first party," then neither the employer nor the hired hands could keep the claim.[60]

Dame Shirley, on the other hand, saw this type of rule bending as benign and said that it was generally tolerated since "the holding of claims by proxy is considered rather as a carrying out of the spirit of the law than as an evasion of it."[61] The hired workers themselves were not unhappy with the arrangement. They were the purported claim holders and could, in theory, have taken advantage of the situation and declared themselves the owners, in a sense jumping the claim on which they were at work; but according to Dame Shirley, that was seldom, if ever, done. Some such system was even necessary for penniless miners to build up the sums necessary to buy a claim.

Given the miners' facility for running and participating in meetings, it is not so surprising that they enacted mining codes in the form of a preamble and resolutions because codes are similar to laws. But we have seen here meetings used as the preferred form for resolving disputes over mining claims. The meetings took direct democracy to its extreme, involving the entire community in every question of law. In addressing novel questions regarding the rules, the meeting acted like an appellate court that, through its findings, created new legal precedents and in effect changed the local code. That this was a time-consuming process for resolving disputes does not seem to have bothered the miners; at any rate, they preferred it to electing a reputable judge.

Meetings were especially valuable because of the American propensity for violence. Where the discoverers of new diggings claimed too much for themselves, the response of later comers was to hold a meeting to pass new rules, assuming they outnumbered the original claimants. Having a peaceful way to resolve issues like claim size and number of claims per person was particularly helpful in California because a battle between claim holders and new arrivals was not unthinkable.

# CHAPTER 6

# Cooperation and Conflict with Mining Companies

The story thus far has been about small, individual mining claims, the kind of claim most people have in mind when they think of the miners of '49. These had a beautiful simplicity: one claim per miner, all claims of equal size, and no need for special equipment. Given the conditions of easily accessible gold, something like the claim system will emerge every time. The system was stable too, in part because an individual miner who tried to take another's claim was vastly outnumbered by surrounding claim holders. Although there was extensive and time-consuming litigation—full miners' meetings every Sunday—violence was rare to nonexistent. No wonder this form of claim has received almost all the literary and scholarly attention.

But as early as 1849, a half year into the gold rush, miners also engaged other kinds of mining projects that required them to work in groups and to invest heavily in one location. River turning was the first of these. The earliest miners reasoned that if the banks of streams and rivers were rich with gold, the riverbeds would be richer still. By turning the water out of its channel into a canal running alongside the water course, they could uncover a literal goldmine.

De Tocqueville wrote that he "often admired the extreme skill with which the inhabitants of the United States succeed in proposing a common object to the exertions of a great many men, and in getting them voluntarily to pursue it," and this talent was on full display in the formation of companies for large-scale mining endeavors.[1] It was all but inevitable that the lone miners who carried their blankets, picks, and pans from diggings to diggings eventually joined dozens or even hundreds of others to carry out large-scale operations, first forming companies to divert the rivers from their beds and, later, building machinery for crushing gold-laced quartz, tunneling deep into the hills, and transporting water via canals, flumes, and aqueducts to diggings many miles from the nearest source of water.

The particular form of organization for these endeavors was the joint-stock company and—at a higher level—associations of companies to coordinate efforts along a particular river. But the rivers did not enjoy the spontaneous equilibrium of the dry diggings, especially when companies in the river clashed with individual miners working on the riverbanks. This was the rare circumstance that precipitated fighting over claims because here there were two groups with conflicting aims. The miners working the land along the river outnumbered those in river turning companies, but the latter were more organized and had a great deal more at stake because of their investments in dams and flumes. This created clashes that miners' meetings—with one man, one vote—could not resolve.

Needless to say, turning a stream or a river out of its bed was an enormous undertaking. Daniel B. Woods, secretary and treasurer of the Hart's Bar Mining Company—organized in May 1850 to turn a portion of the Tuolumne River—kept a suitably secretarial record of its progress. To turn the river, the company had to divert the water out of the riverbed and channel it alongside the bed to the end of the claim, where it would either be released back into the bed or decanted into the canal of the company below. Woods's company was fortunate that its upstream neighbor on Paine's Bar had built a dam to force the river into a canal. Less fortunately, it was not possible to continue the Paine's Bar company canal; the only place for a canal on Hart's Bar was on the other riverbank. The company therefore had to build an aqueduct to carry the river from one side to the other. The canal, when finished, was 638 feet long and 16 feet wide. In some places, it passed through ledges of solid rock, while in others, where the river had carved a hollow in its bank, the men built a wall filled with clay to hold back the water. Woods calculated that he himself pushed his wheelbarrow 420 miles, back and forth, bringing clay from a distance to the canal. The aqueduct was also an enormous project. The men felled trees in the mountains and rolled them down to the river, where they sawed them by hand; they could then construct crates of logs filled with large stones. The sleepers of the aqueduct were laid across these filled crates, and the end product was 102 feet long and 12 feet wide. On September 20, some fifty days after they began their work, the men turned the river into their aqueduct and laid bare the whole channel of the river. Then they could finally begin to dig for gold.[2]

Four days later, however, on September 24, the river began to rise. The Hart's Bar Company rushed to remove its mining equipment from the site, then anxiously watched as the Paine's Bar dam, a quarter of a mile above them, was breached and "the river ran foaming over the entire length of the wall, which bowed and sank before the irresistible force." The water quickly reached Hart's Bar, rising until it poured over the top of the aqueduct. "Gently and gracefully it yielded, swayed forward, and moved away with the ease and rapidity of a thing of life." One thousand twenty-nine days of labor were swept away. Within five minutes, "a meeting of the company was called, and a resolution presented to proceed with our work by means of wing-dams," that is, the company agreed to build a dam down the middle of the riverbed and thereby partially drain at least part of the channel—and finally discover how much gold was there.[3]

Clearly, river turning required a huge outlay in man-hours and lumber before the miners knew whether their claim was rich or not, and in that sense, it was even more uncertain than work in the dry diggings. "We are working blind folded now," as one miner put it.[4] And then if there was gold, it was uncertain whether the company would have enough time to get it out. In a dry year, the miners had three months to dig in the riverbed, but in a bad year, they might have only a few weeks. If individual claims were like a lottery, river turning was Monte Carlo: "the most risky of all the styles of mining," one miner said. "The company either made a fortune or lost one, and being in the nature of gambling, and taking long odds, suited the Californian miner exactly."[5]

"As this is an operation requiring the united labor of many individuals," Daniel Woods wrote, "it is customary to form companies, which elect their officers, form their laws, and mutually share the expense and labor of the preparatory work, and also divide equally the profits." Woods added that "the mining associations enjoy[ed] all of the privileges and immunities of corporate bodies," by which he meant their claims and rights were recognized and would be protected by their fellow miners and that they could sue and be sued. They were, in fact, joint-stock companies with a highly egalitarian flavor.[6]

Americans were familiar with joint-stock companies from home; in fact, many of the emigration companies that set out from the East to make the journey to California and to engage in mining took this form. Constitutions of overland companies from the four corners of the United States show that the joint-stock form of association was widely known; companies from Massachusetts, Missouri, and (West) Virginia were strikingly similar.[7]

The overland companies intended to stick together once they arrived in California and to engage in mining or trade as one concern. They made equal contributions to the company before setting out from home and bound themselves to share equally in the profits and, once in the gold mines, to engage in no individual interests or trade. But mutual support went far beyond the financial. The company was a community, pledged "in all cases of danger [to] be ready to defend each other and in all cases of sickness administer to each other's wants and use all possible means to restore each other to a usual degree of health."[8] The morals of the company were also considered. Some had rules forbidding alcohol, gambling, and working on Sundays. A member of the Hartford Union Mining and Trading Company went so far as to say, with humorous exaggeration:

There were to be no bloated stockholders—all should be equal in interest and profits; one share to each man and no more. We were a *commune*—a socialistic order—who believed in the old Spartan division of all spoils. The sick, and the weak, were to be on one common level with the strong and the well.[9]

This description appears in a somewhat humorous account about a company that took the sea route to California. Some of its members had brought a barrel of cider brandy with them onboard ship, which they intended to sell, privately, in California. The ship's crew drank from the barrel en route and became tipsy; when the captain sought out their source of liquor, the attempt at "private speculation" was discovered. The writer does not disclose what happened to the remaining brandy or the errant members. Joint-stock companies were not exactly communes or socialist, but they were supposed to be all for one and one for all.[10]

Nevertheless, all of the emigrant companies broke up as soon as they arrived at their destination or even before. Only two held together long enough to do any mining, and one of those disintegrates before the reader's eyes in the diary of a member, George Allen. The company held innumerable meetings, which was not a problem in itself because meetings could be very short. As the work progressed, however, the votes became more and more frequent; the company met to change the working hours to 4:00–9:00 in the morning and 3:30–7:30 in the afternoon, met again to change the morning starting time back to 6:00, and yet again to move the afternoon shift back to its original time of 2:00–6:00 p.m. When some members went off prospecting on their own, the rest met and voted to count someone absent if he was not at work five minutes after the whistle blew. Once there were four meetings in one day, including one that:

> had Frank over the coals for speaking disrespectfull of the Co. as some of the verry learned and high minded Gentlemen thought—and wished an explanation or acknowledgement and after some verry laboured arguments + elequent speaches with some threats from the verry sensitive an agreved ones— they wring A sort of aporgy or acknowledgement from Frank and passed A vote excusing him.[11]

Allen wrote, "[M]ay I soon be delivered from this Company," but he stayed on. As the season drew to a close, however, he said, "I think we shall not hold together many days longer + I hope we shall not for I have got tired of working to support Loafers." Indeed, the members voted to dissolve the company at a meeting a few days later.

In contrast to these overland companies, those formed in the mines were not for mutual support: they were all business. Daniel Woods's advice was to "*avoid companies formed at home!* They work badly; they cramp your energies; they entangle all your operations." Instead, he counseled his readers to join companies organized in the mines to carry out a specific project. "These associations are formed and terminate with the necessity of the occasion."[12]

Forming associations was Americans' strong suit anyway; they could literally make the necessary arrangements before breakfast. Miner William Miller, working on the Tuolumne River, recorded in his diary that "this morning before turning too, we formed ourselves into an association called the Tullamah Daming Co. Resolutions where drawn up and a President and Secty and Treasurer chosen and the resolutions read and excepted [*sic*] and signed by all conserned [*sic*] in this joint Stock Co."[13] Remember, too, that Daniel Woods's company voted on a new plan of action five minutes after seeing their aqueduct and canal swept away.

River turning companies were not communes, but they were strongly egalitarian, requiring the undivided loyalty of their members and equal contributions of labor and money from each. Exit was made difficult, in the sense that one lost one's investment. These restrictions were necessary to keep men at work until the claim started to generate some income. Constitutions therefore contained provisions about exactly when everyone had to be at work. For example, the Articles of the Hart's Bar Company stipulated that all members work equal hours; and if a member was absent for part of the week, his distribution would be reduced proportionately. Substitutes were not allowed; members had to do their share of work themselves. The workday was fixed at 7:00 a.m.–12:00 p.m. and 1:30–5:30 p.m.; members who were absent during that period were charged three dollars per hour for the time they missed, to be paid at the next meeting. The directors of the company were charged with recording the hours worked by each man under their charge—and submitting the account to the treasurer at the end of the week.[14] Members of other companies mention a roll call at the start of the workday.

The Star Mining Company was not a river turning operation but rather an association of fourteen men working "Union Flat": it was, however, a joint-stock company organized along the same lines as a river turning company.[15] It required its members to work ten hours a day, six days a week, and all to "commence and quit at the same time." Like all river turning companies, the Star Mining Company took a tough position regarding absences; a miner who missed work could make it up by supplying a substitute or paying a penalty—six dollars for one missed day and sixteen dollars for two in a row.

Exit from a company was made difficult. The rule of the Hart's Bar Company was that "[a]ny member wishing to sell his share, the company shall have the first right of purchase; which if they decline, he may sell it, but only to such person as the company approves."[16] A member who wanted to quit had to go to the trouble of finding a suitable replacement or lose his investment. Shares did change hands, however. Isaac Barker bought a share in a wing dam from the wages he had made working for Southworth, a member of the Beal's Bar Company.[17] Upton bought a share of the Union Mining Company for seventy dollars, which he agreed to "work out" or pay for with labor.[18] Both of these demonstrate flexibility in the admission of new members. Barker went from doing wage labor for a member to membership in his own right; while Upton agreed to pay his entrance fee from future earnings. There was more turnover than the company constitutions might suggest.

Unlike the company rules drafted back East, those of the mining region were surprisingly tough on members who were sick. The Hart's Bar Company's rule was that "in cases of sickness or unavoidable absence, substitutes may be employed, if approved by the directors."[19] On the other hand, miner Warren Sadler's little river turning company passed an interesting rule: "[T]o charge each one who lost a day, sick or not $12 per day and divide what was washed equally among us."[20] The week before, five members had earned an average of just over twelve dollars per day, surprisingly much given that they were still building their dam. In this case, the charge appears to approximate the amount that the group would have made if the sick man had been able to work. The members of a company did not necessarily enforce the rule against a well-liked colleague or in a sympathetic case, however. A miner named Elias Lothrop was sick with mountain fever for many months, yet he seems not only to have been supported by his companions but also to have been given a share of the season's proceeds.[21]

On the other hand, it was difficult or impossible to get rid of a troublesome member who had not violated any particular rule. C. C. Mobley, who belonged to a river turning company at Oregon Bar, wrote in his diary, "There is one of the laziest kind of men in our company. It seems to be a dead drag for him to moove. Wouldn't be as lazy as he for a kingdom." Social pressure made no difference to him. Mobley added, "All the company make sport of him but he's so lazy he don't mind it."[22] If the slacker had been an employee, he could have been dismissed, but members had rights. The most the company could do was buy out the offender. George Allen's company faced this problem when one of its members was suspected of stealing, although there was no solid evidence against him. The others arranged to "settle with him and purchase his shair in the Co."[23]

For all the equality and solidarity of the river turning companies, however, they did not shrink from exploiting noncitizens. Deep into his description of the Hart's Bar river turning operations, Daniel Woods introduces two individuals he had not mentioned before. "There are two servants, belonging to members of the company, at work with the rest," he says, "and right hard-working men they are."

> One of them, who is from Mississippi, is as athletic and vigorous a man as I have ever seen. If any work is to be done which requires great strength, he is called upon; and he always engages in it singing some merry song. The other servant is an old man, named Allen, belonging to our president, who tells me he shall give him free papers when he leaves the country.

Daniel Woods was a clergyman, born in Massachusetts and living in Philadelphia when he caught the gold fever.[24] It is a small mystery that he touches so lightly on the two slaves working for his little company. A little later, he mentions that they hired laborers in the final stages of their operations, including more than fifty Mexicans. "The heavy tax upon foreigners has driven them to seek employment from companies," Woods notes. "They may be hired at $4 and $6 a day."[25] In other words, the Spanish speakers had been prohibited from mining for themselves and became laborers willing to take relatively low wages. Woods notes the injustice, but his company took advantage of it nevertheless.

According to the Scot Borthwick, the Americans' talent for self-organization gave them a great advantage over the miners of other. Frenchmen, he said, never attempted combinations of fifteen or twenty men. "Occasionally half-a-dozen or so worked together, but even then the chances were that they squabbled among themselves, and broke up before they had got their claim into working order, and so lost their labour from their inability to keep united in one plan of operations."[26]

While almost all of the river turning companies were American, however, there were also companies on the river whose members were all or mostly French or Spanish speaking.[27] In addition, at least one company was composed mainly of Chinese members. Consider this entry in the Placer County Records:

> Notice
>
> Know all men by these presents that we the undersigned hold a claim of one thousand feet in the banks & bed of the north Fork of the American River downward from the point of Rock on the right hand side of the River which claim we commenced working in the summer of 1852 & intend continuing our labor so soon as the water in the river will admit. We hereby forewarn all persons from trespassing on this claim or taking any liberties with the lumber &c connected with it.
>
> Dec. 1st, 1852
>
> | Wm Guymen (?)   | Ayake      |
> |-----------------|------------|
> | George McIntyre | Akching    |
> | A. Chip         | Aying      |
> | Aton            | Aqua       |
> | Ahee            | Quing Chin |
> | Arching         | Atching    |
> | Aling           | Apon       |
> | Ake             | Aruot      |
>
> Recorded Dec. 18, 1852[28]

The two first names are presumably American, but the fourteen other members of the company were Chinese. And while they did not call themselves a company, and there is no hint of how they were organized, they had been working one thousand feet of a tributary to the American River and their group, of whatever form, planned to continue working together in the next year.

The French and majority-Chinese river turning companies suggest that although the Americans were good at self-organization, they were not, after all, unique. If Americans had not prohibited Spanish-speaking miners from holding claims, either on an ad hoc basis or through resolutions, there might have been more Mexican or Chilean mining companies. It is a surprise to see even one majority-Chinese company, not because they were bad at organizing—we know nothing about how they were organized—but because Americans tolerated Chinese miners only so long as they worked claims that Americans did not want. What form of organization these non-American companies adopted—or would have adopted—is, of course, entirely a matter of speculation.

## Codes

The mining rules of the dry diggings were not suited to river turning. They were drafted for a society of individuals; the main provisions specified the maximum size of a claim and the work requirements necessary to hold the claim so that all parties knew when it was legally abandoned and could be jumped. River turning raised different issues. One of the main sources of conflict was when one company's dam backed water onto another company's claim, as explained by Peter Decker. "A number of dams are partly in," he wrote, "& much dificulty expected in back water & claimants locating too close—some have their claims overflowed by other claims."[29]

The other big problem was that the interests of the river turning companies conflicted with those of the miners working on the banks of the streams. Under the mining codes, the latter's claims extended to the middle of the stream. "[I]t sometimes happened," as miner John Steele wrote, "that a company [holding claims on the bar] would work . . . until the water of the river prevented their going farther; but, when the river had been turned, so as to clear the bar of water, the company would return and demand the privilege of working out their claim."[30] This was not pure opportunism: after all, the miners on the bars had calculated that water levels would fall over the course of the summer and more ground would become workable. The companies could not claim credit for all of the ground uncovered by their operations. But they were naturally unhappy when individual miners moved into the riverbed, and skirmishes ensued.

Not only did the members of a company have to organize and work together, the companies themselves also had to cooperate with one another. They did this in part by forming associations through which they could agree on the rules of interaction. The problems they faced were different from those in the dry diggings, where one man's work generally had little impact on his neighbors—with exceptions, of course, especially regarding the disposal of waste dirt and water. The companies, in contrast, were strung along a river, sometimes for miles. They cooperated in handing off the water flow from each company's canals and flumes to the next, but in other aspects of their operations, one party might harm another by encroaching on its claim. Particularly, damming the stream—as was necessary for diverting it into a canal or flume—inevitably inundated a part of the claim above. The upper claim, even though it was prior in time, might then have to suspend its operations until the following year.

The companies along a river therefore met to pass agreements governing their interactions with one another. Some of these meetings were just for the mining companies to agree to rules among themselves, while others were open to all and, in effect, created mining codes or laws that applied to everyone working on or near the river, whether they were parties to the agreement or not. Such conventions were held "on most of the rivers in the country."[31]

A grand "Convention of Miners" was held at Mormon Island on the American River on July 28, 1851, bringing together companies and individuals working along thirty miles of river.[32] On July 27, the miners of Mormon Island held a preliminary meeting at which they catalogued some of the problems that arose in the absence of rules. First, dams built by downstream companies backed water onto the claims above them. Second, some companies held river claims from year to year without working them. Third, "[n]ew comers have been driven from one line of 'diggings' to another, by those whose motto was 'might makes right,' . . . simply for the want of general established rules." This referred to men who wanted to dig in the bars of the rivers but were driven off by the companies working the bed. And finally, there was too much litigation. "Companies and individuals, after having spent the mining season in litigation, have been compelled to go to day labor, to pay the judge—the lawyers, as usual, dividing the disputed claims among themselves."[33]

The report of the grand meeting itself on July 28 called it "a mass meeting of miners," rather than, say, a meeting of companies, and three of its provisions applied to individual claims on the banks and bars of the river.[34] John Steele, who with thirteen others had a river turning operation half a mile below Mormon Island, was at the meeting and wrote, "While there were delegates from all parts of the district, it was really a mass convention, as every mine owner was not only entitled to speak but to vote."[35] He wrote that one reason for the convention was precisely "the conflicting interests of river, bar, bank, and gulch claim," that is, the tension between individuals working on the riverbanks and companies turning the river. According to Steele, the rules and regulations passed that day were subsequently recognized in the courts—as, indeed, were most of the mining rules adopted by the miners themselves.

These conventions adopted something like a law code that applied to all of the miners working in or along the river, whether or not they had participated in the convention. There were also "associations" of companies. Alonzo Delano described a "general convention" on the Feather River to form an association, open to existing and future companies as well as individuals. "Every man or company making a claim," wrote Alonzo Delano, would first put up a notice and begin work. "He then registered his name or bar on the books of the Association (thus formed) and became a member, and in the event of others attempting to drive him off, he was entitled to the protection of all the companies constituting the Association." Delano gives the impression that all willing parties entered into a sort of contract of mutual protection. He goes on to say, however, that "this is looked to and spoken of along the river with as much deference and respect as if it was the law of the land," which suggests either that it was binding on nonsignatories as well—or that no one would be so foolish as not to join.[36]

There are far fewer preserved rules for river companies than for dry diggings, probably because rivers covered only a fraction of the territory in the mines and river mining lasted only a few years while the dry diggings continued to adopt codes into the 1860s. In addition, the records of the associations were not well maintained, perhaps because companies along a river lacked a center or main town. Alonzo Delano, working on the Feather River, said that he could not get a copy of the laws. "I appealed a few days ago to the President of the Association for a copy of the law for the purpose of sending it home for publication," he wrote. "After a diligent search, it was ascertained that but a single copy existed, and that was ten miles distant."[37]

## Conflicts between Companies

The basic rules applying to companies' interaction with one another were very simple. One, the first company to post notice of its intention to mine a particular stretch of river got the claim; two, a lower claim had the right to back water onto an upper claim. That was about it.

As in the dry diggings, the existence of rules in and of itself prevented some disputes. This was true of notice. The Placer County Records include many copies of claim notices posted by river turning companies up to a year before they could start work, and remarks by George Allen show that the notices were respected. "This afternoon another Com. With Mules + Packs made their appearance to take possession of the Bar," he reported with satisfaction. "But we were too soon for them as we had got our License from the Justice + stuck upon a tree."[38] Similarly, the first claimant's right to back water onto a later upstream neighbor was generally honored. The later company simply had to put off its operations until the next season. Several claims in the same Placer County Records state that a company had to postpone its operations because its claim was flooded by another company: "Whereas the said Union Canal Co. have been prevented from working the above named claim this season in consequence of the Kentucky Dam we therefore intend to commence working this claim as early in the season of 1852 as the water will admit."[39] The third rule, however, that the company was entitled to all of the riverbed that its dam laid bare, was accepted by the other members of the association or confederacy, but met with bitter resistance from others who felt shut out.

When disputes did arise, they came either before a miners' court or the district court; and two codes included provisions for trials before a jury of twelve miners.[40] The Scottish miner Borthwick painted the scene of an orderly trial before a miners' court. A river turning company was ready to turn the river into its race when nearby miners objected that the water would inundate their claims. Because the parties could not reach an agreement between themselves "as was usual in such cases, they concluded to leave it to a jury of miners." Miners two or three miles up and down the creek were requested to attend, and "[a]lthough a miner calculates an hour lost as so much money out of his pocket, yet all were interested in supporting the laws of the diggings; and about a hundred men presented themselves at the appointed time." The litigants picked six jurors each from the crowd, and these "squatted themselves all together in an exalted position on a heap of stones and dirt." The plaintiff and defendant made speeches, called witnesses, and cited mining rules that supported their cases, "while the general public, sitting in groups on the different heaps of stones piled up between the holes with which the ground was honeycombed, smoked their pipes and watched the proceedings." The jury then examined the ground, called some more witnesses, and, finally, declared that the company should wait six days before turning the river to allow the miners along the race to work out their claims. The hundred men who attended to "support of the law of the diggings," to use Borthwick's expression, presumably represented public pressure on the litigants to accept the outcome.[41]

We have seen that disputes over individual claims were often decided at miners' meetings, and while such trials are rarely described in detail, decisions appear to have been made by the assembled miners. In disputes over river turning claims, however, a jury trial like the one Borthwick described was not unusual; the miner Peter Decker wrote that the rules at Irishman's Bar on the South Yuba provided for the settlement of disputes by twelve jurors. If the jurors split, then the judge would cast the deciding vote.[42]

But the loser did not always accept the verdict of the miners' court. Peter Decker's company on Irishman's Bar was asked to stop backing water onto its upstream neighbor, Mull & Company, which asserted that it had the older claim. A committee drawn from the two companies failed to reach a compromise, so the case was submitted to the miners:

> 100 miners were present Mr. Lyons of Ioway was lawyer— Mr Slater council for plaintiffs. Pease Moderator or Judge— rules as in court. Had 12 jurymen examined some 20 witnesses, agreed in written rules that a majority of jury should decide or when evenly divided the judge to give casting vote. Which being the case the judge decided in our favor.[43]

Although the two parties had agreed in writing to accept the decision, Mull & Company were "much exasperated" and later threatened to tear down the other company's dam, and the latter prepared to put up a fight. In the end, however, the companies settled, and Mull & Company was allowed to run a race along Decker's company's claim. Mull & Company's resistance to the verdict delivered after such an elaborate process is a hint at how ungovernable mining companies could be.

State court records show that there was more litigation in the district court than one would ever have known from the miners' letters and diaries. River turning companies definitely benefited from the court's powers to enforce its verdict. A company at Coloma sued its downstream neighbor, called the Tunnel Company, for backing water onto its claim. Judge Robinson of the district court held that the Tunnel Company should pay $200 and lower its dam within ten days.[44] Instead of complying, the Tunnel Company armed itself and "declared that they would resist any man or set of men, who should attempt to molest them."[45]

The judge sent Sheriff Rogers to remove the Tunnel Company's dam, but 150 men—40 members of the company and 110 supporters—were ready for him and threatened to shoot the first man who touched it. Sheriff Rogers therefore gathered a force of his own. The 120 members of the upstream company volunteered their services, and Sheriff Rogers also summoned citizens of Cold Spring and Placerville to assist him. These preparations so alarmed the Tunnel Company that it began lowering its dam, and by the time the sheriff and his posse returned, the situation was calmer. The water was still six inches too high, but the *Sacramento Daily Union* predicted that "the law will in the end be enforced to the letter, as the citizens are unanimous in their determination to support the Sheriff."[46]

"The Park's Bar War" was the *Marysville Daily Herald* headline for a similar incident. A claim dispute being litigated in the courts caused some difficulty; evidently one or both of the parties were dissatisfied. The sheriff "issued a proclamation" saying that a body of armed men at Park's Bar had resisted the law and his authority. He called upon the citizens to raise a "force . . . to aid in sustaining the law."[47] The sheriff picked a small force from the hundreds who were summoned and, in the end, the defiant company backed down and the deputy sheriff arrested two men "without resistance."[48] Doubtless the miners of the various bars could have held a meeting and achieved the same result, but the court and the sheriff—with the support of the miners—did so more efficiently.

## Codes and Miners on the Bars

The rules of the associations or confederacies seem to have worked well between river turning companies because the rules were clear, the companies were stable—and probably signatories to the association—and there was too much at stake to resolve difficulties through fighting. It was the miners on the bars who resented and clashed with the mining companies. Indeed, these clashes were one of the motivators for the mining convention. Part of the problem was asymmetry: organized groups encountering individuals. Another was the fact of overlapping jurisdictions. The association of companies along the river formed a jurisdiction of sorts that could be many miles long but only one hundred feet wide, and this jurisdiction passed through multiple mining districts. And finally, in each district, individual claim holders both outnumbered and, it seems, resented, the river turning companies.

Although the miners' conventions were held in part to settle the main point of tension between companies and individual miners— namely, where the riverbed ended and the bars began—they decided on different rules, suggesting that there was no obvious solution to the problem. The companies on the Yuba limited themselves to the riverbed "between low water marks," but the low water mark varied from season to season. If the winter had been very dry, it could be very low indeed. Writing about Mormon Island in the fall of 1849, Felix Wierzbicki said, "From the middle of September till the end of November is the best season for mining on the banks of rivers, as it is then that the lowest bars are uncovered, and even sometimes one may work in the very bed of the river itself."[49] Companies on the Feather River agreed that "[e]veryone is to have the privilege to work in the banks above a medium height of water, a provision to accommodate those who do not belong to any company"; while the resolutions passed on the American River stated unhelpfully that "all damming companies shall, before draining the bed of the river, stake off their claims at the edge of the water immediately before turning the water into their race or flume."[50] (And who was to say, later, that the water was as high as claimed on the day that the stakes were driven?) Finally, the companies on the Mokelumne failed to specify any limit to the width of a river claim.[51] So, the demarcation could be the low-water mark, medium height of the water, wherever the edge of the water happened to be when the company staked its claim, or undetermined. It is clear that there was no customary rule or consensus on the line between riverbed and bar.

While the mining companies may have considered it generous to leave any part of the bar to individual miners because, as miner John Steele wrote, they "at large expense, had drained the river" and "naturally claimed all from which they had removed the water"—the individual miners did not see it this way.[52] Few of these individuals can have attended the meetings that established the new rules, and they all, no doubt, preferred the old rules that claims on the bars extended to the middle of the river. At any rate, many moved their operations closer to the middle as the water fell.

Companies called miners who crossed their line trespassers and tried to eject them. Officers of the Union Canal Company, for example, sent a committee to ward off intruders on their canal. "[H]ave had much trouble with them this morning," wrote Upton, a member of the company. "[T]he aggressors swore they would not leave and defied the whole company to put them off they raised the American flag," and Upton talked about "walking over ded bodies pistols bowies knives &c."[53]

The tension between the river turning company and the miners on the bar could indeed turn violent in a flash.[54] A company of eighty men diverted a river into their ditch, but it proved too small to contain the water, which overflowed onto neighboring claims. The victims demanded compensation, and when they did not get it, they moved onto the enemy's territory, the riverbed itself. This started a fight in which "knives, picks, rifles and pistols, were freely used." William Shaw, an Englishman who witnessed the battle, "was horror-struck at the sanguinary atrocities which had been committed: some men lay with their entrails hanging out, others had their skulls smashed with the pickaxe, and bodies lopt with the axe; while a few lay breathing their last, seemingly unscathed, but shot to death with bullets."[55]

But while miners working on their own regarded the companies as the bullies, the companies also feared the aggrieved miners on the bar because the dams, flumes, and water wheels were vulnerable to vandalism.[56] Some companies took the highly pragmatic step of absorbing their adversaries. The Canal Company, after trespassers raised the American flag on their property, decided to sell fourteen shares in the company for fifty dollars each and to divide the proceeds among the original members. "One object in selling the canal property," Upton wrote, "is the improbability of [the] company being able to work it out before the river rises and to strengthen the company so that we can repel invasion." In other words, it seems, the company realized that it had nothing to lose by accepting new members and that it was in fact too small to protect the claim it already had.[57]

The Horseshoe Bend Company did the same, but on a much grander scale. The original company of twenty men held a claim on the Middle Fork of the American River where it made a large bend around a mountain.[58] With six months hard labor, they managed to tunnel through the rock, exposing one and a half miles of rich riverbed. The rules of the day gave a company the right to work that portion of the riverbed that it actually exposed, but this case was extraordinary in that the claim was large enough to employ 1,200 men. George Applegate, who later purchased a share in the company, wrote, "The claim being so large and persons knowing it to be so rich has produced quite an excitement against this Co. other miners say they have no right to so large a Claim

&c. and the Co say that it is all the result of their own labor, &c." The company decided, however, that it would "let out Claims in the bed to such an extent as will prevent further dificulty [sic] on that score." It in effect became the landlord of a thousand miners. Applegate and his father eventually bought two of the original shares for $6,000 down and $3,000 when they had earned that much.[59]

Even so, the Horseshoe Bar company was worried enough about the security of its title during the winter of 1850–1851 that it sought to make it official. It employed Applegate's father to lobby the legislature in January 1851 for a charter that would give it "the exclusive privilege of working our whole claim and give us sufficient time &c."[60] This is the only time such a charter is mentioned, and we do not learn whether the company succeeded in obtaining it, or indeed, whether the other miners would have respected such a grant. The attempt proves only that the company itself was afraid that its excessively large river turning claim would not be respected by the community.

There is one example of a river turning company throwing another off its claim because race, personal differences, and regional differences threw a spanner or two in the works.[61] On October 21, 1849, the Tullamah Daming Company identified a promising claim and, having been assured by their neighbors-to-be that damming the river there would not cause them an injury, decided to work it. Five members of the company were African American. After a while, a swaggering Texan "came along all tough" and said that "he allowed that a white man might come in but a black man could not no how." He also said that "he was agoing into the same opperation on the last of the week with 24 others." The Tullamah Company conferred for half an hour and decided that the Texan would try to bluff them off, but they would start working on their dam anyway.

The Texan had given two reasons why Miller's company had to leave: first, because of the Black members, and second, because the Texan's company planned to work the claim. Neither carried any weight. Studies of African Americans in the mines describe other mixed-race partnerships and companies engaged in various form of mining, though they also record the hostility of Southern whites, in particular, against free Black miners.[62] Furthermore, the Texans had not posted notice of their intention to mine—hence, the Tullamah Company's conclusion that the interloper was bluffing.

Most of the company returned to their old camp for the night. The Black members slept at the new claim, however, and began working in the morning. Then twenty-five Texans arrived, "armed to the teeth with rifles revolvers bowie knives and one pick ax," and ordered the miners to get off, for the Texans "claimed the spot and they where Southerners and might was right and they whould rule." When the rest of the Tullamah Company got back and confronted the Texans, they got the same treatment: "[T]he ground they claimed and they whould have it they allowed that they where under no alcada and they did not care a d–d."[63]

The Tullamah miners nevertheless asked the alcalde for help, and he told them "that if they wished he would send down the Sheriff and order them off." Considering that "it was a going to accumilate considerable expense on the Co," however, they "concluded to give up to them and went to work further down the river." The Texans had won. But it seems that winning was enough, and they did not stick around to turn the river after all. Two days later, a portion of the Tullamah Company, including at least one Black miner, was "digging in the Texen Territory" and making good money.

Despite the shaggy-dog ending, the story has a lesson. The Texans' bigotry was so important to them that they were willing to fight although they had no material interest in the claim; the Tullamah Company did care about its Black colleagues, but not enough to battle the (admittedly crazed) Texans—though Tullamah did stick together as a mixed-race company.[64] This was the asymmetry of passion that would also result in the extermination of the local Native American population.

River turning showed another facet of Americans' skills and techniques for organizing on a large scale, as well as a willingness to compromise when necessary, as when a river turning company absorbed its challengers—that is, allowed them to join the company—to defuse a threat and to boost the company's ability to repel future threats. A company was also inclined to cooperate with its neighbors because they were, to some degree, dependent on one another. It proved difficult, however, to set rules that satisfied both the individuals mining on the bars and the companies in the river because the two groups had conflicting interests and, therefore, different ideas of fairness. And racists were ready to fight to keep others from mining even where the former had no intention of mining themselves, just as other racists were eager to spend a day shooting the native population for no reason whatsoever. Miners' meetings and conventions could not bridge these differences.

# CHAPTER 7

# Lynch Trials and Frontier Criminal Law

The murder trial of Easterbrook, described in the beginning of the book, followed basic common law criminal procedure. The prosecution and the defense were represented by counsel; witnesses testified; the jury of twelve citizens, having heard the testimony of the witnesses, withdrew for deliberation; and the jury ultimately returned a verdict of guilty and pronounced the sentence of execution by hanging. There was no judge, or rather, the assembly of miners *was* the judge. It decided all procedural questions, such as whether there was to be a jury and, if so, how it was to be selected and whether to give the defendant an attorney. This was a meeting acting as the judge of a criminal court.

The most detailed accounts of miners' trials show the meeting voting on every particular, including whether there would be a trial at all, whether the defendant should have counsel, who that counsel should be, the number of jurors, how they were to be selected, and whether the jury or the crowd would decide the sentence. When it came to the sentencing phase, every detail of that, too, was voted on separately. In the matter of Dr. A. Bardt for theft, which was not a trial because Bardt had confessed, the meeting made the following resolutions:

> On motion, it was resolved that Dr. A. Bardt be whipped for the said thefts.

On motion, it was resolved that Dr. Bardt should receive
thirty-nine lashes on the bare back, and leave the mines in
three days.

It was moved and seconded that Dr. Bardt should be cropped.
The motion, on being put, was negatived unanimously.

On motion, it was resolved that Dr. Bardt be whipped by the
Constable, Mr. Thompson, with a rope.

On motion, it was resolved that the Constable should proceed immediately to the discharge of his duty.[1]

In other words, the crowd voted separately not only on the question of
whether he should be whipped, but how many lashes he should receive,
who was to administer them, and when. All of the motions passed, apart
from the one especially cruel motion—to crop the ears of the convicted
criminal—which was duly seconded but rejected by the assembly. This
suggests that the votes were meaningful.

These trials were often called lynch law or the court of Judge Lynch,
but they do not fit the term *lynching* as it has been understood for the last
150 years, namely, a racist attack on a Black person or a member of another minority group. It does fit the early-nineteenth-century usage of the
term, which was, in Christopher Waldrep's words, "violence sanctioned,
endorsed, or carried out by the neighborhood or community outside
the law."[2] In the Easterbrook and Bardt incidents, the "acts of violence"
were the former's execution and the latter's whipping. Both were not only
sanctioned by the community but approved by a vote of all of the persons
present. And they were obviously outside the law. Lynch trials before 1851
were outside the law in the sense that there was no law in the gold region
at the time—no written laws, no government, and no courts. In 1851, the
year of Easterbrook's trial, California did have courts, although they were
short-staffed and inefficient. By the time of Bardt's punishment in 1852,
there was even less justification for lynch law; the miners' argument then
was that although there was a criminal justice system, the courts sat so
infrequently and jails were so insecure that crime went unpunished.

In trying suspects and punishing criminals, the miners assumed a
power reserved to government. This was the ultimate exercise of popular

sovereignty, and the participants knew that they would be criticized by family and friends in the East. The legitimacy of the process, in their eyes, derived from the participation of the whole community—"the people"—through the meeting. In the early days of the gold rush, there were no courts, so it was trial by miners' meeting or none at all, but when the state courts were established, the miners refused to surrender their suspects because, they said, there were too many escapes from the jails and the judges too often let guilty men go free. From this short summary alone, it should be clear that the use of meetings could provide an approximation of a fair trial, but the participants' certainty that they always got things right ultimately led them to commit great wrongs.

This chapter places California lynch trials in the context of America's long history of extralegal punishment. It first offers a brief history of the word *lynch* up to the time of the gold rush and distinguishes lynch trials from other forms of lynching or lynch law, namely, vigilantism, self-help, and racist attacks. "Regulators," or vigilantes, defended—or claimed to defend—the community from gangs that preyed on it, rather than addressing the problem raised when Farmer Smith accused neighbor Jones of theft or murder. The latter circumstance required careful consideration, fairness, and procedural safeguards; it required a proper trial or, in the absence of courts, trial by Judge Lynch. This subset of lynching has gone unnoticed until now. Writers who do mention cases on the frontier have often conflated them with hate crimes. Later chapters will look at lynch trial procedure and punishments and the degeneration over four years from good-faith trials into something more akin to lynching as we know it today.

The earliest formal definition of the word *lynch* appeared in Noah Webster's dictionary of 1848, the year of the gold discovery. It defined *lynching* as "[t]he practice of punishing men for crimes or offenses by private, unauthorized persons, without a legal trial." This covered vigilante movements and trials like that of Easterbrook as well as mob justice. The primary meaning of the word today, namely, mob executions of Black Americans and other minorities, only displaced the other usages in the late nineteenth and early twentieth centuries. As historian William D. Carrigan explained, this is because the first studies on lynching—the *Chicago Tribune*'s annual publication of lynching statistics beginning in

1882 and Ida B. Wells's seminal publications of 1892 and 1895—were undertaken to draw attention to those atrocities.[3] The *Chicago Tribune*'s numbers became the definitive data for researchers and activists from then on.[4] As a result, the other meanings of the word *lynch* fell out of use.

The broader phenomenon of organized community punishment outside of the law goes back to the colonial period, however, when neighbors roughed up men who beat their wives ("those dear regulators," as one wife called them).[5] The term *Lynch's law* itself was coined by Charles Lynch, a colonel in the militia in Virginia during the Revolutionary War. Lynch tried and punished criminals on his own authority because the nearest court was some two hundred miles away.[6] If Lynch and his colleagues found a suspect guilty, they sentenced him to thirty-nine lashes; if they acquitted the suspect, they released him, sometimes with reparations.[7]

By the 1820s and 1830s, the term *lynching* applied to the activities of regulators, also known as vigilantes, who organized against gangs that preyed on the community. Their justification, like Lynch's, was that the accused were beyond the reach of the courts, either because there were no courts, the nearest court was too far away, or the authorities were unwilling to act against the outlaws. Vigilantes were organized: they had officers, their members signed a constitution or manifesto, and they disbanded when they had achieved their aims. A number of frontier vigilante groups held trials very similar to those in the mines, with a judge and jury, counsel for the accused, and a final vote on the sentence by the crowd. Whipping was a more common punishment than execution. The regulators did sometimes kill one or several members of the gang, but if this sufficed to drive off the others, the vigilantes were satisfied.[8]

Like Charles Lynch in Virginia, frontier regulators operated in an institutional vacuum. But some regulators acted in states that had sheriffs, jails, and courts, claiming that weak or corrupted law enforcement forced to take these extreme measures. Historian Richard Maxwell Brown therefore divided regulators into two groups. "Good," or "socially constructive," vigilance committees were disciplined and focused and disbanded when they had completed their self-appointed tasks;

"socially destructive" vigilante movements furthered their personal ends or operated without a community consensus.[9]

The mid-1830s saw an explosion of violence in settled communities.[10] An article in the *Niles' Weekly Register* of September 5, 1835, stated, *"Society seems everywhere unhinged,"* a state of affairs captured by the wild use of italics and exclamation marks in the description of the troubles. "We have *executions,* and murders, and riots to the utmost limits of our union! The character of our countrymen seems suddenly changed, and thousands interpret the law in their own way—sometimes in one case, and then in another, guided apparently only by their own will!"[11]

Two separate atrocities captured the zeitgeist and made the word *lynching* synonymous with mob killings. The first took place in Vicksburg, Mississippi, in 1835, where the rowdy behavior of a group of gamblers had long disturbed the peace, so the people of Vicksburg held a meeting and passed resolutions to expel them and prohibit future gambling.[12] The gamblers resisted and fired four or five shots from their house, killing a respected citizen. At this, the crowd burst in through every door, dragged out five gamblers, took them straight to the scaffold and hanged them. There was no trial.

The other notorious lynching was more brutal and more easily told. It happened in St. Louis on April 28, 1836. Francis J. McIntosh, a man of mixed race, attacked two policemen who were trying to break up a fight between two boatmen. McIntosh was arrested, taken before a justice of the peace, and committed to jail. As the same two police officers escorted McIntosh to the jail, he drew a long knife, killed one officer, and badly wounded the other. A large mob seized McIntosh, chained him to a tree, and burnt him to death.[13] McIntosh's horrific death caused a national sensation.

The events at Vicksburg and St. Louis made lynching a household word and crystalized opposition to all forms of extralegal punishment.[14] The same issue of *Niles' Register* that described the events at Vicksburg called them an "outrage" and said, "[T]here is neither mercy nor justice in the *decisions* of a mob, and when mob-law is tolerated, statute and moral *law* will become a dead letter."[15] Historian Christopher Waldrep offers several reasons why Vicksburg and St. Louis captured the public imagination in a way that generations of mob actions had not. First,

newspapers had recently begun printing stories of lurid crimes. The
year 1835 provided plenty of copy; it and the following years saw un-
precedented levels of riots, mayhem, and mob violence generally.[16]
Lynching was a novel category of crime, and, of course, both burning a
man alive and hanging five men at one time were sensational events.[17]
Second, Waldrep says, newspapers affiliated with the Whig Party, which
positioned itself as the law and order party, played up news of the outrages and associated them with Jacksonians and the elevation of popular sovereignty over the Constitution.[18] The new word, *lynching*, ac-
centuated the danger. At the same time, abolitionists seized on lynching
as "part of a larger pattern of lawlessness" in the South.[19]

In short, by the time of the gold rush, *lynching* meant mob law and
atrocities. Many California journalists and letter writers were themselves Easterners and anticipated criticism from home. "It will be difficult for people in the Eastern States to fully realize our condition here,"
wrote the *Alta California* after a description of a recent lynch trial.
"They will therefore, probably condemn by wholesale this summary
mode of arraigning and punishing for a most heinous offence." But, the
article continued, California labored under extraordinary conditions
with criminals from every corner of the globe and an inadequate penal
system. "Lynch law is not the best law that might be," the paper concluded, "but it is better than none, and so far as benefit is derived from
law, we have no other here."[20]

California apologies for lynch law were published in Eastern papers,
but they failed to persuade, even though the readers understood that
lynch trials in the gold mines were different from the murders in Vicksburg and St. Louis. On the related subject of vigilance committees, the
*Weekly National Intelligencer* in Washington, DC, noted that "[t]he
newspapers of California . . . fully justify the outrage." Yet the editors of
the *National Intelligencer* were unimpressed. The secret committees of
San Francisco reminded them of the terrible and accelerated proceedings of the Star Chamber. And they wrote that this opinion was general:
"[T]he press here on the Atlantic border most earnestly and unreserv-
edly deprecate this mob-law rule."[21] There was nothing the Californians
could say that would justify justice straight from the people in the eyes
of their countrymen.[22]

The Californians, in their turn, read in newspapers from the East that their arguments and explanations were rejected. "I see, by late intelligence from home, that the Atlantic papers, with few exceptions, have taken grounds against the Vigilance Committees in California and denounce them as 'mobs' and 'lynchers,'" wrote Enos Christman on the separate but related issue of vigilantism. "We cannot blame them much for this course; but they do not understand the causes."[23] Since almost all Californians agreed on the absolute necessity of lynch law, and no one in the East "got it," the problem seemed to be one of communication or perhaps of the lack of imagination of the citizens in settled parts of the country. The armchair philosopher in Boston or London simply did not know what he was talking about. "[N]o doubt many sound theories may be brought forward against the propriety of administering Lynch law," wrote Borthwick, "but California . . . was no place for theorising upon abstract principles."[24]

How could a young man like Enos Christman from West Chester, Pennsylvania, be converted to the institution of the vigilance committee? And how could Theodore Johnson from New Jersey, who traveled to California and back in 1849, having spent only two weeks in the mines, write that the general application of lynch law was "both necessary and useful," adding, reassuringly, that "since the less frequent resort to the extreme punishment of death, except only for murder, it has been more justly applied"?[25] Or how did any of the young men, who had felt the same as their families and friends only a few months before they arrived in the mines, come to defend lynch trials in letters home?

It was because the new arrivals found themselves in a foreign country, the frontier, where community-held trials had long been the norm, and they accepted that they did things differently there. One rarely thinks of the California gold region as belonging to the frontier, but in many respects it did, especially in the early years. As discussed in the Introduction, California was remote from the rest of the United States, sparsely populated, and without a civil government until December 1849.

Settlors from Oregon were among the first to reach the mines in 1848, and they brought their form of trial with them. G. B. Stevens of New York was among those who attributed the good order in California in 1849 to those pioneers: "Everything is safe. No thieves. No robbers. The Oregon people have given a character & tone to society and things here."[26] Similarly, at a lynch trial at Spanish Bar in the summer of 1849, a "rough Oregon Man" acted as sheriff. Prior to the trial, this man "said he had had some experience both in Oregon and in California in certain lynch cases where the accused were condemned and hung."[27]

In later years, men from Missouri, Arkansas, Texas, and other states on the edge of the frontier made up a large proportion of the mining population. They did not leave much of a record because they wrote few letters home and did not keep diaries; to us, they are a kind of dark matter of the mines, undetectable but exerting gravity. They, too, must have had some experience in lynching and lynch law before California and certainly voted at lynch trials there.

It has been suggested that the defense of lynch trials in California newspapers and in the letters from articulate young men to their families was picked up by Southerners and, thus, indirectly helped to make later racist lynching acceptable. William Carrigan and Clive Webb, for instance, write that letters from the mines "convinced family and friends back in other parts of the country that, given the proper circumstances, vigilantism could and should be condoned." Carrigan and Webb further note that justifications for lynching were especially well received in Texas and New Mexico "before, during, and especially after the Gold Rush."[28] It is more likely, however, that the justifications were going the other way: it was the frontiersman from Texas and other frontier regions who introduced the forty-niners to the concept of lynch law and not the reverse.

## Lynch Trials on the Overland Trail

The majority of descriptions of frontier lynch trials come from California and the Overland Trail because of the hundreds of trials recorded in emigrants and miners' letters and diaries as well as newspaper accounts. Those run by wagon trains were studied by John Phillip Reid in rich detail as part of his virtuoso study of crime, punishment, and social behavior on the trail. Reid documented the emigrants' efforts to replicate common law criminal trials as closely as possible. Since the accused murderer was often a member of the same company as his victim, a unit that had been traveling together for weeks or months, the emigrants sought to recruit impartial jurors from outside their own group to ensure a fair trial. The defendant's own train, and any other trains who provided jurors, had to stop for these sometimes full-day trials at an enormous cost to themselves in time and resources. If there was a lawyer or judge present, he was asked to take a lead in the proceedings, and the defendant was always allowed to hire counsel. Many further procedures of a proper trial were observed: the judges instructed the jurors; the jurors retired for deliberation; when they were agreed, they submitted a written verdict to the court; and the participants in the trial used the phrases and vocabulary of American courts.[29] A number of defendants were acquitted on the grounds that they acted in self-defense or had been provoked. In short, everything possible was done to assure the legitimacy and fairness of the trial and to deal with offenders "not by vengeance but by applying the remembered trappings of a partly understood judicial process."[30]

Reid's thesis was that the emigrants recreated the institutions they left behind, including the forms and safeguards of American criminal law. "[T]he attitudes of the emigrants toward the judicial process," Reid writes, "and the consistency with which they appealed to legal principles, were more indicative of those of the average American than those of 'frontiersmen.'"[31] He interprets the orderly trials on the Overland Trail as a bubble of Eastern values that the Easterners carried with them, evidence that Americans had internalized the values of the common law and adhered to them when they were beyond the reach of official courts. And given the loaded history of the term *lynch*, it was practical of Reid to focus not on the word but on the actual proceedings.

But the similarity to criminal trials in the states does not mean that they were not frontier trials. Emigrants' trials looked like those at home because all Americans, those in the states and those on the frontier, respected certain norms of the common law criminal trial, most importantly, the right to a jury. Lesser rights, such as a right to counsel or a right to confront witnesses, were open to negotiation. As Reid wrote, "throughout all of American history . . . westward settlers have always carried with them their traditions, their customs, and their law."[32]

In fact, the criminal law of the Overland Trail was precisely that of the frontier: it was lynch law and would have repulsed friends at home. Reid quotes multiple uses of the term *lynch* in overland diaries, but downplays them, noting that "[w]hen an emigrant used the expression 'lynch law' it seldom meant condemnation."[33] As an example, he quotes an emigrant who wrote that "[s]ome of the men on the plains ... seemed to think there was no law on the frontier and that they could do as they pleased, but that is not a country for that way of doing things, for Judge Lynch invariably gave justice."[34] The emigrant was saying that Judge Lynch was law—law as the frontier applied it.

The consciousness of being on the frontier and part of frontier culture is most evident from the dates after the gold discovery, when many of the emigrant companies were bound straight for the mines, with names like the California Banner Company. Emigrants described the Overland Trail itself as "in California," and as soon as they left Missouri, they said that "California laws" prevailed.[35] Presumably some of these emigrants had heard of lynch law from friends in the mines or through publications and absorbed the basic idea that, in the absence of courts, the accused should be given an approximation of a regular trial with the community playing the part of the judge. And while the emigrants tried to replicate regular trials, some seemed to be in transition to what they believed was California law. One man, while not calling the emigrant trials lynchings, was speaking the language of the mines when he wrote that "[t]he tedious, tardy, and often doubtful manner of administering what is called justice in the States has but few admirers or advocates on the plains."[36] Clearly, some emigrants had acquired the ways of the frontier with more conviction than others.

## Lynch Trials Elsewhere on the Frontier

There is dramatically less evidence of lynch trials beyond California and the Overland Trail, but enough to show that they happened across the frontier. Stephen Leonard and Darlene Cypser have studied the known instances in frontier Colorado.[37] Leonard describes eleven trials by the People's Court in Colorado in 1859 and 1860, before that preterritory had any official government. In each case, an unofficial judge presided, an attorney represented the accused, and a jury decided the verdict. Everything was public and orderly, and four of the trials resulted in acquittals. "The People's Court may not have been fully legal," Leonard writes, "but it was the best the isolated community could do and it was better than mob law," although, he adds, the trials "put the community on the slippery slope to the 'secret, often disorderly monster' of vigilantism."[38] Cypser summarizes and analyses almost thirty trials in the People's Courts, in the same period, including those described by Leonard.[39] She makes a strong argument that in one case, there was both a coroner's inquest and a jury trial, each with a different judge.

Leonard and Cypser draw heavily on regional newspapers, which gives hope that the criminal law of other, relatively populous frontier areas can be documented in similar detail. Even without deep research, however, one can find further citizen trials north, south, east, and west of the frontier.

To begin in the East: the community of lead miners in Dubuque, Iowa, had much in common with the California gold miners. They, too, were working in a land without law, in their case because their claims were on Indian land and therefore illegal. The miners assembled on June 17, 1830, to appoint a committee of five miners to draft "rules and regulations by which we, as miners, will be governed." There were only two rules: each claim should be two hundred yards square and be worked one day in six; and the miners should elect an arbitrator to decide disputes.[40]

When, on May 29, 1834, a miner named Patrick O'Conner shot and killed his partner, George O'Keefe, the citizens immediately held an inquest, at which a jury delivered a verdict that the former had killed the latter. The trial took place the next day. A jury of twelve citizens was "taken from the multitude." The accused was allowed to choose a friend as his counsel and to object to as many of the jurors as he chose. Witnesses testified that O'Conner's housemates, including O'Keefe, came home from "the village of Dubuque" to find that he had locked them out. As they pushed open the door, O'Conner fired, killing O'Keefe. There was some evidence of premeditation and testimony that O'Conner said after the shooting that he was glad that he had killed O'Keefe. The jury retired for two hours and returned a unanimous verdict of murder in the highest degree, signed by all twelve. They recommended that Patrick O'Conner be held for three weeks and then "conducted to the place of execution, and there be hung by the neck until he is dead."[41]

Three days before the execution, the "citizens of Dubuque's mines" held a meeting to adopt the necessary measures for the hanging. Through resolutions, they chose a man to command a company of volunteers to guard O'Conner; the chairman was enabled to appoint a committee of three men to make the arrangements for the execution and subsequent burial; they appointed a sheriff; and they appointed a committee of three to collect funds to pay for "keeping, executing, burial, &c. of said O'Conner." One thousand five hundred people witnessed the hanging itself. Everyone observed the utmost restraint and good order. "By mutual consent of all, every coffee house was kept closed, and not a drop of spirits was sold until after the execution."[42]

*Niles' Weekly Register* added its own observations on the trial and execution. "[A]s law, in every country, emanates from the people, and is in fact, whether written or not, nothing more nor less than certain rules of action by which a people agree to be governed," the unanimous agreement by the citizens of Dubuque to execute O'Connor for murder "rendered the act legal to all intents and purposes."[43]

Although the hanging of O'Connor in Dubuque was not called a lynch trial by the local paper, the *Galenian*, it got a surprising amount of coverage as an example of lynch law. Charles Augustus Murray, who was visiting the United States from the United Kingdom at the time of the event, used the Dubuque trial as an introduction to the term for his readers. Although "few could pity the miscreant, or blame his executioners," Murray felt that from a broader perspective, "it is impossible to conceive a more horrible outrage upon law, justice, and social order, than this kind of self-constituted court."[44]

The year after the events in Dubuque, 1835, a similar citizen trial took place in Mexican California, among a small group of Americans who had settled at the Pueblo de Los Angeles. Richard H. Dana described the events in *Two Years before the Mast*. He said that a Yankee who had settled there was sitting in his house with his wife and children when a Mexican man with whom he had quarreled entered and stabbed him to death. The Americans who happened to be living nearby seized and confined the killer while they appealed to the governor-general for justice. He, however, refused to act in the matter. "Seeing no prospect of justice being administered," the Americans resolved to try the man themselves. There happened to be "a company of some thirty or forty trappers and hunters from the Western States, with their rifles" at the pueblo, and "these, together with the Americans and Englishmen . . . proceeded to try the man according to the forms in their own country." They chose a judge and a jury, and the man was "tried, convicted, sentenced to be shot." Twelve men were chosen by lot to form a firing squad and, when the word was given, shot him dead.[45]

In the year of the gold discovery, 1848, an Indian was prosecuted for murder on the Northern frontier near Balsam Lake, Minnesota. "H. H. Perkins acted as judge," a jury was impaneled, and "[a] prosecuting attorney and counsel for the accused were appointed." The Indian suspect confessed to the murder and said that a man named Miller had hired him. The jury brought in a verdict of guilty, and by "unanimous consent" the murderer was hanged the next day. The crowd also gave Miller fifteen lashes and then put him on a steamboat and told him not to come back. The author of the account thought this last was "unexpectedly lenient," given that Miller was the principal in the affair.[46]

Finally, the 1863 trial of George Ives in Nevada City, Montana, was the most elaborate of the known lynch trials. As in California, it was run by a meeting that made all procedural decisions. After some debate, the crowd agreed that Ives should have the assistance of counsel; after more debate, they decided that he would be tried before two twelve-person juries—one jury from Nevada City and one jury from Junction, the nearest settlement—who would give an "advisory" verdict, which the crowd could affirm or reverse. By the time of the trial, the crowd had swelled to 1,500 men. Ives's lawyers—there were five—made forceful objections to the admission of hearsay and irrelevant evidence, but the crowd overruled the objections. Ultimately, the juries split, twenty-three guilty to one not guilty. Their advisory verdict of guilty was affirmed by the crowd in a voice vote; by a second voice vote, they sentenced Ives to hang.[47]

The Ives trial led to the formation of a committee of vigilance. It emerged that Ives and his companions had committed many robberies and murders and that capturing and trying them one by one was impracticable. Twenty-four men therefore joined to form the most famous Montana Vigilante Committee. They pledged in writing to form "a party for the laudable purpos [*sic*] of arresting thievs [*sic*] & murderers & recovering stollen [*sic*] property" and swore to reveal no secrets and never to desert one another. The difference between a popular trial and vigilantes could not be clearer; whereas the trial was public and attracted a thousand people, the vigilance committee was small, it had a founding document, and its members took an oath of secrecy.[48] It was also implied that their trials would be more efficient than the unwieldy, democratic people's court. In short, the community held a lynch trial and formed a vigilance committee in quick succession, and these differed significantly in their proceedings and aims.

In short, the popular trials are *there*. The known trials are scattered over a wide area, however, and many are documented only by a single eyewitness account or, worse, in reminiscences and local histories. They put the California material in context, but, more importantly, the gold rush lynch trials put them in context. This is because the California sources are so numerous and so detailed that they include the fine points of procedure and the struggles between participants who favored quicker trials and harsher punishments, on the one hand, and those who inclined toward more procedure and lenient sentences, on the other. What emerges from everything combined is a pan-frontier criminal law system that was run by popular meetings, followed parliamentary procedure and adhered to basic common law forms. At their best, these citizen trials were, in fact, sober and fair: and at their worst, they slipped into mob law, that is, execution with, at most, the pretense of process. In California, the trajectory over time was toward chaos, as will become clear.

## Lynch Trials versus Vigilantism and Self-Help

Although modern accounts of California lynch trials sometimes describe them as vigilantism or mob law, they were fundamentally different, though this difference is rarely noted. California gold rush trials did not even overlap with vigilantism, the former being public and democratic, and the latter being run by an organized group that reached its decisions behind closed doors. Vigilantes were community leaders who organized to hunt down and punish "outsiders," such as gangs of horse thieves, counterfeiters, and gamblers, who preyed on society.

Lynch trials were for neighbors. The whole community participated in the proceedings, and the aim was to punish the guilty party rather than to drive out a gang of outlaws. The object was justice rather than self-defense. The originally justification for citizen trials was the lack of courts. Then, when courts were first established, lynch trials were still deemed necessary because of government incompetence, setting up a competition between the miners and the courts that led to abbreviated trials and hangings.

## Self-Help and Mob Law

From the beginning, there were also instances of self-help, which could be classified as mob law, when a group punished a criminal caught in the act. Lynch trials could merge into mob law when the trial became an empty formality; one might call lynch trials a gateway drug to mob law. Defenders of lynch trials emphatically distinguished it from mob law, however, because the latter was the act of individuals and not the community as a whole.

The best documented instances of self-help in California were those in which the victim of theft or the friends of a murdered man punished the perpetrator themselves. Self-help did happen in the mining camps and fell under the general heading of lynch law, although it is not nearly as well documented as lynch trials. The constraint on summary punishment was that it was only accepted when the criminal was caught in the act. Englishman William Kelly wrote that as theft increased in 1851, "the code of the famous Judge Lynch was unanimously adopted, and under its oral provisions any person caught 'in flagrante delicto' was shot down without ceremony."[49] Another observer suggested that permission to kill was not so much a rule as an excusable deviation from the norm. Ordinarily, he wrote, "all culprits were tried by a jury," but "[t]wo or three [thieves] who had stolen largely had been shot down by the injured party, the general feeling among the miners justifying such a course when no other seemed available."[50] I have not come across any examples of a thief shot by his victim, so it was indeed rare.

Death, the extreme summary punishment, seems to have been reserved mainly for murderers; and then it was, of course, not the victim but the bystanders who executed the offender on the spot. An individual or individuals could do the deed. A Mr. Beach was shot by a man who owed him money. A man in a nearby looked out when he heard the report and saw the murdered Mr. Beach, "got his gun & shot the other man."[51] Usually, however, it was a group of bystanders or the whole community that seized and executed the killer, and with more passion than displayed by Beach's avenger. When a Spaniard killed a man named Hawkins in a saloon at Goodyear's Bar, the murderer was at once "fiercely attacked by the spectators, who cut and hacked him without mercy, causing his death almost instantly."[52]

Hanging was more common than hacking. At Curtis Creek, a certain Bowen shot Alexander Boggs in the head without provocation. Some of the bystanders "thereupon seized Bowen, put a lariet around his neck, dragged him to a butcher's shambles, and hung him on the scaffold erected for the butchers to hang their slaughtered animals upon." The newspaper offered a very mild reproof to these proceedings, noting only, "This was some what summary."[53]

Another killer, Macy, who stabbed an old man to death in his own home, was "pursued and taken by a crowd, who took him a short distance out of town, on the emigrant road, and hung him up, without judge or jury."[54] And a final example involved a man called Devine, who had a habit of gambling away his family's money. One day, he demanded that his wife hand over the money she had hidden to keep him from squandering it; she refused, and he shot her dead. "An enraged crowd, several hundred strong, assembled forthwith, set Devine on a horse and rode him off to a tree." They made him kneel upon the horse's back, put the rope around his neck, and drove the horse off, leaving him hanging from a branch of the tree.[55]

For thieves, as opposed to murderers, the bystanders invented various penalties.[56] One technique was to give the accused a taste of hanging, either instead of or in addition to whipping. When three "rascals were caught in the act" of attacking a Chinese man in his sleep with the intent to rob him, "one of them was immediately strung up, and was kept suspended some minutes, but was taken down before strangulation could take place."[57] Another was given a hundred lashes on his bare back, and the third was still at large at the time that the newspaper appeared. Similarly, two cattle thieves "detected in the act of stealing stock" were "hung for a short time, and taken down before life became extinct."[58]

At Rough and Ready, some gamblers accused a man of stealing a $200 lump of gold, but "[u]nder the most severe thrashing, and even after threats of hanging, he continued to deny the theft." The newspaper, which reported the incident under the title "Judge Lynch," noted that a "majority of the people did not sanction the movement," but not that they tried to stop it.[59] Similarly, Alfred Peabody, who arrived in San Francisco on June 1, 1849, heard that a man suspected of stealing had recently been "taken by several persons to a tree nearby, a rope put round his neck, and he was hoisted nearly from the ground, but his earnest protestations of innocence moved the hearts of his accusers, and they felt that they had made a mistake in the person and let him go." Peabody observed that "if mistakes of this kind should often occur, I felt that even a quiet man from Salem would be hardly secure."[60] Both of these incidents were really acts of torture to extract a confession rather than punishments.

The men who caught a thief and gave him a hundred lashes—a horrific, potentially fatal injury—or strung him up until he was almost dead were not themselves committing a crime. The community did not bring a criminal case against them—just as it did nothing about the men who slaughtered Native Americans, or took Mexicans' claims from them, or beat up anyone at all. They did not even drive the offenders out of the diggings. The miners of Smith Flat were so incensed by a man who decided to tie up a chicken and roast it alive on his campfire that they "immediately called a meeting, and unanimously adopted a resolution to the effect that the chicken-roaster's presence was no longer desirable in that camp." He was given fifteen minutes to get out: "[A]nd that fifteen minutes be given him, after due notice from a committee appointed to notify him."[61] Shooting a murderer on the spot was evidently not as shocking as cooking a live chicken.

Paradoxically, some of these examples of self-help seem less offensive to us today than lynch trials because they were committed in the "heat of passion," in reaction to crimes against sympathetic victims—the old man in his home, the wife hiding the savings from her gambling husband. And yet, where a group carried out the deed, they were lynchings as we understand the term today.

## Vigilantism

Vigilance committees had a brief floruit in California mining region in 1851. (The most famous and the most influential vigilante movement of all, the San Francisco Committee of Vigilance of 1856, is a good example of vigilante organization and tactics, but is less relevant to our story because of its late date and because it targeted a different sort of gang, namely, an entrenched political machine.)[62] Elsewhere on the frontier, however, they were the most familiar form of organized crime control. Unlike lynch trials, vigilantism has been studied in great depth, both as it functioned on the frontier generally and in San Francisco specifically. One modern view is that vigilantism cannot be distinguished from lynch trials, that vigilantes were simply lynch parties, or that lynching was "instant vigilantism."[63] Certainly, vigilantism was a form of lynching in its broadest sense of extralegal punishment. As this section discusses, however, vigilantism differed from lynch law in its hierarchical organization and its goal of ending a specific, ongoing threat to the community rather than punishing individual criminals.

Richard Maxwell Brown explained in a learned analysis of the subject that vigilante movements formed on the frontier in response to gangs of horse thieves and counterfeiters, inadequate law enforcement hampered by shortage of officers, and the lack of secure jails. Prominent men in the community led the movement, while farmers, craftsmen, traders, and others of relatively modest means made up the rank and file. Brown noted that vigilantes organized in "command or military fashion and usually had a constitution, articles, or a manifesto to which the members would subscribe."[64] Their goal was that of reestablishing order, which could generally be accomplished by trying and executing a couple of the outlaws and expelling the rest.[65]

In California, there were two classic vigilante movements during the gold rush period. The first was the Law and Order Party of 1849, formed to rid the city of "the Hounds," a gang of ex-servicemen discharged in California after the war with Mexico. The gang was a general menace to society, and the last straw was a violent attack on the Chilean community of San Francisco. The vigilantes tried and convicted eight of the Hounds and banished them from San Francisco.[66]

An increase in crime and the perceived inadequate response of the courts led citizens of San Francisco to form a second committee of vigilance in 1851, this time in response to a rash of crime by, for the most part, Australians. Membership of the committee and its internal working were secret to the rest of the population, although the public had a general knowledge of what was happening and could see members coming and going from the committee headquarters. Fortunately, the committee kept meticulous records as well as every scrap of correspondence that crossed the secretary's desk, all of which have been published.[67] More than seven hundred members signed their names to the constitution, which stated the committee's purpose, "for the maintenance of the peace and the good order of Society and the preservation of the lives and property of the Citizens of San Francisco." There were a president, secretary, and treasurer, as well as standing committees of finance and of membership; committee police and police chiefs; and a sergeant at arms who lived in the committee rooms so that someone was always present to receive reports made to the committee.[68]

The conventionality of the committee was also reflected in its decor, as described in the *Daily Alta California*. Its rooms "are handsomely furnished. The floor is carpeted. At one end is a handsome rostrum, containing an elegant chair for the President. . . At the eastern end, opposite the rostrum, the daily papers are to be found on file. The windows are neatly curtained; while hanging against the wall are pictures and maps."[69] The rooms were respectability made manifest.

In the course of the summer of 1851, the committee tried and executed four of the men brought before it: Jenkins, Stuart, Whittaker, and McKenzie. The members ran the trials, much like the lynch trials in the mines: they selected a jury, appointed a prosecuting attorney, and summoned witnesses. After the convictions and sentencing of Jenkins and

Stuart, the committee "felt that it was necessary to ascertain whether or not the community at large would support them in their self-assumed office." In Jenkins's case, Sam Brannan addressed the crowd in the public square, recounting the evidence against the prisoner, the conviction, and the sentence of death. He asked the crowd whether it approved this action. "The response was a tumultuous cry of 'Yes!' mingled with cheers and some dissenting 'Noes!'" There was no vote, though a witness later reported that a third of those present favored releasing Jenkins. The committee, assured of public support, proceeded to hang Jenkins on June 11, 1851. James Stuart was hanged on July 11 after similar proceedings.[70]

The San Francisco Committee of Vigilance of 1851 encouraged other towns to form branch committees, and nearly every county had a committee by December of that year. Stockton, Marysville, Sacramento, and Sonora had their own committees before the end of June 1851, and Nevada City followed suit in July. These assisted the San Francisco committee by sharing information and hunting down the criminals who had escaped the metropolis as well as holding trials and punishing a handful of thieves and murderers.[71]

One hundred twenty-seven of Marysville's "principal merchants and business men" formed a committee of vigilance in June 1851 and adopted a constitution modeled on that of San Francisco. It provided information about various criminals to the San Francisco committee, and that was about all. When the committee decided not to take action against two Mexican men accused of knifing another Mexican, possibly fatally, the *Marysville Herald* approved. "It is no part of the Committee's business to take cognizance of private quarrels, however fatal their consequences," it wrote. Instead, the purpose of the committee was to punish "such crimes as are more extended in their consequences, and the extent of which cannot be known when they are committed." Fortunately, no such threat presented itself.[72]

One glance at the resolutions passed at the first meeting of the Sonora Vigilance Committee shows how different its organization was from that of a miners' meeting:

*Resolved,* That no members be admitted to this association except they be unanimously elected.

*Resolved*, That ten gentlemen be selected to act as a police for the night.

*Resolved*, That the police have a private watch word, "Action!" . . .

*Resolved*, That secrecy should be observed as to the doings of this committee by the members thereof . . .

*Resolved*, That if called upon by the People's Police of Camp Seco, this committee respond by lending their aid.

*Resolved*, That a committee of five be appointed to draft constitution and bylaws and report tomorrow evening.[73]

Where miners' meetings wanted to be inclusive, only men who had been "unanimously elected" could join the Sonora committee. Where miners' meetings met spontaneously and dispersed when their work was done, the committee created a standing police force. Where miners' meetings were open, the committee was committed to secrecy.

The documented vigilance committees in California were almost exclusively based in towns, although multiple sources mention that mining camps also formed committees. Enos Christman, who was secretary of Sonora's committee of vigilance and therefore in a position to know, wrote, "[I]n almost every camp and city in the country, the most respectable portion of the community have formed what are called 'Vigilance Committees' which appoint officers, organize courts, catch rascals, try them and, when found guilty, punish them by whipping, banishing or hanging."[74] But these mere mentions are almost all that is known about the committees in mining camps. Mary Floyd Williams wrote, "[T]he references [are] so brief and so disconnected that it is impossible to say whether the societies were permanent in character or were temporary associations formed to meet particular emergencies."[75] A rare exception is Dame Shirley's account of the vigilance committee at Indian Bar, which was elected by the miners—also exceptionally—following a battle between Spanish speakers and Americans. The committee was charged with ridding the community of the Spanish-speaking threat. It ordered two Spanish ringleaders whipped and expelled the rest, which, while probably unjust (the facts are not entirely clear) was less severe than the punishment that they would have received after a lynch trial.[76]

In short, vigilante movements sought to break up and expel criminal gangs. Insofar as they executed a few of the worst offenders, it was *pour encourager les autres* to leave. Their goal was security, not justice. The trial format, in contrast, was used to address crimes committed by members of the community. Neighbors who committed crimes—like the man who killed his wife or the man who stole from his partner—had to be punished; but they were entitled to a public trial. In the absence of courts, the community provided this themselves. As the *Alta California* said, lynch trials, while "harsh and of a character not legalized by the law, have frequently to be adopted in new countries, where the law can, from the nature of things be but imperfectly administered."[77]

Lynch trials were not about terrorizing Indians, Spanish speakers, or Chinese people in the mines. What the Americans did to those groups was much worse even than lynching: it was genocide, open season, mass expulsion, and theft without repercussions. Lynch trials were not self-help or mob law, that is, punishment without process. Californians believed that the miners' trials were preferable to self-help. Australian gold miners, in contrast, tolerated self-help but rejected citizen trials because the latter usurped the authority of the state. Lynch law also did not include vigilantism, whether in the form of vigilance committees aimed at breaking up criminal gangs, a sheriff and his posse, or regulators who expelled undesirables without process.

Finally, lynch trials could be remarkably formal, following parliamentary procedure and Anglo-American criminal procedure. Some, especially in the first year of the gold rush, were fair to the point of error, acquitting individuals whom the participants believed to be guilty and who were later discovered indeed to be guilty. Other miners' courts rushed through empty formalities to amateur, botched executions.

Recognizing lynch trials as a distinct genre is important mostly because they constitute the true criminal law of the frontier, the purpose of which was to see justice done as opposed to chasing off outlaws. Christopher Waldrep noted that Westerners—or, at least, Western defenders of lynch law—used the term to mean an orderly trial.[78] But most authors conflate lynch trials with either mob law or vigilantism.

For example, Rodham Paul, whose book *California Gold* is one of the clearest descriptions of the gold rush, wrote, "A 'lynching party' was usually a mob that came hastily together to deal with a particular crime."[79] Similarly, David A. Johnson used the phrases "popular tribunals, lynch courts, and vigilance committees" interchangeably. He described all of them as forms of a ritual in which the protagonist was the undifferentiated mass—the "people"—whose collective rage stemmed from "an inherent, natural sense of justice, unreachable through the procedures of due process."[80] The climax of the ritual was the execution of the alleged criminal, in which the "moral authority" of the people triumphed over the "morally alienated individual."[81]

Johnson's description fits some of the most famous accounts of trial by Judge Lynch and most if not all lynchings after 1852, when the courts were well established. But it is not accurate with respect to others, which most certainly mention individuals by name—the chairman, secretary, attorneys, jury members, and witnesses. The "minutes" of at least one meeting that conducted a trial were so long and boring that the newspaper printed only extracts. Many abbreviated accounts of lynch trials mention a jury or counsel in passing, hints of due process that are easily missed if one is looking for enraged crowds.

On a different note, the focus on lynch trials of Mexicans diverts our attention from the real wrongs against immigrants. Very few Mexicans were subjected to lynch law; the overwhelming majority of defendants in the court of Judge Lynch were whites. The real danger to Mexicans was that lynch law did not punish a white man for robbing or killing them, so that it was open season on that minority. Paradoxically, the absence of Mexicans from the lynch law record is disturbing because it indicates that whites were getting away with murder.

Meanwhile, good-faith trials that are not called lynch law are studied separately from those that are. John Phillip Reid largely omitted the word *lynch* from his work on criminal trials on the Overland Trail, even though he noted occasional references to them as lynch law or California law and although they fit the dictionary definition of "punishment for crimes or offenses by private, unauthorized persons, without a legal trial." Reid's thesis was that the trials on the emigrant trail were not lynch law in the *modern* sense; perhaps, therefore, he felt that the further argument that lynch law on the frontier was different would confuse readers rather than enlighten them. The effect, however, has been to exclude these hundred or so trials from the corpus of trials by Judge Lynch.

Similarly, descriptions of lynch trials submitted to the California newspapers often omit the word *lynch;* Easterbrook's trial is not labeled lynch law. Scholars using the keyword *lynch* in a search engine would miss these cases. I am sure that I have missed many descriptions of lynch trials myself for that reason, despite searching also for *trial, theft,* and *lashes,* as well as *lynch.* Moreover, the most exciting lynch trials are easier to find than the boring ones, skewing our perception of the phenomenon.

In the long run, the respectability of lynch trials was a bad thing. The justification for lynch law rested on the absence of government and settled society, on small communities in the wilderness who had no defense but self-defense. That justification disappeared when California became a proper state and appointed judges and sheriffs, built jails, and established a regular court schedule. It took time, however, for those institutions to get up and running, and in the meantime, few accused criminals were convicted, either because they escaped or because the witnesses against them had moved on. The miners' confidence in their ability to determine guilt or innocence now became a danger, as they literally fought the authorities for control of prisoners—habeas corpus in reverse. At this point, lynch trials turned into something less like trials and more like lynchings. First, however, we turn to the rules and procedures of Judge Lynch's court in the mines.

# CHAPTER 8

# Trial by Judge Lynch

I n March 1851, a slight dispute at Shasta City suddenly escalated, and one of two messmates seized a gun and shot the other so that "the victim made a leap, the blood gushed forth, and he fell dead." The murderer was seized, and the next morning, a "court of the people was formed on Sunday—a judge appointed—witnesses examined—and the murderer showed all the clemency he could have obtained in a legal tribunal."[1] The accused was sentenced to hang the same afternoon. That was a lynch trial, and the writers of the account approved the measures taken to punish the guilty party.

The reader might well ask what kind of a trial "the people" could have given the accused under the circumstances. This chapter examines the trials that Californian Joseph Warren Wood had in mind when in 1852 he said, "The form of a court most dear to Americans has always been adopted, and the prisoners have been allowed the widest construction of the privileges usual on such occasions."[2] There were trials that even Joseph Warren Wood, had he known about them, would have had to admit were debacles, and the proportion of those increased as the miners became more comfortable with their creation, crowds got larger, and trials were speeded up. Sometimes the trial was reduced to a mere formality, as when the crowd took the suspects "from the Shireff [sic] choose a Jury try them and have them strung up in an hour or two."[3] Where prominent citizens pleaded with a frenzied crowd to let them hold a trial with the promise that the accused would be convicted and executed as a result, no jury could have been impartial. These lynchings were similar to our modern idea of lynching. Our focus here, however, is on the mechanics of an "ordinary" lynch trial.

Unlike either summary punishment or vigilantism, trial by Judge Lynch mirrored the proceedings of a regular American criminal trial. The only preserved mining code to include rules for criminal procedure, namely the Jacksonville Code of January 20, 1850, provides that "[i]n the administration of law, both civil and criminal, the rule of practice shall conform, as near as possible, to that of the United States, but the forms and customs of no particular state shall be required or adopted." For criminal trials, this meant that at the very least, the accused would be "tried by a jury of eight American citizens," or twelve, if he so chose, "who shall be regularly summoned by the sheriff, and sworn by the al-calde, and shall try the case according to the evidence."[4]

The best starting point for understanding what this meant is a relatively complete description of a single trial sent to Charles Dickens's magazine, *Household Words*, by "a University Graduate who was an eyewitness," which almost certainly means an Oxford or Cambridge man.[5] This particular account is interesting for being in plain English. Americans often used a kind of shorthand in the passive voice, as if they were taking minutes of a meeting—as, in fact, they were: chairmen were elected, juries selected, counsel appointed, and motions made and voted upon, with few details about how these things were done or descriptions of the participants or the surroundings. The English observer, describing the process for the first time, paints a lively and detailed picture of the proceedings. He had acclimatized to California so well that the *Household Words* article opens with the same statements of mutual incomprehension that appear in all Eastern reports of lynching: the editor—perhaps Charles Dickens himself—writes that the author "seems to approve of it more than our readers will be likely to do," while the author says defensively that "[y]ou have, in England, but a vague idea what this Lynching is; how absolutely essential it is at present." Indeed, he is clearly impressed by the proceedings while mildly amused by their rustic setting.

"Picture yourself on the top of a hill in a pine-forest," the author says, "the stumps of felled trees lying round." The assembled miners, "a crowd of rough-looking men in beards, felt hats, red flannel shirts, and long boots" begin the proceedings by appointing a president by accla-mation. One man climbs on a stump and "explains that the object of the meeting is to try certain men for stealing a purse of gold-dust out of a store in the town." The three men are now in the custody of the sheriff, "and their committal to the prison at Marysville has been made out (here a laugh and a growl)." The listeners laugh because the authorities at Marysville were notoriously bad at holding on to their charges. Was it "the will of the meeting," the speaker asks from his stump, "that men *suspected* of such crimes be let loose, &c.?" The answer must have been no because we are next told that "[g]uided always by their president (the Americans are peculiarly apt in the conduct of public meetings), they elect a sheriff pro tem., and a committee of safety." The crowd or-ders these appointees to take the prisoners from the real sheriff and bring them before the meeting, where *orders* almost certainly means that a motion was made and passed; perhaps the president called for the motion and in that sense "guided" the meeting.

This move, taking suspects from the sheriff, or even refusing to sur-render them to him, was controversial. It could not happen without ma-jority support since such questions were voted upon; and it was staunchly defended in letters to the editor and private diaries. Sometimes, however, a few but influential men argued vigorously against lynching a suspect when it was possible to hand him over to the authorities to be tried before a proper court. The case at hand is therefore on the border between the early lynch trials and the later, less easily justified ones.

The miners' own sheriff and his committee of safety did indeed seize the prisoners from his official counterpart despite the latter's resist-ance and brought them before the meeting, and a space was cleared for the accused to sit, surrounded by guards. "Counsel are appointed by the meeting, and are paid one hundred dollars for their services." The plural suggests that two lawyers were hired, one for the prosecution and another for the accused. The prisoners claimed that they could not pay, and the article does not explain who in fact paid the attorney's fees.

The account also provides a fascinating detail about the jury: "[S]everal jurors named, object; their pleas are put to the vote, and ac-cepted or refused." Clearly they had not volunteered for job. But their unwillingness to serve was not in and of itself an impediment; the meeting took upon itself the task of deciding who had legitimate reason to be excused and who should serve despite his objections. In other words, the meeting, which consisted of all the miners present, held a kind of *voir dire*.

The meeting also chose a judge, and, remarkably, all of the men proposed for the job refused it, "for those named who have held commissions in the States, protest against the legality of the proceeding, and say they are sworn to defend the constitution." I have not seen another case in which a lawyer spoke out against lynch law on the ground that it was illegal and unconstitutional; here, apparently, more than one did so. The refusal to participate for the stated reasons was a blunt rebuke to the assembly. Then an elderly man stands up and "tells the meeting plainly that they are doing wrong" by holding this trial. Strangely, the university graduate who describes the scene is impressed not with the arguments against the proceedings but with the crowd's tolerance for criticism, observing of the old man that "[s]o far from being molested, he is listened to." In the end, the assembly appoints its president as judge, "and the court opens."

The author glossed over the rest of the trial rather quickly, saying only that it lasted two days (an exceptionally long time), that witnesses testified both for and against the defendants, and that the jury found all three guilty and sentenced them to thirty-nine lashes each. That the jury determined the sentence was a departure from the norm, namely that the crowd usually voted on the sentence. Two of the defendants then made statements. One blamed another for inciting him to commit the theft while he was in his cups; the second denied corrupting the first but offered to hand over his share of the money in return for a reduced sentence. "The jury re-assemble and reduce the sentence accordingly" for these two.

The punishment was carried out the day after the sentence was announced and left the criminals "half fainting, curled up, sick and moaning." The author writes that "[t]hey are hardly allowed to stay in the town till their wounds heal, and one dies." This is a startling ending. Many convicted thieves were given thirty-nine lashes, but they could be more or less severe, depending on who applied them. No other accounts that I know of report a man dying of thirty-nine lashes.

The first lesson from this case is that the typical summary of a lynch trial—that the crowd chose a judge and jury, which, after a fair trial, found the prisoner guilty and sentenced some number of lashes or to execution—does not necessarily mean that the trial was choreographed, that is, that the miners went through some ritual motions before reaching a foregone conclusion. The crowd made choices at each step of the way. Choose a judge to run the trial, or do it themselves? If a judge, should it be someone with legal training or a locally prominent individual? There was always a jury, but how were its members to be appointed? Should the defendants be given counsel? Who served as counsel for the prosecution and defense? Were they qualified lawyers, were they paid, and, if so, by whom? Each trial was different, depending in part on the willingness of "the crowd" to take the time to do things thoroughly.

The case also raises questions about the extent to which individuals were able and willing to influence the process. The resistance to the lynching just described was unique in that learned individuals chosen to be judge actually denounced the proceedings; but it was not rare for men of conscience to take a strong position at the sentencing phase of the trial and, indeed, to succeed in getting the punishment reduced from hanging to whipping. On the other hand, hooligan types acted as rabble rousers, arguing for harsher penalties and carrying out the actual punishments, whether whippings or executions. In between were the well-intentioned but timid men who did no more than vote their conscience on the question of whether to provide counsel for the defense or, in the sentencing phase, on the severity of the punishment. Although many accounts attribute actions to "the crowd," the primary actors were individuals, and every person present had to cast his individual vote.

## The Crowd

The question, then, was who was present at the trial: Who made up the "crowd"? A lynch trial was a form of miners' meeting, and generally, everyone in the community participated, at least in the sense of showing up. When a trial that began at Indian Bar was moved to Rich Bar, nearby, "[e]verybody went to Rich Bar," Dame Shirley wrote, adding in her dry way, "[n]o one remained to protect the calico shanties, the rag huts, and the log cabins, from the much talked of Indian attack."[6] The diary of one miner, Daniel Kleinhans, records two occasions on which he was requested to attend a lynch court. The first occasion was at Spanish Bar in the summer of 1849 and was his first experience of the kind. The next year, when Kleinhans was camped near Fiddletown, a horseman stopped by and told him to come to a lynch trial that evening, several miles downstream. This time, he did not bother to go. The organizers of this second trial were casting a wide net for their meeting.[7]

The size of the crowd varied greatly depending on the density of population. "Several hundred participated" at the trial of Rigler, Allen, and Miller for theft at Nevada City in April 1851, at the end of which the defendants were convicted and sentenced to be whipped.[8] Fifty voted for the execution of five Mexicans convicted of cattle theft in May of that year.[9] And a mere thirty-three participated in the dubious trial of Jones and partners for the alleged theft of "two sacks of flour, one keg of butter, and some other articles."[10]

In a small community, a proper "assembly of the miners" could in fact be just the friends and neighbors of the victim. Once, a group of gamblers roughed up a man named Kelly; Kelly came back the next day and shot the ringleader in the head. The other gamblers pursued Kelly, "took him & tried him & was to hang him the next day"; but local miners rescued Kelly and handed him over to the authorities for trial.[11] It is fascinating that the gamblers thought that trying Kelly would legitimize his execution, but this was not the only case of its kind. Vicente Pérez Rosales, a Chilean, scornfully recounted the "trial" of one of his countrymen by a company of miners en route to the diggings. The latter had discovered that one of their shovels was missing, and their suspicions fell on the Chilean because the so-called "descendent of Africans" was the only foreigner present. "Without any further ado the barbarians became the jury,"[12] wrote Rosales, and they were in the process of hanging the fellow when Rosales arrived at the scene. If he had not managed to talk them down by pretending to be a Frenchman and vouching for the prisoner's good character, the man would have been executed. Rosales may have embellished this story, as most witnesses to lynchings probably did, but the fact remains that "the community" could be a very select body.

The trial of a group of Chileans accused of murder at Iowa Log Cabins was carried out by a particularly biased group, namely, the Americans who had been trying to take the Chileans' claims and who lost two of their countrymen in the ensuing struggle.[13] The Americans arrested fourteen Chilean suspects, and a jury found them all guilty of murder in the first degree. The sentencing was put off to the next day; but before it took place, some ninety men arrived from the neighboring river, the Mokelumne. Thus augmented, the crowd voted not to sentence the accused after all, but instead "to empanel a jury and give them a fair trial, from Disinterested persons, and cappable [sic] men from the other River." This is a very rare intervention by one community in another's criminal procedure. The denizens of the Mokelumne also supplied the defendants with "a young and smart Lawer [sic] from the City of Boston, by the name of Melville." Two of the Chileans were discharged before the trial, including a boy who had "turned state evidence." Nine of the remainder were found to be peons whose masters had forced them against their will to participate in the murders. These nine were sentenced to one hundred lashes and to have their heads shaved, and one was also sentenced to have his ears cut off. Only three men, the masters, were sentenced to be shot. In short, the original lynch trial was considered by the other miners to be illegitimate, and the crowd was "persuaded" to place the matter in the hands of outsiders and to accept their verdict. As a result, the number of executions was reduced from fourteen to three.[14]

## The Location

Judge Lynch's court met in the most public and convenient place available. In isolated settings, judicial architecture was picturesque but lacked variety; trials were held "on the top of a hill in a pine-forest," as the article in *Household Words* reported; the "top of an adjacent hill . . . under a tree,"[15] "under a tree,"[16] and "an old pine log, of gigantic dimensions."[17]

If the camp was large enough to support a store, saloon, or hotel, this was the obvious place for a trial: as one observer wrote, "gambling houses are often turned into court rooms on account of their size."[18]

These tents or buildings were where the population naturally congregated and had the added advantage that they served refreshments. Dame Shirley explained this best. In October 1851, Little John, as he was called, was suspected of stealing $400 from Mr. B, proprietor of the Empire Hotel at Rich Bar. Little John was arrested at the Humbolt Hotel at Indian Bar. The next morning, a miners' meeting was held at the Humbolt not to hold the trial, but to vote on Mr. B's proposal to change the venue to the Empire "for the convenience of his wife, who could not walk over to Indian Bar to give her evidence." Dame Shirley could not see what was happening but heard "the rapidly succeeding 'ayes' and 'noes,'" in response to various motions.[19]

## The President or Chairman

The first step of a lynch trial, as at any meeting, was to choose someone to preside over the meeting, that is, a president or chairman. As noted earlier, the choice rarely fell on the obvious candidate, that is, the man whom the miners had elected alcalde long before the event. Future Supreme Court Justice Stephen Field, when he was alcalde of Marysville, was concerned that the onlookers at a trial might take the prisoner from him if he did not give a harsh enough punishment, so it is no surprise that the crowd pushed aside other alcaldes, ones who were not so highly respected, when a suspected thief or murderer was captured.

Dame Shirley described the background to the ouster of the local alcalde in rich detail. This otherwise mild and ineffectual man, known to all as the Squire, had gone to county seat to be sworn in as justice of the peace of Indian Bar. (Justice of the peace was an approximate equivalent to the alcalde after the California Constitution took effect.) The Squire either acted on his own initiative or perhaps after a kind of secret election held by his friends, but though some respectable people said they would have opposed his candidacy if they had known about it, no one actually challenged him once the deed was done.[20] When Little John was to be tried, however, "the people, the mighty people ... commenced proceedings by voting in a president and jury of their own, though they kindly consented (how *very* condescending!) that the Squire might *play at judge* by sitting at the side of *their* elected magistrate!"[21] Shirley thought he acted almost too meekly in accepting this offer, but also recognized that if he had insisted on running the trial himself, the crowd would simply have excluded him from the proceedings altogether. And she conceded that he did not have what it took for the job. "Although the Squire is sufficiently intelligent, and the kindest hearted creature in the world, he evidently does not possess that peculiar tact, talent, gift, or whatever it is called . . . which is absolutely necessary to keep in order such a strangely amalgamated community, representing as it does the four quarters of the globe, as congregates upon this river."[22] The man the people elected to serve as judge at the trial of Little John presumably had at least more of this quality than did the Squire.

## The Jury

The one responsibility that the assembly almost never took upon itself (there are exceptions to every rule) was that of deciding the guilt or innocence of the accused; this was always the privilege and duty of the jury. When miner Joseph Warren Wood said that "[t]he form of a court most dear to Americans has always been adopted," he meant trial by jury;[23] and, indeed, in almost every trial, the verdict was delivered by the jury. The sentence might be decided by either the jury or the crowd, and more often than not it was the latter, but question of guilt or innocence was left entirely to the former.

Most reports of trials state that the jurors were selected, appointed, voted, called, or empaneled without specifying who did this or how this was done.[24] One early source, from January 1849, explains that "twelve jurymen were drawn by ballot."[25]

The most detail about jury selection comes from the minutes of the trials sent to the newspapers. In the Easterbrook case, the reader may remember, a committee selected the jury. The list of jurors was printed in the newspaper report, and it included Josiah Roop, postmaster of Shasta and brother of the chief witness, Isaac Roop.[26] Roop was elected by the jurors as their secretary. This looks bad.

In two cases, however, the accused himself participated in the jury selection. At the trial of Rigler, Allen, and Miller (charged with having stolen $2,500), which was run very much along the lines of the Easterbrook

case, a motion was made, and apparently agreed to, for "a jury of twelve
disinterested citizens to be selected as follows: a committee of three con-
sisting of the chairman, Dr. Edmonston, Dr. Clark and Adam Smith, who
were to make out a list of fifty names, when the prisoners were to select twelve of the fifty to act as a jury."[27] And in the trial of Samuel Allen
for the murder of William Schay, "[t]he prisoner was permitted to walk
through the crowd for the purpose of selecting the twelve men to whom
he was about to commit his fate."[28] There was no doubt that Samuel Allen
would hang: he confessed to the crime of beating his sixty-year-old victim
to death and asked to be tried "then and there" rather than be taken to the
nearest town. It hardly mattered who was on the jury.

Nevertheless, the Allen case provides a striking example of the jury's attempt to be diligent and impartial. When the twelve withdrew
for deliberations, they discovered that one of their number had been
absent during the witnesses' testimony. The foreman informed Allen of
the lapse, and he agreed that the jury could proceed with eleven men.
But then, another juror made unspecified objections and "with the prisoner's consent, was released from serving as a juror."[29] The remaining
ten men found Allen guilty; thirty minutes later, he was executed.

Some kind of *voir dire* appears to have been normal, judging from
an account of a court trial at Sonora in July 1850. The proceedings were
speeded up because the miners were "in a state of high excitement," and
"a jury was impaneled from among the miners present, without asking
any questions in regard to prejudice or preconceived opinions."[30] The
unscreened jury was evidently worth commenting on.

Sometimes a jury was selected to be representative of two communities that claimed jurisdiction. There was a special effort at impartiality
in the jury selection for a trial of a Mexican accused of killing one of his
countrymen; it was in effect a double jury of "twelve Americans and
an equal number of Mexicans." At the end of the trial, "[t]he Mexicans
were requested to return their verdict, which they did, finding the prisoner guilty, which the Americans assented to."[31] Possibly the Americans
were a backup in case the Mexican jury convicted the defendant against
the weight of the evidence. Similarly, at the lynching of Nicholas discussed below, the jury included eight men from Columbia, where the alleged murder occurred, and four from the victim's home, Pine Lodge.[32]

Jurors were supposed to be paid for their service. The Jacksonville Code specified that "[t]he fee of the jury shall be to each juror half an ounce in each case," to be paid by the accused; but it also said that when "a criminal convict is unable to pay the costs of the case, the alcalde, sheriff, jurors, and witnesses shall render their services free of remuneration."[33] Since the alcalde and sheriff were entitled to one ounce each, and the code provided for eight jurors unless the accused requested twelve, this would amount to costs of at least six ounces, or ninety-six dollars, not including the judge's fees for issuing writs or search warrants. Doubtless—but also evidenceless—a defendant who was completely innocent would not have to pay the fees. On the other hand, at Spanish Bar in 1849, a man was accused of stealing a bag of gold from his partner; the jury was convinced of his guilt, but had to acquit him for lack of evidence. Despite the acquittal, the jury decided that the defendant should pay the court costs and leave the bar.[34]

## Legal Representation

Legal representation was the third requirement of a scrupulous lynch trial. A trial "conducted with the utmost coolness and impartiality" meant that "[a] jury of twelve men was empaneled, Judge selected, and counsel allowed the prisoner."[35] Even at the lynching of Peter Nicholas, who was seized from the authorities by an excited crowd, "counsel was allowed the accused, and the usual forms were observed."[36]

Counsel was "allowed," but not all mining camps provided a lawyer. The question of counsel for the accused was put to a vote, like every other element of procedure: the miner known only as Sam, who was present at the lynching of Frederick Roe in Sacramento, but disapproved of the whole affair, said, "I refrained from participating in all proceedings against him, and only voted with the citizens once, and that was in the affirmative on the second proposition to give him a lawyer."[37]

The defendant had to pay his counsel's fee, as he did all of the court costs. If he could not pay, the Jacksonville Code, quoted above, provided that the judge, jurors, sheriff, and witnesses would serve without remuneration—but says nothing about counsel.[38] Nevertheless, in some cases, the community did bear the cost of a lawyer for the accused.

This may have been the case at the trial described in *Household Words*, above, which mentions that counsel were appointed and paid one hundred dollars. Stephen Field also gave the impression that the community paid for the lawyer if the defendant could not when he wrote that "in all [criminal] cases I appointed an attorney to represent the people, and also the accused, when necessary."[39] Surely, it would only be "necessary" to appoint counsel if the defendant could not do it himself.

The importance of counsel is somewhat surprising because, on the whole, the mining community had nothing good to say about lawyers and, indeed, thought that the legal profession was the biggest obstacle to justice in the California and even in the Eastern states. J. H. Carson, writing in 1852, reflecting fondly on the first years of the gold rush (then three years in the past), said, "We were not blessed at that day with statutes as unintelligible as a Chinese Bible or with hordes of lawyers who, for a pittance, would screen, under the plea of informalities in indictments of proceedings, villains from just punishment."[40] It was a source of great satisfaction that lynch law had put lawyers out of a job. "Lawyers stand but poor chance to do anything; they must dig or starve," wrote one correspondent to the *Sacramento Transcript*; and another miner, Delano, wrote to his wife that lynch law had "stoped [*sic*] about all murder and robery [*sic*] for villins have no chance so it is a poor place for lawyers."[41] Evidently, it was not advocacy as such that the miners rejected, but what they thought of as irrelevant technicalities or the lawyers who profited from them.

The names of the counsel for the prosecution and defense are rarely given, but several of those who are named were already lawyers or would become attorneys in later years. Their participation shows how normalized the lynch trials were and also suggests that the accused's representation was real rather than token. In the Nevada City trial of Rigler, Allen, and Miller by a public meeting, "Wm. T. Barbour was appointed counsel for the People, and E. F. W Ellis for the Prisoners."[42] Both of these had addressed the meeting when it opened, whether to see justice done or to build their reputations is unclear. As persons who were already involved in the proceedings, they were obvious choices to serve as counsel. Ellis, representing the accused, was an attorney and, later, a member of the California State Assembly.[43] The counsel for the

people, William T. Barbour, would in a few months' time be elected
judge of the Tenth Judicial District, comprising Yuba, Nevada, and
Sutter Counties.[44] Stephen Field had a low opinion of him: he thought
Barbour "possessed a fair mind . . . but he was vacillating and indo-
lent."[45] Still, he won the case.

Almost two months after this trial, another took place at Park's Bar.[46]
The accused were two Mexicans charged with assault and battery with
intent to kill. "H. C. Hodge. Esq, of Nevada City being present, was selected by the meeting as attorney for the people, and C. N. Lamison, Esq.,
for the defendants." Hiram C. Hodge, counsel for the prosecution, was
admitted to the bar in 1850.[47] In June 1851, a week after the Park's Bar
case, he was elected treasurer of Nevada County.[48] Perhaps he happened
to be at Park's Bar campaigning for that office. I have not yet been able to
identify C. N. Lamison, but the title "Esquire" suggests he was a lawyer.
The defendants were found guilty and sentenced to forty-five and thirty-
five lashes, respectively, which was a relatively light penalty, considering
that they had stabbed Barbour, the future judge, three times in the back
with a bowie knife.

A third named attorney, James W. Coffroth, served in several trials
either as prosecutor or as counsel for the defense. Coffroth later studied
law and became an accomplished criminal defense lawyer, thanks in
part to his eloquence on the subject of mercy when life was at stake.[49]
During their tenure as a member of the California Assembly, 1852–1853,
Coffroth and Ellis were among the primary movers behind the bill, radical at the time, granting married women the right to transact business
in their own names.[50] Coffroth was, in short, the person whom a man
about to be lynched would most want on his side and most dreaded to
see with the prosecution.[51]

In the case at hand, the accused was Peter Nicholas, who, without
provocation, had stabbed a Captain Parrott from Pine Lodge. The
judge committed Nicholas for trial, but fifty or sixty of Parrott's friends
managed to seize the prisoner, notwithstanding that he was chained to
staples driven into the floor of the courthouse and guarded by ten or
twelve special constables. They took Nicholas to a tree and would have
hanged him, but Coffroth and some others persuaded them to hold a
trial instead. A jury was selected—the four men from Pine Lodge and

eight from Columbia; Thamas M. Cazneau was appointed for the prosecution, and Coffroth with another attorney, by the name of Gillespie, was for the defense. The jury's verdict was "We, the jury, find the prisoner guilty of assault and battery, with intent to kill Captain John Parrott, but as Parrott is not yet dead, they agree that the prisoner shall be given up to the civil authorities."[52] Parrott was later convicted by a proper court and sentenced to death, but the governor commuted the sentence to seven years in prison.[53] This meeting appointed Coffroth as counsel for the defense even though he was a known opponent of lynch law; and his eloquence helped to save the man's life.

Thomas Cazneau, the prosecutor in this last case, had been a notary and insurance adjuster in San Francisco and was a delegate from Tuolumne to the State Democratic Convention in July 1852—as was James Coffroth.[54] In short, he was a man of some standing. Eugene F. Gillespie is named in several newspaper articles, at least once as "Esq.," so he is also likely to have been a lawyer.[55]

In more remote camps, real attorneys might not be available, but that did not mean the accused did not get a spirited defense. The trial of Little John for theft at Rich Bar was described in detail by Dame Shirley. She wrote, "A young Irishman from St. Louis was appointed counsel for John, and a Dr. C. acted for the prosecution. Neither of them, however, was a lawyer."[56] Even after John was convicted and sentenced to thirty-nine lashes, indeed, after the punishment had been inflicted, his lawyer was perfectly convinced of his innocence and continued to seek evidence to exonerate him.[57]

Lawyers seem to have been given a lot of latitude in their efforts to represent their clients. Two of the few accounts of lawyers' methods happen to involve Americans accused of shooting or stabbing Germans, and both describe base appeals to the jury's prejudices. William Shaw, an Englishman, witnessed a trial in Stockton in 1849, when it was still more of a camp than a town, with "comparatively few wood buildings, the stores and taverns being mostly of canvass nailed on to frame work." The American and German in this case had argued about "the merits of their respective countries": the German "passed certain severe strictures upon America," was thrown out of the tent where they quarreled, and returned to retaliate, and as he advanced on the American, the latter shot him in the abdomen. The attorney for the prosecution, "who was apparently a gentleman," stated the case and called witnesses who established the prisoner's guilt. The lawyer for the defense, on the other hand, was what Shaw called a "popular man": instead of "attempting to disprove the evidence, he skillfully pandered to the passions of his audience; representing his client as a martyr, who endangered his life in defending the reputation of the republic." The prisoner was acquitted— a perversion of justice, Shaw felt.[58]

The second incident happened two years later. A German and an American gambler argued, and the latter plunged a knife into the former. "They tried him & his lawyer on the trial would [ask] one ju- ryman and then another if he was justifiable in stabing the german." Needless to say, this is not acceptable procedure. The author blamed the judge for allowing the defendant's lawyer to pervert justice. Better to have no trial at all, he said: "Their is the Vigilance Committee in San Francisco they hang a man up if they know he is guilty."[59]

The lynch trial of Frederick Roe in Sacramento in February 1851 is of interest even though it was not held in the mining district and was not a trial by meeting; instead, the crowd deputized the trial to a com- mittee. But it does give a fuller picture of lawyers at work and of the jury's impatience, at times, with zealous advocacy.[60] Roe was accused of shooting a Mr. Chas. Humphrey Myers, "a quiet and most respectable citizen," who had tried to break up a fight between Roe and a miner. Over the vehement objections of the city marshal and Justice Bullock, an immense and angry crowd voted that Roe be tried by a committee, also called a jury, in the Orleans Hotel, and it is this committee's report that furnishes the details of the proceedings.

One of the jurors "moved that the prisoner or his friends select counsel," and a Mr. Kewen was chosen or volunteered to appear for Roe.[61] This must have been Colonel Edward J. C. Kewen, a practicing lawyer and California's first attorney general, who had recently resigned that position to practice law in Sacramento.[62] Kewen made an opening statement, to which someone objected, suggesting that he was speaking against time, that is, in the hope that the authorities would rescue Roe. "Steps were taken to enter at once upon the investigation—Mr. Kewen speaking—and much confusion." At this point, a committee from the people arrived. "They reported that unless quibbling was dispensed with and the jury proceeded to come to a prompt decision, the people would take the prisoner out and hang him at once." Shortly thereafter, a second committee appeared, desiring that all lawyers be removed, with which the jury refused to agree. Kewen's role from then on appears to have been limited to calling witnesses for the defense, the gist of whose testimony was that Roe did not aim at Myers or that he fired by accident; and that he was drunk, had been fighting, and did not know what he was doing. "The counsel for the prisoner here rested the case." Roe was found guilty and executed before five thousand spectators—but Kewen appears to have used his position as the only lawyer in the room to insist on a small modicum of due process.

As so often, information about defense counsels at lynch trials also raises new questions. Many of them were trained lawyers, and some were destined for high-profile careers. This is impressive; it means that at least some defendants in some lynch trials were well represented. On the other hand, it also means that some highly reputable individuals were involved in lynch trials. Did they believe in the integrity of the proceedings? Or did they participate in a bad process hoping to get a reduced punishment for their clients? The evidence above suggests that they did at least use every trick in the book to try to save the defendants.

## Jury Deliberation

The last stage of the trial was the jury deliberation. When all of the evidence had been presented, the jury retired to consider its verdict, *retiring* being perhaps a fancy word for moving from one tree to another. Sometimes they were absent for only a few minutes before returning a verdict,[63] but in other cases they deliberated for one or even two hours.[64]

During this time, they were probably drinking. Many trials and executions were held near a general store or hotel, which was the only equivalent to a public building; these generally sold liquor and naturally hoped that the jury and crowd would partake. Dame Shirley reported that it was Mr. B, the proprietor of the Empire Hotel at Rich Bar, who asked the miners to move the trial of Little John from the Humboldt

Hotel at Indian Bar to his own premises. "Malicious people *will* say," she added, that Mr. B hoped to make money from the trial, "as it was well known that at whichever house the trial took place the owner thereof would make a handsome profit from the sale of dinners, drinks, etc., to the large number of people who would congregate to witness the proceedings."[65]

Some storekeepers also served as the local alcalde or justice of the peace. The trial of Bill Lomax for murder in 1854 took place at the "Old Daily Adobe" hotel, run by the local justice of the peace.[66] Another defendant, Corrigan, was tried in 1849 in "a large tent, kept as store and hotel" owned by James & Co., in Jamestown, where Mr. James, the alcalde, "dispenses grub and justice to the satisfaction of all."[67] These storekeepers/alcaldes made double profits on legal cases.

Jurors took breaks for drinks in the course of the trial. During a civil trial at Rich Bar, the justice of the peace himself "stopped the court twice in order to treat the jury."[68] Stephen J. Field turned the mellowing effects of alcohol to advantage during a criminal trial at which he was a mere spectator. While watching the proceedings, opposite "a small lodging-house and drinking-saloon," he was persuaded that the accused was innocent. When there was some delay in the proceedings, he invited the jury into the saloon for drinks, ostensibly as a vote-seeking candidate for the legislature but really in hopes of persuading them to deliver the prisoner to the sheriff. The trial was interrupted while the jury enjoyed two rounds of "smiles." (Let us pause to consider how many violations of law and ethics figure in this one incident.) Field took one of the jurors aside and gently urged him to be merciful. Then:

finding they were about to go back to the trial, I exclaimed, "Don't be in a hurry, gentlemen, let us take another glass." They again acceded to my request, and seeing that they were a little mellowed by their indulgence, I ventured to speak about the trial . . . and I appealed to them, as men of large hearts, to think how they would feel if they were accused of crime where they had no counsel and no friends. "Better send him, gentlemen, to Marysville for trial, and keep your own hands free from stain."

"A pause ensued; their hearts were softened" . . . and they sent the man to Marysville.[69]

Drinking during trials also occurred elsewhere on the frontier. Regarding the trial of an Ojibway Indian alleged to have murdered Alfred Aitkinin in Wisconsin Territory in 1837, one of the jurors wrote that they were locked up in a grocery during breaks in the proceedings and, for seventy-five cents each, could drink all the liquor they wanted, provided that they took none away with them. Juries pretty much always drank. "Imbibing was quite prevalent among all classes in that day," according to this juror, "and if each of the jurymen drank his seventy-five cents worth, the judge and counsel could not have been far behind, and some individual was heard to say that the prisoner was the only sober man in the court-room."[70] It would be nice to think that the officers of the court and the jury were "mellowed by their indulgence," as Field said, but drink takes people different ways.

Sometimes, the prisoner was tipsy too. Indeed, the defendant was the person whose drinking was most understandable. Miner David Brown, who had confessed to stealing $1,800 in gold and knew what fate had in store for him, "exhibited, during the trial, the utmost recklessness and nonchalance, had drank many times in the course of the day, and when the rope was placed about his neck, was evidently much intoxicated."[71] If the accused was drunk when he committed his crimes, a generous judge would postpone the trial until he sobered up.[72]

When they had finished their deliberations, the jury returned its verdict. Usually, it was "guilty," but in a significant number of cases—I have counted at least ten—the defendant was acquitted. The least surprising are those in which the jury found that the shooting was an accident or that a killer acted in self-defense. For instance, Henry J. Freund shot and killed Roderick M. Morrison in a quarrel at Carson's Creek in May 1849. "Freund was tried for the murder, and acquitted on the ground of 'justifiable homicide,' it appearing that he acted in self-defense."[73] If there was no doubt of his innocence, a killer might even have welcomed a trial to clear his name. A newspaper article titled "A Most Melancholy Death" reported that a miner shot his partner, mistaking him in the night for a thief. He was tried, and the jury returned a verdict of accidental homicide; the onlookers then passed a resolution of sympathy with the victim's family and with the killer himself, adding that they concurred fully with the jury's decision.[74] It is almost unimaginable that he would have been convicted under the circumstances.

There were also multiple acquittals for lack of evidence despite a general belief that the defendant was guilty. Sometimes the case did not even reach a jury. The notorious robber Jim Hill, when he had been caught and convicted, named his accomplices because, he said, he wished "those who led him into crime to be hung along with him."[75] All of the men he named were already suspected of complicity in his crimes. Search parties set off in various directions; they managed to capture one suspect and bring him back. "A form of examination was gone through and no positive evidence other than that of the doomed man appearing against him, he was honorably acquitted."[76] Similarly, a Virginian named Middleton was accused of stealing $2,000 to $3,000 from Mr. Blacksmith at Long Bar: Middleton was the only person who had recently gone down the trail to the river where the money was found. Kimball Webster wrote that "Judge Lynch" was soon summoned, a court was organized, and the Virginian was arraigned. After noting that the evidence was damaging but circumstantial and not positive, Webster concludes, "The verdict of the court was to the effect: That he was probably guilty of committing the robbery, but as there was room for a little doubt, he was entitled to that doubt."[77]

In other cases, it is clear that a jury did the acquitting. A miner was accused of stealing a bag of gold from his partner; the miners elected an alcalde and a sheriff, and "[t]he trial proceeded, but no evidence of a positive nature appeared against the accused. Even his gold was emptied out and examined to see if the loser could identify it as having been his, but it could not be so identified." The jury believed the man guilty but could not convict him given the lack of evidence. He was ordered to pay all costs of court and jury and leave the bar.[78] Another bona fide acquittal by a jury was summed up by miner Clark's diary entry for February 1854: "M'Candless is stabed in a row at the french house Spanish Jack was arrested + I being the recorder he was brought before me for trial a Jury of 12 selected 30 witnesses examined and Jack cleared."[79]

At least one acquitted defendant was, in fact, guilty. William (David) Brown, a Swede, fell sick at Rich Bar in the fall of 1851, and two German

miners nursed him back to health. Soon after Brown's recovery, his ben-
efactors found that $1,600 had been stolen.[80] According to the *Alta Cal-
ifornia,* Brown was "suspected, brought before a court and examined."
He was released because "proof sufficient to convict him could not be
obtained."[81] Dame Shirley, who was at Rich Bar, also wrote that Brown
and an accomplice "were tried before a meeting of the miners" and "acquitted" because the "evidence was not sufficient to convict them."[82]

A few weeks later, Brown returned to the bar looking for a place to
mine, so he said. The two Germans had piled brush around the place
where they suspected Brown of hiding the gold, however, and saw that
it had been disturbed; they found a money belt, freshly cut open. They
confronted Brown, and he admitted his guilt. The news of Brown's return
and confession spread like wildfire: "[A] meeting of the miners was immediately convened, the unhappy man taken into custody, a jury chosen,
and a judge, lawyer, etc., appointed." After hearing the evidence, the jury
retired for a few minutes, "returned, and the foreman handed to the judge
a paper, from which he read the will of the people," namely, that Brown
was guilty of theft and should be hung by the neck until dead.[83] The suspicions against Brown in the first trial were therefore entirely justified.

Lynch trial reports sometimes state that the jury's verdict was unanimous.[84] When it was not—when the jury was hung, as we would say—
the result was a mistrial, and the accused was either released or had to
be retried. Theodore Johnson, who published the first eyewitness account of the gold rush, met a man who had deliberately shot and killed
another for a minor offense. "A jury was empanelled under the forms of
lynch law, to try him, but they could not agree. Another was then empanelled and this time they acquitted him."[85] Johnson could tell by the
man's face, he said, that "the knawing worm of conscience was eating
into his soul." Another example comes not from the mines, but from a
lynching in San Francisco, the notorious trial of Stewart and Wildred in
February 1851. "After the charge of the Judge, the jury were out about
one hour, and said they could not agree; nine being for conviction, and
three for acquittal. The jury were then discharged and the 'Court' dissolved, amidst the angry growlings of the multitude."[86]

At trials where the jury decided the punishment as well as the verdict,
this could be a topic of fierce debate. Sutton, the man who was chosen to

serve on a jury an hour after he returned to camp, having been gone for a week, got his fellow jurymen to sentence the prisoner to twenty lashes, although at the start of deliberations, the majority had wanted to hang him.[87] It could be that the members of the jury were unable to reach an agreement, but in such a case they could compromise. A jury that was "equally divided—six for whipping and six for hanging" the convicted man, eventually agreed to whip him and tell him that they would hang him if he ever returned.[88] In another case, a twenty-two-man jury "stood ten for, and twelve against hanging." Their compromise was to shave one side of the convicted man's head, brand him with HT on his right arm, and give him fifty lashes on his bare back. Just as in more regular sentencing proceedings where the crowd decided the punishment, milder men outnumbered harsher ones, but the latter did influence the outcome.

## Timing

The whole process—selection of the judge and jury, appointment of counsel, witness testimony, and the final verdict—happened quickly. Speed was thought to be the great advantage of lynch trials over the state courts when they were established. It was not uncommon for a suspect to be caught in the morning, tried in the afternoon, and hanged before the day was done. People said that "one to two hours was all the time needed to determine the guilt or innocence of the accused,"[89] and that was probably true in many cases; but the trials that were reported in detail were the more elaborate ones and took longer. One trial took three hours altogether, another six hours.[90] The trial described in *Household Words* lasted two days. That of Rigler, Allen, and Miller for stealing $2,500 ranged over three days. At the meeting on the first day, the miners decided to try the accused. The actual trial took place on the second day, and Allen and Miller were convicted; but Rigler's case was put over for an extra day to give time for a fuller examination. The final verdict was delivered at two o'clock in the afternoon of the third day.[91]

An acquittal was the end of the process, but after a conviction, there remained the sentencing phase and the punishment itself. Sometimes the jury determined the sentence, but more often the crowd decided the fate of the accused.

Lynch trials are the ultimate example of self-government through parliamentary procedure. In trying and punishing criminals, the miners assumed a basic function of the state, and they ran their trials by means of parliamentary procedure. The format enabled moderate individuals to influence the proceedings, first by persuading the crowd to provide a semblance of a trial and then by arguing for a lesser sentence. In particular, letting the crowd decide the sentence by vote had the advantage that the milder and perhaps quieter members of the crowd could outvote the wild characters who were ready to hurry the defendant to his death.

This chapter presents lynch trials in their most positive light, that is, as real trials in which the crowd sought to provide the accused with competent counsel and an unbiased jury which, in its turn, took its job seriously and tried to reach a just verdict. That there were such lynch trials at all is surprising and has gone largely unnoticed. It goes without saying, however, that criminal trials by the whole population of a mining camp could go badly wrong and *did* go badly wrong: Chapter 10 describes the degeneration of lynch law as it came into competition with the newly founded State courts. Moreover, while a handful earlier lynch trials resulted in acquittals, the great majority of defendants were found guilty. There were no doubt members of the crowd who favored a proper trial, just so long as it was understood that the defendant would be convicted; this was certainly the case in the final years of lynch law. Finally, lest this chapter has overpersuaded the reader into believing that lynch trials were pretty good, the next chapter describes the barbaric punishment that the miners visited upon the men, and one woman, whom they convicted.

# CHAPTER 9

# Whipping, Branding, and Hanging

I f the jury found a defendant guilty, the next step was sentencing. In modern trials, the judge determines the punishment; in the mines, the crowd assumed the role of the judge. It decided the sentence by vote, as it did everything. In the few cases where the jury suggested a sentence, the crowd voted on it and either approved it or modified the punishment.[1]

Like every other step of the trial, the sentence phase was a series of motions and votes, as illustrated by the transcript of the sentencing phase of the trial of Dr. A. Bardt reproduced in the Introduction.[2] Arguments over sentencing are interesting because they occasionally demonstrate one advantage of parliamentary procedure, namely that it gave moderate members of the crowd a means to stand up to the rabble and obtain a lesser sentence for a convicted thief. For example, after William Brown was first acquitted of robbing the men who nursed him back to health, then convicted after he was caught recovering the loot, the jury sentenced him to be hanged one hour after his trial; but "the persuasions of some men more mildly disposed" got this extended to three.[3]

Sentencing and punishment also provide a reality check, however. Although trials were better than mob action, the punishments—hangings,

169

whippings, and branding—were horrific and make sickening reading. Hanging was done by volunteers, who were almost by definition the most barbaric members of the crowd; while the more "moderate" punishments of whipping, branding, and mutilation were not only atrocious but made worse by the clumsiness of the amateurs who administered them. The participants themselves were sometimes appalled and readers may wish to skip much of this chapter. The descriptions are included lest the relative formality of legal procedure described in the previous chapter leave an impression that lynch trials were not all that bad.

Convicted murderers were hanged; there was no room for negotiation except with respect to the timing of the execution and, in the worst cases, whether they should be both whipped *and* hanged.[4] The sentencing phase of a murder trial, therefore, holds little interest.

Assault and battery, in contrast, were not even prosecuted, apart from a few very serious cases of stabbing, and in these cases, the punishment was whipping rather than execution. For example, miner J. D. Breyfogle reported that on the Fourth of July 1850, a man was tried for stabbing a man eight times. "[H]ad the man died he would have been hung," Breyfogle wrote, "but as it was he received 40 lashes on his bare back . . . and it nearly killed him."[5] Two Mexicans, Alberto Dela Cruz and Martin Lopez, committed an even more egregious assault. Unhappy with the ruling of a certain Squire Barnard regarding a disputed donkey, the aggrieved men tried to seize the animal and, in the process, attacked Barnard. "Squire Barnard was stabbed three times in the back by Dela Cruz with a large bowie knife, the blade of which was broken off near the handle at the third stab, the point of the blade hitting a rib bone." The next day, a twelve-man jury found both Mexicans guilty of assault and battery with intent to kill and sentenced both to be whipped on the bare back.[6] The penalty seems almost lenient, given that this seems to be the most egregious assault possible from the Americans' point of view—Mexicans trying to kill a judge without provocation. No wonder, then, that common assault was not even prosecuted.

The conflicts arose with respect to the punishments for theft, which varied enormously. It was widely believed that thieves were executed—Charles Henry Randall told his parents not to worry about his safety because "a man here is hung for stealing everything in the streets or at the mines is perfectly safe left out doors good order prevails."[7] In fact, however, fewer than half of the convicted thieves were hung; the rest suffered a range of possible punishments, including hanging, lashes, branding, shaving the head, and cropping (cutting off the ears). Whether a convicted thief would hang depended in part on factors such as the date of the trial (penalties grew harsher over time) and the ethnicity of the defendant (non-Americans being more likely to be hanged than Americans). No factor was determinative, however. Contrary to expectation, the amount stolen seems to have had no bearing on the sentence. One can only suppose that the thief's fate depended mainly on the mood of the crowd.

Reaching agreement on what penalty fit the crime was the most contentious stage of the trial. The death penalty as punishment for theft was controversial in California. Those who supported it urged that it was necessary to deter criminals in a territory without police or jails, while opponents felt that it was excessive punishment. The dynamics of the crowd in trials for theft therefore best illustrate how the use of parliamentary procedure could moderate the convicted man's punishment.

## Sentencing

Not all crowds were the same. Some lynch trials were conducted "with solemnity and decorum," while others degenerated into "the hungriest, craziest, wildest mob standing round that I ever saw anywhere."[8] Much depended on the horribleness of the crime and on how much the participants had been drinking. Any given crowd also contained great variety within itself because it could include hardworking miners, storekeepers, and gamblers; frontiersmen and New Englanders; newcomers and old hands. The crowd was a collection of individuals; sometimes milder men won out, while at other times the bloodthirsty ones got their way.

There was a significant difference between the crowds at the *trial*, where the attendees were participants in a meeting and made decisions by motions and votes, and those at the *punishment*, where they were mainly spectators. The second crowd was prone to be larger, less disciplined, and more reckless so that even a so-called good lynch trial might be followed by a terrible hanging. Or the crowd might change the original sentence by a simple vote without a trial; and while any change was welcome to a man convicted to hang, some prisoners who were supposed to be handed over to the sheriff were instead executed.

One reason for the difference between the two crowds is that the men at the trial were from the immediate neighborhood, while the execution could draw a larger audience. The trial was usually held within hours of the arrest, so there was not enough time for men to come from a distance.[9] One trial was held in the middle of the night, a certain Milus Gay reported: "I was called up last night 11 or 12 o'clock to assist in taking and trying a man for stealing . . . Tryal [*sic*] occupied the night—Jury rendered their verdict about sun up—took him out—tied him up and applied the lash—required him to leave by 3 p.m."[10] Alternatively, the culprit could be confined until a more convenient hour. The people of Weaverville arrested an accused thief late in the evening, but when they woke up the judge, he refused to hear the case until morning. This "judge," Colonel Johnson, formerly of the Empire House in Weaverville, was not an official judge; he had been chosen to preside over a related trial the day before and was therefore the judge of the moment. The crowd assembled anxiously around his tent and watched him make his slapjacks, eat them, and do his dishes before he metaphorically returned to the bench.[11]

In a big mining town, the assembly would be larger than at an isolated digging. There were "several hundred" at the trial of Rigler, Allen, and Miller by miners' meeting,[12] while at the other end of the scale, thirty-three men endorsed a jury verdict against an Englishman named Jones and two others for stealing provisions,[13] and a group of fifty sentenced to death a Mexican gang of cattle rustlers.[14]

The sentencing phase began when the judge asked the assembled miners what punishment the convicted man should suffer. Someone usually shouted, "Hang him!"[15] In any case, the death penalty formed the backdrop for the discussion; it was a point of departure inviting a counterproposal from less vicious members of the crowd. The alternative had to be harsh enough to get a majority. Dame Shirley, writing of a punishment applied by the short-lived committee of vigilance at Indian Bar was almost unable to bear the sound of two Spaniards being whipped for their part in a fight with the Americans on the bar. She nevertheless added, "[I]n my very humble opinion, and in that of others more competent to judge of such matters than myself, these sentences were unnecessarily severe, yet so great was the rage and excitement of the crowd that the vigilance committee *could do no less.* The mass of the mob demanded fiercely the death of the prisoners, and it was evident that many of the committee took side with the people" (italics added).[16] Stephen Field made the same argument when he, as alcalde, sentenced a thief to fifty lashes. "Imposing a fine would not answer; and, if he had been discharged, the crowd would have immediately hung him." Whipping was therefore the only possible punishment, and "however repugnant it was to my feelings to adopt it," Field wrote, "I believe it was the only thing that saved the man's life."[17] So the men who shouted, "Hang him!" were a force to be reckoned with even when they did not get their way. A sentence of thirty-nine lashes—horrific though that was—was the best the moderates could do for the convicted man.

Not surprisingly, information that made the convicted thief seem more sympathetic might induce the crowd to spare his life. These included appeals by his friends, testimony as to his character, and his own contrition and appeals for mercy. Chilean Pérez Rosales managed to save an acquaintance from execution by pretending to be a Frenchman and vouching for his soundness.[18] Similarly, a young man named Close who stole $3,000 was sentenced to death, but "[t]he desperate effort of [Close's] friends got him cleared on the grounds of his former respectability, as also that of his family and friends"—cleared, that is, apart from getting fifty lashes, having his ears cut off, and being banished from the mines.[19] And finally, Englishman Henry Clark, also convicted of theft, was sentenced to receive two hundred lashes, being branded with an R, and having half his head shaved: many had been "in favor of hanging him, but on account of his youthfulness, he received the above punishment instead."[20]

This principle worked the other way around too: the unsympathetic were more likely to hang. Englishman William Shaw described the fruitless attempts to stay the execution of an Australian who stole a few small items: "Appeals were made for mercy, but not even a respite could be obtained for the culprit."[21] Shaw thought the reason for the harsh sentence was the American prejudice against Australians, and he may have been right—non-Americans were more likely to be hanged for theft than Americans.

Some voted for execution simply because they wanted to see a man hang. The anonymous men who shouted, "Hang him!" did not explain themselves. Buffum described one of these as a "brutal-looking fellow in the crowd," not someone he recognized, let alone one of the main actors. Franklin Buck, from Maine, observed—probably in jest, but intriguingly nonetheless—that the people hanged and those most strongly in favor of harsh penalties were drawn from the same pool. Describing Irishman Michael Grant's trial for murder, Buck wrote:

> After the sentence was read a dispute arose as to whether he should be hung right up the next morning or have ten days. Although a majority of the people voted for ten days the minority held on to hang him the next day. High words ensued. Pistols were drawn and I thought for sometime that half a dozen more lives would be lost in discussing this point. But finally the few bloodthirsty scoundrels (who will probably be hung themselves) were ruled down and ten days were given him.[22]

So Buck supposed that the criminal types most wanted to see a hanging. This was certainly the case at a lynch trial in 1848 at Balsam Lake: "Of the more active participants in the hanging, Pat Collins, who officiated as hangman, and who flogged Miller, was undeniably a hard citizen. He had a bitter grudge against Miller, and administered the strokes with a will. He was himself hanged some years later in California for highway robbery."[23]

Perhaps guilty men were extra tough on criminals to deflect attention from themselves, as was true of a man named Carrico, who had robbed $900 on Sherlock's Creek in 1852. The mob suspected someone else of the robbery—an old man named Johnson. They did not hold a trial, but sought to extort a confession by whipping Johnson brutally and hanging him by his neck until he lost consciousness. When this did not work, the real thief, Carrico, advised them to place Johnson's "bleeding and lacerated body upon hot embers, and to extract the nails of his fingers and toes with a pair of bullet moulds."[24] None of the other men supported this proposal, and Johnson was set free. Carrico himself was later arrested for the robbery and was found to be carrying some of the stolen gold. Fortunately for him, he was tried in an official court and sentenced to five years in prison; his fellow miners would not have been as lenient.

Maybe some men who shouted, "Hang him!" did not really want the defendant to hang; they were like the idiots who shout, "Jump!" when a suicidal person is standing on a ledge. They just want to stir the pot. This could explain what happened at the trial of Dr. Bardt discussed in Introduction. Someone moved that, in addition to being whipped, his ears should be cut off; and someone else seconded the motion. But "[t]he motion, on being put, was negative unanimously."[25] Evidently, even the men who made and seconded the motion did not vote for it.

In the case of William (David) Brown, the defendant who was drunk at his own trial, the people participating in the execution did not really believe it would happen. "Almost everybody was surprised at the severity of the sentence," wrote Dame Shirley, "and many, with their hands on the cord, did not believe even then that it would be carried into effect, but thought that at the last moment the jury would release the prisoner and substitute a milder punishment." Dame Shirley had not spoken with anyone who approved of the proceedings: "[I]t seems to have been carried on entirely by the more reckless part of the community."[26] The "men more mildly disposed" had managed to grant the convicted man an extra three hours; if they had exerted themselves, they probably could have stopped the hanging altogether.

## The Crowd at the Punishment

The sentence was often executed on the spot or after a short delay if the condemned man was to be hung and needed time to write his last letters or to meet with a minister. David Brown's execution was originally scheduled for one hour after he was sentenced, but some "more mildly disposed" got it extended to three.[27] An instant launch into eternity was considered harsh, however, and moderate members of the crowd sometimes pushed for more time, such as the ten days that the majority granted Michael Grant, or at least a delay until the following morning.[28]

If the whipping or hanging took place a day or several days after the trial, the crowd could be much larger than that at the trial since people could come in from a distance.[29] The town of Downieville filled with people to see Pajo the Indian hanged for killing a Chinese man in September 1853.[30] Six or seven hundred men attended the hanging of three murderers near Dunbar's ranch in July 1852.[31] In June 1851, three thousand men looked on while a murderer was hung in Sonora.[32]

Even the well-socialized men who kept diaries and journals were curious to see the spectacle and could write matter-of-factly, "A man was hung here this afternoon for murder I went to see him, determined to see a murderer die I watched him from the moment he came from prison till he was dead."[33] Similarly, Edward Gould Buffum, the Quaker, wrote, "Never having witnessed a punishment inflicted by Lynch-law, I went over to the dry diggings on a clear Sunday morning, and on my arrival, found a large crowd collected around an oak tree, to which was lashed a man with a bared back, while another was applying a raw cowhide to his already gored flesh."[34] Buffum was appalled by what he saw and tried to stop the ensuing degeneration into mob law, as described below. Finally, David Ferson told the folks back home, "I thot I would go and see him hung so we all went down."[35] None of these men had been present at the trial. Hangings as semirespectable entertainment are, of course, well documented. In San Francisco, some parents took their children to see hangings; and an article in the *Daily Alta California* criticized Eastern papers for creating, in effect, a genre of hanging reportage that resembled "very nearly in its reading and arrangement, some of the popular light literature."[36] The article's (ironic) title was "The Romance of Hanging."

Naturally, hangings also attracted the worst of the population. Jim Hill was executed on Sunday, June 29, 1851, at six in the evening: "Since early morning, people from the various camps had been on their way to Camp Seco and an immense number of accomplices and other villains had collected." Freewheeling crowds at executions were responsible for some of the most shambolic, amateur hangings. Two of the best-known California lynch trials—best documented at the time and most widely cited today—were held in exceptional circumstances: before crowds that were, for different reasons, both very large and very drunk. The *Californian* newspaper said in its report of one of these that "the second sober thought of the people is always right and never wrong"—an unintentionally ominous choice of words in light of the setting of many trials. Oscar Wilde might have changed it to "the second thought of the people is rarely sober and seldom right."[37]

The first of the two wild lynchings took place on January 20, 1849, at Dry Diggings—later known as Hangtown, thanks to this incident in particular.[38] It began with a conventional lynch trial of five men who robbed a Mexican gambler named Lopez.[39] They broke into his room at night, held a gun to his head, and were rifling through his trunk when a group of citizens burst in and arrested them. The following day, they were tried to a jury and sentenced to thirty-nine lashes to be administered the day after. This punishment was horrible but normal for the crime; in fact, the men were lucky not to have been hanged, given that some were foreigners and they were caught in the act.

The flogging happened to take place on a Sunday, the miners' day off, and a crowd of about two hundred men came into town to see it.[40] After the five robbers had been whipped, someone raised new charges against three of them, two Frenchmen and a Chileno—namely, that they had attempted robbery and murder on the Stanislaus River in the fall of 1848. The crowd resolved to try them then and there—in their absence, since they were nearly unconscious from their punishment and were lying on the floor of a nearby house. The whole crowd declared itself a jury and elected a judge. Within thirty minutes, the crowd had heard the evidence and the judge called the vote: Had they been proved guilty? Two hundred men answered, "Yes!" Then he asked: How should they be punished? "A brutal-looking fellow in the crowd, cried out, 'Hang them.'" The motion was seconded and passed almost unanimously—so some miners must have voted against it. Buffum wrote that at this point:

> I mounted a stump, and in the name of God, humanity, and law, protested against such a course of proceeding; but the crowd, by this time excited by frequent and deep potations of liquor from a neighbouring groggery, would listen to nothing contrary to their brutal desires, and even threatened to hang me if I did not immediately desist from any further remarks.

The convicted men were given thirty minutes to prepare for death. They tried to speak, but since they spoke no English, no one understood them; they called for an interpreter, but "their cries were drowned by the yells of a now infuriated mob." The nooses were put around their necks, the wagon driven out from under them, and they were dead.[41]

What is interesting about this incident is not that it shows there were bad lynch trials—because that is old news—but what a difference the crowd made. Here, the same defendants, tried in the same mining town, were given a conventional trial on Saturday and a travesty of a trial on Sunday—thirty minutes total, no jury, no chance to make a defense, and no interval before the hanging. Buffum wrote that "the charges against them were well substantiated," but even this is dubious, when the crime in question happened months earlier and many miles away.[42]

The lynching of Juanita or Josefa, a Mexican, at Downieville, was the best-known lynch trial in the mines because it was the only case in which a woman was executed.[43] "The press of the whole country" had published articles about it before the end of 1851, as had the *London Times*.[44] She was accused of murdering an American named Cannon on the night of July 4 to 5, 1851. On the day of the incident, the town was packed with men who had come to celebrate the Fourth of July and to hear an address by John B. Weller, later a US senator. This is critical because it explains the size, composition, and mood of the crowd.

Accounts of the alleged crime differed substantially. The *Marysville Herald* published three days after the trial that Cannon and his friends entered Juanita's house in the night and created a riot and a disturbance, and when he came back the next morning to apologize, she plunged a knife into him.[45] David Pierce Barstow, a miner at the trial, said the drunken men pushed her door in during the night and she jumped out of bed and stabbed one of them at that time.[46]

Five or six hundred attended the trial and execution; David Barstow called it "the hungriest, craziest, wildest mob standing about that ever I saw anywhere," and all of the accounts agree that the crowd was exceptionally impatient and aggressive.[47] On the other hand—and this is what makes the case so interesting—half-a-dozen or more prominent men worked hard for her acquittal, despite being harassed and threatened by the onlookers. (One who failed to act, John Weller, the visiting dignitary, did not object and in fact sat on the stand during the trial. This "haunted him politically for many years.")[48] Because there are many accounts of this trial, the identities and actions of the participants are known in more detail than those of almost any other lynching in the mines, as is the involvement of the crowd.

The format of the trial was exemplary. The jury foreman, Amos Brown, and the jurymen were said to be sober, candid, intelligent, and honest. John Rose served as judge; this could have been the John Rose who came to California in 1841 and gave his name to Rose Bar on the Yuba River, in which case he would have been one of the oldest American residents of California.[49] William S. Spear, who acted for the prosecution, was one of the first members of the bar of Sierra County.[50] Two lawyers acted for the defense: Messrs. A. W. Brockelbank (probably the A. M. Brocklebank who later became a lawyer and then a judge) and Pickett, unidentified.[51]

The crowd, on the other hand, though it had presumably voted to hold a trial by jury, objected and interrupted at every stage. It was so wild that it had to be held back with ropes; and the lawyers for the *prosecution* "appealed to them, calling on them to remember their wives, mothers, and daughters, to give the woman a fair trial, and in that way they were kept quiet."[52]

One of the lawyers for the defense was standing on a barrel: it was kicked out from under him, and he fell into the crowd, where he was punched and kicked from all sides. The crowd threatened to hang Dr. Aiken, who testified that the defendant was pregnant, and it did vote him out of town. (Aiken returned, however. A year later, he won the election for coroner and in 1854 was appointed doctor for the indigent sick.)[53]

Although the hanging of Juanita is today the paradigm of gold rush lynchings and their horrors, it attracted fierce criticism in its own time as a shocking miscarriage of justice—lynch law gone wrong. Downieville never recovered from the ignominy. What shocked America was the hanging of a woman under any circumstances, but it was the unruliness of the crowd that was an ominous portent of things to come. In the earliest lynch trials, the population walked on eggshells to ensure a legitimate result; by 1851, the legitimacy was widely accepted, and the mining community had gained an alarming amount of confidence and efficiency: "[T]he excited people seized the prisoners, took them to the top of an adjacent hill, selected a jury under a tree, tried and found them guilty, and sentenced them to be hung."[54]

## Hanging

The death penalty was carried out by hanging, except for one instance of execution by firing squad.[55] In later years, hangings involved a drop long enough to break the condemned person's neck, but at the time of the gold rush, the rope was put around the prisoner's neck and he was pulled up, or he was placed on a wagon and it was driven away, leaving him suspended in the air. The latter methods killed by strangulation, which is slow and painful. Californians had never known anything but this suspension technique, and their hangings were correspondingly gruesome.[56]

A tree limb usually served as a gallows. The prisoner might be placed on a block, from which he swung himself or was made to swing by removing the support; or placed on a wagon, or on an animal that was led away. Some men who had voted for the execution were distressed when "with scarcely any fall [the prisoner] hung some time gurgling + quivering."[57] In that particular case, a bystander tried to help the man along by tightening the rope; and when that didn't work, "a rough looking customer drew his revolver stepd up + shot the swinging Man through the body and one more flaunce (?) ended [his] career."[58] It is a pity that did not happen more often.

It was difficult to get decent men to manage the execution. In Stockton, according to Ramón Gil Navarro, the jury selected an executioner because no one would volunteer for the job, even for pay. Once the choice fell on a Mr. Sparrow, a friend of Navarro, "and the poor man had to run madly all over the place trying to find someone to replace him for a tidy sum." He managed to find a substitute who would do the job for $200, "but he would have given him a thousand or would have preferred to die before doing it himself."[59] Maybe that is why the prisoner was sometimes made to launch himself into eternity by jumping off a tree or bridge or giving the signal for a wagon to be driven out from under him.[60]

Those who volunteered for the job were the least likely to do it hu-
manely. Dame Shirley describes the hanging of William Brown at Rich
Bar, where "all who felt disposed to engage in so revolting a task lifted
the poor wretch from the ground in the most awkward manner possible." They tried to hasten the death "by hauling the writhing body up
and down, several times in succession."[61] Adolphus Windeler described
the same event; his partner had been one of Brown's victims, and both
Windeler and partner prepared the noose and participated in the
hanging. Windeler wrote, "[W]e hoisted him up & I belayed the ropes
end round a stump," and "then he was forked up & down several times
to break his neck."[62] Most executions must have been equally horrible.

## Whipping

Death was the maximum penalty. Lashes were the minimum, but lashes
were also horrific.[63] They were applied with a whip—rawhide or cat-o'-
nine-tails—on the convicted man's bare back. A leather lariat was said
to be particularly terrible: a prisoner sentenced to thirty-nine lashes
with one of these "held in until the third blow came down, when he
screamed out for mercy."[64] The sufferers naturally did not publish accounts of their ordeals, but the onlookers who did were agonized by the
mere sight and sounds of the punishment. Dame Shirley was particularly distressed, although she only heard the thwack of the lash on flesh.
"O Mary!" she wrote to her sister:

> [I]magine my anguish when I heard the first blow fall upon
> those wretched men . . . nothing can efface from memory
> the disgust and horror of that moment. I had heard of such
> things, but heretofore had not realized that in the nineteenth
> century men could be beaten like dogs, much less that other
> men not only could sentence such barbarism, but could ac-
> tually stand by and see their own manhood degraded in such
> disgraceful manner.[65]

Some men could *not* stand by, like members of the committee charged
with supervising the whipping of horse thieves who had been sentenced

to one hundred lashes each. The criminals suffered such torture that the committee stopped the flogging after fifty lashes and remitted the balance; a Presbyterian deacon on the committee, in particular, was shaken by "the piteous groans of the culprits . . . as the quivering flesh turned black under every stroke of the riata."[66] Even Dimmick, "first Judge in the mines," told his wife, Sarah, that Americans, Spaniards, and Indians unanimously approved his sentences of twenty-five lashes for one thief and fifty for another, but also that he "never saw men so severely whipped before, and never wish[ed] to again."[67]

And yet, because lashes were considered the minimum punishment, good and reasonable men thought they could not get away with proposing a lesser sentence, as shown above. What is strange is that prisoners were sentenced to so *many* lashes—that Field regarded fifty as the minimum acceptable number. A few really minor thefts were punished with twelve lashes: they included the theft of a pick,[68] of barley from a neighbor,[69] and of twenty-seven dollars.[70] All other thieves received at least twenty-five lashes, and most got thirty-nine or more, up to 150, whether they stole $50 or $5,000. (Thirty-nine was a common number because it was the maximum punishment under Jewish law.) The sentence could also be enhanced with branding or cutting off the ears; or hanging; but it was never reduced to ten lashes.

The cruelty of a whipping depended not only on the number of lashes but also on the zeal of the man holding the whip. Stephen J. Field ordered lashes to appease the mob, but he adds in his memoir, "Privately, I ordered a physician to be present to see that no unnecessary severity was practiced."[71] The lashes might be less harsh if the thief was well liked or if he was not clearly guilty, as in the case of Eustis and Grant. Eustis had sold stolen cattle to Grant, who insisted he did not know they were stolen. Nevertheless, the jury sentenced both to fifty lashes and to be branded with an R. "Eustis was branded deeply, whilst Grant's brand was light," and, as for the whipping, "frequently the knot was buried out of sight in the flesh, so severe was the lashing of Eustis, though Grant's was much more moderate."[72] Grant continued to protest his innocence right up until the whipping began, and the public, having second thoughts, voted to stop the whipping at thirty lashes. Someone must have told the old Indian who applied the punishment to go easy on Grant.[73]

Differences in the manner of whipping may explain why thirty-nine lashes affected some sufferers much more than others. The five men who robbed Lopez, the Mexican, in his room, were "so weak from their punishment as to be unable to stand" and lay stretched out on the floor of a neighboring house while they were tried again, in absentia.[74] In contrast, three hours after he had been given thirty-nine lashes for theft, Little John, a Swede, was "singing loudly, and apparently very gayly, a negro melody." Dame Shirley remarked that Little John's "punishment was very light, on account of his previous popularity and inoffensive conduct."[75] Since Dame Shirley found whipping revolting—it was she who was so appalled that "men could be beaten like dogs"—she did not mean that thirty-nine lashes were trivial, but that the man who whipped Little John had a light touch.

It was one thing for a man to vote for thirty-nine lashes—or branding, as discussed below—and another to watch the whipping, let alone wield the whip. Who would want that job or even to witness the punishment? Some sadists relished it, but most men tried their best to avoid it, so this was the stage of the lynch trial with the greatest variation and the most eccentric outcomes. If the community had a sheriff, he had to apply the lashes as one of his duties.[76] At least one constable, John D. Scellen, was distressed when he had to give fifteen lashes to a Chinese man at Goodyear's Bar in 1853. Scellen, "who was a gentleman," tried to evade the task, without success; and in the end, he "laid on the blows as lightly as possible," however, "giving the Chinaman about as severe a lashing as the stage Uncle Tom gets from his master in the theatrical performance of 'Uncle Tom's Cabin.'"[77]

If there was no sheriff, a non-American might have to do the job. Eustis and Grant, mentioned earlier, were whipped by "an old Indian who was a vaquiero on Rhode's ranch,"[78] while two horse thieves tried by miners and ranchers near the Old Daily Adobe hotel were sentenced to one hundred lashes, and "an Indian employee was ordered to do the whipping."[79] Both Indians were underlings who could be made to do the dirty work, but the second Indian apparently did his job with gusto— this was the case in which the committee, including a deacon, stopped the whipping after fifty lashes because it was so severe. In December 1850, near Daylor's Ranch, a horse thief was sentenced to fifty lashes, and "a Spaniard volunteered his services to execute the sentence."[80] *Spaniard* was used loosely for any Spanish speaker; the volunteer could have been Mexican or South American.

One convict was actually allowed to choose the man to inflict his punishment.[81] This unexpected arrangement may have been a concession to the prisoner, who would obviously prefer a friendly torturer, or it may have been because no one on the jury or in the crowd was willing to do the deed. Ordering the accusers to do the whipping, as a jury did when it found John M. Jones guilty of theft, was another quirky choice: "We, the jury, find the prisoner, John M. Jones, guilty of theft: and assess the punishment at four dozen lashes, well laid on upon the bare back, with a cowhide, to be laid on by his accusers—Robert McGarvey, S. M. Miller, L. Gillman, and deputy constable Curtis."[82] If this really was a job that no one wanted, then there was a certain fairness in making the men who accused the prisoner also do the dirty work of punishing him.

In one case, American volunteers were forthcoming. When an Australian, or "Sydney Bird," was given twelve lashes for stealing "$21, a pair of gold scales, and a razor," two men carried out the sentence: "One man, who was left-handed, administered six, and a right-handed man the remainder."[83] Evidently the miners of Condemned Bar, where this happened, had a sick sense of humor.

The miners seem to have been less bothered about carrying out a hanging—except that in one case they were. When Pijo, an Indian, was sentenced to hang for killing two Chinese men, the sheriff was uncomfortable about carrying out the execution. Another man offered to do it for fifty dollars:

> The volunteer executioner, to escape the opprobrium which he was aware would attach to his conduct, appeared in disguise. But his *ingognito* was readily discovered; and when he that evening frequented a gambling saloon, staked his fifty dollars on a game of chance and lost it, even the gamblers themselves refused to take the price of human life.[84]

Later that night, some of the gamblers beat up the man and banished him from Downieville, where the hanging took place. One might dismiss this as gamblers being gamblers, except that the volunteer knew he would be despised for what he did. Possibly it was the pay, the fifty dollars, that made his bargain despicable.

The shame of the man who applied the lashes was, of course, nothing compared with that of man who received them. Men with a particularly high sense of honor preferred death. "A finelooking man, well dressed and gentlemanly in appearance," who was sentenced to be branded and to receive one hundred lashes on the bare back, "begged to be hung instead."[85] Similarly, the lashes that Dame Shirley was so distressed to hear were given to a group of Spanish speakers, including a "very gentlemanly young Spaniard," who pleaded to be killed instead of whipped: "He appealed to his judges in the most eloquent manner, as gentlemen, as men of honor, representing to them that to be deprived of life was nothing in comparison with the never-to-be-effaced stain of the vilest convict's punishment to which they had sentenced him."[86] His captors were probably *not* gentlemen in the sense that the young Spanish speaker meant; they did not regard degradation as worse than death.[87] In one incident—a case of mob law rather than lynch law, though that makes no difference for present purposes—the "court" gave the accused "two desperate choices, either to be hung at once, or to have his head shaved, branded on the check and receive one hundred and fifty lashes." The man, whose name was Starkey, was a rancher, a man of property, yet "[h]e chose the latter sentence, and was immediately tied up and received one hundred and twenty-five—the balance being remitted."[88]

It would be interesting to know whether Starkey, who always protested his innocence, had the courage to stay on at his rancho after his punishment. Lashes were usually accompanied by a sentence of banishment, although, as Stephen J. Field said, "[t]he latter part of the sentence . . . was supererogatory; for there was something so degrading in a public whipping, that I have never known a man thus whipped who would stay longer than he could help, or ever desire to return."[89] The miners sometimes took up a collection to help them get to another camp. This was as much enlightened self-interest as kindness because the criminal would otherwise be forced to steal to feed and clothe himself.[90]

## Branding and Cutting off Ears

Several new arrivals in San Francisco who had not yet been to the mines reported that the penalty for theft was hanging, receiving a hundred lashes, and having one's ears cut off or the latter and also being branded on the cheek.[91] In fact, cutting off ears and branding were much less common punishments for theft than either hanging or whipping; but they did happen, and to fail to describe them, at least briefly, would be to play down the barbarism of the system.

Lashes plus cutting off the ears or branding was the harshest punishment short of death for criminals in the colonial and early national period and for slaves while there was slavery—and that is clearly what it was in California: a compromise offered when the defendant was sympathetic or too young for hanging or an enhanced punishment for a second offense.[92] There were no particular racial or ethnic associations to cutting off the ears.

Cutting off ears was the rarest penalty; only a handful of cases were reported. Two of these were ones at which persons "more mildly disposed" persuaded others to reduce the sentence from hanging to whipping and cutting of the ears, as mentioned above. Bayard Taylor met the first coming down from the mines on his way to Stockton—"a man whose head had been shaved and his ears cut off, after receiving one hundred lashes."[93] G. B. Stevens saw the second, a man named Close, in San Francisco.[94] William Kelly saw a third victim at Weber Creek, a "lad shorn of the rims of his ears, and seared deeply in the cheek with a red hot iron, for the theft of a small coffee tin."[95] This is an incredible punishment for stealing a *small* coffee tin; one almost suspects the young convict of pulling Kelly's leg—unless the tin had money in it. And finally, a man named Grant, after being whipped and branded at a lynch trial on the Cosumnes River, returned to his home in Sacramento only to find that his fellow citizens wanted him gone. "Grant says he has no place to go to—that if he should go to Placerville, they might not believe him innocent, and if he should go to Marysville, the brand would point him out as a marked character; and that he will remain, trusting to futurity for a full refutation of the charge."[96] These poor men must have had to tell their stories over and over.

There is one description of how cutting off ears was actually done: the prisoner had been convicted of stealing a paltry fifty dollars' worth of gold dust and was sentenced to having his ears cut off, fifty lashes, and banishment:

> Then lots were drawn to discover who should cut off his ears, and it fell upon a person named Clark. The prisoner prevailed upon a doctor sojourning there, to do the job instead of Clark, knowing that he could do it more skillfully and with less injury; but the difference was that between a little hell and a big hell. The doctor complied with great good nature and willingness, and with a well sharpened glittering razor, cut the scoundrel's ears off close to his head.[97]

The drawing of lots suggests that no one wanted the job; and the chosen person, Clark, was happy to hand it over to the doctor. The well-sharpened glittering razor was a godsend. But cutting the ears close to the prisoner's head was an extreme form of an already extreme penalty. In the Anglo-American tradition, ears were usually "cropped," or cut off partially, just as the lad who stole the coffee tin was "shorn of the rims of his ears."[98] Either the miners of McNeil's diggings were particularly harsh or the doctor took his instructions too literally.

Branding was marginally more common than cutting off ears; there are about a dozen examples in the material collected for this book, including the lad who was both cropped and branded for the theft of a coffee tin. Two further prisoners were branded for stealing money, and the rest were horse thieves. The money thieves were whipped and branded as a compromise between those for and against hanging, just like the men whose ears were cut off. Persons sympathetic to Englishman Henry Clark managed to talk his punishment down "on account of his youthfulness"; at the other man's trial, the jury split on the sentence, and the question was referred to a committee.[99] In both cases, the deal was that they should be whipped, branded with an R, and told to leave the diggings. Half of Henry Clark's head was also shaved.

The remaining seven or eight cases of branding almost fall outside of the category of lynch law in the mines. They all, or almost all, involved

large-scale and repeated horse thefts from ranchers between January
and July 1851. The accused were caught and punished by ranchers and
their neighbors, in several cases without a proper trial. In other words,
they had nothing to do with gold mining, although they took place
within the gold mining region; and in a number of cases, there was no
trial, so they could be described as mob law rather than lynch law.[100]

This business of branding was not *quite* as strange to Californians
as it is to us because they were not as far removed from the time when
the punishment was on the books (Rhode Island still used branding
in 1826), and it was still being used to punish slaves. But it was still
strange and rare. There is the question of who did it and how, particularly since it is unlikely that many people carried human-sized brands
in the mining region. The miners of Mississippi Bar branded an R on
Henry Clark's arm in 1851, as did those at Rough and Ready in 1852.[101]
The ranchers used R for *rogue* and HT for *horse thief*. Thomas Jenkins,
who was found guilty of horse stealing but escaped before he was punished, was later caught by a crowd and "branded on each cheek—the
letter 'R' on one, and the letter 'S' on the other—so people are now allowed to call him 'Rogue' or 'Scoundrel,' according to their tastes."[102]
Did they have a branding alphabet at their disposal?

It is conceivable, but unlikely, that there *were* no brands, that all of
these letters were inscribed with a hot iron, just as the lad with the coffee
tin was seared with a red-hot iron. Some slave owners branded their
slaves this way.[103] The reason that it is more likely that the ranchers did
have proper branding irons is that the Vigilance Committee of Sonora
reported that they had decided to brand a horse thief with the letters
HT and, separately, that they had given twenty-five lashes each to two
Mexicans for passing counterfeit dust. The correspondent quipped,
"The Committee are having a T brand made, to enable you to distinguish between the H. T. (horse thief) and those engaged in the retail
trade."[104] If you want a brand, in other words, you have it made. The
ranchers naturally had a blacksmith around for doing general iron-
work, including making their cattle brands. This could be a reason why
branding was a much more common punishment among ranchers than
miners—this, and a kind of lex talionis, in that the convicted men had
stolen branded animals.

Like lashes, branding could be deep or less deep. Eustis, remember, was branded deeply, while the brand of Grant, his confederate, was light. There is no description of how the branding was done or who did it. If miners were unwilling to apply lashes, it is hard to imagine that ranch hands would willingly brand a man. Maybe that is why two sentences of branding were remitted, although in one case the remission was said to be "in consideration of certain confessions made by the prisoner."[105]

## Redress against Lynchers

Although state officials tried to stop lynchings, they did not investigate them after the fact, let alone punish the participants. This was in part because it was impossible to prosecute a whole community, but it may also have been because whipping and branding were, at worst, forms of assault; and assault was not treated as a crime. They were, however, grounds for a lawsuit, and in a small handful of cases, the victim sued for compensation in the district court. These lawsuits were taken seriously and treated like any other matter before the court, but astoundingly, the defendants could plead justification if the plaintiff was guilty of the crime for which he had been lynched.

At least two cases were fully litigated, both involving alleged cattle rustlers whom ranchers had tried, convicted, and whipped. One was an action brought by Henry Gage against three ranchers, Sheldon, Lewis, and Terry. The ranchers had accused Gage of helping a horse thief, by the name of Hamilton, to escape. They tried and convicted Gage and sentenced him to thirty lashes upon the bare back. Gage then sued them for damages, pleading "innocence of the charge made." The case was tried to a jury before Judge Parsons. Each side was represented by three attorneys, and a large number of witnesses testified. The lawsuit came to an abrupt halt, however, when a witness for the defendants testified that Gage had confessed to assisting in the escape of Hamilton. "This produced a surprise and embarrassment in the proceedings, and resulted in non-suiting the plaintiff and entailing upon him the paying of the costs already incurred."[106]

The other, similar case was brought by the friends of two men, James and Staggers. The ranchers of Cache Creek had tried the two men for stealing stock and, having found them guilty, punished them with hanging (briefly) and lashes. The "jury and persons who tried" the alleged thief James, eighteen or twenty men in all, surrendered themselves to the court. The case was heard over two days before Justice Cretcher. "The defense admitted the assault and battery, and took the grounds of its being justifiable, under the circumstances," that is, that James had stolen from them. After hearing the defendants' case, James's lawyer, Mr. Morrison, dropped the suit; and the prosecuting attorney, Mr. Wambo, dismissed the case.[107]

In other words, court did not consider the lynch trials and punishments of Gage, James, and Staggers wrongful if those individuals were indeed guilty of stealing stock. This puts lynch trials in a different light. It seems unlikely that a lynch trial resulting in the execution of the accused would be similarly excusable; indeed, the officers of the law went to heroic lengths to try to stop such trials. But it is conceivable that trying and hanging a man for murder would be equally acceptable to the courts, if the defendant was indeed guilty. Indeed, this would explain the apprehension expressed when Judge Lynch executed a suspected murderer before his victim had actually expired.

The vigilance committee of Indian Bar voluntarily remunerated a man whom they mistakenly arrested for murder, although they caught their error before there were serious consequences. Dame Shirley wrote that they compensated the individual by "making him a handsome apology and present, and paying his expenses at the Humboldt [Hotel]."[108] Any vigilance committee or group of lynchers would be mortified to discover they had the wrong man, but the knowledge that they could be sued for their mistake no doubt made them extra generous.

In the first years of lynch law, trials themselves were invariably described as orderly. At the sentencing phase, however, the rowdier elements of the crowd and their shouts of "hang him!" pulled the assembly toward a harsher punishment that it might otherwise have chosen. The men more moderately inclined often proposed a more moderate penalty, but not too moderate because they needed a majority vote. At least these respectable citizens were allowed to speak and the crowd listened, and at best they persuaded a majority to approve a lesser punishment of whipping, cropping, or branding. "Lesser" is a relative word, of course: these penalties were barbaric.

Whatever respectability that the trials had was a double-edged sword, however. The miners prided themselves on their formality and adherence to common law procedural safeguards, and they were never confronted with their mistakes because there was no avenue for appeal—except in the handful of cases where the accused sued the participants in the lynch trial. Because of this self-confidence, combined with the weakness of the early California courts, the miners continued to hold lynch trials in defiance of the criminal justice system. In their confidence, they also came to regard the procedural formalities as signals of their respect for law and order. Working quickly to execute their man before the sheriff could snatch him away, they settled for the motions of a trial that was little more than window dressing. Chapter 10 describes this degeneration of lynch trials into mob trials.

# The End of the Hangtown Oak

hatever legitimacy lynch trials may have had at first was lost when California had a government. Worse, as the miners came into competition with the actual state courts, the crowds grew larger, emotions ran higher, and the process was speeded up to execute the criminal before the sheriff could rescue him. Mary Floyd Williams, the great expert on the San Francisco Vigilance Committee of 1851, suggested that the mining population abandoned its commitment to due process after 1850. Before the California Constitution was enacted, she argued, the miners felt the responsibility of their position. But after the creation of the courts, the miners' tribunals "lost their dignity and their ideals of deliberate justice. . . . Inevitably, they degenerated into angry mobs, that hastened to whip or to hang the accused before the sheriff could intervene."[1] In other words, Williams suggested that good-faith popular trials lasted only from 1848 to 1850.

Williams was right that the miners' trials were more volatile after they came into competition with the courts. But it was not as simple as "the miners" and "inevitable angry mobs." With few exceptions, the men involved in lynch trials, even those who seized the prisoner from the sheriff, still made their decisions by proposing resolutions and voting; and they usually gave the defendant at least the semblance of a trial. At the same time, the crowd's act was now clearly illegal, and some brave men rejected the majority position and tried to save the prisoner. There are, therefore, two stories here: that of the crowd, disciplined or rowdy; and that of the individuals.

This chapter first describes the serious deficiencies of the new state courts, which gave the population reason to believe that criminals were going unpunished and led them to take back prisoners who had been arrested. It then summarizes a particularly orderly and well-documented trial of one prisoner kidnapped from the authorities before looking at more fragmentary accounts and straight-up lynchings of others. Although the breakdown of good order at lynch trials was less clear-cut than Williams suggested, the miners' ideas of popular sovereignty had shifted to something more dangerous. Where they had formerly claimed a right to adopt laws and punish criminals in the absence of courts, they now maintained that they could hold their own trials even when there were courts, if these were not effective. The idea that citizens can punish prisoners on their own authority not only in the absence of courts, but also where the courts supposedly failed them, was peculiarly American; it was also used to justify the lynchings of abolitionists and Blacks in the Eastern states. It stands in stark contrast to the Weltanschauung of Australians, for instance, who considered trial by the miners worse than self-help.

When the California courts were fully up and running, and citizens were confident that accused criminals would get a real trial and, if convicted, suffer a real punishment, lynch trials came to an end. This coincided with the beginning of lynchings of minorities, a completely separate phenomenon, the purpose of which was to terrorize minority groups and reinforce the dominance of white Americans. Lynching of minorities has been the subject of multiple meticulous works of scholarship and, since it falls outside the scope of this book, is not included here.

## Lynch Law and the Courts

The justification given for the lynch trials described in the preceding chapters was the absence of government and a natural law right to self-protection. After the first district courts were established and ready to hear cases in the summer of 1850, lynch law was defended on the slightly different ground of the absence *effective* government.[2] This was what so infuriated Josiah Royce—that those who participated in these later lynchings were not only unembarrassed by their deeds, but effectively blamed lynch trials on the courts for not doing their job. A portion of the miners had become too comfortable altogether about their ability to carry out a trial—or in some cases, even to skip the trial and proceed directly to punishment.

It was generally agreed that the state justice system was unsuited to the situation in the mines and unable to bring criminals to justice. Newspaper editorials, grand jury findings, and contemporary observers listed the same systemic problems. The first of these was topographical: the courts were too far away from the mines.[3] Since the justices of the peace had no criminal jurisdiction, even in misdemeanor cases, all suspects had to be brought to town and held until the next session of the court.[4] Getting them from remote mining camps to the county seat was difficult in itself. Stephen Field faced this problem as alcalde of Marysville. He would have liked to send a convicted thief to San Francisco to work on the chain gang instead of whipping him; but he decided that this was quite impracticable because "at that time the price of passage by steamer from Marysville to San Francisco was fifty dollars, which, with the expense of an officer to accompany the prisoner, and the price of a ball and chain, would have amounted to a much larger sum than the prosecution could afford."[5] It was certainly more than the community was willing to pay.

The second problem was that the courts met so infrequently that when a prisoner *was* jailed, he faced a long wait before trial. The lowest court with criminal jurisdiction, the court of sessions, was supposed to meet six times a year in the county seat, but it did not always adhere even to this light schedule. The district court, which tried murder cases, served a large area but met only three to five times per year.[6] It failed to meet in Marysville on April 15, 1851, because one of the two judges was away in San Jose and the court was being adjourned from day to day until his return. "There has been no term of the District Court held here this year," the *Marysville Herald* complained, "and we are now in probability to be deprived of a term of the Court of Sessions."[7] By the time a case came to court, the witnesses—who in any case would have had to interrupt their work and travel to town—often had moved to distant diggings and could not be traced. Those who did appear in court received no compensation for lost work, although they might have to be available for days at a time. Not surprisingly, when the trial finally took place, key witnesses were often absent.[8]

Finally, California's legal institutions were so shoddy that miners believed, with good reason, that no criminal had ever been brought to justice. In fact, many escaped before trial because the jails were shoddy or the guard had been bribed.[9] Governor Riley wrote in August 1849, "Prisoners have escaped so frequently that on several occasions the people have risen in masses and executed the criminals directly after the trial."[10] Marysville got its first proper jail in January 1851, built of twelve-inch timbers and lined with heavy sheet iron. Five months later, the *Marysville Herald* announced, "General Jail Delivery—Escape Extraordinary!" in which ten prisoners broke out. It was widely believed that the guards were complicit in these escapes. Accused murderer Marianna Hernandez, for instance, escaped when he was taken to give a deposition in the night on the orders of an individual who also saw to it that the prisoners manacles were removed.[11] It is almost impossible to imagine a reason to take a jailed suspect for a nighttime deposition except to engineer a getaway. The ease of breaking out of jail meant also that accused criminals who did make it to trial would not stay locked up for long.[12]

The incompetence and corruption of the officers of the law was a constant source of complaint. The *Evening Picayune* reported in August 1850, little more than half a year after the state constitution had gone into effect, that there was scarce a political officeholder "who has not entered upon his duties and responsibilities as the means of making money enough to carry him home."[13] In the same month, the *Marysville Herald* wrote that "magistrates and judges are tainted with scoundrelism and corruption . . . successful crime of [every] character goes unpunished."[14] More colorfully, Charles Henri Doriot wrote to his brother in Virginia, "This country is in a Reched Condition the State is a Bankrupt a part of her officers occasionally runs away with her money and the balince are paid with script of sixty percent discount."[15]

Because of these delays resulting in absent witnesses and escaped prisoners, there were calls to speed up criminal trials. A letter to the editors of the *Sacramento Transcript* signed by "Economical Justice" argued that if the courts of criminal jurisdiction "were constantly in session, or if the judges of them were required to call a term, whenever there is an untried charge—thus making the trial as speedy as possible—every county would annually save thousands and the guilty would seldom escape conviction." Quick, certain justice would not only save money but would also check the "dangerous disposition to lynch." The punishment for theft should be flogging, Economical Justice went onto argue, because it was more certain than jail, more merciful than hanging, and cheap.[16]

For all three reasons—topography, infrequent court sessions, and corrupt officials—the miners had no faith in the courts and either refused to hand suspected thieves over to the authorities or, if they were already locked up, took them from jail and tried them by lynch law. Forty-niner Enos Christman explained, "The people were compelled for their own protection to take upon them the responsibilities they did."[17] With the crowd and the sheriff sometimes fighting, literally, over the possession of the prisoner, the miners speeded up the procedural formalities and hanged suspects as quickly as they could.

The many descriptions of these trials by the people show that some were wild affairs, but others were surprisingly formal. On March 30, 1851, a butcher by the name of Napper was robbed of $2,500 in gold dust that he had stored in a trunk: the trial of the three robbers is one of the most elaborate of all of the lynching accounts from the mines. George Allen and John Miller, described as "a fellow attached to the Circus," had been seen dividing gold that same night, so Allen was searched and found to be carrying one of the two purses that had held Napper's dust. Judge Edwards of the district court immediately issued a warrant for the two men's arrest as well as that of an alleged accomplice, Henry Rigler, and all three were taken into custody.[18]

As Judge Edwards was examining the accused on the next day, Tuesday, a large and increasingly excited crowd gathered outside, and before long, "the people arose in their might," as one newspaper put it, "and demanded that the prisoners be handed over to them for trial."[19]

Judge Edwards, of course, refused—multiple times. Finally, the crowd of several hundred men managed to seize the prisoners as they were being moved from the courtroom to the jail and immediately held a meeting to give them a trial in "Judge Lynch's Court."[20]

The proceedings lasted three days and, afterwards, the secretary of the meeting sent the full transcript of the minutes to the newspapers. It was so long that the *Sacramento Transcript* said that it could not print even half of it; but even in its abridged form, it is the most complete surviving account of a lynch trial. But for the fact that the crowd had seized the defendants from the officers, it could serve as a model of the genre and an even better introduction to trial by Judge Lynch than the case of Easterbrook that opens this book. It was naturally run by a meeting:

> Doc. Edmonston was called to the chair, whereupon he stated the object of the meeting . . . The meeting was then addressed by Wm. T. Barbour, E. F. W. Ellis, H. C. Hodge, and others, when a motion was made that the prisoners be tried before a jury of twelve disinterested citizens to be selected as follows: a committee of three . . . were to make out a list of fifty names, when the prisoners were to select twelve of the fifty to act as a jury.

The names of the chosen jurors followed. Then, "Wm. T. Barbour was appointed counsel for the People and E. F. W Ellis for the Prisoners— Dr. Edmonston still acting as chairman of the meeting, by the request of the council and others—Dr. Voorhies, Reporter."[21]

When the evidence had been presented, the jury deliberated and decided unanimously that the prisoners were guilty and each should receive thirty-nine lashes, but that Allen's and Miller's sentences would be decreased to twenty lashes if they produced the stolen money. Those two did, in fact, reveal where the gold was hidden, and their punishments were reduced accordingly. Napper had his fortune back.

The emphasis on procedural protections for the defendants in this trial is striking, as is Judge Edwards's inexplicable disappearance from the record after the prisoner was taken from him—in many cases, the

authorities did their best to take back the prisoners. Other such prosecutions are reported in less detail, but still use the vocabulary of both
meetings and trials.

Even a Mexican taken from the courtroom by a vast mob was formally tried, though the guilty verdict was no doubt a foregone conclusion. Jesus Sevaras, also known as Charley the Bullfighter, was alleged
to have been involved in the gruesome murder of Jacob Mincer. He was
in the courtroom being tried by the civil authorities when the "[f]ive
or six hundred miners standing round" decided to take him from the
courtroom where he was being questioned and try him themselves.
They took him to the edge of town, where they selected twelve jurymen;
and "a justice named A.J. Lowell, of St. Louis Council, administered
the oath." A string of witnesses identified the knife found at the scene
as Charley's. The jury retired briefly, returned a verdict of guilty, and
"asked the people to pass the sentence. Several hundred rose to their
feet & declared he should be hung in one hour," which he was.[22]

At the other end of the spectrum from these formal proceedings were
cases where the crowd took the accused from an officer and hanged him
without trial. Henry Vere Huntley, an Englishman, described a crowd
in Marysville in 1852 trying to take an accused thief from an officer.
"I have seen a pack of hounds baying round the huntsman who holds
up the fox," he said, "and so now did the mob round the recorder who
held the thief: revolvers were cocked on both sides."[23] In that case, the
recorder won and hung on to his prisoner, but in others, the crowd got
its way. A man in Hangtown was to be tried for murder, but instead
the judge merely examined him and, presumably, remanded for trial. At
that point, "the mob raised the cry 'Bring him out! [H]ang him!'" and
made a rush for the prisoner. He "was seized by the hair and dragged a
short distance to an oak tree—a rope was put around his neck and over
the limb of the tree—some men took hold of the end and hoisted him up
as they would a hog to be dressed where he hung until he was dead."[24]

Another crowd, after hanging one thief for theft, decided to keep
going and execute two Sydney men in the jail. "Someone shouted, 'Let's
hang the Sydney Convicts.' The excited crowd rushed over to the jail,
pushed in the door, brought the men out, and hanged them on the same
tree."[25] In a third case, where a jealous husband shot a man who was

too friendly with his wife, the husband "was put into jail, and the crowd took him out and hung him forthwith."[26] These were lynch mobs, not lynch trials.

The competition over the prisoner speeded up some proceedings, but the option of returning him to the sheriff for a trial at law—or "allowing" the sheriff to seize him—offered a third outcome when the miners were divided. The choices were now acquittal, conviction, or return to the authorities. At Columbia, a large crowd of miners captured a prisoner from the officers, dragged him to a tree, and were in the process of hanging him when the limb broke. "[I]t was then decided to give him a trial by jury": presumably, this means that someone made a motion and the assembly voted for a jury trial. The witness testimony lasted five or six hours, "at the expiration of which time, the Sheriff succeeded in obtaining the malefactor, and carried him to Sonora."[27] The sheriff had tried unsuccessfully to rescue the prisoner at the very beginning of the trial, so it seems that the hours of testimony had reconciled them to handing the man over. Similarly, in a stabbing case in 1853, the jury was unwilling to sentence the convicted man to death while his victim was still alive and "advised" that the prisoner be handed over to the authorities. "A majority of the meeting sustain[ed] the decision of the jury [and] it was carried into execution."[28]

Much depended on the character and persuasive power of the sheriff and the members of the crowd who supported him. Officers of the law in the East were accused of making only half-hearted efforts to save the prisoner from the mob. William Defensor Thomas, writing in 1835 about lynchings of abolitionists in the East, describes Judge Lynch's methods as reasonable on their surface, but actually orchestrated to bring about the whipping of the accused. Rabble were planted in the crowd to shout out at critical points and eventually to take matters into their own hands, leaving the leaders in a position to write to the newspapers that they did their best to preserve order, but the righteous indignation of the community was such that saving the prisoner's life was the most they could do.[29]

In California, however, there were citizens, sheriffs, and judges who did literally fight for possession of the accused. It seems that one man, or a small group, could stop a mob if the conditions were right, that is, when the men who intervened were well respected and good speakers, when part of the crowd already had reservations about the lynching, and when there was a pause in the proceedings that gave the representatives of the law a chance to be heard. Even if all of these factors were in place, the sheriff and those who supported him might have to use physical force to get possession of the accused.

Sheriff George Work stands out as a model of what one man could do to prevent a hanging. He certainly saved the three Indians and a Mexican who were discovered burning the bodies of two Americans, on July 10, 1850. The men were murdered at Green Flat Diggings, eight miles from Sonora, and the suspects were brought to the town to be arraigned before a judge. During the proceeding, the crowd was already shouting, "String 'em up," and, "Hang them," and the officers tried, with little effect, to calm them. Sheriff Work threatened to shoot the first man who interfered with the prisoners, while Judge Marvin "in a forcible address" promised the crowd that justice would be done and reminded them of the heavy responsibility they would bear if they took the law into their own hands.[30]

At the arraignment, the evidence was favorable to the defendants; they said the Americans had been dead for several days when they found their bodies and that they had burned them in accordance with their funeral customs. The prisoners were calm and respectful; and the Mexican, at any rate, was good-looking. Nevertheless, the multitude was so wild that the court briefly retired to consider its next step, and in its absence, several hundred persons elected their own judge, took the accused to a hill outside the town, empaneled a second jury, found the men guilty, and sentenced them to hang.[31]

The first prisoner was already suspended by the neck when Judges Tuttle, Marvin, and Radcliffe arrived. Judge Tuttle urged the people "in a powerful, feeling, and eloquent address" to respect the law. "[B]y flinging themselves boldly into the crowd," the county clerk and others "succeeded in effecting a diversion that enabled the proper officers to regain possession of the prisoners, and contrary to expectation . . . succeeded in lodging them in jail."[32]

On the day of the trial, July 15, almost two thousand armed men poured into Sonora from all the surrounding diggings, intent on executing the prisoners. But when the trial began, the scene suddenly became a farce. One of the guards dropped his gun, which went off, and "instantly numberless revolvers were drawn, bowie knives flashed forth and the tumult became indescribable." The examination was postponed, and the mob spent the night drinking. In the morning, many left for their diggings, and the examination of the men resumed. "There being no evidence against them, they were acquitted."[33]

All accounts had special praise for Sheriff George Work for his courage in protecting the prisoners against the mob, "our active and worthy sheriff," the *Alta* called him; *The History of Tuolumne County* described him as "the redoubtable Sheriff, a man of the steadiest courage and iron nerve, who never quailed in the discharge of his duty."[34]

Work had also demonstrated these qualities two weeks earlier when he rescued Jim Hill from a lynch trial at Camp Seco, near Sonora, on June 29—a Sunday, the very worst day for law and order. Hill was a member of a gang that stole an iron safe at gunpoint. Shortly thereafter, when any reasonable criminal would have been keeping a low profile, Hill shot and robbed a man at a Spanish house of ill repute and was arrested. The next day, a dozen men arrived in Sonora and took Hill from the jail to stand trial in Camp Seco. "A fair and impartial trial was given before a jury of twelve men who rendered a verdict of guilty unanimously," and he was sentenced to hang by a general vote—note again all of the formalities of a lynch trial. Oddly, the opening for those who opposed lynching happened at the execution itself, when Hill addressed the vast crowd that had gathered to see a hanging. Hill threw himself on their mercy:

This appeal to the people caused the question to be put amongst them, "Shall he be hung?" A large number answered aye, but an equal number responded in the negative. Immediately some hundreds of pistols were drawn and a universal stampede occurred. Horsemen plunged through the crowd and over them, and the people ran in every direction.

Sheriff Work appeared at this moment of maximum confusion and asked the crowd to hear him as conservator of the peace. "He pledged his own life that the prisoner should be forthcoming at the District

Court, if the people would deliver him into the hands of the civil authorities." He got no answer, but in the confusion that followed, some men managed to take Hill from the stand, his hand still bound behind him, and "thrust [him] into a wagon which was immediately driven off at a rapid rate for Sonora."[35] Miner David G. Ferson, who was present at the hanging, described the events very similarly: "[A] lot of tham that didn't wont him hung mad a leep at at [sic] him and got him on to a hors and started for Sonora."[36]

When the wagon reached Sonora, with two armed outriders, a crowd was waiting at the entrance to the town. Christman wrote that the driver continued at full tilt into town until it hit a post in the dark. George Work then jumped out with the prisoner, holding him by the collar, and both ran at full speed for the jail, plunging through the arroyo, while the crowd behind was shouting, "Stop him in front. We are afraid to shoot, lest we may kill our friends. Stop him in front!"[37] They made it to the jail, but found Colonel Cheatam (a good Dickensian name) blocking the door. As Cheatam and Work faced each other, both with cocked revolvers in their hands, the crowd caught up with them. One man took hold of the sheriff, another grabbed the prisoner, and it was all over for Jim Hill. He was hung within the hour in spite of the sheriff's heroic efforts.

I have provided all of these details because, together with George Work's reputation and his role in saving the men caught burning the bodies of two men, they suggest that one sheriff, at least, made a heroic effort to prevent a lynching and almost succeeded and also that he had supporters in the crowd. But then Christman's account of Jim Hill's trial concludes, "Sheriff Work was not inimical to the hanging of the robber Hill, but owing to his official position, he could do no less than make an effort to lodge the prisoner within the door of the jail."[38] Make an effort? Against his inclinations? Perhaps Work, like many lawmen after him, was secretly sympathetic to the lynchers; or perhaps Christman was attributing these sympathies to him. It is not clear what more Work could have done if, as David Ferson wrote, two to three hundred men were waiting at Sonora and took Hill from him.[39]

There are other accounts of individual men using persuasion and force to rescue prisoners from miners' justice and deliver them to the authorities, some successful and some not. The arrest of Franklin

Sanford, accused of stealing cattle from various ranches, attracted an excited crowd, a portion of which was strongly inclined to punish him in the court of Judge Lynch; but "Mr. Shelden assumed a most decisive course in favor of bringing the man to town for a regular trial, and his motion finally prevailed."[40] On the other hand, when the miners convicted an eighteen-year-old Mexican man, Flores, of the brutal stabbing of a countryman and sentenced him to hang, "[o]bjections were made to the summary mode of proceeding, and an attempt was made to have him turned over to the civil authorities and sent to Jackson: but it did not succeed."[41] And at Stockton, the marshal rescued a thief who was in the process of being given one hundred lashes.[42] In short, for those readers who are wondering whether they could have made a difference if they had been present at a lynching in the mines, the answer is, it was worth a try. No one was ever penalized for trying to stop a hanging, and under the right conditions, some even succeeded.

## Lynch Law: An American Institution

The worst lynchings described in this phase of California's history began to look like the lynchings of Vicksburg and St. Louis that had caused such outrage in the Eastern states. They happened especially—though not exclusively—where these miners were competing with the nascent courts, while the more remote camps were still experiencing frontier conditions. Some of the young men who, at home, had presumably believed lynching to be unacceptable were witnessing and perhaps participating in proceedings that would be much more difficult to justify to their parents.

The excuse for lynching now shifted from the absence of courts to the inadequacies of the courts, stating, with respect to horse thieves recently imprisoned, that "so little confidence is placed in the authorities . . . that it was suggested last night, by one of the best citizens of the place, to take the thieves out and call on Judge Lynch to preside."[43] This justification resembled that of ordinary lynchers in the settled portions of the United States. As Michael Pfeifer puts it, Americans believed "that citizens might reclaim the functions of government when legal institutions could not provide sufficient protection to persons or their property."[44] In California, the alleged failure of the courts was not that they failed to do what they were supposed to do, but that what they were "supposed to do" was unsatisfactory: they provided procedural safeguards for the defendant that undoubtedly allowed some criminals to go free. These safeguards included the presumption of innocence, the requirement of proof beyond a reasonable doubt, and the rules of evidence.

Multiple historical studies have documented the nineteenth-century dissatisfaction with the criminal justice system and justifications of lynching. The historian Richard Maxwell Brown explained in his pioneering book, *Strain of Violence*, that lynchers "made the old familiar complaint that the American system of justice favored the accused rather than society."[45] Michael Pfieffer and William Carrigan, among others, have gathered extensive evidence supporting this thesis that Americans have long been impatient with the criminal justice system because it seems to include too many openings for an actual offender to go unpunished. The adversarial system sometimes appears to let off defendants on a technicality of evidence or procedure; and convicted prisoners are permitted appeals to distant and inscrutable—or at least, unobservable—courts.[46]

It is, of course, a tenet of the criminal justice system that it favors the defendant on the principal that is better ten guilty men go free than one innocent man be executed; but the Californians did not see why any guilty man should go free, and they believed that they could recognize a guilty man. The number of men tried by Judge Lynch and found innocent could be counted on one hand. Some participants may have regarded the trial as a ritual that turned the punishment of the criminal into a formal and public act rather than an act of vengeance. When the crowd was induced to grant the prisoner a lynch trial only on the promise that he would be hanged, it was not a trial as we understand it, but an empty formality.

## The Australian Gold Rush and Lynch Law

The miners' justification of lynch trials was rejected in the Eastern states, as shown earlier, and also in the near contemporary gold rush in

Australia. Californians might have expected more understanding from their counterparts in the Australian mines given that the Australian gold rush partially overlapped with that in Californian, both chronologically (it began in 1851) and in population, since some miners had also been in California. Despite the very similar circumstances, however, it was only the Americans who practiced lynch law: lynching was truly an American institution.

As David Goodman has shown, the Australian government worried about what gold meant for order from the time of its discovery in 1851. Australian officials understood law and order to mean social stability and, especially, respect for law, institutions, and class distinctions. Disorder could be summed up in one word: California. More specifically, the Australians hoped to avoid the supposed American conditions of republicanism, turbulence, violence, and, above all, lynch law. The newspapers wrote endlessly about the barbarity of Californians and lynch law and also about the good order and respect for law among Australian miners.

The different attitudes toward lynch law are illustrated in an account, quoted by Goodman, of an incident in Victoria. In the writer's story, a crowd caught a robber but did not know what to do with him because there were no police in the area. "A voice came out of the crowd which unmistakably from its nasal drawl proclaimed itself to be Yankee, 'do as we do in California. Lynch him.'" The crowd was silent:

Then a man, a noble earnest looking fellow he was, enquired, "Where is the man who spoke last?" Then a tall lean looking fellow stepped forward . . . "Hiram Jones, late of Californy and California born." The previous speaker said in a quiet earnest way, "Look here, Hiram Jones late of California, California born. We are law abiding subjects of the British Queen Victoria, if a man is accused of breaking the laws of the Realm, if caught, he is handed over to proper judicial authorities to have a fair trial, if found guilty, he has to suffer the penalty. We have no sympathy with mob law in the Queen's dominions nor do we, Hiram Jones, tolerate California ruffianism in this land."[47]

This story is almost too good to be true, and, as Goodman suggests, whatever facts might underlie it were no doubt improved in the retelling. But that is all the more reason to believe that it captured the Australians' idea of how they differed from Americans.

Australians did not necessarily object to self-help. When miners in Australia caught a thief, they inflicted on him any kind of corporal punishments short of hanging, including flogging, holding over a fire, and chaining to a tree for days. Historian Geoffrey Serle writes that one thief "was soused in sludge, stripped to his underpants, branded with a red-hot chisel 'Caught Stealing Mates' Gold', and banished."[48] George Henry Wathen, an English visitor to the gold fields, wrote that the Australians never went so far as lynch law, but things did get very bad, "and I have myself seen a ruffian, who had just shot a man, being dragged along by an infuriate crowd, many of whom fiercely shouted, 'Hang him up!'"[49] These were as gruesome as some of the penalties inflicted by lynch law; the difference was that the Australian miners did not pretend to be sitting as a court, and executions were almost nonexistent. For the Australians, it would seem, self-help—short of killing—was more acceptable than a citizen trial.

Australian miners did not execute criminals, but there was one exception. In February 1852, a man was hanged for murdering his mate with a pick; the execution took place over the hole that was the subject of their quarrel.[50] A second report was called a rumor by Chief Justice A'Beckett his charge at the opening of the Supreme Court: "[A] man who had stolen gold was seized, bound, thrown into a waterhole, and left to drown." If the rumor proved to be true, the chief justice said, "it is to be feared that the ranges of Mount Alexander are not altogether free from the stigma that attaches to the name of California."[51] Americans in the Eastern states would have agreed: no matter how careful their trials, lynch law was a stigma on the name of California.

In the modern state, only the government has the authority to punish crime; it is said to have a monopoly on violence. By holding criminal trials and executing the men they found guilty, the miners took on the role of the state. This was a bold move, and the miners at first appeared to be aware of the responsibility that they had assumed: their first trials were earnest and careful and occasionally resulted in acquittal. When they continued to hold lynch trials and execute prisoners after California had a government, judges, and jails, however, they themselves were acting criminally. Now the sheriff was coming for them, or at least trying to stop them, and they dropped some of their self-imposed constraints in the name of executing their prisoner while they could. The worst of the lynch trials began to resemble the lynchings of the East.

The wonder was that the lynch trials continued to be run by meetings using parliamentary procedure and that these were occasionally dignified, like the trial of Rigler, Allen, and Miller. That they held a trial at all, rather than just stringing up their prisoner, shows that they still regarded themselves as "the People"—*l'etat, c'est nous*. Non-Americans found it astonishing. The Australians punished criminals through self-help, and the Australian government was apparently willing to overlook such incidents, but they never usurped the prerogative of the state to run a criminal court.

Whether lynch trials of Americans simply died out or were actively stopped varied from place to place. Colonel Norton reported that at Placerville in 1853, "some eighty in number [organized] in the interest of law and order, and determined that promiscuous hanging should be stopped, and that the laws of the country should be enforced in all cases, criminal as well as civil."[52] Soon afterwards, one man killed another in a drunken brawl. The civil authorities arrested the accused, and, predictably, a mob of several thousand demanded that he be surrendered to them. Norton writes that he and his compatriots managed with great difficulty to hold on to the prisoner and take him to Coloma, the county seat, where he was in due course tried, convicted, and hanged. According to Norton' this marked the end of lynching in El Dorado County. "The old Hangtown Oak was cut down and principally manufactured into canes, which are carefully kept in remembrance of the days of gold excitement, riot, and blood-shed."[53] For Spanish speakers in California, however, the other kind of lynching—racial terrorism—was just beginning.

CHAPTER 11

# Massacring Indians and Ejecting Spanish Speakers

So far, almost all of the descriptions of meetings, claim jumping, and dispute resolutions concerned Americans interacting with each other. Everything was different when Americans dealt with non-Americans: they refused to give foreigners the protection of the law and, worse, passed special laws depriving them of their rights. The great historian of the California gold rush, Josiah Royce, said of the maltreatment of foreigners, "This tale is one of disgrace to our people."[1] Americans massacred the Indians, expelled the Mexicans, fought the French, and tolerated (at best) the Chinese, so long as they only worked on land that Americans considered worthless. As for Black Americans, their right to mine on equal terms was recognized by their countrymen, except for a few Southerners who "allowed that a white man might come in but a black man could not no how."[2]

This chapter focuses on American use and abuse of meetings in their interactions with Native Americans and Spanish speakers during the gold rush proper, 1848–1852. American miners used meetings to ban Spanish speakers from the diggings, while here is only one example of a vote that *prevented* the expulsion of minorities from their claims. Equally importantly, the mere handful of criminal prosecutions of Americans who robbed or assaulted Spanish speakers suggests that

208

perpetrators rarely suffered legal consequences. In effect, these minorities were outlaws, that is, Americans could commit crimes against them with impunity.

As for the Native American population of the mining region, they were massacred, man, woman, and child. Miners shot and killed individual Indians, and groups of miners combined to wipe out villages. What they did has rightly been called an American genocide, and the full extent of its horrors have been documented by Benjamin Madley in *An American Genocide.*[3] As with other genocides, one asks, Who were the men who killed Indians? Who, if anyone, opposed them? To what extent did decent people act to protect the intended victims? And, finally, were conscientious miners ever able to prevent such outrages?

Americans were experts at self-organization: that has been the theme of this book until this point. Entire diggings cooperated to settle legal questions; and in the case of criminal trials, moderate miners stood up to their bloodthirsty fellows, sometimes successfully and sometimes not. They could certainly have tried murderers of individual Indians in Judge Lynch's court, but they did not do so. The massacres were different. In principle, if the decent men outnumbered those who set out to destroy an Indian village, they could have called a meeting and . . . what? Passed resolutions condemning the slaughter, and that is about all. It is unlikely that the miners who opposed the genocide could have stood up to the perpetrators. There were too many of them, and they were violent. Oregonians and Texans were prominent among the killers, and they intimidated other Americans.[4] Perhaps miners from the East even felt that the frontiersmen had a score to settle or that they knew more about Indians than New Englanders. In point of fact, however, there is not enough information about what other Americans thought, and that in itself indicates that they did not consider it an important question. The stories of atrocities in letters and diaries are disapproving, but not very much so. This was a great failure of self-government in the mines.

## Indians

It was not even illegal to kill Indians. In fact, government policy favored the moneyed interests that profited from the massacres and the

de facto enslavement of much of the Indian population. In 1770, the
native population is thought to have been 310,000. By 1848, the numbers had been reduced to 125,000–150,000 by disease and the disrup-
tion of families and communities by the missions and later by ranches.
In 1855, only some 50,000 natives remained.[5] Murder and the loss of
territory, leading to starvation, caused this last precipitous drop. Contemporary observers called this extermination; modern scholars label
it genocide.[6]

   Federal law governed Indian relations, and had the law been applied
in California, many more Native Californians would have survived,
though probably not prospered. When Americans moved into Indian
territories west of the Mississippi, the government negotiated treaties
with the native populations, under which they promised loyalty to the
United States and surrendered most of their land in return for guaranteed reservations and certain services and annuities.[7] In California,
however, the federal government did too little, too late. Congress took
no steps on behalf of the native population until late in 1850, more than
two years after the discovery of gold, when it provided for three agents
to report on the Indian situation and to make peace. The word *treaty*
did not appear in the mandate from Congress, but the secretary of the
interior directed the agents to "make such treaties and compacts . . .
as may seem just and proper."[8] The three agents did, in fact, negotiate
eighteen treaties that set aside 8.5 million acres for reservations on
terms similar to earlier treaties with Indians.[9] But all treaties must be
ratified by the United States Senate, and due to intense resistance by
the white people of California—it was too much land, they argued, and
some of it was in the mineral region—the Senate tabled the treaties in
1852.[10] There was, therefore, no place where the Indians were safe.

   Meanwhile, in 1850, California adopted laws with the Orwellian title,
"Act for the Government and Protection of Indians," which stated that
any citizen could bring about the arrest of an able-bodied Indian who
was found "loitering and strolling about." That Indian would then be
hired out, his or her labor sold to the highest bidder for a period of up to
four months.[11] In addition, any person obtaining an Indian minor from
its parents or friends could be granted "the care, custody, control and
earnings of such minor, until he or she obtained the age of majority."[12]

In 1860, the laws were revised to create indentured servitude of adult Indians for up to ten years.[13]

The law also prohibited Indians from testifying against a white person in court, which meant that they could not seek justice for crimes against them. A white man who killed an Indian would not be punished unless there were white witnesses, and often not even then.[14] Moreover, the state retaliated for alleged crimes against whites by sending multiple military expeditions, some of which engaged in the indiscriminate slaughter of men, women, and children and the destruction of their villages.

Some miners were more than willing to kill Indians, whether in revenge for crimes or supposed crimes or simply because they hated all Native Americans. That some Indians had killed some Americans was enough reason for a campaign against the whole race. Henry Sturdivant's journal entry for July 2, 1851, recorded that he was leaving Clear Creek because of poor diggings and a shortage of drinking water and because Indians had killed some Americans, including a friend of his. And it was also, perhaps, because he did not want to participate in an upcoming massacre: "The miners intend in this place to celebrate the 4th by seeing how many Indians they can kill," he wrote. "[A]las, for the red mans, they are hunted by the miners as though their salvation depended on their extermination of the Indian race—Their will be a fearful account to be settled when at the court of heaven justice shall be done to this unfortunate people."[15]

Men who wanted to exterminate the Indians were almost entirely successful. Although William Kelly warned emigrants in remoter parts of the mining region not to camp near shrubs or bushes that Indians could use as cover from which to shoot animals and sometimes people, he added that this danger was quickly disappearing. The Indians were "fast dwindling in numbers," he wrote, "for trappers and travellers shoot them down without hesitation or remorse wherever they meet them."[16] Kelly was wrong that Indians hid in the shrubs to take potshots at miners unless they were taking revenge for atrocities against their village; but his statement that the population was "fast dwindling" was accurate.

Oregonians were responsible for the earliest atrocities.[17] In 1848, the miners were primarily Americans who were in California at the time of the discovery, Indians, and settlors from Oregon. The first group had dealt with the native population mainly as laborers; they had had a low opinion of Indians, but no desire to kill them. The Oregonians, however, had fought with the indigenous peoples among whom they had settled, and they were determined to carry on the fight against any Indians they encountered, of whatever tribe.[18] "The Oregonians, especially, hunt them as they would wild beasts," said William M'Collum. "An Oregonian will leave a rich placer to wreak his vengeance on one of a race that he has learned to regard as his foe, by the outrages they have committed upon the whites in Oregon."[19] Later, other frontiersmen joined enthusiastically in the slaughter. Miner Warren Sandler thought that they were entirely to blame for the clashes between Caucasians and Indians:

> The trouble with the Indians is caused by the Oregoners and the Missourians—they shoot them down whenever they can get near them and even hunt them like wild beasts. Thus they drive the poor Indians into the mountains where there is nothing for them to eat, consequently they are forced to come down and get whatever they can find to eat . . . then there is a great noise made—"them damned Indians have stolen my cattle & mules"—the first thing is a party out after them, running them down on horse-back, scattering the families all about the mountains. Little children are left to wander about alone while their parents are hunted and shot.[20]

Borthwick's comment that these frontiersmen "thought about as much of shooting an Indian as of killing a rattlesnake" hits the mark; they regarded the native population as vermin.[21]

But frontiersmen were not the only ones who attacked Indians for little or no reason. The gold rush attracted other lowlifes who relished killing for its own sake. Heinrich Lienhard encountered a group of forty-niners he described as "the scum of large cities of the east." On seeing some nearby Indians, these men said they would like to try their guns on them. "What flashed through their minds was something like this," Lienhard wrote, "'See that black devil. Look at his wild eye. Why not blow his brains out.'"[22] Lienhard first came to California in 1846, was an associate of Sutter's, and had worked with the native workmen at Sutter's Fort, so he was naturally disgusted by such crazy talk. Others said that "nearly all the difficulties with the Indians in this country have originated in outrages upon them by the unhung rascals who disgrace our nation and our race, a white minority that did not represent the general population."[23]

On the other hand, punitive expeditions against Native Americans who had allegedly murdered white miners or threatened an attack were broadly accepted. Some accounts even suggest that when the miners voted to "punish" a group of Indians, everyone in the diggings was expected to participate, whether he had voted in favor or not. The Chilean miner Vicente Pérez Rosales reports that a meeting was called to organize an expedition against the Indians, who, it was learned, had planned an attack on the miners. "Because I had not gone to the meeting, something that really surprised them about a Frenchman (that is what they thought I was), their committee came looking for me," Pérez Rosales wrote. The committee assumed that he would join in the operation, but he told them a white lie: "They found me, *naturally*, very sick but strongly desirous of accompanying them." They did not make him get up from his supposed sickbed, "but were content to accept . . . a contribution of gunpowder and lead." So, even Pérez Rosales, who opposed the preemptive strike against supposedly hostile Indians, felt obliged to donate to the cause.[24]

Punishment and retribution might seem like a version of the native population's own practice of feuds, but it was not. Alonzo Delano, who took such an interest in the Indian village near his store, said that when someone from another tribe murdered one of them, they in turn killed someone of that person's tribe; and if the killer was a white man, "they determined to take vengeance on any of the white man's tribe they could find."[25] But Delano notes that they killed *one* person, where the Americans would have massacred a whole village. Furthermore, many observers agreed that the whites were generally the aggressors and that "as a matter of course the Indians retaliated whenever opportunities occurred; and in this way several unarmed or careless Oregonians had become, in turn, their victims."[26]

Moreover, many of the supposed Indian transgressions for which the whites were taking revenge never happened: the allegations were based on lies or unfounded rumors or the assumption that if livestock went missing, Native Americans must have stolen them. Delano wrote that in early 1850, on the Feather River, a group of miners missed several head of oxen. Fifteen men grabbed their guns and set out for an Indian rancheria some twelve miles away, shot fourteen of the inhabitants, and demolished the houses. "When they had nearly reached home," wrote Delano, "their sense of justice was a little shaken, by seeing every ox which they had supposed stolen, quietly feeding in a somewhat isolated gorge, whither they had strayed in search of grass."[27] He notes that if Indians had made a similar mistake, the white population would have launched a war of extermination against them.

Most obviously, the whites were responsible for the hostilities because they had made the first move when they threw Indians off their lands. In his 1851 annual message, the governor of California noted, "We have suddenly spread ourselves over the country in every direction, and appropriated whatever portion of it we pleased to ourselves, without [the Indians'] consent, and without compensation."[28] This was wrong in itself and had also left the native population without the means of subsistence. The governor rightly said that they were necessarily driven to steal stray animals from time to time. "This leads to war . . . and creates in the Indian bosom a hatred against the white man that never ceases to exist." In short, many commentators of the time agreed that the Americans bore the blame for the hostilities between the Indians and themselves.

These same commentators who opposed the attacks on Indians also believed that they would continue until the whole race was exterminated because the whites would not stop killing while an Indian was left alive. There had always been miners who said that the Indians were in the way and that "it will be absolutely necessary to exterminate the savages before they can labor much longer in the mines with security."[29] More humane observers saw the ongoing genocide as a tragedy that was, unfortunately, unstoppable. In the same annual message in which Governor Burnett faulted the killers, he added that "[w]hile we cannot anticipate this result but with painful regret, the inevitable destiny of the race is beyond the power or wisdom of man to avert."[30]

The feelings of some white Americans went beyond regret to shame and guilt. In an article on "Our Indian Policy" published in the *Alta*

*California* in 1850, the author noted that present conflicts would snowball into in a war of extermination. "We cannot but yield to the conviction that such is the destiny of that miserable race," he continued, "and that we are but fulfilling our own by the enactment of scenes on the Pacific similar to those which have stained with blood our Indian history on the shores of the Atlantic, from the first dawnings of civilization."[31] The scuttling of treaties that would have saved many thousands of Indians, however, shows that such honorable men were greatly outnumbered.

The general picture was therefore as bad as it could be. White miners deliberately exterminated the Indian population; and while enthusiastic frontiersmen committed many murders on their own, other punitive expeditions were undertaken by the miners en masse. What, then, of the men who opposed the killing of innocent Indians?

Individuals would have found it difficult or impossible to confront frontiersmen about their mania for revenge on the native population. Silas Weston, newly arrived from Rhode Island in the spring of 1853, described his reaction to an attack on an Indian village. Twenty-two men from Kelly's Bar set out to punish an Indian village, armed with bowie knives and enough guns so that "the company could fire more than two hundred times without stopping to re-load." The Americans approached the Indian settlement from behind a hill and, just after sunrise, when the villagers were at their breakfast, dashed down the other side, "pouring upon them a most deadly fire." The Indian men grabbed their weapons and fought with "great courage" until forced to retreat. The Americans shot some of them in the back as they fled, and then, Weston wrote, "with their bowie knives they passed around among the wounded and slain, and where life had not become extinct, they extinguished it!" In all, the attackers killed about thirty Indians and wounded about thirty more. Weston added, "[W]hat followed is too revolting for any but a savage mind to contemplate." He was probably alluding to scalping, since he adds that some of the attackers returned to Kelly's Bar with several scalps dangling from a bundle of bows and arrows.[32]

For once we know who participated in the slaughter and who stayed home. The twenty-two attackers belonged to a company of forty-one men from one of the Western states, possibly Missouri, since one of the attackers was brought back to "Missouri House," a bar. Other Indians had attacked them on the Overland Trail—not without cause—and had killed almost half of their number. The survivors swore to shoot every Indian they encountered, and they acted upon this vow almost as soon as they reached the mines, when one of them "shot dead on the spot an innocent little Indian girl as she sat upon a log." The raid on the Indian village was part of this vendetta.[33]

Meanwhile, the majority of miners did not participate in the attack; they stayed in camp and "very generally disapprove[d] of the conduct of the young victors, especially those acts of cruelty perpetrated upon the wounded after the enemy had fled," wrote miner Weston, but it was "unsafe to say much against the uncivilized treatment" of the Indians.[34] This is clear also from an incident that took place after the massacre at Kelly's Bar, when one of the company narrated the history of their clashes on the plains. When he finished, a listener said softly to the man standing next to him, "The whites are more to blame than the Indians, for they were the first aggressors." The narrator spun round and shouted, "Who dares take sides with the vagabond Indians who spilt the blood of my friends! I'll fight him! I'll fight a dozen of the wretches who dare do it!!" Fearing that there would indeed be a fight, Weston and a companion quietly withdrew.[35]

It is understandable that individuals shrank from confronting frontiersmen fresh from a massacre. This is where the miners' meeting should have come into its glory, by providing a forum where even ninety-eight-pound weaklings could safely speak out against a proposed attack or punish the attackers after the event. But that did not happen. The miners almost never voted on decisions relating to Indians; and when they did, it was the aggressors—not the peacekeepers—who carried the day.

Belligerent miners were often in the majority. For example, after a miner was found murdered and his partners were missing and presumed dead, the camp held "a sort of general inquest into all the circumstances."[36] There was no doubt that the perpetrators were Indians, according to William Kelly, a participant, and at a second meeting "[i]t was *unanimously* agreed" that a party should set out for the Indian village and "by inflicting summary punishment teach them a lesson."[37]

Half of the men who signed up to join the expedition later dropped out, but only because of the awful weather, not because they had second thoughts about the justice of their cause.

Caucasians who killed Native Americans were almost never prosecuted. A rare exception followed a meeting between settlers and Indians at Taylor's Ranch, Indian Valley, in November 1853, where representatives of both sides pledged that "equal justice should be meted out to white man and to Indian when any wrong had been done." The assembly was arranged by the rancher Jobe T. Taylor, after he himself shot an Indian thief and realized the importance of cultivating the goodwill of the local tribes. A month later, George Rose, a blacksmith, entered Jobe Taylor's own establishment, of all places, and seeing an Indian sitting by the fire said, "What business has that d–d Indian in this house?" and shot him dead. Rose was given a full lynch trial. The verdict was, "We, of the jury in the case of George Rose for shooting an Indian on the 18th inst., find the prisoner guilty of murder in the first degree," signed by all eleven jurymen; and Rose was executed the next day. Of course, this incident had several unique features, including the very recent undertaking to give Indians justice, the ruthlessness of the murder, and the fact that it took place in Taylor's house and in his presence.[38]

Usually, there was no appetite for trying murderers of Indians, and if some individuals were brave enough to argue for a trial, they were voted down. In December 1850, a white man murdered an innocent Indian. He had first shot at a different Indian who had drawn a knife on him, but missed; two or three other Indians then came running around the corner of the house to see what was happening, and the American emptied his gun into one of those, killing him. If the victim had been white, the murderer would have been tried by Judge Lynch and hanged. In this case, "[s]ome of the citizens were in favor of delivering the offender up to the Indians for them to punish, & others were for arresting him by the law while others were in favor of letting him run at large," wrote William Tell Parker, adding, "the latter counsel prevailed & the man has 'vamosed.'"[39] Notably, the suggestions did not include a lynch trial.

In fact, an article in the *Alta California* of October 4, 1851, suggested vaguely that lynch law's purview did not extend to attacks on Indians and foreigners. A "class of reckless, inhuman, mercenary and selfish men . . . has produced more trouble among the tribes of Indians in this country than all the other influences of rapid settlement and 'border' civilization combined," the paper stated. But their crimes were "of a species not accessible to the law, as the people have undertaken to administer it."[40] Anyone who thought an Indian killer should be treated like any other murderer faced a mountain of inertia.

A year later, this same William Tell Parker wrote about an expedition against local Indians to retaliate for the deaths of two Americans—although the Indians that they targeted were probably not the guilty parties. When the whites had captured an Indian, "[a] few of those present thought it unworthy of Americans to kill a prisoner without a trial, but a majority were in favor of shooting him." Parker himself was one of the men who disapproved of the whole operation, and he wrote, "I did not go with this party myself as such work is very uncongenial with my feelings." But he did not feel that this absolved him of responsibility for the crime because he agreed with his partner Harry Mitchell that the latter would go while Parker and another partner stayed behind and worked and that they would share the profits equally among the three of them. "I mention this to show that I am committed with regard to the transaction," Parker wrote, "and must bear a proportion of the blame that will eventually attach to the perpetrators of the deed." This was true of anyone who associated with the killers, but Parker was perhaps the only one who admitted it to himself.[41]

Even a meeting resulting in a vote against attacking Indians did not settle the matter: the murderous types did what they wanted anyway, with no repercussions. In November 1851, a William McGee staggered into Bean's Bar, badly injured, and before he died, he managed to say that he and his partner Dickinson had been attacked by three Indians. A search party organized to find Dickinson met a chief of the Uno tribe, who told them Dickinson had been killed and thrown into the water. At this point, the *Sacramento Daily Union* reported, "[a] council was called to decide whether a war of extermination should be commenced," and a captain was in fact chosen to lead the mission; "but as there were twenty dissenting voices the party disbanded." This was a victory for the moderates, but the case was not closed. A few days later, another company of forty men set out, "determined to slay every Indian they can find in that section of country."[42] The fact that the miners' meeting had voted against the expedition did not stop them from acting on their own authority.

Similarly, in April 1854, two Indians suspected of murder were given a jury trial at Columbus House and acquitted; but "then the mob dissatisfied with the decision caught & hung them."[43] Nowhere else do we see a mob kill men who were acquitted by Judge Lynch, but as these victims were Indians, the usual rules did not apply.

So there were at least three reasons for nonviolent men to keep their counsel: the ferocity of some of the men who wanted to kill Indians; the knowledge that they, the moderates, were in the minority and would be outvoted anyway; and the futility of meetings and criminal trials, which the Indian haters were free to ignore anyway.

No wonder that principled men chose passive resistance when called to join an expedition against a native group: Rosales, who feigned illness, but did contribute gunpowder for the cause; Parker, who refused to participate himself, but shared his earnings with the partner who did go; and Weston, who wrote that the majority of miners opposed an attack on Indians and refused to join in, but were afraid to confront the killers directly. Daniel B. Woods similarly reported that when a messenger asked the miners of Rattlesnake Creek to contribute men and guns for an expedition against Indians who had attacked them, that "[n]ot having any inclination to join in the fight, I remained at the camp."[44] This was evidently the best that Americans could do when confronted with genocide: stay home.

## Spanish Speakers

Ramón Gil Navarro recorded that "about 200 Americans made up an armed force and, as is custom among them, shamefully threw out all the Chileans, Peruvians, Mexicans, and anybody else who speaks Spanish. . . . There is no other tyranny or arbitrariness as great as that carried out by this nation of free and republican people."[45]

The extermination of the Indians was unique; the Americans did not try to wipe out other ethnicities or even carry out massacres of any note. But neither did they extend their principles of self-government, fairness, rule of law, majority rule, or property rights to these other groups; instead, they operated on the principle that might makes right, particularly with respect to possession of desirable mining claims. The main use of meetings here was to pass resolutions prohibiting Spanish speakers from holding claims, which meant they had to leave or work as hired labor. The miners used their law in other ways too. Americans who committed crimes against Mexicans were not prosecuted before Judge Lynch, and disputes between Americans and Spanish speakers came before the American alcalde, who always ruled against the foreigner. The foreign miners' tax was enacted by California's government, but citizens took it upon themselves to help enforce the rules. Overall, there was a veneer of legality that was missing from the treatment of Indians, but it was manipulated to serve American ends.

Excellent works exist about the gold rush experience of major ethnic groups, including Spanish speakers, the French, and Chinese miners, and many chapters could be devoted to how American self-government played out in relation to these populations. Here, I will focus on the American interaction with Spanish speakers, the largest and most successful foreign presence in California and the most frequent target of American hostility during the gold rush proper. In later years, the Chinese held that status, but immigration from China was relatively low before 1852.[46]

Spanish speakers were a diverse group. American accounts often fail to distinguish between them, calling them all Mexicans or Sonorans, which accounts in part for wildly different descriptions of their customs and habits.[47] The largest group was the actual Mexicans, most of whom were working-class men who came to California for the mining season but returned home for the winter.[48] Also included under the heading "Mexicans," however, were the Californios. These were Mexicans who lived in California before the Americans arrived, who had the right to become American citizens, and whose property was protected by the Treaty of Guadalupe-Hidalgo. Some had great wealth and political influence in the territory's formative years; they were the aristocrats who figured in the tales of Zorro—the rancheros and vaqueros who went to fandangos "dressed in the style of country gentlemen, black or green velvet jackets, richly embroidered; wide pantaloons, open at the sides, ornamented with rows of silver buttons; a red sash around their waists and a great profusion of gold filigree on their vests."[49] Californios, however, did not engage much in mining; there were better ways for men of wealth and connections to profit from the gold rush.

Very ignorant Americans lumped miners from Chile in with "Mexicans," while moderately ignorant miners used "Chileans" to refer to all South Americans because they sailed to America via Chile. Needless to say, there was great variety among the South American population in the mines. The actual Chileans included wealthy, educated young men and the laborers, or peons, they brought with them, as well as traders who imported Chilean goods and produce. The Chilean laborers caused particular resentment among Americans not because they disapproved of servitude as such, but because as employers they enjoyed advantage over independent American miners. Their use of peons would be used as an excuse to expel Chileans from the mines. Argentinians were a race apart. William Perkins, himself a Canadian with Argentinian friends and who later married an Argentinian, said of them, "These people are very reserved, mixing little with other Spaniards . . . They hold in contempt the Peruvians, Chileans and Mexicans, to all of whom, at least those we have here, they are in truth vastly superior."[50] Most Americans were oblivious to this superiority.

Two of these South Americans, Argentinian Ramón Gil Navarro and Chilean Vicente Pérez Rosales, wrote vivid accounts of their adventures. Unlike the Indians and Mexicans, whose personal thoughts and feelings are lost to us, these two South Americans did describe American harassment from the victims' point of view and flesh out the picture of American-Spanish relations. The young men turn out to be—surprise!—very similar to literate American diarists. Like American forty-niners, they had heard that California was a land of equality, where "it made no difference whether you were master or servant because in this land aristocrats and commoners were treated the same."[51]

The Americans did not hate the Spanish speakers as they hated the Indians. In the first year of the gold rush, members of the two cultures peacefully worked alongside each other; in later years, Americans were happy to employ Mexicans as miners or hire them to transport goods to the mines. There was, in fact, considerable praise of Mexicans—as workers. That did not preclude critique, however.

Some criticisms of Mexicans were trivial. A miner called Robert wrote to his wife about the ladies at a "Mexican" fandango at Sonora (they may in fact have been Californios): "[T]hey dress elegantly and waltz beautifully, but do not know much about cotillions."[52] Other grounds for complaint against Mexicans were more serious, though the tellers themselves did not recognize the implications. For instance, it was said they took too many cigarette breaks. Daniel B. Woods, who employed fifty Mexican workers, had to explain the novel concept to his readers. "Many times in the day," he wrote, "they will stop, take out a small, square piece of white paper, and putting upon it a small pinch of loose tobacco, roll it into a cigarito, and lighting it with a piece of punk or a match, smoke with apparent relish."[53] Giving Americans a taste for cigarettes may have been the Spanish speakers' ultimate revenge on their oppressors.

There was also, of course, deep prejudice and racism. Joseph Warren Wood conceded that his Mexican employee "knows his business well" but added that he was "a consumate hog & so are all of them . . . I have a worse opinion of Mexicans than I had before I had to do with them."[54]

One newspaper article made the case, chillingly, that all Mexicans had to be expelled because their presence itself would hamper California's progress. The author stressed that most Mexicans were descended from Native Mexicans, or Indians, as he called them; and he argued that America was able to become a great and prosperous nation only through the "complete annihilation of the Indian tribes" of the East Coast. In fact, he added, Mexico "might at present be the finest and best cultivated region of the American continent" if only it had exterminated its native population because the Spaniards who conquered Mexico in the sixteenth century were at least as sophisticated as the English of that time. Californians should take heed. Although "the measures of the American miners in driving the half Indian Mexicans and Chilians from the soil, may at first sight appear hard and difficult to justify, yet in the end it will doubtless prove conducive to the best interests of California," the author wrote.[55]

This lunatic point of view was not widely shared. Most Californians did not want to expel all the Mexicans; they just wanted them to stop mining. The real objections to Spanish speakers were that they were too many, occupied too much ground, and earned too much. It was galling to Americans like John Hovey to go "up the Gulch a prospecting to find a better place, but soon returned, as it was all taken up with Mexicans and Spaniards."[56]

The American population in the mines persecuted the Spanish speakers by two means: naked aggression in the form of robbery, harassment, attacks, and murder; and clothed aggression in the form of meetings and resolutions that gave legal cover for expelling Mexicans from the diggings. Moderate men should have been able to use those same meetings to counter the aggressors, and, in a few instances, they did manage to pass resolutions prohibiting attacks on foreigners or affirming the right of noncitizens to remain in the mines. In most diggings, however, the anti-Mexican element had the advantage of numbers and of passion.

## Spanish Speakers and the Miners' Courts

In conflicts between Spanish speakers and Americans, American law applied, and somehow it always favored the Anglophones. The American alcalde would not give the Mexicans justice. Rosales said of the alcalde in San Francisco that if an American and a Spanish speaker come before him, "his job is to declare the Spaniard guilty and make him pay the court costs."[57] The alcalde was chosen by the Americans, of course, and therefore likely to take their side against foreigners. Charles De Lambertie, a Frenchman who had a lot to say about how the Americans abused law to deprive foreigners of their claims, experienced the problem firsthand. Some Americans just start working on his claim, De Lambertie writes. He protests, but they ignore him, so he complains to the collector of the foreign miners' tax, who tells him to wait for the alcalde. When the alcalde arrives, he wants to hear from the collector. After a three-hour wait, the collector appears. The collector has a sudden lapse of memory: he says it is De Lambertie's claim, he *thinks* so, anyway, but he can't quite remember. The alcalde eventually assigns De Lambertie only part of his claim. What annoyed De Lambertie most was that the other Americans were standing around laughing like imbeciles, and no one stood up for him.[58] These Americans, at any rate, did not care to protect the foreigners' property rights.

The criminal law discriminated against Mexicans too, but in its own peculiar way. Mexicans were less likely than Americans to come before Judge Lynch, who was regarded as harsh but fair. Those who killed Americans were often killed by the mob without any trial at all. Americans who killed Mexicans, on the other hand, were tried in state court, the miners' equivalent of getting off lightly. Or, according to Argentinian Ramón Gil Navarro, if a man who killed a Chilean was arrested, "a jury of his friends was formed, and he was promptly declared not guilty." Gil Navarro wrote that he himself had seen this "in the case of a man named James Wilson who had murdered Benegas, a Chilean, along with a Mexican from Sonora." This was presumably a trial by Judge Lynch.[59]

When Mexicans were accused of killing an American or Americans, they were more likely to be killed by the mob than an American suspect was.[60] For example, two Mexicans murdered their employer, Captain George W. Snow, and then fled. They were arrested in Sonora, but "so great was the excitement amongst the people, that an immediate determination was made to hang them, not waiting for the action of the law." The crowd brought the accused back to Shaw's Flat, the scene of the crime, and strung them up.[61] I count eight such incidents in which a Mexican was hanged without a trial, representing about a quarter of the punishments meted out to Spanish speakers in my admittedly incomplete collection of cases. In contrast, when Americans were threatened with summary justice, law-abiding types usually persuaded the mob to allow a quick trial for form's sake; indeed, men of conscience went to desperate lengths to wring this concession from a furious crowd. Where were these men when the mob was about to hang a Mexican? Perhaps they felt less strongly about due procedure for Spanish speakers, or perhaps they believed the mob was less open to persuasion when it was bent on hanging one of them.[62]

A Mexican accused of a crime against another Mexican, in contrast, was more likely to be arrested than lynched. Of the hundreds of criminal cases that I have collected, Mexicans were the *victims* in about ten. In six of these, the accused was also Mexican and was arrested for trial by the district court. The circumstances of each case were different, of course, but it seems that Americans cared less about Mexican-on-Mexican crime than about crimes against Americans. They were willing to hand over the suspect to the authorities even though that meant he might escape or be acquitted. From the Mexican point of view, this was a good thing: a Mexican accused of killing a Mexican was less likely to receive a lynch trial than an American who killed another American.

But the record contains relatively few crimes either by or against Mexicans, and this is a puzzle. Mexican-on-Mexican crime was probably settled within the Spanish-speaking community; that would account for the small number of such incidents that came before either Judge Lynch or real judges. There are hardly any cases of Mexicans killing English speakers, though there were a few lynch trials of Mexicans charged with theft.[63] What was most dangerous to Mexicans was that Americans could kill them without repercussions, and that was the reason that most such incidents went unrecorded.

Americans could throw Spanish speakers off their claims without fear, although they could never get away with doing the same to Americans. Ramón Gil Navarro wrote that "[a] Yankee would invade the claim of a Sonoran with his revolver in hand . . . put his pistol to his head and order him off."[64] There are almost no firsthand accounts of this—it was not something that decent men wrote home about—but John Hovey did describe one incident:

> This morning commenced on our new Clame we had not got it fairly clear'd of[f] before two Mexecans came up and clamed our ground they tryed to make a great fuss, but we told them to vamos that they had no business here no how and if they did not keep still and Clear out, drawing our revolvers, we should put them through, they were terrible frightened and clear[e]d out, we than sunk our hole down and here'd no more from them.[65]

It is almost as though Hovey did not recognize a Mexican's possible interest in the claim as a matter of principle. And after all that, the claim turned out to be a bad one, and the Americans abandoned it.

If an American murdered a Spanish speaker, as undoubtedly happened, that, too, was unworthy of note. Dame Shirley said that the

gamblers and rowdies at Indian Bar "commit the most glaring injustice against the Spaniards" but "it is generally passed unnoticed."[66] I
do not know of any American who was punished for killing a Mexican
or Chilean; indeed, in the only two cases where such a murder is even
mentioned, the sympathies were all on the side of the killer. One of the
injustices that Dame Shirley had in mind was the reaction to a Spaniard
who respectfully asked an American to pay him a few dollars that the
latter owed him: he "received for answer several inches of cold steel in
his breast."[67] Nothing was done about it. Heaven forbid the friends of
a Spanish-speaking victim should think of punishing the perpetrator
themselves. In a letter to his brother on April 20, 1851, David Ferson
wrote with some relish:

> som of the mericans kild too or three of the mexican and
> that mad than mad so tha went and took the mericans and
> was agonto hang than but tha got a little taken in about that
> tim thar was for or five houndred americans collected thar
> and went at the mexicans and tak ther guns and pistols and
> kifes from them and shot some five or six of those and drove
> the rest of tham of out of the plase.[68]

The Americans punished Mexican murderers, but not their countrymen
who murdered Mexicans.

What were responsible Americans to do in the face of predations by
the likes of John Hovey and the rowdies of Indian Bar? They did once
use the tools of meetings and resolutions. The miners of Rodger's Bar
on the Tuolumne River passed a set of resolutions on August 9, 1850,
warning people who attacked Mexicans under the pretext of defending
themselves or enforcing the law. "Many persons of Spanish origin,
against whom there had not been a word of complaint, have been murdered by these ruffians," we read in the preamble, while "[o]thers have
been robbed of their horses, mules, arms, and even money, by these persons, while acting as they pretended under the authority of law." The
resolutions go on to condemn this brutality, stating that the miners of
Rodger's Bar voted unanimously "[t]hat the citizens of this Bar will dis-
countenance any act of violence committed against peaceable persons

of any race living or traveling in this community, and will use every means in their power to bring all men guilty of offences against such persons, to speedy punishment" and "[t]hat we will suffer no person who may be associated with these American guerrillas, to remain on this Bar." The term *guerrillas* expressed strong disapproval, of course; but it also likened the rogue Americans to Mexican bandits, for whom the title guerilla was generally reserved.[69]

These resolutions were highly unusual; I have not found anything else comparable, so it appears that Americans elsewhere attacked, murdered, and robbed Mexicans with impunity. This was more dangerous to Spanish speakers, and more shocking, than lynch trials, at least in the period from 1848 to 1852, when few Mexicans came before Judge Lynch and when lynch trials were relatively orderly—with emphasis on *relatively*.

In sum, Spanish speakers did not enjoy the benefits of American miners' law: they could not seek redress against Americans who took their property or cheated them in transactions, and they did not benefit from the so-called protections of lynch law, as crazy as that sounds. But all of this was secondary to the mass ejections of Spanish-speaking miners from the diggings, first by resolutions passed at miners' meetings and later by California state legislation that imposed a severe foreign miners' tax.

## Resolutions to Expel Spanish-Speaking Miners

Americans began expelling Spanish speakers from the mines in the late spring of 1849, which is surprisingly early because Americans had only just begun to arrive from the East and the supply of gold was believed to be almost infinite. The *Placer Times* of July 21, 1849, could already report that "Peruvians and Chileans have been pretty thoroughly routed in every section of the Middle and North Forks, and the disposition to expel them seems to be extending throughout the whole mining community."[70] Naturally, expulsions began with meetings to pass resolutions to prohibit "foreigners" from mining. The decrees did not specify Spanish speakers, but there was no doubt that these were the ones targeted. As Ryan recorded, "there was a wide distinction made between the Europeans generally, and persons tinctured with Spanish blood," due, he said, to lingering animosity from the recent war with Mexico.[71] The miners gave several reasons for expelling Spanish speakers. Two of the main ones were, first, that, unlike other immigrants, the Mexicans did not intend to become citizens; and second, that they were allegedly responsible for the alarming increase in crime in the mines.

Why did they need to invent any reason for prohibiting non-Americans from holding a share of America's gold mines? It was partly because they cared about the opinion of other Americans, some of whom opposed the expulsions; but also, oddly, it was because they themselves believed in America as a land that welcomed immigrants. The tension was acknowledged by Governor John Bigler in a message to the Senate and Assembly of the State of California on April 23, 1852, although he was speaking of the Chinese who had by then become the main target of American hostility. "[W]e have thrown open our ports and the bosom of our far-famed America as an asylum to the oppressed of all nations," he said, "that they may, by our naturalization laws, reap the rewards of our institutions, and bask in the sunshine of 'eternal liberty.'"[72] But, he argued, the Chinese were different: they were not Christian and therefore could not swear the oath required for testimony in the law courts. He did not wish for any change in America's generous immigration policy in so far "as it affects Europeans or others capable of becoming citizens under our laws," but the Chinese could not assume the duties and privileges of citizenship.

Two weeks later, the miners of Little York district assembled to hear the governor's message read and passed a mining code that excluded foreigners generally. They quoted the passage about basking in the sunshine of "eternal liberty," but, they added, the first law of nature is self-preservation. Therefore, "Resolved, that no foreigners shall hold mining claims in this district"; but it was also resolved that anyone who declared an intention to become a citizen would have the same rights as current citizens.[73]

So let the Spanish speakers become citizens, one might think. Chilean Vicente Pérez Rosales wrote that this idea did occur to some well-intentioned Americans, who proposed that their Chilean friends become full US citizens with all the advantages thereof; and, besides, the process was cheap—only ten dollars. But even documentary evidence of citizenship would not protect Spanish speakers from all hostile American miners. "[T]his safe conduct was only halfway effective: it worked only where it was accepted," Rosales noted. "In other places it was treated as a joke."[74] Chileans remained foreigners in American eyes.

Moreover, even actual bona fide American citizens of Mexican descent were harassed. Under the terms of the Treaty of Guadalupe-Hidalgo, Mexican citizens then living in California, that is, Californios, could choose Mexican or American citizenship; and if they failed to choose, they automatically became American citizens one year after the treaty was signed. They also had the right to remain in the state, whether or not they took American citizenship, so there was no question at all about their right to mine. Yet Bayard Taylor wrote that miners on the Mokelumne expelled all foreigners, including Spanish-speaking Californians and that "Don Andres Pico, who was located on the same river, had some difficulty with them until they could be made to understand that his right as a citizen was equal to theirs."[75] Ryan similarly said that he had heard many Spanish-speaking Californians say "that they had been deterred from going to the mines by the apprehension that they would be mistaken for Chileans, and their lives and property sacrificed."[76] In short, the argument that Spanish speakers should leave because they were not willing to become citizens was bogus, as anyone could have guessed.

The other main justification for ejecting Spanish-speaking miners from their claims—namely, that they were responsible for the spike in crime—was equally unpersuasive. Horrific murders were definitely being committed; the newspapers reported an endless stream of highway murders (at least forty) of the kind described by German miner Friedrich Gerstäcker: "In all sorts of places, as also in their own tents, diggers were found in the morning killed with their short crow-bars, which were lying about. . . . Others were attacked and murdered on the high roads, or from behind bushes, without the murderers being detected in one single instance."[77] The preamble to resolutions to expel foreigners from Sonora in July 1850 accordingly stated that Americans had to take drastic measures because they were "in danger from the bands of lawless marauders of every clime, class and creed . . . and scarcely a day passes but we hear of the commission of the most horrible murders and robberies." Therefore, it was resolved that "all foreigners in Tuolumne county (except persons engaged in permanent business and of respectable character) be required to leave."[78] They were given fifteen days to get out.

The great weakness of this justification—or rationalization—is the lack of evidence that foreigners committed more crimes than anyone else. In fact, given the size of the Mexican population in California—second only to Americans—the number of reported murders by Mexicans was small, suggesting that they were less homicidal than average. Moreover, there were no grounds for attributing the unsolved murders to Spanish speakers; the criminals who killed miners in their beds or on empty stretches of road left no trace of their identity. Friedrich Gerstäcker wrote that some Mexicans were put on trial, but "there was not the least thing brought home to them."[79] Judge Lynch had the wrong men. Furthermore, if crime had been the Americans' real objection, they would have ejected the Mexicans from the mining region, whereas the decrees usually prohibited them from holding claims but allowed them to stay in the area.[80] Finally, prohibiting them from mining could only induce them to commit crime. Gerstäcker indeed believed that "[m]any of these hotblooded sons of the south were, by the unmerited ill-treatment of brutal Yankees, goaded into . . . a pitch of despair and revengefulness" and became bandits.[81]

On the other hand, there is persuasive evidence that the miners' motives for expelling Spanish speakers were greed and envy. William Redmond Ryan put it delicately when he wrote, "The influx of strangers created great discontent . . . as the enormous increase of the population interfered everywhere with the interests of the Americans."[82] The *Alta California* was more direct: the main reason for "this antipathy and prejudice" was "the superior and uniform success of these Mexicans among the gold hills of California."[83] Seeing allegedly inferior people mining in your country and doing it better than yourself was irritating. The resolutions citing crime as the reason for the expulsions were pretexts: Gerstäcker states, plausibly, that the Americans wanted to "make the affair an American cause and, at the same time, protect the individuals from the revenge of those who were to be deprived of their lots."[84] They were closing ranks and wrapping themselves in the flag.

When the Spanish-speaking miners were ordered to leave, they sometimes waited to see what the Americans did next. Gerstäcker—again, because he is one of the few foreigners to describe these episodes—wrote that the zeal to rid Carson's Creek of foreigners fizzled out. Placards announcing the order were posted, but nothing happened. About fifty "easily frightened" Mexicans packed up and left. "All the other foreigners quietly remained where they were; and the committee, expressly appointed last evening for the carrying out of the law, were wise enough not to notice it."[85] The same thing happened at diggings called the Pines early in 1849: Antonio Franco Coronel said that notices went up and the foreigners prepared to defend themselves, but after a standoff of three or four days, "everything calmed down and we returned to our work." Coronel qualified this anticlimax with the following: "[A]lthough daily some of the weak were despoiled of their claims by the stronger."[86]

Plenty of other diggings did force the Mexicans to go, however. In a letter of July 1849, miner G. B. Stevens wrote, "The Chileans are coming in from the mines daily. Our people are driving them out—also the Sandwich Islanders."[87] Stevens added that two Chileans had been shot recently: "A party of them had been ordered off the grounds, two hours were given them to leave; they declined going, were fired into & two of them killed."[88] So, unless they were ready for an all-out war with the Americans, the Spanish speakers had no choice but to obey. Some "made no resistance, but quietly backed out and took refuge in other diggings."[89]

## American Aggressors and American Peacemakers

The actors in all these accounts are "the Americans" and "the Mexicans," although we know that every individual experienced events differently: there were leaders, followers, and objectors. In the case of the Indians, it seemed that the leaders of the massacres, at any rate, included a high proportion of Oregonians and Missourians; and while the kind of men who wrote letters home to Mother deplored the whole business, they were not able or motivated enough to try to stop it. The Mexicans were different. The Americans used a kind of law to get rid of them: they held meetings, elected chairmen, drafted resolutions, and, most importantly, adopted them by majority vote. Majority vote means that most Americans present were in favor of ejecting the Mexicans. This again raises the question of who pushed for expulsion and what could good men do to sway their angrier fellow Americans.

Several sources described the leaders of the expulsion movement in general terms, though they differed radically on which groups were involved. Miner William Ryan wrote that in 1849, it was "the Oregon men, and some of the Yankees" who were determined to drive out the foreigners.[90] In 1850, the *Alta California* blamed "characters from the convict colonies, and other quarters, whose purpose was robbing and plunder so soon as the Mexicans were disarmed"; but in 1851, the same paper suggested that it was an "almost distinct species of Americans, coarse, ignorant, self-willed and unscrupulous, that have provoked disturbance, and bred disorder frequently, among the foreign laboring classes of California—among the Mexican miners, particularly."[91] There were Americans in California, the *Alta* said, who left honor and decency behind and who "robbed their countrymen and accused the Mexicans of the crime."[92] Meanwhile, the *Stockton Times* stated "that the principal enemies of the Mexicans is the foreign population in the mines."[93] The only point that these theories had in common was that the average American was not to blame for the hostility, which suggests that the writers either wanted to assign responsibility to some disreputable subgroup rather than Americans generally, or, in the case of the newspapers, to make miners feel like rowdies if they supported the resolutions to eject Mexicans from the mines.

As for good men, they were usually conspicuous for their absence. The resolutions of the miners' meeting in Nevada County, prohibiting foreigners from holding claims in that district, were "unanimously adopted."[94] But there are several reports of dissent at other meetings, as best recorded by the Frenchman Charles De Lambertie, who described the process with the eyes of an outsider. In fact, he did not speak English, so someone else had to act as his ears. De Lambertie wrote that the foreigners bothered the Americans, so one evening they deliberated under a tree whether "to chase us out or to let us stay on the Mokelumne."[95] They decided to give the foreigners eight days to leave and posted notices to that effect on many trees. "Has there ever been anything more ridiculous and more illegal?" De Lambertie wrote. The government had decided that foreigners could work in the mines so long as they paid a tax, and here a handful of selfish men had the audacity to consider whether they should be chased out. But it transpired that many of the Americans had been absent from the meeting and opposed the measure. They held a new meeting just like the first, De Lambertie said, and he heard them and saw them talking and gesticulating. Finally, the president said, "All right! Those who want to expel them go to the left, and those who want them to stay move to the right." Almost everyone turned to the right, to the great disappointment of the anti-Mexican group, and that was that.

De Lambertie's account offers two new insights. First, the French and Mexicans thought it was ridiculous that the Americans presumed to make law, especially law that affected them. The Americans felt that meetings legitimized their decision to expel foreigners even though this violated state and federal law, but—as they should have known—the foreigners found the idea laughable. The second point is that the Americans on the Mokelumne who wanted to expel Spanish speakers were in the minority and held a private meeting to achieve their ends—as though a miners' meeting legitimizes an illegal action even if it is held in the dead of night or privately among friends.

This Mokelumne incident represented the moderates' most effective intervention on behalf of Mexican miners, but there were others.[96] The *Sacramento Transcript* of August 10, 1850, reported with approval that "[t]he inhabitants of Georgetown have taken a position directly opposed to that assumed by the town of Sonora." They "unanimously adopted" the following resolutions:

1. Resolved, That all men shall have permission to live in this camp, without being in any way molested.

2. Resolved, That the civil law shall be sustained, and that all those under the civil law shall be supported.

3. Resolved, That two hundred and fifty copies of these resolutions be printed in English and Spanish, and distributed through the various diggings.[97]

Georgetown was in the northeast area of the gold region and may not have had many Mexican miners, but it was signaling its opinion to the other diggings. The meetings and resolutions were published by the newspapers and Georgetown held up as an example of good sense in a time of shameful xenophobia.[98]

Friedrich Gerstäcker, like De Lambertie, provided a glimpse of the discussion at such meetings, fleshing out the formal preambles and resolutions of American reports. The miners of a rich diggings had decided to evict the Spanish speakers and were hammering out the details. Someone moved that the Mexicans should be given twenty minutes to get out. "This mad resolution did not certainly pass, owing to some of the more sensible Americans—of whom there seemed, however, but a few to have been present that evening—having objected against it; that indeed they had no power whatever to enforce such a law; and that they would only make themselves ridiculous if afterwards it were not obeyed."[99] So there were some Americans who were more moderately disposed—too few to change the course of the meeting, but ready to put in a word when the proposals went completely off the rails. Ultimately, however, they could not prevent the end result, though they did manage to extend the deadline for departure to twenty-four hours.[100]

The one group who regularly stood up for Mexican miners was the commercial men. In an article, "The Alta California and the Sonorian Troubles," that newspaper wrote that "[e]very merchant and trader is diametrically opposed to the recent movement, and each, heart and soul condemn, the narrow minded, narrow souled views of the anti-foreigner party."[101] The *Alta* bolstered its appeal to Californians' better natures with an argument that Mexicans were good for the economy because they did the kind of work that Americans did not want to do, such as working for four to eight dollars per day in the dry diggings. They developed California's resources without putting Americans out of work. At a meeting at Sutter's Mill, merchants and traders spoke out against expulsions. The miners, however, were not sympathetic to the merchants' plight or the economy generally; they voted the Mexicans out.[102]

## Foreign Miners' Tax

In the same summer that miners were expelling Spanish speakers on their own authority, those foreigners were also leaving the diggings of their own accord because they could not or would not pay the new foreign miners' tax. The state legislature enacted "An Act for the Better Regulation of the Mines" that required all noncitizens to hold a license to mine at a cost of twenty dollars per month, beginning May 13, 1850.[103] Actual enforcement began in the various diggings as the tax collectors reached them; in Columbia, it was June 1, 1850.[104] The alleged reason for the tax was to raise revenue, and it targeted foreigners because they enjoyed the privileges and protections of living in California without the duties that came with citizenship.[105] There is ample room for doubt about whether this was the true reason for the tax. First of all, citizens had no particular duties except serving as jurors, and few miners did even this. Secondly, legislators revealed their anti-Mexican position in debates on other topics.[106]

Most importantly, however, the *effect* of the tax was that the Mexicans and Chinese were unable to continue as independent miners and either had to leave the diggings or become wage laborers. This effect was so dramatic that the legislatures should have predicted it and probably did so. The *Alta California* wrote, "[i]f the exorbitant tax of twenty dollars per month on all foreign miners was intended to drive this population out of the mines, the end of the law is about being accomplished, they are leaving by the hundreds, and since the Sonora meeting, are no doubt going by thousands."[107] By June 1, a little over two weeks after the law went into effect, the merchants of Stockton were already suffering from loss of custom because so many Spanish speakers had left the mines. "[N]early every merchant in Stockton, there being but one dissentient," signed a petition to Governor Burnett stating that the effect of the tax "has been to stop the labor of thousands of miners" because "vast numbers of the foreign miners are unable to pay it."[108] The businessmen asked the governor to call an extra session of the legislature to lower the tax to five dollars. That did not happen, but in the next regular session, which began on January 6, 1851, the tax was repealed, to the *Alta California*'s great satisfaction. "It was a very unfortunate enactment," the newspaper said, "violative of private rights, constitutional guarantees, our national policy, considerations of expediency, and the professions which we have made to the struggling and oppressed world, for more than half a century."[109]

The tax was reintroduced more than a year later, on May 4, 1852, at a more sustainable three dollars per month.[110] Meanwhile, some Americans took advantage of the tax to defraud Spanish speakers. "Evil disposed Americans, without authority, are taking the arms away from Mexicans, and levying contributions upon them," the *Daily Alta California* wrote in August 1850. "They represent themselves as tax gatherers."[111] Citizens were always ready to come to the aid of the real tax collector too, if the Mexicans gave him any trouble, without enquiring much into the rights and wrongs of the matter. In September 1850, the tax collector went to call on thirty to forty Mexicans camped at Savage's Diggings on the Merced River. On his way there, he met the group en route to Stockton. Although they were not mining at the time and may even have been leaving the country, the collector tried to stop them, at which point the Mexicans seized him, tied him to a tree, and continued their journey at double speed. They were also carrying knives, which was forbidden to Mexicans if they crossed a river, as they presumably had done or planned to do. "[T]hen the miners were on a hunt," wrote John Hovey, always hostile to Mexicans; "finely they overtook them with their rifles and shot down three of them, and wonded one, and the rest ecaped in to the woods were nobody could find them, and luckily for them for if taken they would have been hung."[112]

In fact, Americans felt entitled to enforce or abuse any rule against Mexicans. A supposedly humorous poem, "The Great Greaser Extermination Meeting," which mocked the resolution to eject foreigners from Sonora, included the following awful rhyme:

> The gentry from Sydney, they laughed in their sleeves;
> And the pickpockets loudly applauded it;
> For they knew there would be a fine harvest for thieves,
> And none could complain—because law did it.[113]

In short, the Mexicans were constantly in violation of one or more of the rules passed against them and in danger of being "punished" by any American or, evidently, Australian.

The Spanish speakers' response to the attempts to drive them from the mines, both by force and through the foreign miners' tax, was to appeal to state officials. The *Alta California* published a letter from Sonora by "Leo," the pen name of William Perkins, future brother-in-law of Ramón Gil Navarro.[114] Perkins reported that on May 19, 1850—six days after the tax went into effect—"large bodies of Mexicans, Chileans, and Frenchmen . . . assembled outside the town, holding meetings and consulting on means to evade the payment of the imposition of $20 per month."[115] "Evade" was poorly chosen; Perkins went on to say that what the foreigners actually did was request a meeting with officials to explain that many miners were unable to pay such a high fee and to "ascertain if any action of the Governor could arrest the consummation of the contemplated taxation: or at least, to have it explained to them, and the justice of it shown to them."[116] Nothing came of this, and, in any case, there was nothing local authorities could do.

In this same letter, Perkins wrote that the foreigners addressed a petition to Governor Peter H. Burnett, translated from the Spanish. It read, in part, "Without assuming any tone other than that of the deepest respect for the government under which we live and are protected, we beg humbly to suggest to your excellency that a larger state income could be raised, and that too, without causing the slightest dissatisfaction, by the imposition of four or five dollars per month, instead of the large sum of twenty."[117] It was at least the second such petition to reach the governor's desk. The first, dated May 1, 1850, was provoked by American attempts to expel the miners of Jesus Maria on the Calaveras. "We your humble petitioners being Chileans, Sonorinos and other Mexicans," they wrote, "and now being threatened to be driven off from our present encampment not wishing to resist the Americans or do any act contrary to the laws of your nation humbly beg your protection, and should it be contrary to your laws that we work in the mines, we will peaceably retire, but if it is lawful for us to remain and work in the mines, we earnestly beg your speedy intercession."[118] The petition was signed, "Yours with much respect."

Perversely, the Americans were enraged by these appeals. "Persistingly [*sic*] as our people in the mines believe the enactments of our State Legislature, regarding the taxation of labor, unjust, severe, and productive of the greatest evil," the *Daily Alta California* reported,

they nevertheless "frown[ed] indignantly down [*sic*] any and every attempt on the part of aliens to incite opposition to its laws, or impede,
by a show of resistance, its early political prosperity."[119] Considering the
American miners' own willingness to ignore the laws and state officials
by expelling foreigners, taking prisoners from the sheriff and trying
them before Judge Lynch, and massacring Indians, to name just a few
examples, this anger over a petition to the governor is inexplicable.

## Iowa Log Cabins Incident

The American attempts to eject Spanish speakers en masse highlighted
the differences between the legal attitudes of the two groups. The
Americans believed that law derived from the people and that even the
smallest community could make its own laws. They had no faith at all in
the state's courts, judges, sheriffs. In matters like ejecting foreigners,
they did not care whether they violated state or federal law or not, just
as in criminal matters they were ready to seize suspects from the authorities and try them before the court of the people. To Chileans and
Mexicans, meanwhile, state officials represented the law. They would
have submitted to the decisions of a proper alcalde, but they ridiculed
the American version of this officer—elected on the spot, deposed at
will, and biased in his decisions. Whether or not they thought that their
appeals to the governor would do any good, they did believe that he
could command an end to the American attacks.

The clash between Chileans and Americans at Chili Gulch, and Iowa
Log Cabins on the North Fork of the Calaveras near Mokeumne Hill,
in December 1849, illustrated many of the preceding points, including
the Americans' use of meetings and "law" to take foreigners' claims. Remarkably, it was described in detail by two of the American participants
(John Hovey, the man who also recorded that he threw two Mexicans
off their claim at gunpoint; and Ayers, in a document written forty years
after the event)[120] and also by the Chilean Ramón Gil Navarro.[121] Problems began when several Americans started digging in Chili Gulch,
though Hovey claimed that they had merely been "prospecting" near
the Chilean diggings. The Chileans chased them away; according to
Hovey, they also threatened the Americans with guns and then smashed

their mining equipment. When the news reached the American camps at Iowa Log Cabins, "[t]he cry of the people was, "call a meeting, elect an Alcalde, and drive the foreigners off!"[122]

It was typical of Americans that, roused to avenge an affront to their honor, they began with calling for a meeting and an election. But the miners at Iowa Log Cabins were keen to do everything by the book, as they understood it. They enacted a full mining code with twelve articles, five of which created unremarkable rules regarding claim size and notice and water usage. The other seven, however, were aimed straight at the miners of Chili Gulch. The first resolution was, in fact, "that no foreigners shall be permitted to work at these mines after the 10th day of December," that is, the next day; the second, that Americans working for themselves were entitled to thirty feet of ground; and the third, that no individual could hold more than one claim. The Chileans had taken claims in the name of their peons, which this rule made illegal. Other resolutions included a unique provision that the miners would elect a "Judge to preside over trials, and that he shall give a trial by Jury," creating a legal-looking way to enforce the clause against foreigners, and one authorizing the judge to call out miners to execute the provisions of the code. The miners elected L. A. Collier, a former steamboat captain, to be their judge.[123]

Hovey explained why, in the heat of the moment, the miners paused to enact a full mining code, including not only prohibitions on foreign miners but also mundane mining rules—namely, because he thought that he and his confreres "might possibly be charged with an ungovernable spirit of revenge by some, if I did not, . . . by publishing the entire business of the meeting, prove that our countrymen felt that they should have laws & officers to govern their conduct." And yet he also wrote, with no apparent cognitive dissonance, that the president's first words on taking the chair at the meeting were "that in his opinion, the foreigners, and especially these d-d copper hides, every s-n of a b-h of 'em, should be driven from our diggings."[124]

Evidently Hovey believed that throwing out the Chileans was justified and even lawful, provided that the miners first passed suitable rules. But this was not true; the miners had no authority to exclude foreign miners. Commenting on similar resolutions passed at Sonora in July 1850, the *Alta California* wrote, "The law is virtually set aside by the people, and their own regulations substituted as the criminal code of the country."[125] This was exactly right: the miners of Iowa Log Cabins were creating law for the purpose of taking the Chilean's rich claims. It is another example of the American idea that a popular vote made anything legal, even when it conflicted with state law.

## Spanish Speakers after the Great Exodus

Many thousands of Spanish speakers left the mines in summer of 1850 because of the expulsions and the foreign miners' tax. Some stayed on, moving to remote locations where the tax collector was unlikely to visit or working for those who held permits; others came back after the tax was repealed on March 14, 1851. "It is said that there are eight thousand Sonorians at Los Angeles about to migrate into the Southern mines," the *Alta California* reported on March 21, 1851, an implausibly high number, given that they would have been ready to go before the legislature had voted on the tax.[126] But California remained inhospitable to Spanish speakers: Americans continued to drive them off desirable claims and various diggings and passed further resolutions prohibiting them from holding claims.[127]

While the extortionate tax was in effect, many Mexicans switched from mining for themselves to working for others. Americans had no objection to having them in the country so long as they did not hold claims in their own name; in fact, the abundance of cheap labor was very useful. Bayard Taylor wrote that after Mexicans were driven from the Mokelumne River, they quietly returned and most of them worked for some American. He added that they "labor steadily and faithfully, and are considered honest, if well watched."[128] The river turning company to which Daniel B. Woods belonged hired fifty Mexicans to mine the riverbed once it had been uncovered—work that had to happen quickly before the fall floods washed away the dams. "The heavy tax upon foreigners has driven them too seek employment from companies," he wrote, and [t]hey may be hired at $4 and $6 a day."[129] It was in this context that Woods described the Mexican habit of stopping what they were doing to smoke a cigarette. He seemed unaware or indifferent to the fact that his company was profiting from an injustice committed by his countrymen.

The equality and spontaneous order among Americans in the California gold rush was typical of gold rushes around the world; and the tension between ethnic groups is common, if not universal. But in their hostility and violence toward Indians, Spanish speakers, Hawaiians, and Chinese, Americans were exceptional and possibly unique. It was, as Josiah Royce wrote, "a disgrace to our people."

# CHAPTER 12

# Outside Capital and the
# End of the Gold Rush

Astute observers had predicted from the beginning that when miners finally gave up hope of big money, outside capital could begin to invest in the mines. Thomas Hart Benton had looked forward to that day from the beginning of the gold rush. In January 1849, he had recommended that the government not issue licenses to miners or in any way try to profit from the gold rush. The sooner the surface gold was exhausted, the better, he said. "I care not who digs it up I want it dug up," Benton said. "I want the fever to be over. I want the mining finished. . . . Then the sober industry will begin which enriches and ennobles a nation."[1]

Indeed, as placer mining became less and less profitable, wages came down, towns acquired settled populations, and innovators developed technology for processing huge volumes of mineral ground at small cost. Hydraulic mining captured gold by using powerful jets of water to dissolve the ground and wash it down into a ribbed channel, making even very poor ground pay for its investors. Quartz mining, too, recovered from its false start thanks to heavy machinery and expertise, brought by Cornish miners. At this point, the gold rush was definitely over. As historian Maureen Jung put it, "During the 1850s, California mining was quickly transformed from individual adventure to an industry organized by corporations and worked by wage laborers."[2]

Before that, however, there was a period when independent miners could not work without water supplied by water companies. Gold mining had always required water, so much so that mining was often called gold washing, but in the first two years, miners rarely required an artificial supply. At first, miners swished their pans in the stream itself, and then, when they adopted cradles, they added water by hand while rocking the machine. During this stage of the gold rush, the men worked along rivers or piled up dirt in the dry diggings and waited for the rains to fill small gulches and streams nearby.

By the spring of 1850, running water was used for new, more efficient methods of processing, namely, the long tom and the sluice. The tom was a long box into which the miners turned a stream of water; the sluice was a series of boxes attached end to end. The running water washed down the conduit, where riffles nailed along the bottom trapped the gold while the lighter gravel was carried off by the flow.[3] It was estimated that the long tom reduced the cost of washing dirt by 75 percent as compared to a rocker, even when the price of water was taken into account, amply justifying the investment of digging a ditch to deliver water.[4]

Moreover, the miners had discovered that although the gold was especially accessible near flowing water, it was not confined to those areas. In fact, there was more gold in "them thar hills" than there had ever been in the gulches, but most of it was in low concentrations, distributed equally throughout much larger volumes of dirt and rocks. This had its advantages and disadvantages. The chance of a big find was less—almost zero, in fact—but steady labor yielded a steady return, so long as there was water.

Although dependence on water companies was the first step in the miners' loss of autonomy, it was not predetermined that the miners *would* become dependent in this way. Indeed, the miners did everything in their power to prevent it as much as possible, using all of the organizational tools that they had perfected over the preceding years. They passed rules that favored individual miners over companies; formed joint-stock companies to compete with those owned by capital; organized strikes; and, in a few cases, destroyed company property. And, in the miner-owned Stanislaus Water Company, they very nearly fulfilled their vision of a joint-stock water company, built and owned by working miners, that charged a fair price for its product. When that project failed, the second marvel of the gold rush, namely, the dominance of labor over capital, ended with it.

## Early Diversions: Local and Small Scale

The first water companies were small and locally owned; the main issue was whether they were legally obliged to leave enough water in its natural course so that the mining along the streambed could continue. The conflicts were addressed, if not resolved, by combinations of state courts, miners' meetings, and violence, just like the problems raised by river turning. It was later, when the water had to be transported for fifty of miles or more from rivers high in the mountains, that investors took control of the water companies. At that point, the problem was not one of conflicting rights, that is, riparian versus prior appropriation, but of "monster monopolies" squeezing the maximum profit from hardworking miners. I return to this below.

Miners initially dug ditches to bring water to their own claims a few hundred yards from the stream. The first such ditch was said to have been at Yankee Jim's in Placer County in 1850.[5] The first commercial ditch, in the sense that the owners rented out long toms and water, was operational in March 1850 and brought water one and a half miles to Coyote Hill near Nevada City.[6] In the course of 1850, ditches grew longer to service claims further and further from the streams and rivers.

"I wish that you could see this ditch," wrote Dame Shirley, describing a channel a foot wide, a foot deep, and three miles long. "I never beheld a *natural* streamlet more exquisitely beautiful. It undulates over the mossy roots and the gray old rocks like a capricious snake, singing all the time a low song with the liquidest murmur."[7] Even such pretty ditches required a big investment, however, and could potentially generate huge profits. Dame Shirley's "sparkling thing" had cost $5,000 to build. The owners planned to recoup their investment by selling the water over and over. They charged the first user 10 percent of their earnings. The same water then went to other groups for 7 percent; and finally, if there were any takers, to third parties for 4 percent.

Creating these commercial ditches and flumes required organization and cooperation—which was the miners' métier. The early water
companies, like river turning companies, took the form of joint-stock
companies of miners who sought to supply their own claims and also
to make money by selling water to others. In July 1851, for example, the
*Sacramento Daily Union* reported:

> A company of ten men have been formed for the purpose of
> turning the water of Dry Creek on to Long Bar, for the pur-
> pose of sluice washing. The ditch is between three and four
> miles in length; one-third of it has been already dug. This
> work completed, the miners will be enabled to sluice wash
> the large flat back of the river on Long Bar.[8]

In October 1851, companies of miners were at work in every direction, conducting water from the rivers to the dry diggings. Anyone
could join one of these "young companies," said Frank Marryat, "for
by taking your coat off and helping to cut the ditch, you could in six
months work yourself into a very respectable stockholder."[9] The companies were doing well, selling water at about forty-five cents per day.

Water was becoming property. The miners working along a stream
argued for the traditional law of riparian rights, that is, the right of
landholders along a stream to the natural flow of water. Of course, the
miners were not landholders, so they had no rights at common law. The
water companies naturally favored a right to divert water from a stream
based on first possession, or "prior appropriation," that is, that the first
individual or company to claim a flow of water by digging a canal or
registering with the local recorder had a right to the flow for as long
as he was actively using it.[10] They functioned as if this was the rule,
and it was in due course recognized by the courts, as the great majority
of miners worked not along the streams but at distant dry diggings.
The members of the company registered their water claims with the
recorder like any other claim. A company could claim a fixed amount of
water, like the "Sullivan's Creek Water Company" of twenty-five members, which claimed "the right of taking four hundred inches of water
under one foot head, from Sullivan's creek . . . and also claim the right

of way to cut a ditch . . . to convey the water to Shaw's & Columbia flats hence to Chinese Diggings."[11] Alternatively, the company could assert a right to all of the water in the stream. For example, on October 25, 1852, a group of four mines claimed "the exclusive privilege of conveying water for mining purposes from Shirt Tail Canon to Wisconsin and King's Hills." They describe their ditch, two feet deep and two feet wide and six miles long, "all of which is now well nigh completed and at a cost of about thirty thousand dollars." And as a final flourish, they add, "We do claim all the water in said Canon above the ditch together with all that may flow from the various tributaries along the line of the same."[12]

The idea that the first user to claim and divert water acquires an exclusive right to it was invented (or reinvented) in California.[13] Subsequent upstream users could not diminish the senior claimant's flow by taking water even for their own use, while subsequent downstream operations took their rights subject to the prior claims. This right of prior appropriation was necessary to a water company to protect its investment against upstream rivals who might take all of the water and render the original ditch valueless. The doctrine was a sharp break from the older rule of "riparian rights," which guaranteed a steady and undiminished flow of water to all landholders or claimants along the stream or river.

Californians did not question the possibility of diverting water; they all recognized that it opened up vast new fields for gold mining and that was a good thing. The great issue of the early days was whether there was still such a thing as riparian rights. Naturally, claimholders on the stream who used its water for their work had a right to that water by prior appropriation as against ditch owners, upstream or downstream, who later sought to divert the water. The company had to leave enough in the bed for those existing miners. The issue was whether individuals who later took claims below an existing ditch could demand that the company leave enough water in the stream for their use. This question pitted water companies and their clients against miners along the stream.

The miners along the river insisted that riparian rights were not only common law but natural law. They summarized their position in resolutions passed at a meeting at Ophir in Placer County, on January 22,

1854, which denounced "the manifestly unjust and monstrous assumption of an absolute fee simple title to running water by certain ditch companies; such ditch companies intending and endeavoring thereby to deprive all miners of their natural, legal and inalienable rights to make use of such water as would naturally flow through the gulch or valley of the stream in which they worked, as was necessary to work their claims."[14]

The stage was set for a series of conflicts: between individual miners and water companies, between different water companies, between miners of different diggings, between operations on the streams and those in the dry diggings, and between rules announced at miners' meetings and those decided in the courts. As we have seen, self-government through meetings and parliamentary procedure did not work well for groups whose interests were diametrically opposed to one another: not only could they not reach agreement, but there was no majority that could enforce the consensus on bad actors. Self-employed miners continued to use their tools of meetings and resolutions, but to less and less effect.

## Codes and Arbitration

Local clashes between prior appropriation and riparian rights were historically significant because from them, prior appropriation would emerge as the law not only of California but of the West generally.[15] The following discussion follows Donald Pisani's thoughtful and well-supported argument that during the gold rush, water law was local, shaped by the topography of the area and the interests of the parties working there. Its history is of conflict and politics rather than steady development toward a simple rule of prior appropriation.

The riparian claim holders' weapons were, as mentioned earlier, mining codes that made riparian rights the rule of their diggings and miners' meetings as the local arbiters of disputes. The California Practice Act of 1851 authorized judges in mining claim suits to admit proof "of the customs, usages, or regulations established and in force at the bar or diggings embracing such claims; and such customs, usages, or regulations, when not in conflict with the Constitution and laws of this State, shall govern the decision of the action."[16]

Some codes granted "[t]hat any person or company may divert the water from any creek gulch or ravine, for mining purposes, providing that enough water be left in the natural channel to work the bed of such creek, gulch, or ravine."[17] But quite a few phrased the rule not as permission, but as prohibition, such as "[t]hat no Company shall monopolize a Stream of Water for Speculation or unnecessarily use it to the injury of others."[18] Special miners' meetings were called when such a diversion was imminent, as at Greenhorn Creek, Siskiyou County, in February 1855. The miners "immediately on the Creek . . . adopted a series of resolutions, declaring that no person or persons shall divert the water from the Creek for mining or other purposes until the rains have raised it."[19] The miners declared that they would "support this law by every means in their power," but according to the newspaper report on the incident, "the canal and ditch companies appear determined to persevere in taking water as formerly."[20]

Historian Douglas Littlefield, who collected a number of early water disputes, observed that decisions by committee or arbitration by local miners tended to reject claims to exclusive water rights in favor of giving access to all.[21] It was a miners' committee that first heard the dispute that later became Irwin v. Phillips (1855), in which the Supreme Court of California established prior appropriation as *the* law of the mining region and effectively abolished riparian rights. The committee of miners had held the opposite, that the defendant, Robert Phillips, was justified in cutting through the water company's dam to release water for his own mining use because, as a riparian claim holder, he was entitled to water and even to take the water by force.[22] In another arbitration regarding water rights in Stuart's Gulch, Trinity County, in 1853, the arbitrators divided the water between the contestants instead of deciding for one or the other.[23]

Not surprisingly, "thare [we]re difficulties ariseing allmost dayly amont the miners respecting claims or water," as miner Perry Gee recorded in his diary in 1853. And, also not surprisingly, the miners called meetings to settle those difficulties. The rules of Siskiyou County, for instance, specified that "all disputes or difficulties about claims or Water privileges occurring in this mining district shall be settled by a majority of the miners in a miners meeting, or by a jury as the parties may agree."²⁴ Gee himself wrote that he "was under the necessity of calling a miners meeting today to recover water that was taken away from me out of spite and through selfishness such difficulties are of almost every day occurrence."²⁵ But arbitration was also an option. Dame Shirley, writing about the "exquisitely beautiful" little ditch built by her acquaintance that served five or six toms, said that the "water companies are constantly in trouble, and the arbitrations on that subject are very frequent."²⁶

Disputants could also take their case before the state courts. The trial courts tried to strike a balance between the legitimate expectations of mining companies and those of miners along the river.²⁷ Pisani argues that judges did not seek bright-line rules but tried to tailor their holdings to circumstances in the case. As both he and Littlefield show, district court judges were sensitive to the arguments of the local population that elected them and gave juries wide latitude. Instructions to jurors like "[n]o given rule can be laid down that will govern each controversy of this kind" allowed them to favor local, joint-stock water companies over corporations.²⁸ Not until Irwin v. Phillips in 1855 did the Supreme Court draw a bright-line rule by which miners along a stream took their claims subject to prior appropriations, and miner-owned companies were not favored over those owned by outside capital.

Meanwhile, mining districts shaped local law, or tried to, through their codes, miners' meetings, and local dispute resolution. Individual miners also turned to self-help when they felt that a ditch company had done them wrong and thought they could not get satisfaction through the regular channels. The case of Dr. William Ware's race is the best-documented struggle between miners on the stream and clients of a ditch company, and it is one that illustrates the use of all of the different tactics. The action took place near Weaverville in the spring of 1853. Aspects of the dispute are described in newspaper reports, in King's *Mining Laws*, and in an early *History of Trinity County*. The whole affair has also been the subject of several studies, most notably that of Donald Pisani, which I follow here.²⁹

Ware's ditch, begun in 1850, brought water from West Weaver River to McKenzie's Gulch, a mile or two away, where he sold to miners. All was well until the dry summer of 1853, when the ditch diverted almost all of the water in the river, leaving none for the miners downstream, who, however, had arrived at West Weaver Creek a year after Ware's ditch was completed.[30] The parties were unable to reach a compromise, and, at last, the downstream miners held a meeting "and resolved to cut the dam out by force, and fight if necessary." As per parliamentary procedure, "the meeting resolved itself into a committee of the whole" and proceeding to the dam, demolished it and returned the water to its natural channel.[31]

Dr. Ware entered a complaint against nine of the miners' leaders, whom the sheriff at Weaverville arrested and jailed. Their confederates, however, who numbered more than a hundred, insisted that they were equally guilty and demanded to be locked up with their leaders. The sheriff (rolling his eyes, no doubt) indulged them; but when miners streamed into Weaverville from other diggings to support their colleagues, and when the sheriff, meanwhile, had calculated the cost of feeding a hundred prisoners, he flung open the doors and exclaimed, "Get out of here, every mother's son of you!"[32] This was just what happened when the authorities tried to hold a whole community to account for a lynch trial—they found that it could not be done; the same problem would also prevent the legal system from punishing miners who later damaged the flumes of the "monster monopoly" water companies.

Ware's customers, however, the miners of the dry diggings, depended as much on the doctrine of prior appropriation as the ditch destroyers did on riparian rights; and they held their own meeting on June 7, 1853, at Weaverville, "for the purpose of finally settling the claims to the water of West Weaver." After denouncing "some malicious persons" for causing serious injury to Dr. Ware and the miners whom his race served, they adopted a preamble and resolutions by a "seventh eighth" vote. Among other things, they resolved "that we the miners of Weaver assembled, en masse, do hereby repudiate and frown upon any and every such act of agrarianism as . . . the burning of the reservoir."[33] Agrarianism has several meanings, of which the most likely here is opposition to the ownership of natural resources or an equal division of natural resources. The Weaverville miners took a conventional—indeed, riparian—position on water rights in principle, namely, that ditch builders "are entitled according to their priority of right to so much of the water of said creeks as their respective Races will convey. Provided always that a sufficient quantity be allowed to run in the natural beds of said creeks for the benefit of miners at present working or who may hereafter work said beds." In practice, however, they resolved "that four tom-heads shall be deemed sufficient for that purpose."

In a letter to the *Shasta Courier,* quoted by Donald Pisani, a miner calling himself "West Weaver" objected vehemently to this arrangement. First, the miners at the meeting had no authority to divide the water, he said; and second, four tom-heads would not even reach the downstream claims before it had evaporated, let alone furnish enough water for 120 claims. The miners along the channel had suggested splitting the water equally with those in the dry diggings, according to "West Weaver," but their offer had been turned down. They were told "that their diggings were worthless, and that of the diggings at Sidney were rich, that Sidney of course should have the water. Not only insulting our poverty, but robbing us because we were poor."[34]

This—the exhaustion of the diggings along the water courses—was the core of the problem. When the case reached the district court as Davis v. Ware, Judge McCorkle noted that "the beds of most of the creeks and streams of the mineral regions have been worked out, while extensive gold fields lie unoccupied and untouched yet for want of water but which by the construction of canals for the conducting of water on and through them, will . . . furnish thousands with constant employment."[35] Economic considerations alone would not justify the district court in departing from the common law, but California's legislature had given "the usages and regulations" of the miners the status of law, and in this case, the miners' meeting at Weaverville on June 7, 1853, had established that the usage of the mining district in question was . . . that the miners on the stream were entitled to four tom-heads. The plaintiffs themselves had attended this meeting and were, no doubt, among the one-eighth of those present who voted against the resolutions. The shift to the dry diggings enabled the miners there to outvote those on the creek.

## Monster Monopolies versus Miners

Dr. Ware and his partners were early investors in water as a commodity, and his ditch carried water for only a mile or two. From small, private ditches like Dr. Ware's, the water companies grew to "monster monopolies" and sank into obsolescence in a short amount of time. As sparkling little channels expanded into miles and miles of ditches, tunnels, and flumes, they consumed hundreds of thousands of dollars' worth of labor and materials. The largest ditch and flume networks brought water from rivers high up in the mountains for hundreds of miles: in the words of J. D. Borthwick, who was in the mines 1851–1854, "Hollows and valleys were spanned at a great height by aqueducts, supported on graceful scaffoldings of pine-logs, and precipitous mountains were girded by wooden flumes projecting from their rocky sides."[36]

These projects required an enormous investment not only of labor, but also of cash for the timber for scaffolding to carry flumes. Some water companies continued to be run as joint-stock companies by miners for miners, but the business was ripe for capital investment and, eventually, takeovers by investors from outside the mines. The Tuolumne County Water Company was the first to raise capital outside the mines, in 1852.[37] In that same year, the newspapers reported that the treasurer of the South Fork Canal Company had received $40,998 to that date and that "non-resident stockholders" would be interested to know that the work was progressing finely.[38]

Initially, these commercial companies were greeted with open arms. They effectively created the most important diggings of the mid-1850s. News of a new ditch company or an extension of an existing ditch generated great excitement, and miners took up claims in dry diggings long before the promised ditches reached them.[39] "When the canal now under construction, from Trinity River, is completed," wrote miner Franklin Buck in August 1853, "there will be 500 tons of water to work with which will give employment to several thousand men."[40] By 1855, half of California's gold was produced with artificial water.

But inevitably, there were also conflicts over access to water—conflicts between companies and between companies and their customers. Miners and corporations were dependent on one another; if a water company invested hundreds of thousands of dollars to bring water to new diggings and nobody came, it would be a disaster. And claimholders could not work without water, although they could more easily pick up and leave for other diggings than the company could. In other

ways, however, the interests of the two groups were adverse. Corporations charged as much as they could get away with and sought to drive
miner-owned water companies out of business. And corporations did
not vote in miners' meetings or subject themselves to miners' law.

It had been a source of great satisfaction in the early gold rush that
"neither business nor capital can oppress labor in California" and that
"the laboring class have now become the capitalists of the country."
There simply were no opportunities for capital investment in those
days. The speculative frenzy in quartz mining from 1850–1852, in which
investors from San Francisco to London burned their fingers, discouraged further forays into mining for some years. When investors poured
money into water companies, some miners therefore feared the worst.
Miners at Yankee Jim wrote in a letter to the *Placer Herald* in October
1853 that capital control of water was "a tyrant in the form of a lamb,
[that] has gradually assumed the form of a two horned beast, whose
right horn is bread, and the left horn water, and the community are
gored into surfdom [*sic*]."[41]

The miners wanted water, of course, and news that a company was
starting a new ditch was a matter for great rejoicing. The expected the
company to charge reasonable rates, however. A monopoly had to offer
water cheaply enough so that miners would come to the area it served;
if the price was too high, the miners would go elsewhere and the company's valuable infrastructure would stand idle. In theory, however, a
company could "allow" miners to make a good wage—say, five dollars
a day—and set its rate to absorb any earnings over that amount. For
example, if miners averaged twelve dollars a day, the company could
charge seven dollars for water and still attract customers. The richer the
diggings, the richer the company, while the miner's wage remained the
same. The miners of Butte County, whose reaction to Irwin v. Phillips
was quoted earlier, presumably had this in mind when they said that
"these water sharps aim to control the industrious, the frugal and the
enterprising . . . to make hewers of wood and drawers of water of the
miners, for a grasping and soulless monopoly."[42]

There is, in fact, enough evidence of sharp dealing to account for
the miners' anger at some powerful water companies. The Tuolumne
County Water Company, which is the best documented and was, in the

miners' view, the most monstrous of the monster monopolies, charged more at Columbia, where it had a monopoly, than it did at Shaw's Flat, which was also served by a joint-stock company.[43] Dividends on successful companies could be amazingly high: 12 percent *per month* for the Tuolumne Water Company in September 1853,[44] and 4 percent per month for April 1854.[45] A canal from the Trinity River to Cañon Creek was projected to pay 20 percent per month in August 1853, although it is not known whether that projection was realized.[46]

In contrast, miner-owned companies charged their customers much less. The seminal case of Eddy v. Simpson (1853), involved two competing companies; the Grizzly Company was a cooperative venture by four miners, who built their ditch primarily to water their own claims, while the Shady Creek Company was primarily a business venture.[47] The Grizzly sold its water at one dollar per sluice head, which the historian Littlefield surmised was close to its operating cost; while the for-profit company charged $2.50 in the same diggings. Littlefield suggested that the miners' company was "more concerned with providing water to miners than in profiting by this service."[48] At Rich Bar, according to Dame Shirley, a company that built a ditch to water its own claims also sold water to others for a percentage of their earnings.

Another source of resentment against the corporations was that they bought up joint-stock companies that ran into trouble. This was not, strictly speaking, the fault of the stockholders; but the miners who had put their own labor and savings into the joint-stock companies were naturally resentful when they found themselves paying for the water that was brought to the diggings on flumes they had built themselves. The problem was illustrated by the fate of the Miners' Cosumnes and Deer Creek Water and Mining Company. Like most joint-stock companies, the members of this one invested capital, but their main contribution was labor, for which they were to be paid in water when the project was finished. Of course, they had had to borrow substantial additional sums. However, they underestimated the amount of time and money necessary for the completion of the project: "[N]ew and larger loans must be effected to meet the demands of creditors, and before the company have had time to realize any actual nett proceeds from their canal, it is levied on and sold under execution, or passes at private sale into the hands of capitalists at from one-fourth to one-half its actual cost and value."[49] The Deer Creek Company's canal cost $75,000 to construct and was expected to yield an annual net revenue of from $20,000 to $25,000; but it was to go under the hammer on May 4, 1854. "Capital is power," wrote the author of the article in the *Sacramento Daily Union*, "and those possessing it step in and enjoy the labor of their less favored or more unfortunate neighbors." This was a bitter lesson.

Just as the struggle over Dr. Ware's race exemplified the competing interests of riparian claim holders and those in the dry diggings, and weapons that each party had at its disposal, so the history of the mighty Tuolumne County Water Company illustrates the confrontations between a major corporation and its clients. Donald Pisani, again, wrote the best account of these events.[50] The Tuolumne County Water Company brought water from the Stanislaus River to Columbia and surrounding diggings in 1852; thousands of miners had work thanks to the company—which is also to say that they were completely dependent on it.

In 1853, the miners claimed that they were barely earning enough to live and asked the Tuolumne County Water Company to reduce its rates by half, but their request was refused. In fact, John Wallace, superintendent of the company, wrote to a relative in England that when a miners' deputation called on him, he said, "[I]f any gentleman could not afford to pay the price he was not compelled to use it . . . . A few of the more rabid ones were marked, and for some time we refused to sell them water at any price, that took the shine out of them, and deterred others from acting in a similar manner."[51] In reaction to the company's intransigence, a large group of miners formed its own joint-stock company, the Columbia and Stanislaus River Water Company, to free themselves from grip of the Tuolumne County Water Company. The project took them four years to complete.

Meanwhile, resentment against the Tuolumne County Water Company grew as the mines were worked out and earnings decreased. One response was violence. As a group of 126 miners at Pine Log Crossing said in a petition to the company, "[I]f yous [*sic*] don't comply presently, we will find means in supplying our wants."[52] In 1856, miners on the San Antonio Creek, angry at another water supplier, the Table

Mountain Company, "tore down a mile of TMC's flume, and the dam in mainstream, and shattered the timber. Damage about $8,000."[53]

In 1855, the miners launched another weapon against the corporation: strikes—what we would call boycotts—to be continued until the company reduced the price of water to four dollars per day.[54] This action drew upon all of the organizational tools that the miners had perfected since the beginning of the gold rush. Three thousand miners participated in a mass meeting to agree on their measures and encouraged all miners to withdraw their money from the bank, "so that it will be impossible for it to be used against us by the controlling cormorants of this monster monopoly with which we are now at war."[55]

Work requirements only kicked in when the claim was actually workable.[56] The laws of the Ohio Flat District, for instance, subtitled, "A coad [sic] of laws for the better security of the interests of the miners holding claims in the Ohio Flat District of Yuba County," included a provision that all Ravine Claims must be worked in ten days after water can be had at a reasonable price."[57] The ability to walk away was always a powerful weapon against extortionate water companies.

In addition to violence and boycotts, the striking miners had a third tool, namely, encouraging the Columbia and Stanislaus River Water Company to accelerate its construction work. They held a meeting and resolved "that the officers of the new water company be requested to commence their canal at the earliest possible day, so as to give immediate employment to the miners who may be thrown out of work by the present strike."[58] The Columbia and Stanislaus would be the ultimate answer to the monster monopoly: a cooperative effort, built by the miners for the good of the miners and not for "foreign stockholders." Pisani notes that it survived the Tuolumne County Water Company's effort to crush it with lawsuits and to buy up its stock, and by the end of 1855, it was delivering the greater share of water to Columbia. "Miners working on the ditch supplied their own provisions for months on end, and local merchants loaned the company money to see the job through to completion."[59] The final completion of the ditch in 1858 was celebrated as a great victory: Pisani aptly called it "a symbol of what free men in a free society could accomplish." But the victory came too late;

the diggings at Columbia were exhausted, and "not even free water" would keep them profitable.[60]

If the Columbia and Stanislaus Water Company had succeeded, labor might have continued to control the diggings for a few more years. It was not to be. But the American habit of and commitment to self-organization continued in California, elsewhere on the frontier, and in the East, for decades. Even today, we are in some degree obliged to the Californians of the gold rush era every time we participate in faculty meetings and teacher-parent organizations and charitable boards. Henry M. Robert himself began writing *Robert's Rules of Order*—the definitive American work on how to run a meeting—after he was unexpectedly asked to serve as chairman of a meeting in San Francisco. The year was 1863, five years after the completion of the Columbia and Stanislaus Ditch. Robert was so embarrassed by his ignorance of procedure that he resolved to teach himself parliamentary law before he attended another such event.[61] And so we cite regularly rules that, in a small way, reached us via California.

# Conclusion

With the opening words of the mining rules of Warren Hill, "We the miners and citizens of Warren Hill," borrowed from the Constitution of the United States, the miners declared themselves legislators for themselves and "all others that may come among us." The words "We the miners" are grandiose and faintly ridiculous given that what followed was a set of relatively mundane rules about the size of mining claims. But from a bird's-eye perspective, it is remarkable that a group of ordinary people governed themselves by procedures originally developed in the British Parliament, and that they undertook to enact "Laws," a function that is in principle reserved to the state. The miners did, in fact, consider themselves lawmakers. Their rules would apply to everyone in the district, and moreover, "[a]ll miners or other persons residing now within this district shall be considered citizens of Warren Hill and have the right to vote in our assemblies." The mining code was not just a contract between the men who adopted it, but a set of general rules applicable to everyone who lived in or moved to Warren Hill.[1]

The meeting that adopted the code of Warren Hill was characteristically American. The Scot J. D. Borthwick wrote that Americans were "of all the people in the world the most prompt to organize and combine to carry out a common object."[2] Other visitors to the United States—from Alexis de Tocqueville to Frenchmen in the California gold mines—agreed that Americans were extraordinarily skilled at organizing to get things done. The basis of this proficiency was something simple and almost boring, namely, a universal competence with the rules of running a meeting, also called parliamentary procedure and known today as *Robert's Rules of Order*. The miners had practiced it back East in their Bible societies, reading groups, and charitable associations and in their frontier towns where settlers had no resource except each other. In California, the skill and discipline required for meetings was a kind of superpower because it enabled groups of miners, often complete strangers to one another, to organize on the spur of the moment to adopt a mining code or organize and run a large mining project.

In itself, a superpower is neither good nor bad. The miners used their organizing skills to good effect in forming and running mining companies that accomplished amazing things. But they also organized to expel Spanish speakers from the diggings in contravention of the law. And they did *not* organize to stop their countrymen from massacring the Indians. The Americans were not heroes; they exerted themselves when it suited them and not otherwise.

First, the good: there were the mining codes, of course, and the next most obvious example of useful self-organization after that was the mining company. Companies were of the joint-stock form in which the members had equal shares and made decisions about the work through company meetings. They were used for operations that required a large investment of labor, first for moving rivers out of their beds so they could mine the bottom and later supplying water to rich diggings far from the nearest rivers. American miners could organize companies like these in a matter of minutes and run them efficiently.

Their greatest venture was taking on the highly capitalized Tuolumne Water Company, which charged monopoly prices. The miners used meetings to organize to strike against the company, and they changed their own local mining rules to enable claimholders to leave their claims unworked in the meantime. Most importantly, they formed a rival to the investor-owned company, the Columbia & Stanislaus River Water Company, which was the costliest, most complex, and most impressive joint effort of California miners. Unfortunately, they succeeded in delivering their miner-supplied water just as the diggings were worked out—but the years-long struggle had been a triumph of organization and cooperation.

Now the middling and the bad: the mining camps were in effect a pure democracy, meaning that "the people" governed directly and not through representatives. The danger was that of any pure democracy:

the miners recognized no authority except the will of the majority. There was a reluctance to delegate decision-making capacity, so that instead of resolving claim disputes through arbitration or before an elected judge, litigants often chose to go straight to full miners' meetings, with the result that everyone devoted their Sundays to litigation.

Another problem was that a meeting of individual miners was badly positioned to reach a compromise with large companies whose interests conflicted with theirs. A water company, for instance, that diverted a stream to distant diggings caused harm to the individual miners near the river who needed that water. The individual miners outnumbered the members of the company, but the latter was not about to let the small-claim holders' votes decide the matter. These conflicts occasionally ended in violence. Meetings worked best when the voters were roughly similarly situated.

Furthermore, because the miners were the ultimate authority, the native population and foreigners in the mines were unprotected; their rights were not guaranteed, and they were not represented at meetings. As far as the majority of Americans were concerned, they had no rights and no status. A large number of miners *wanted* to kill Indians; they did not bother with meetings and consensus, but went out and slaughtered whole villages. Although some writers of letters and journals deplored this, they did not care enough to organize—their specialty—to stop the murders; they had a cost-free tool for pushing back against the genocide but did not use it. There were bigger forces at play: killing Indians was not a crime, and at various times, government policy was, in fact, to exterminate the native Californians. One would think, however, that men who passed resolutions at the drop of a hat to express sympathy or to organize a celebration could have done at least that much to censure the man who shot and killed a young Indian girl sitting on a log. To their shame, they did not even bother do this much the only protest recorded is that some miners stayed home.

Interactions with Spanish speakers were more complex. It was perfectly legal for them to mine in California, and Americans did not hate them as they did the native population. The goal was not to kill them, but to prohibit them from holding claims—in effect, to reduce them to wage labor. This did require miners' meetings, almost all of which voted to eject the Spanish speakers from their claims. Here pure democracy was a kind of tyranny, unchecked by fundamental rights or judicial review.

The advantages and disadvantages of the miners' organizational skills, or rather, their *faith* in their skills, were most striking in the area of criminal trials, the so-called lynch trials. These were least objectionable in the first two years, when the participants were intimidated by the responsibilities they had assumed, especially with that of pronouncing a death sentence. This caution was also evident on the Overland Trail, where emigrants took great pains to provide a fair trial. The rules of parliamentary procedure were helpful in that they imposed a certain degree of good order and gave a voice to the moderate majority. Individuals might have been afraid to stand up to the rowdies, but as a group, they could outvote them and bargain a death sentence down to a whipping,

The miners' confidence in their ability to hold a fair trial turned to overconfidence, however, especially when state courts tried to take over criminal trials and punishment. The state's criminal justice system was weak in the early days, when courts sat infrequently, jails were insecure, and witnesses had moved on by the time of trial. In response, the miners speeded up their popular trials, confident that "the people" had an unerring instinct for guilt or innocence. Eventually, procedural safeguards took on the role of procedural theater: the miners fought the sheriff for control of the suspect and were only induced to give him a lynch trial because the more conservative among them promised that it would result in a hanging.

Parliamentary procedure is a tool or an instrument that enabled Americans to reach group decisions and work together. It was not a character trait or an ideology, but a skill that enabled Californians to do big things in the absence of formal government. The "big things" they chose to undertake were naturally determined by their culture and values. Some of them were impressive; they could not move mountains, but they did move rivers. Others were despicable, such as ejecting non-English speakers from the diggings in violation of California law and tolerating the extermination of the Indians. Since everyone had a vote, the population owned those choices in a way that few citizens could claim today.

NOTES

ACKNOWLEDGMENTS

INDEX

# NOTES

## Introduction

1    All details of the Easterbrook trial are drawn from "The Tragedy at Shasta City," *Sacramento Transcript*, April 3, 1851.

2    Hubert Howe Bancroft, *History of California: 1848–1859*, vol. 6 (San Francisco: History Co., 1888), 6. Also published as Bancroft, *Annals of the California Gold Era* (New York: Bancroft Company, 1880). Monterey also had about eight hundred inhabitants. Bernarr Cresap, "Early California as Described by Edward O. C. Ord," *Pacific Historical Review* 21 (1952): 329–330.

3    Letter K. H. Dimmick to his wife, January 1, 1848, Correspondence (manuscript, Bancroft Library at MSS C-B 847).

4    Rodman W. Paul, *California Gold*, 2nd ed. (Lincoln: University of Nebraska Press, 1967), 7, on the topography of the valley. See also Bancroft, *History of California*, vol. 6, 3. Bancroft estimates the American population in 1848 at "somewhat over 6,000" and the Hispano-Californian population as around seven thousand. "The great valley of the interior, at the opening of the year 1848, remained practically undisturbed by civilization."

5    Heinrich Lienhard, *A Pioneer at Sutter's Fort, 1846–1850; The Adventures of Heinrich Lienhard*, trans. and ed. Marguerite Eyer Wilbur (Los Angeles: Calafía Society, 1941), 102, estimated some forty to fifty pioneers and livestock owners in the Cosumnes and Sacramento valleys.

6    Albert L. Hurtado, *John Sutter: A Life on the North American Frontier* (Norman, OK: University of Oklahoma Press, 2006), 129, quotes Larkin in a letter to the secretary of state: "All parties by land from Oregon or from the United States to California touch at this establishment first." Bancroft, *History of California*, vol. 6, 12.

7    Sutter had been granted the unusual power to make land grants to settlers, and he did give eighteen deeds to immigrants. Hurtado, *John Sutter*, 140.

8    US Constitution Article IV, Section 3. See Gary Lawson and Guy Seidman, "The Hobbesian Constitution: Governing without Authority," *Northwestern*

*University Law Review* 95 (2001): 581 at 609. California was ceded to the United States by the Treaty of Guadalupe-Hidalgo, which was formally effected on May 30, 1848. "Treaty with Mexico," Serial. 521, 30th Cong. 1st Session, H. Exec. Doc. 69, [1].

9   "Meeting at Sonoma," *Alta California*, March 1, 1849.

10   Peter H. Burnett, *Recollections and Opinions of an Old Pioneer* (New York: D. Appleton & Company, 1880), 294.

11   Andrea McDowell, "Criminal Law Beyond the State: Popular Trials on the Frontier," *Brigham Young University Law Review* (2007): 335.

12   Dame Shirley (Louise Clappe), *The Shirley Letters from California Mines in 1851-52* (San Francisco: T. C. Russell, 1922), 48.

13   For an overview of literature on women in gold rush California, see Glenda Riley, "Feminizing the History of the Gold Rush," *Western Historical Quarterly* 30, no. 4 (1999): 445–448.

14   Hubert Howe Bancroft, *Popular Tribunals*, vol. I (San Francisco: History Co. Publishers 1887), 124.

15   Carl Sandburg, *The American Songbag* (New York; Harcourt, Brace, and Co., 1927), 106–107.

16   Dame Shirley, *The Shirley Letters*, 81–82.

17   Daniel B. Woods, *Sixteen Months at the Gold Diggings* (New York: Harper & Brothers, 1851), 86–87.

18   Alexis de Tocqueville, *Democracy in America*, trans. Henry Reeve (Oxford: Oxford University Press, 1952), 376.

19   Robert D. Putnam, *Bowling Alone: The Collapse and Revival of American Community* (New York: Simon & Schuster, 2000).

20   Peter Clark, *British Clubs and Societies 1580-1800: The Origins of an Associational World* (Oxford: Oxford University Press, 2000).

21   De Tocqueville, *Democracy in America*, 380. The same was true in Canada; see Jeffrey L. McNairn, *The Capacity to Judge: Public Opinion and Deliberative Democracy in Upper Canada, 1791-1854* (Toronto: University of Toronto Press, 2000), 63–115.

22   De Tocqueville, *Democracy in America*, 387.

23   On "common parliamentary law," see "Advertisement to the First Edition" in Cushing, *Manual of Parliamentary Practice* (1845), 4; Henry M. Robert, *Robert's Rules of Order: Pocket Manual of Rules of Order for Deliberative Assemblies* (Chicago: Griggs, 1876), 14.

24   Henry M. Robert and Sarah Corbin Robert, *Robert's Rules of Order*, 10th ed. (New York: Perseus Press, 2000), xviii.

25   Thomas Jefferson, *Manual of Parliamentary Practice* (Columbus, OH: J. Phillips, 1842), 18.

26    Letter Thomas Jefferson to John Page, May 25, 1766. Wilbur Samuel Howell, ed. *Jefferson's Parliamentary Writings: Parliamentary Pocket-Book and a Manual of Parliamentary Practice*, 2nd series (Princeton: Princeton University Press, 1988), 4.

27    Henry M. Robert, *Pocket Manual of Rules of Order for Deliberative Assemblies* (1876), 102–105.

28    *National Advocate* (New York), Monday, March 3, 1817, col. E.

29    Letter to the editor, *Edgefield Advertiser* (South Carolina), April 27, 1842, 3, cols. 1–2.

30    *Proceedings of a Meeting of Citizens of Nashua upon the North Side of Nashua River, March 10, 1842* (Nashua, NH: A. Beard, 1842).

31    Luther S. Cushing, *Manual of Parliamentary Practice: Rules of Proceeding and Debate in Deliberative Assemblies* (Boston: Reynolds, 1845), 3.

32    The quotation is from the Notices before the title page of the seventh edition of Cushing's *Manual* (Boston: Reynolds, 1854). On associations as schools of parliamentary procedure, see Don H. Doyle, "The Social Functions of Voluntary Associations in a Nineteenth-Century American Town," *Social Science History* I (1977): 333–355 at 350.

33    Joseph Warren Wood, "Diaries of Crossing the Plains in 1849 and Life in the Diggings from 1849 to 1853" (manuscript, Huntington Library HM 318), January 20, 1850. This was the Jacksonville Code reproduced in Woods, *Sixteen Months*, 125–131.

34    Joseph Warren Wood, "Diaries of Crossing the Plains in 1849," June 25, 1852.

35    John David Borthwick, *Three Years in California [1851–1854]* (Edinburgh and London: William Blackwood and Sons, 1857).

36    Borthwick, *Three Years*, 369.

37    Frank Marryat, *Mountains and Molehills* (New York: Harper & Brothers, 1855), 216.

38    Clifford H. Bissell, "The French Language Press in California," *California History Quarterly* 39 (1960): 8, quoting the journal of Albert Bernard de Roushaile.

39    "California—The French View," *Placer Times*, December 1, 1849.

40    Borthwick, *Three Years*, 369.

41    Paul, *California Gold*, 164.

42    Wood, "Diaries of Crossing the Plains," entry for June 25, 1852.

43    For the five hundred mining districts, see J. Ross Browne, James W. Taylor, and United States Department of the Treasury, *Report of J. Ross Browne on the Mineral Resources of the States and Territories West of the Rocky Mountains* (Washington, DC: GPO, 1868), 226. About 150 codes were collected for the Department of Interior as Clarence King, *The United States Mining Laws and*

*Regulations Thereunder, and State and Territorial Mining Laws, to Which Are Appended Local Mining Rules and Regulations* (Washington, DC: GPO, 1885), 47th Cong., 2nd Session, H. R. Misc. Doc. 42, 279 (1885); alternative title: *Tenth Census of the United States*, vol. 14 (1880). For further publications, see Umbeck, *Theory of Property Rights*, 104–105, Table 8.1.

44    Regulations of Warren Hill, Plumas County, October 22, 1853. King, *United States Mining Laws*, 279.

45    Declaration of Independence, "And for the support of this Declaration, with a firm reliance on the protection of divine Providence, we mutually pledge to each other our Lives, our Fortunes and our sacred Honor."

46    King, *United States Mining Laws*, 300.

47    King, *United States Mining Laws*, 271.

48    Enos Lewis Christman, *One Man's Gold: The Letters and Journal of a Forty-Niner*, ed. Florence M. Christman (New York: McGraw-Hill, 1930), 192.

49    Jean-Nicolas Perlot, *Gold Seeker: Adventures of a Belgian Argonaut during the Gold Rush Years*, trans. Helen Harding Bretnor, ed. Howard R. Lamar (1985), 105 (Mariposa Code 1851); Woods, *Sixteen Months*, 125–130 (Jacksonville Code, January 20, 1850).

50    William Binur, *Wooded Up in Log Town: A Letter from the Gold Fields* (Berkeley: Bancroft Library Press, 1986), 12 (letter to Sarah, March 8, 1851).

51    A. P. Nasatir and J. Lombard, "A French Pessimist in California: The Correspondence of J. Lombard, Vice-Consul of France, 1850–1852," *California Historical Society Quarterly* 31, (1952): 139–148 at 144. For more on the French in the gold rush, see Malcom J. Rohrbough, *Rush to Gold: The French and the California Gold Rush, 1848–1854* (New Haven, CT: Yale University Press, 2013).

52    Josiah Royce, *California: A Study of American Character: From the Conquest in 1846 to the Second Vigilance Committee in San Francisco* (Berkeley, CA: Heyday Books, 2002; first published Boston: Houghton Mifflin, 1886), 253–255.

53    John Hovey, "Journal of a Voyage from Newburyport, Mass. to San Francisco, Cal. in the Brig Charlott by a Passenger Commencing Jan. 23, 1849, and ending July 23, 1849" (manuscript, Huntington Library at HM 322). Entry dated December 10, 1849.

54    Allen Varner, Letters (manuscript, Huntington Library at HM 39975-39986 & Fac 685), specifically, HM 39980, March 5, 1850; Joseph Warren Wood, "Diaries of Crossing the Plains," Jacksonville, July 28, 1850; John Hovey, Historical Account (manuscript, Huntington Library at HM 4384; transcribed from Hovey, Journal (manuscript, Huntington Library at HM 322), January 1850.

55    Jason Lothrop, "A Sketch of the Early History of Kenosha County Wisconsin, and of the Western Emigration Company," *Collections of the State*

*Historical Society of Wisconsin*, Vol. 2 (1855): Appendix No. 14, 450–479. The minutes of the meeting and constitution are at 472–475.

56    John Phillip Reid, *Policing the Elephant: Crime, Punishment, and Social Behavior on the Overland Trail* (San Marino, CA: Huntington Library Press, 1997).

57    On problems with sources, see Kenneth Owens, introduction to *Riches for All* (2002).

58    C. C. Mobley, "Diary of a Miner at Oregon Bar, California etc. 1850–1851" (manuscript, Huntington Library at HM 26612), 85 (August 16, 1850).

59    Edward Austin, Letters 1849–1851 (manuscript, Bancroft Library at MSS C-B 621); Letter to George, September 24, 1849.

60    Editorial, "Judge Lynch," *Daily Alta California*, October 13, 1850, 2.

61    "Arrests, Trial and Execution," *Placer Times*, August 18, 1849, 1. On the *Placer Times*, see Edward C. Kemble, *A History of California Newspapers, 1846–1858*, ed. Helen Harding Bretnor (Los Gatos, CA: Talisman Press, 1962 [1858]), 137.

62    Kemble, *History of California Newspapers*, 145.

63    On the unreliability of various accounts, see Erwin Gudde, ed., *Bigler's Chronicle of the West* (Berkeley and Los Angeles: University of California Press, 1952), 94nn11–12; Will Bagley, ed., *Scoundrel's Tale: The Samuel Brannan Papers* [Kingdom in the West, vol. 3] (Spokane, WA: Arthur H. Clark, 1999), 135; Owens, *Gold Rush Saints*, 35.

## 1. Before Property

1    *The Larkin Papers. Personal, Business, and Official Correspondence of Thomas Oliver Larkin*, vol. 7, ed. George Hammond (Bancroft Library, 1960), 285.

2    Kenneth N. Owens, *Gold Rush Saints: California Mormons and the Great Rush for Riches* (Spokane, WA: Arthur H. Clark Co., 2004), 93.

3    Letter Marshall to General R. Jones, August 17, 1848, *United States Congressional Serial Set*, Ser. 573, 31st Cong., 1st Sess. (1849), 57.

4    Americans could not legally mine on land still in Indian hands, but no authority in California was able to stop them. See Albert L Hurtado, *John Sutter: A Life on the North American Frontier* (Norman, OK: University of Oklahoma Press, 2006), 224.

5    That there was no "American" mining law, see Charles McCurdy, "Stephen J. Field and Public Land Law Development in California, 1850–1866," *Law & Society Review* 10, no. 235 (Winter 1976): 235–266. Mason's abolition of Mexican gold mining law is quoted by McCurdy, ibid., at 8n; Gregory Yale, *Legal Titles to Mining Claims and Water Rights in California* (1867), 17.

6    *Larkin Papers* vol. 7, 263.

7    Letter Larkin to Christie, May 18, 1848, *Larkin Papers* vol. 7, 264.

8    Letter Larkin to Buchanan, March 28, 1848, *Larkin Papers* vol. 7, 212–213.

9    Hurtado, *John Sutter*, 222–223; According to the unreliable James Stephens Brown, Marshall tried to establish preemption rights even before Sutter arrived by ordering his employees to mark off two 160-acre parcels, one for himself and one for Sutter, and to lay the foundations of a cabin on each. James Stephens Brown, *California Gold: An Authentic History of the First Find* (Oakland, CA: Pacific Press Publishing, 1894), 11.

10    Hurtado, *John Sutter*, 221; Kenneth N. Owens, ed., *Riches for All: The California Gold Rush and the World* (Lincoln: University of Nebraska Press, 2002), 20.

11    Hurtado, *John Sutter*, 222.

12    Hurtado, *John Sutter*, 223–224.

13    William Tecumseh Sherman, *Recollections of California, 1846–1861* (Oakland, CA: Biobooks, 1945), 41.

14    There are many accounts of how the news leaked out. Hurtado suggests also that Sutter deliberately misled newspaperman Edward Kemble when he visited the site of the sawmill. Hurtado, *John Sutter*, 226.

15    Henry William Bigler, *Bigler's Chronicle of the West*, ed. Erwin G. Gudde (Berkeley, CA: University of California Press, 1962), 92–93. See also Brown, *California Gold*, 13–14, quoted in Owens, *Gold Rush Saints*, 112.

16    Owens, *Gold Rush Saints*, 35n10, 35n39.

17    Owens, *Gold Rush Saints*, 58; Joseph Wheelan, *Invading Mexico: America's Continental Dream and the Mexican War, 1846–1848* (New York: PublicAffairs, 2007), 218–219. The attrition to 260 is my calculation based on the attrition mentioned in various sources.

18    John D. Unruh Jr., *The Plains Across: The Overland Emigrants and the Trans-Mississippi West, 1840–60* (Champaign, IL: University of Illinois Press, 1993), 317.

19    On these three sources, see Owens, *Gold Rush Saints*, 81–82, 94–97.

20    Will Bagley, ed., *Scoundrel's Tale: The Samuel Brannan Papers* [Kingdom in the West, v.3] (Spokane, WA: Arthur H. Clark Co., 1999); Owens, *Gold Rush Saints*.

21    Gudde, *Bigler's Chronicle*, 99n1.

22    Gudde, *Bigler's Chronicle*, 93.

23    Gudde, *Bigler's Chronicle*, 99.

24    Brown, *California Gold*, 13–14, quoted in Owens, *Gold Rush Saints*, 112.

25    Ibid.

26    Letter Larkin to Buchanan, July 20, 1848, *Larkin Papers* vol. 7, 286.

27    Harlan Hague and David J. Langum, *Thomas O. Larkin: A Life of Patriotism and Profit in Old California* (Norman and London: University of Oklahoma Press, 1990), 169.

28    Hurtado, *John Sutter,* 224; Gudde, *Bigler's Chronicle,* 105; Owens, *Gold Rush Saints,* 119–121.

29    Owens, *Gold Rush Saints,* 125.

30    Bagley, *Scoundrel's,* 266, quoting from *San Francisco Chronicle.*

31    Bagley, *Scoundrel's Tale,* 266.

32    Letter Larkin to R. B. Mason, May 26, 1848, in Hammond, *Larkin Papers* vol. 7, 279.

33    Willis and Hudson discoverers of Mormon Island, Owens, *Gold Rush Saints,* 119; Bagley, *Scoundrel's Tale,* 263.

34    Bagley, *Soundrel's Tale,* 259–260. Bagley notes the *Star* was the source of the August 1848 *New York Herald* article that started gold fever in the East.

35    Gudde, *Bigler's Chronicle,* 100, 103, 109n15; see also letter Robert Baylor Semple to Larkin, May 19, 1848, in Hammond, *Larkin Papers* vol. 7, 267, reporting that one of the workers at Sutter's Mill gathered three pounds of gold, working only on Sundays.

36    Owens, *Gold Rush Saints,* 130.

37    Hubert Howe Bancroft, *History of California,* vol. 6 (San Francisco: History Co., 1888), 62.

38    Letter Larkin to Buchanan, June 28, 1848, in Hammond, *Larkin Papers* vol. 7, 304.

39    Letter Thomas O. Larkin to Richard B. Mason, May 26, 1848, in Hammond, *Larkin Papers,* 279.

40    Gudde, *Bigler's Chronicle,* 110.

41    Owens, *Gold Rush Saints,* 139, quoting Borrowman, Friday, May 19, 1848.

42    Owens, *Gold Rush Saints,* 138, quoting Borrowman, Tuesday, May 30, 1848.

43    Sherman, *Recollections of California,* 41. Owens, *Gold Rush Saints,* 143, notes that the payments to Brannan did stop after Mason's July visit.

44    Not all the Mormons stayed at Mormon Island. In June 1848, some Mormons left the South Fork for richer deposits. They found Spanish Bar on the Middle Fork, which was the center of the gold rush in 1849. Edward Gould Buffum, *Six Months in the Gold Mines: From a Journal of Three Years' Residence in Upper and Lower California. 1847-8-9* (Philadelphia: Lea and Blanchard, 1850), 77.

45    Chester S. Lyman, *Around the Horn to the Sandwich Islands and California, 1845-1850*, ed. Frederick J. Teggart (New Haven: Yale University Press, 1925), 267-268, diary entry for July 7, 1848.

46    Lyman, *Around the Horn*, 269, entry for July 11, 1848.

47    William Jackson Barry, *Up and Down; or, Fifty Years' Colonial Experiences* (London: Sampson Low, Marston, Searle & Rivington, 1879), 102.

48    Letter Mason to General R. Jones, August 17, 1848, in G. G. Foster, ed., *The Gold Regions of California: Being a Succinct Description of the Geography, History, Topography, and General Features pf California: Including . . . The Gold Regions of That Fortunate Country* (New York: Dewitt & Davenport, 1848), 9-16 at 13.

49    Letter Charles Bolivar Sterling to Larkin, San Francisco, July 9, 1848, in Hammond, *Larkin Papers* vol. 7, 312, said he could only get a poor prospect until he bought a prospect from a Mormon.

50    Letter Kimball Dimmick to Sarah H. Dimmick, September 3, 1848, Correspondence, (manuscript, Bancroft Library at MSS C-B 847).

51    See letter Talbot H. Green to Larkin, October 15, 1848, in Hammond, *Larkin Papers* vol. 8, 14.

52    M. Collette Standard, "The Sonoran Migration to California, 1848-1856," *Southern California Q* 58 (1976), 333-357.

53    Rodman W. Paul, *California Gold: The Beginning of Mining in the Far West* (Cambridge: Harvard University Press, 1947), 22-23.

54    Walter Colton, *Three Years in California* (Cincinnati: A. S. Barnes, H. W. Derby & Co., 1850), 291.

55    C. Howard Shinn, *Mining Camps: A Study in American Frontier Government* (New York: Scribner, 1885), 166.

56    Colton, *Three Years*, 287 (on October 13, 1848).

57    Bigler, *Chronicle of the West*, 109.

58    Bigler, *Chronicle of the West*, 111; Owens, *Gold Rush Saints*, 141.

59    Letter Larkin to Buchanan, July 20, 1848, in Hammond, *Larkin Papers* vol. 7, 321.

60    Letter Larkin to Buchanan, in Hammond, *Larkin Papers* vol. 7, 302.

61    Buffum, *Six Months*, 51.

62    Buffum, *Six Months*, 53.

63    Bagley, *Scoundrel's Tale*, 271, quoting Peckham, *An Eventful Life* (1877).

64    Felix Paul Wierzbicki, *California as It Is and as It May Be* (San Francisco: Grabhorn Press, 1933), 57-58.

65    Letters from George McKinley Murrell (manuscript, Huntington Library in Murrell Collection, 36338-36403), April 24, 1850. Eldorado County,

"between the middle & north forks of the American river & near Burds store." See also Fariss and Smith, *Illustrated History of Plumas, Lassen & Sierra Counties*, 287, who record that the first individuals at Rich Bar, in what was later Goodwin County, in June 1850, staked off claims and then left to get provisions; their claims were recognized even while they were gone and while the diggings were filling up. *History* was written in 1882, however, and is not a firsthand account.

66      Bayard Taylor, *Eldorado, or, Adventures in the Path of Empire*, vol. 1 (New York: G. P. Putnam, 1850), 76.

67      Isaac Barker, "Diary of a Voyage Around Cape Horn . . . and of Life in the Mines Near Mormon Island, California, 2 vols." (manuscript, Huntington Library at HM 19366), entry for April 4, 1850. See also William Franklin Denniston, Journal (manuscript, Huntington Library, catalogued at HM 50660), entry for November 25, 1849, at Rio Agua Frio: "[A]fter breakfast Perry and Bowers went up the brook to leave some tools in the place where we found the gold, which according to the mining laws conferred title."

68      Valeska Bari, *The Course of Empire. First Hand Accounts of California in the Days of the Gold Rush of '49* (New York: Coward-McCann, 1931), 207.

69      Buffum, *Six Months*, 60.

70      Buffum, *Six Months*, 71–72.

71      Both stories in Buffum, *Six Months*, 79.

72      James H. Carson, *Early Recollections of the Mines* (Tarrytown, NY: W. Abbatt, 1931 [1852]), 13.

73      Paul, *California Gold*, 55, estimating average wage around twenty dollars and on earnings generally, 349–352.

74      Letter Kimball Dimmick to Sarah H. Dimmick, August 2, 1848, Correspondence (manuscript, Bancroft Library at MSS C-B 847).

75      Colton, *Three Years*, 292.

76      Lyman, *Around the Horn*, 272.

77      Jean-Nicolas Perlot, *Gold Seeker. Adventures of a Belgian Argonaut during the Gold Rush Years*, trans. Helen Harding Bretnor (New Haven, CT: Yale University Press, 1985), 104.

### 2. Powerless Judges and Discharged Soldiers

1      Gary Lawson and Guy Seidman, "The Hobbesian Constitution," *Northwestern University Law Review* 95 (2001): 609n110.

2      Lawson and Seidman, "Hobbesian Constitution," 622–623.

3      Theodore Grivas, "Alcalde Rule: The Nature of Local Government in Spanish and Mexican California," *California Historical Society Quarterly* 40

(1961): 11–32; Myra K. Saunders, "California Legal History: A Review of Spanish and Mexican Legal Institutions," *Law Library Journal* 87 (1996): 487 ff.

4    Walter Colton, *Three Years in California* (Cincinnati: A. S. Barnes, H. W. Derby & Co., 1850), 249. See also Richard Henry Dana, *Two Years before the Mast: A Personal Narrative* (Boston: Houghton Mifflin, 1911), 79: "[S]mall municipal matters are regulated by the alcaldes and corregidores. . . . Capital cases are decided by the [governor]."

5    Neal Harlow, *California Conquered: War and Peace on the Pacific, 1846–1850* (Berkeley: University of California Press, 1982), 284–285.

6    Letter Colonel Richard B. Mason to Colonel Stevenson, August 20–28, 1848, Ser. 573, 31st Cong., 1st Sess., 645–646.

7    *A Letter from [William Tecumseh] Sherman to Colonel Stevenson with an Introduction by Wilbur J. Smith* (Los Angeles: Privately Printed, 1960). Dated from Monterey, August 26, 1848.

8    This section draws from William B. Secrest, *California Desperadoes: Stories of Early Outlaws in Their Own Words* (Clovis, CA: Word Dancer Press, 2000), 3 ff. and the accompanying bibliography.

9    Secrest, *California Desperadoes*, 12. On Joseph Lynch, see William Redmond Ryan, *Personal Adventures in Upper and Lower California, in 1848–49*, vol. 2 (San Francisco: W. Shoberl, 1850), 52–54.

10    Like the other California missions, this one had been privatized and now belonged to an Englishman named William Reed. Secrest, *California Desperadoes*, 7.

11    Secrest, *California Desperadoes*, 5.

12    Letter Mason to John Sinclair, October 24, 1848, Ser. 573, 31st Cong., 1st Sess., H. Ex. Doc. 17, 653.

13    Letter Mason to General R. Jones, December 27, 1848, Ser. 573, 31st Cong., 1st Sess., H. Ex. Doc. 17, 629.

14    Secrest, *California Desperadoes*, 23.

15    Secrest, *California Desperadoes*, 23 and 27.

16    Letter Mason to Jones December 27, 1848, Ser. 573, 31st Cong., 1st Sess., H. Ex. Doc. 17, 629.

17    Letter Halleck to Kimball H. Dimmick, 1st alcalde, District of San Jose, May 17, 1849, Ser. 573, 31st Cong., 1st Session, H. Exec. Doc. 17, 744.

18    Letter Mason to Jones, December 27, 1848, Ser. 573, 31st Cong., 1st Sess., H. Ex. Doc. 17, 629.

19    Letter Mason to Dimmick, January 23, 1849, Ser. 573, 31st Cong., 1st Sess., H. Ex. Doc. 17, 667.

20    Grivas, "Alcalde Rule," *California Historical Society Quarterly* 40 (1961): 24, quoting Colonel Richard Mason.

21    Letter Dimmick to Sarah H. Dimmick, October 23, 1848 (manuscript, Bancroft Library at C-B 847).

22    Mary Floyd Williams, *History of the San Francisco Committee of Vigilance of 1851* (Berkeley: University of California Press, 1921), 81.

23    John Boessenecker, *Gold Dust and Gunsmoke: Tales of Gold Rush Outlaws, Gunfighters, Lawmen, and Vigilantes* (New York: Wiley, 1999), 48; James J. Ayers, *Gold and Sunshine, Reminiscences of Early California* (Boston: Gorham Press, 1922), 46–58.

24    Hovey, Journal, 62, Mokelumne River, October 2, 1849.

25    Frank Marryat, *Mountains and Molehills; or, Recollections of a Burnt Journal* (New York: Harper & Brothers, 1855), 290–292.

26    Charles Rossiter Hoppin, *Some of His Letters Home 1849–1863* (Oakland, CA: Privately printed, 1948), 6.

27    Marryat, *Mountains and Molehills*, 141.

28    Alfred R. Doten, *Journals, 1849–1903*, ed. Walter van Tilburg Clark, vol. 1 (Reno: University of Nevada Press, 1973), 64; Correspondence, *Weekly Alta California*, May 31, 1849.

29    Letter Halleck to Alcalde Raymonda Carrillo, May 15, 1849, Ser. 573, 31st Cong., 1st Sess., H. Ex. Doc. 17, 741–742.

30    James H. Cutler, Letters (manuscript, Beinecke Library at WA MSS S-1364 C976), letter to Sister dated "At Sea . . .," in November 1850. See also William Penn Abrams, Diary (manuscript, Bancroft Library at MSS C-F 65), Stockton, Wednesday, October 3, 1849, described drunken revelry following— and perhaps during—the election in Stockton in October 1849.

31    Bayard Taylor, *Eldorado, or Adventures in the Path of Empire*, vol. 2 (New York: George Putnam, 1850), 6–7.

32    Stephen J. Field, *Personal Reminiscences of Early Days in California* (n.p., 1880), 221.

33    Theodore H. Hittell, *History of California*, vol. 3 (San Francisco: N. J. Stone & Co. 1898), 225.

34    Heckendorn and Wilson, *Miners and Business Men's Directory* (Columbia, CA: Clipper, 1856), 6.

35    James H. Carson, *Early Recollections of the Mines* (Tarrytown, NY: Reprinted, W. Abbatt, 1931), 37–38.

36    Marryat, *Mountains and Molehills*, 327.

37    See also Fariss and Smith, *Illustrated History of Plumas, Lassen & Sierra Counties, with California from 1513 to 1850* (San Francisco: Fariss & Smith, 1882), 208–209. Thomas D. Bonner of Butte, elected justice in 1852, always found against the party best able to pay costs—until the "people" rebelled.

38    Rosales in Edwin A. and Carlos U. López, ed., *We Were 49ers! Chilean Accounts of the California Gold Rush* (Pasadena, CA: Ward Ritchie Press, 1976), 46 (entry of March 1, 1849). For a good word portrait of Rosales, see Susan Lee Johnson, *Roaring Camp: The Social World of the California Gold Rush* (New York: W. W. Norton, 2000), 65–67.

39    Rosales in Beilharz and Lopez, ed., *We Were 49ers*, 68.

40    Fariss and Smith, *Illustrated History of Plumas, Lassen & Sierra Counties*, 208.

41    Daniel B. Woods, *Sixteen Months at the Gold Diggings* (New York: Harper & Brothers, 1851),126.

42    Field, *Personal Reminiscences*, 32.

43    Field, *Personal Reminiscences*, 33.

44    Carson, *Early Recollections*, 36.

45    Bernarr Cresap, "Early California as Described by Edward O. C. Ord," *Pacific Historical Review* 21 (1952), 335.

46    Cresap, "Early California," *Pacific Historical Review* 21, 336.

47    Cresap, "Early California," *Pacific Historical Review* 21, 336.

48    Mason asked to be relieved from his post because, among other things, "the soldiers nearly all deserted." Letter Mason to Brigadier General R. Jones, November 24, 1848, Ser. 573, 31st Cong., 1st Sess., H. Ex. Doc. 17, 649.

49    Letter Secretary of State H. W. Halleck to Captain J. A. Sutter, May 5, 1849, Ser. 573, 31st Cong., 1st Sess., H. Ex. Doc. 17, 734; George Edward Faugsted, *The Chilenos in the California Gold Rush* (San Francisco: R and E Research Associates, 1973), mentions General Riley in summer 1849 setting up "Camp Stanislaus," which lasted for about a year, to protect the miners from Indians and to prevent major clashes between American and foreign miners.

50    Colonel Herbert M. Hart, "Cantonment Far West, in Historic California Posts, Caps, Stations and Airfields," http://www.militarymuseum.org/CpFarWest.html.

51    David Goodman, *Gold Seeking: Victoria and California in the 1850s* (Palo Alto, CA: Stanford University Press, 1994), 71.

52    Goodman, *Gold Seeking*, 78.

53    Goodman, *Gold Seeking*, 89.

54    General Riley, "Report on his Tour of the Southern Gold Mines to Major General R. Jones, Adjutant General of the Army," Washington DC, August 30, 1849, reproduced in John Frost, *Frost's History of the State of California* (Auburn, NY: Derby & Miller, 1850), 433–446 at 437.


3. Indian Miners


1    Fariss and Smith, *Illustrated History of Plumas, Lassen & Sierra Counties, with California from 1513 to 1850* (San Francisco: Fariss & Smith, 1882), 108–112.

2      Benjamin Madley, *An American Genocide: The United States and the California Indian Catastrophe, 1846–1873* (New Haven: Yale University Press, 2016); Albert L. Hurtado, *Indian Survival on the California Frontier* (New Haven: Yale University Press, 1988), 107–111; Hurtado notes that some Indians adjusted to the new economy of the gold rush, but this did not mean that a new class of "gold baron" Indians emerged.

3      See, for example, Felix Paul Wierzbicki and George Lyman, *California as It Is & as It May Be: or, A Guide to the Gold Region* (San Francisco: Grabhorn Press, 1933), 18 ("some of the Indians live in the families of the settlers, or near their farms, working for their subsistence and an occasional blanket. These are called in Spanish, very properly, *Indios manzos*—tame Indians.")

4      Wierzbicki and Lyman, *California as It Is*, 18 (on Indian employees); Hurtado, *Indian Survival*, 67.

5      Fariss and Smith, *Illustrated History of Plumas, Lassen & Sierra Counties*, 122, recorded long after the gold rush that the Indians were paid in food and trinkets. See James J. Rawls, "Gold Diggers: Indian Miners in the California Gold Rush," *California Historical Quarterly* 55 (1976): 28–45 at 30–32, on the terms on which the first Indian laborers were taken to the mines. See also Ronald H. Limbaugh and Willard P. Fuller Jr., *Calaveras Gold: The Impact of Mining on a Mother Lode County* (Reno, NV: University of Nevada Press, 2004), 14–15.

6      Letter Richard B. Mason to General R. Jones, August 17, 1848, US Congressional Ser. 537, H. Ex. Doc. 17, 530, stating that Lunol (Suñol) & Co. had about thirty Indians employed whom they paid in merchandise.

7      Ibid. See also Hubert Howe Bancroft, *History of California, vol. 6, 1848–1859* (San Francisco: History Co., 1888), 3, 89 n12.

8      J. S. Holliday, *Rush for Riches: Gold Fever and the Making of California* (Berkeley, CA: University of California Press, 1999), 68.

9      Letter Thomas O. Larkin to Secretary of State Buchanan, July 20, 1848, in Hammond, *Larkin Papers*, vol. 7, 321.

10      Letter Charles B. Sterling to Larkin, August 15, 1848, in Hammond, *Larkin Papers*, vol. 7, 336. "Not clean" may mean that they had dug dirt they thought would yield 150 pounds, although that would be an astounding claim.

11      Letter Sterling to Larkin, August 1, 1848, in Hammond, *Larkin Papers*, vol. 7, 332, gives the impression the group had just started working in earnest a few days earlier. When Sterling wrote on August 15, they would have worked for at least seventeen days.

12      Letter William Rufus Longley to Larkin, September 4, 1848, in Hammond, *Larkin Papers*, vol. 7, 351.

13      Letter John S. Williams to Larkin, September 13, 1848, in Hammond, *Larkin Papers*, vol. 7, 357.

14      Letter Williams to Larkin, October 18, 1848, in Hammond, *Larkin Papers*, vol. 8, 18.

278                                                          Notes to Pages 53–56

15    Letter Sterling to Larkin, July 9, 1848, in Hammond, *Larkin Papers*, vol. 7, 312–313.

16    Letter William Tecumseh Sherman, November 14, 1848, from Camp on the American Fork near Sutters, in William Tecumseh Sherman and Edward Otho Cresap Ord, *The California Gold Fields in 1848. Two Letters from Lt. W. T. Sherman, U.S.A.* (n.p., 1964).

17    Letter Sterling to Larkin, July 14, 1848, in Hammond, *Larkin Papers*, vol. 7, 312.

18    Letter Sterling to Larkin, July 14, 1848, in Hammond, *Larkin Papers*, vol. 7, 316.

19    Simon Doyle, from Bidwell's Ranch, in a diary entry dated October 17, 1849, wrote that Mr. Potter, working with "his Indians," "had made $6,000" (manuscript, Beinecke Library at WA MSS 144).

20    William Thurston, Esq., *Guide to the Gold Regions of Upper California* (London: J. and D. A. Darling, 1849), 40.

21    Edward Gould Buffum, *Six Months in the Gold Mines* (Philadelphia: Lea and Blanchard, 1850), 125.

22    Will Bagley, ed., *Scoundrel's Tale: The Samuel Brannan Papers* [Kingdom in the West, v.3] (Spokane, WA: Arthur H. Clark Co., 1999), 271, quoting Peckham, "An Eventful Life" (1877). Letter Sterling to Larkin, July 14, 1848, in Hammond, *Larkin Papers*, vol. 7, 317.

23    Letter Moses Schallenberger to Larkin, August 16, 1848, in Hammond, *Larkin Papers*, vol. 7, 339.

24    Chester S. Lyman, *Around the Horn to the Sandwich Islands and California, 1845–1850*, ed. Frederick J. Teggart (Freeport, NY: Libraries Press, 1971 [1924]), 284.

25    Buffum, *Six Months*, 125–126.

26    Buffum, *Six Months*, 93–94.

27    Buffum, *Six Months*, 49–50.

28    Theodore T. Johnson, *Sights in the Gold Region, and Scenes By the Way* (New York: Baker and Scribner, 1849), 206.

29    Buffum, *Six Months*, 98.

30    This excerpt from Antonio Franco Coronel's reminiscences is printed in the editor's introduction to *Three Years in California: William Perkins' Journal of Life at Sonora, 1849–1852*, ed. Dale Lowell Morgan and James R. Scobie (Berkeley, CA: University of California Press, 1964), 21 ff. See also Richard Morefield, *The Mexican Adaptation in American California, 1846–1875* (San Francisco: R and E Research Associates, 1971). Appendix A is a translation of Antonio Franco Coronel, *Cosas de California*.

31    Ibid.

32    Lyman, *Around the Horn*, 268–269.

33    Walter Colton, *Three Years in California* (Cincinnati: H. W. Derby, 1850), 277.

34    Alonzo Delano, *Life on the Plains and among the Diggings* (Auburn and Buffalo: Milner, Orton & Mulligan, 1854), 292–320.

35    Delano, *Life on the Plains*, 294, 296.

36    Delano, *Life on the Plains*, 309.

37    Delano, *Life on the Plains*, 310.

38    Delano, *Life on the Plains*, 316.

39    Delano, *Life on the Plains*, 317.

40    Johnson, *Sights in the Gold Region*, 206.

41    Buffum, *Six Months*, 46.

42    Ephraim Delano, *Letters*, Letter to wife dated San Francisco May 15, 1851 (Beinecke Library at WA MSS S-59 D 374). Ephraim Delano is not, to my knowledge, a relative of Alonzo Delano.

43    Katja Werthmann, "Frivolous Squandering: Consumption and Redistribution in Mining Camps," in *Dilemmas of Development: Conflicts of Interest and Their Resolution in Modernizing Africa*, eds. Jon Abbink and André van Dokkum (Leiden: African Studies Centre, 2008), 60–76.

44    Francis Asbury Hammond in Kenneth N. Owens, *Gold Rush Saints: California Mormons and the Great Rush for Riches* (Spokane, WA: Arthur H. Clark Co., 2004); Rawls, "Gold Diggers," 34–35.

45    "California Indian Chiefs," *Sacramento Daily Union*, January 31, 1857, 4.

46    Delano, *Life on the Plains*, 307.

47    Ananisas R. Pond, Journal (manuscript, Huntington Library at HM 19383), entry for October 25, 1849, at the Feather River.

48    John A. Swan, *A Trip to the Gold Mines of California in 1848*, ed. John A. Hussey (San Francisco: Book Club of California, 1960), 5.

49    Swan, *Trip to the Gold Mines*, 15. Swan also sold blankets for 2.5 ounces each.

50    Heckendorn and Wilson, *Miners and Business Men's Directory* (Columbia, CA: Heckendorn & Wilson, 1856), 54.

51    Johnson, *Sights in the Gold Region*, 206–207.

52    Fariss and Smith, *Illustrated History of Plumas, Lassen & Sierra Counties*, 123. Reading told the authors he mined for six weeks with sixty Indians on the Trinity River, after which parties arriving from Oregon "protested against my Indian labor." He immediately packed up and went home. See also Hurtado, *Indian Survival*, 107, 118.

53    For broader studies of attacks on Indians, see Clifford E. Trafzer and Joel R. Hyer, ed., *Exterminate Them: Written Accounts of the Murder, Rape, and*

*Slavery of Native Americans during the California Gold Rush, 1848–1868* (East Lansing: Michigan State University Press, 1999); Madley, *American Genocide, passim.*

54   Johnson, *Sights in the Gold Region,* 207–208.

55   Thomas Butler King, Report on California, March 26, 1850, Ser. 577, 31st Cong, 1st Sess., H. Ex. Doc. 59, 8.

56   Amos Batchelder, Journal (manuscript, Bancroft Library at MSS C-B 614), 164, entry for December 22, 1849. But Rawls, "Gold Diggers," 30, quotes a Major General Thomas Green, who "criticized whites for monopolizing Indian labor for bits of calico when they would have been happy to work for ¼ of what whites made." *Daily Alta California,* May 31, 1850.

## 4. The Mining Codes

1   Gregory Yale, *Legal Titles to Mining Claims and Water Rights in California, under the Mining Law of Congress, of July 1866* (San Francisco: A. Roman, 1867), 58–84.

2   Clarence King, *United States Mining Laws and Regulations Thereunder* (Washington: Government Printing Office, 1885); Charles Howard Shinn, *Land Laws of Mining Districts* (Baltimore: N. Murray publication agent, Johns Hopkins University, 1884). See also Stephen Field's opinion in Jennison v. Kirk, 98 US (8 Otto) 453, 458 (1878).

3   For Australia, see David Goodman, *Gold Seeking: Victoria and California in the 1850s* (Palo Alto, CA: Stanford University Press, 1994). For Canada, see Douglas C. Baker and William R. Morrison, "The Development of Property Rights on the Canadian and American Mining Frontiers," *American Review of Canadian Studies* 29 (1991), 431–446; M. H. E. Hayne and H. West Taylor, *The Pioneers of the Klondyke: Being an Account of Two Years Police Service on the Yukon* (London: S. Low, Marston and Company, 1897), 123–124; William Ogilvie, *Early Days on the Yukon* (London: John Lane, 1913), 245–266. In Brazil, the first discoverer assigned claims to new arrivals: see below. In Papua New Guinea, some claims were holes no more than a shoulder-width across; see Peter Ryan, *Black Bonanza: A Landslide of Gold* (Melbourne: Hyland House, 1991).

4   Thomas Stone, "The Mounties as Vigilantes," *Law and Society Review* 14 (1979), 83–114 at 86–87.

5   Baker and Morrison, "The Development of Property Rights on the Canadian and American Mining Frontiers," 431–446.

6   Hayne and West Taylor, *Pioneers of the Klondyke,* 123–124.

7   John David Borthwick, *Three Years in California [1851–1854]* (Edinburgh and London: William Blackwood and Sons, 1857), 155.

8   Bayard Taylor, *Eldorado, or Adventures in the Path of Empire,* vol. 1 (New York: George Putnam, 1850), 246–247.

9      Daniel B. Woods, *Sixteen Months at the Gold Diggings* (New York: Harper & Brothers, 1851), 131.

10     Walter Colton, *Three Years in California* (New York: A. S. Barnes, 1850), 314.

11     Simon Doyle, Journals and Letters, 1849–1856 (manuscript, Beinecke Library at WA MSS 144), Letter to parents, August 1850. See also "Sacramento and Placer Intelligence," *Alta California*, April 10, 1850.

12     L. M. Schaeffer, *Sketches of Travels in South America, Mexico and California* (New York: J. Egbert, 1860), 184.

13     Joseph Warren Wood, "Diaries of Crossing the Plains in 1849 and Life in the Diggings from 1849 to 1853" (manuscript, Huntington Library at HM 318), entry for June 25, 1852.

14     Borthwick, *Three Years*, 156.

15     Tyrrell Martínez and Frank J. Drummond, *Early Mining Laws of Tuolumne and Calaveras Counties*, (typescript, n.p., 1936), 30 (quoting "Tuolumne," *Sonora Herald*, October 23, 1852).

16     King, *United States Mining Laws*, 279.

17     Isaac Barker, Diary of a voyage around Cape Horn (Manuscript, Huntington Library, HM 19366). Entry for Sunday, April 14 [1850]. Barker arrived at Georgetown on April 13 and attended the meeting the next day, although he did not have a claim. He moved to nearby Ford's Bar on April 17.

18     Regulations of Warren Hill, King, *United States Mining Laws*, 279.

19     Exceptionally, the Jacksonville Code Articles XII–XVI dealt with crime. Daniel B. Woods, *Sixteen Months at the Gold Diggings* (New York: Harper & Brothers, 1851), 125–131.

20     Mining Laws of Butte County, King, *United States Mining Laws*, 296.

21     For example, Woods, *Sixteen Months*, 57. (Ten feet [square] was allowed by custom at Salmon Falls in 1849).

22     John Hovey, Journal of a Voyage (manuscript, Huntington Library, HM 322), 139.

23     Fariss and Smith, *Illustrated History of Plumas, Lassen & Sierra Counties, with California from 1513 to 1850* (San Francisco: Fariss & Smith, 1882), 288.

24     "Letters from the Mountains," *Daily Alta California*, December 21, 1852.

25     For a list of different kinds of notice requirements (without references), see Charles Shinn, *Land Laws of Mining Districts* (Baltimore: Johns Hopkins University, 1884), 12; for the notice requirements of the individual codes, see, of course, King, *United States Mining Laws*, passim.

26     Upper Yuba Mining Laws, April 11, 1852 (five days), in King, *United States Mining Laws*, 277; Weaver Creek Rules and Regulations, June 19, 1852 (ten days), ibid., 277; Warren Hill Act, October 22, 1853 ("at all times . . . (and) in

good faith, not merely as a pretext to hold said claims"), ibid., 280; French Creek Mining Laws, November 12, 1854 (seven days), ibid., 281; Smith's Flat Hill Laws, no date (seven days), ibid., 283; etc.

27    "San Joaquin Intelligence," *Daily Alta California*, September 13, 1851.

28    Barker, Diary. Mormon Island, April 4, 1850. Idem, December 6, 1850, for a similar example.

29    Andrea McDowell, "From Commons to Claims: Property Rights in the California Gold Rush," *Yale Journal of Law and the Humanities* 14, no. 1 (2002): 34n113.

30    See Stephen J. McCurdy, "Field and Public Land Law Development in California, 1850–1866," *Law & Society Review* 10, no. 2 (Winter 1976): 244–245, on the Prosser v. Parks (1861), in which the court held that miners' assemblies "cannot restrict the quantity of ground or number of claims which any person may purchase."

31    Pringle Shaw, *Ramblings in California* (Toronto: James Bain, [1857?]), 132–133.

32    J. M. Hutchings, *The Miners' Ten Commandments* (San Francisco: Sun Print, 1853). Note the relatively late date. This text was reprinted endlessly.

33    William Blackstone, *Commentaries on the Laws of England*, vol. 2, *2–*11 (Baton Rouge, LA: Claitor's Publishing Division, 1976), quoted from Robert C. Ellickson, Carol M. Rose, and Bruce A. Ackerman, ed., *Perspectives on Property Law*, 2nd ed. (New York: Aspen Publishers, 1995), 39.

34    Edmund Booth, *Forty-niner; The Life Story of a Deaf Pioneer* (Stockton: San Joaquin Pioneer and Historical Society, 1953), 57 (letter dated Sonora, CA, May 25, 1852).

35    The seminal article on claim clubs is Allan G. Bogue, "The Iowa Claim Clubs: Symbol and Substance," *Mississippi Valley Historical Review* 45 (1958): 231–253.

36    John R. Umbeck, *A Theory of Property Rights: With Application to the California Gold Rush*, (Ames: Iowa State University Press, 1981). For one of many citations to this work, see Andrew P. Morriss, Roger E. Meiners, and Bruce Yandle, "Finding Better Words: Markets, Property Rights, and Resources," *Washington Journal of Environmental Law & Policy* 11 (2021): 264.

37    Richard O. Zerbe Jr. and C. Leigh Anderson, "Culture and Fairness in the Development of Institutions in the California Gold Fields," *Journal of Economic History* 61 (2001): 114–143. Their article is included in Ellickson, Rose, and Ackerman, *Perspectives on Property Law*.

38    Zerbe and Anderson, "Culture and Fairness," 116–119.

39    Karen B. Clay and Gavin Wright, "Order Without Law? Property Rights During the California Gold Rush," *Explorations in Economic History* 42 (2005): 155–183.

40    William M'Collum, *California as I Saw It*, ed. Dale L. Morgan (Los Gatos, CA: Talisman Press, 1960), 151.

41    Ansel James Mccall, *Pick and Pan: Trip to the Diggings in 1849* (Bath, NY: Steuben Courier Print, 1882), 25–26, Friday Oct 26, 1849.

42    John Hale, *California as It Is* (Privately printed, 1851, 1954), 25.

43    Katherine A. White, ed., *A Yankee Trader in the Gold Rush; the Letters of Franklin A. Buck* (Boston and New York: Houghton Mifflin Company, 1930), 28. On the importance of achieving independence, that is, becoming self-employed as a farmer, shopkeeper, or businessmen in the mid-nineteenth century, see Eric Foner, *Free Soil, Free Labor, Free Men: The Ideology of the Republican Party before the Civil War* (New York: Oxford University Press, 1970), 11–39.

44    McCall, *Pick and Pan*, 17. See also Allen Varner, Letters (manuscript, Huntington Library at HM 3997539986 & Fac 685), November 12, 1849, Rector's Bar. Varner wrote that those who wanted to make money in the mines had to work hard and live rough, "for there is no Aristocracy to contend with here."

45    Pierre Charles Fournier de Saint-Amant, *Voyages en Californie et dans l'Oregon* (Paris: L. Maison, 1854), 582–583.

46    "San Joaquin Intelligence," *Daily Alta California*, June 13, 1851.

47    Henry George, *Progress and Poverty* (Princeton, NJ: Robert Schalkenbach Foundation, 2006), 212.

48    See also "Letters from the Mountains," *Daily Alta California*, December 21, 1852.

49    California Legislature, *Journals*, 1st Session, 1849–1850, 805–806.

50    California Legislature, *Journals*, 1st Session. 1849–1850, 811.

51    California Legislature, *Journals*, 1st Session. 1849–1850, 812.

52    Samuel McNeil, *McNeil's Travels in 1849, to, through, and from the Gold Regions in California* (Columbus: Scott & Bascom, 1850), 5.

53    Andrea McDowell, "Gold Rushes Are All the Same: Labor Rules the Diggings," in *Property in Land and Other Resources*, eds. Daniel H. Cole and Elinor Ostrom (Lincoln Institue of Land Policy, 2012), 99–118.

54    McDowell, "Gold Rushes Are All the Same," 99–118.

55    Goodman, *Gold Seeking*, 69–70.

56    David Cleary, *Anatomy of the Amazon Gold Rush* (Iowa City: University of Iowa Press, 1990), 51, 64.

57    Cleary, *Anatomy*, 69.

58    Michael Schuman, "How Big Mining Lost a Fortune in Indonesia: The Locals Moved In," *Wall Street Journal*, May 16, 2001, 1, 8.

59     John Vail, "All that Glitters: The Mt. Kare Gold Rush and Its Aftermath," in *Papuan Borderlands: Huli, Duna, and Ipili Perspectives on the Papua New Guinea Highlands*, ed. Aletta Biersack (Ann Arbor: University of Michigan Press, 1995), 343–374.

60     Peter Ryan, *Black Bonanza: A Landslide of Gold* (Melbourne: Hyland House, 1991).

61     Tilo Grätz, "Gold Mining Communities in Northern Benin as Semi-Autonomous Social Fields," Working Paper No. 36 (Halle: Max Planck Institute for Social Anthropology, 2002), 3.

62     Woods, *Sixteen Months*, 171.

63     Letter Stephen Woodin to his wife and children, May 17, 1850 (Manuscript, Huntington Library at MS 19369-19381), estimated that not one in twenty would make any money from his expedition. George McKinley Murrell estimated in 1850 that only one in forty would earn enough to pay for his journey to California (letter August 18, 1850, Huntington Library, Murrell Collection, HM 36338-36403).

64     Felix Paul Wierzbicki, *California as It Is and as It May Be* (San Francisco: The Grabhorn Press, 1933), 55.

65     Thomas J. van Dorn, Letters (Beinecke Library at WA MSS S-1319), May 30, 1850.

66     Dame Shirley (Louise Clappe), *The Shirley Letters from California Mines in 1851–52* (San Francisco: T. C. Russell, 1922), 213.

67     Dame Shirley, *Shirley Letters*, 219.

68     Peter H. Burnett, *Recollection and Opinions of an Old Pioneer* (New York: D. Appleton & Co., 1880), 414.

69     Borthwick, *Three Years,*191.

70     Letter George McKinley Murrell, September 15, 1851. See also *A Frenchman in the Gold Rush; the Journal of Ernest de Massey, Argonaut of 1849*, trans. by Marguerite Eyer Wilbur (San Francisco: California Historical Society, 1927). De Massey was employed for two days; after paying his wages and meals, there was nothing left over for the two Irishmen who hired him.

71     Edward Gould Buffum, *Six Months in the Gold Mines: From a Journal of Three Years' Residence in Upper and Lower California. 1847-8-9* (Philadelphia: Lea and Blanchard, 1850), 107.

72     *Alta California*, Steamer Edition, August 31, 1849. Letter signed F.P.W. (Felix Paul Wierzbicki). These words appear again in Wierzbicki's *California as It Is*, 34.

73     Benton's speech in the Senate of January 15, 1849, as reported in the *Alta California*, September 6, 1849, 2, col. 2.

74     William Thurston, Esq., *Guide to the Gold Regions of Upper California* (London: J. and D. A. Darling, 1849), 35, quoting "a correspondent in New York."

*See also* "The Gold Mine," *Californian*, August 14, 1848, stating "the laboring class have now become the capitalists of the country." This edition of the *Californian* was intended for circulation back in the States. Both these remarks were intended to encourage immigration. Samuel Upham, *Notes of a Voyage . . . Together with Scenes in El Dorado, in the Years 1849–'50* (Philadelphia: by the author, 1878), 307.

75    "The Gold Mine," *Californian*, August 14, 1848.

76    Buffum, *Six months*, 107.


### 5. Resolving Disputes

1      Letter James H. Cutler to Haskell, July 25, 1850 (Beinecke Library at WA MSS S-1364).

2      C. W. T. Ballenstedt, *Beschreibung Meiner Reise nach den Goldminen Californiens* (Schöningen: J. C. Schmidt in Helmstedt, 1851), 39.

3      Letter James Canfield to his wife, August 21, 1849, in *Peter Decker, The Diaries of Peter Decker Overland to California in 1849 and Life in the Mines, 1850–1851*, ed. Helen S. Griffin (Georgetown, CA: Talisman Press, 1966), 321.

4      Joseph William Singer, "Property," in *The Politics of Law*, 3rd ed., ed. David Kairys (New York: Basic Books, 1998), 240–257.

5      "Execution of Logan and Lipsey at Coloma," *Sacramento Daily Union*, November 6, 1854.

6      Perry Gee, *Journal of Travels . . . and an Account of Four Months Experiences at the Gold Diggings*, January 6, 1853, manuscript, Beinecke Library at WA MSS 213).

7      John Boessenecker, *Gold Dust and Gunsmoke: Tales of Gold Rush Outlaws, Gunfighters, Lawmen, and Vigilantes* (New York: Wiley, 1999), 47, quoting Chilean miner Ramón Gil Navarro.

8      Frank Marryat, *Mountains and Molehills; or, Recollections of a Burnt Journal* (New York: Harper & Brothers, 1855), 217.

9      "Difficulty at the North. Correspondence of the Transcript," *Sacramento Transcript*, August 6, 1850.

10     Gregory Yale, *Legal Titles to Mining Claims and Water Rights in California, under the Mining Law of Congress, of July 1866* (San Francisco: A. Roman, 1867), 81.

11     Yale, *Legal Titles*, 79.

12     Richard Brown Cowley, "Journal of a Voyage on the Barque 'Canton' from New York to San Francisco via the Horn; Life in the Mines on the Mokelumne River" (March 29, 1849–November 9, 1851) (manuscript in the Huntington Library at HM 26652), 58 recto (entry for September 15, 1850).

13    John Clark, *The California Guide. With Distances & Notes of Travel by Clark & Co in Fifty Two from Ohio to the Sacramento Valley. 1852–1856* (Beinecke Library at WA MSS 83).

14    "Handsome Specimens," *Sacramento Transcript*, December 28, 1850: "Mr. C. informed us that . . . [o]ne claim which Mr. C. abandoned afterwards yielded over $5000."

15    Karen B. Clay and Gavin Wright, "Order Without Law? Property Rights During the California Gold Rush," *Explorations in Economic History* 42 (April 2005): 155–183.

16    Richard Henry Dana, *Two Years before the Mast: A Personal Narrative* (Boston and New York: Houghton Mifflin, 1911), 79. See also Letter Halleck to M. Foley, Willow Bar (Mokelemne River), December 1, 1849, Ser. 561, S. Exec. Doc. 52, 31st Cong., 1st Sess., 29–30.

17    Clay and Wright note that only twenty-four codes include a mechanism for dispute resolution ("Order Without Law" at 165).

18    "San Joaquin Intelligence," *Daily Alta California*, September 13, 1851.

19    Decker, *Diaries*, 219.

20    Daniel Woods, *Sixteen Months in the Gold Diggings* (New York: Harper & Brothers, 1851), 57.

21    Marryat, *Mountains and Molehills*, 217.

22    Stephen J. McCurdy, "Field and Public Land Law Development in California, 1850–1866," *Law & Society Review* 10, no. 2 (Winter 1976): 243–244. McCurdy discusses a series of California Supreme Court decisions about jumping and the kinds of disputes that arose between claim holders and jumpers.

23    Perry Gee, "Journal of Travels," 1852. Entry for December 7, 1842, at Ringgold Diggings near Hangtown. Gee mentions that there were thirty miners at Ringgold Diggings, a manageable size for a meeting.

24    Perry Gee, op. cit., December 28, 1852.

25    See also Fariss and Smith, *Illustrated History of Plumas, Lassen & Sierra Counties, with California from 1513 to 1850* (San Francisco: Fariss & Smith, 1882), 207; in spring 1851, Rich Bar, Miners' meeting decided the question of whether the recorder was to be paid one dollar per claim or one dollar per company (i.e., one dollar for twelve men working together who made twelve claims).

26    "Our Grass Valley Correspondence," *Sacramento Daily Union*, April 18, 1853.

27    "Dame Shirley" (Louise Clappe), *The Shirley letters from California mines in 1851–52* (San Francisco, Printed by T.C. Russell, 1922), 213.

28    Perry Gee, "Journal of Travels . . . and an Account of Four Months Experiences at the Gold Diggings," January 13, 1853.

29    Fariss and Smith, *Illustrated History of Plumas, Lassen & Sierra Counties*, 207; see also below, Chapter 8.

30    *"Our Grass Valley Correspondence," Sacramento Daily Union*, April 18, 1853.

31    Letter Jonathan Wheeler Bryant to brother, Diamond Springs, November 18, 19, or 20, 1852 (manuscript, Beinecke Library at WA MSS 51).

32    Tyrrell Martínez and Frank J. Drummond, *Early Mining Laws of Tuolumne and Calaveras Counties* (typescript), 28 (quoting an article by "Tuolumne" in the *Sonora Herald*, October 23, 1852). Rodman Paul notes that the editors of the *Sonora Herald* were among the chief proponents of selling titles to mining claims. Rodman W. Paul, *California Gold: The Beginning of Mining in the Far West* (Cambridge: Harvard University Press, 1947), 228n44.

33    Fariss and Smith, *Illustrated History of Plumas, Lassen & Sierra Counties*, 207.

34    "San Joaquin Intelligence," *Daily Alta California*, February 9, 1852.

35    Pringle Shaw, *Ramblings in California* (Toronto: James Bain, [1857?]), 73–76.

36    Shaw, *Ramblings in California*, 73–76.

37    "Our Grass Valley Correspondence," *Sacramento Daily Union*, April 18, 1853.

38    Karen Clay and Gavin Wright, "Order Without Law?" Citing US Census (1880), vol. 14 at 323.

39    James H. Carson, "To the Miners of California," *San Joaquin Republican*, March 12, 1853. Reprinted in Doris Shaw Castro, *James H. Carson's California, 1847–1853* (New York: Vantage Press, 1997), 174.

40    Daniel Bates Woods, *Sixteen Months at the Gold Diggings* (New York: Harper & Brothers, 1851), 1850.

41    Woods, *Sixteen Months*, February 22, 1850.

42    Laws of Warren Hill Mining District: "All persons who come here for the purpose of mining or becoming residents shall after the 6th day be considered citizens and have the right to vote in assemblies." See Clarence King, *The United States Mining Laws and Regulations Thereunder, and State and Territorial Mining Laws, to Which Are Appended Local Mining Rules and Regulations* (Washington, DC: G.P.O., 1885), 47th Congress, 2d Session, H.R. Misc. Doc 42, 279 (1885), alternative title: *Tenth Census of the United States*, 1880, Vol. 14, 279. Compare Isaac Barker, Diary of a Voyage around Cape Horn (Manuscript, Huntington Library, HM 19366), entry for April 13, 1850. Barker participated in a meeting about mining claims the day after he arrived at Georgetown.

43    Fariss and Smith, *Illustrated History of Plumas, Lassen & Sierra Counties*, 151.

44    Peter Justesen, *Two Years' Adventures of a Dane in the California Gold Mines*, trans. John Bellows (Gloucester, UK: Bellows 1865), 50.

45    William Jackson Barry, *Up and Down; or, Fifty Years' Colonial Experiences* (London: Sampson Low, Marston, Searle, & Rivington, 1879), 125–126.

46    Peregrine Pilgrim, "The Southern Mines—Mining Laws," *Daily Alta California*, January 14, 1853.

47    King, *United States Mining Laws*, 279–280.

48    "Mining News," *Sonora Herald*, August 10, 1850, 2.

49    King, *United States Mining Laws*, 277.

50    "Letter from the Mountains," *Daily Alta California*, January 3, 1853 (letter dated Sonora, December 24, 1852).

51    John Heckendorn and W. A. Wilson, *Miners and Business Men's Director* (Columbia, CA: Columbia Clipper Print, 1856), 54. Mining Laws of Jamestown District, November 23, 1853.

52    "Correspondence of the Transcript. Difficulty at the North. Taylorsville, July 25, 1850," *Sacramento Transcript*, August 6, 1850.

53    David Cleary, *Anatomy of the Amazon Gold Rush* (Iowa City: University of Iowa Press, 1990), 69–71.

54    See e.g., Felix Paul Wierzbicki, *California as It Is and as It May Be* (San Francisco: Grabhorn Press, 1933), 44.

55    The solidarity of mining partners became proverbial. Charles Henry Randall explained the arrangement in a letter to his parents, San Francisco, September 13, 1849: "We three have formed ourselves into a company for the purpose of digging gold[,] taking care of each other if sick[,] with mutual interest in whatever any of us may obtain" (manuscript, Bancroft Library at 68/40 C).

56    See *Local Mining Laws, Drytown Mining District*, "Resolution 6th," in King, *United States Mining Laws*, 271–272.

57    Ernest Frignet, *La Californie*, 2nd ed. (Paris: Schlesinger, 1867), 107.

58    "San Joaquin Intelligence," *Daily Alta California*, June 13, 1851.

59    King, *United States Mining Laws*, 280.

60    "Thursday Morning, June 9th," *Daily Alta California*, June 9, 1853.

61    Dame Shirley, *Shirley Letters*, 213.


### 6. Cooperation and Conflict with Mining Companies


1    Alexis De Tocqueville, *Democracy in America*, trans. Henry Reeve (New York: Oxford University Press, 1952), 377.

2    Daniel B. Woods, *Sixteen Months at the Gold Diggings* (New York: Harper & Brothers, 1851), 150.

3    Woods, *Sixteen Months*, 152–153.

4    *California Letters of Lucius Fairchild*, ed. Joseph Schafer (Madison: State Historical Society of Wisconsin, Madison, 1931), 76; "Dame Shirley" (Louise Clappe), *The Shirley Letters from California Mines in 1851-52* (San Francisco, Printed by T. C. Russell, 1922), 337, wrote that in the summer of 1852 that "nearly all the fluming companies had failed"; John Heckendorn and W. A. Wilson, *Miners and Business Men's Director* (Columbia, CA: Columbia Clipper Print, 1856), 89: "As a general thing, river turning in 1850 was a failure—since then the mode of operating has been very different, and the bed of the stream in a number of places has paid well for the expense of fluming."

5    J. G. Player-Frowd, *Six Months in California* (London: Longmans, Green, and Co., 1872), 94.

6    Woods, *Sixteen Months*, 143–144. On river turning generally, see Malcolm J. Rohrbough, *Days of Gold: The California Gold Rush and the American Nation* (Berkeley, CA: University of California Press, 1997), 197–215.

7    Massachusetts: Octavius Thorndike Howe, *Argonauts of '49: History and Adventures of the Emigrant Companies from Massachusetts 1849-1850* (Cambridge: Harvard University Press, 1923), 214–217; West Virginia: Constitution of the Charlestown, [West] Virginia, Mining Company, in *Trail to California: The Overland Journal of Vincent Geiger and Wakeman Bryarly* (New Haven: Yale University Press, 1945), 213–222; Missouri: John Philip Reed, "Tied to the Elephant," *University of Puget Sound Law Review* 1 (1977): 144n20. Naturally, the agreements all took the form of a preamble and series of articles. John Phillip Reid, "Governance of the Elephant: Constitutional Theory on the Overland Trail," *Hastings Constitutional Law Quarterly* 5 (1978): 421–443.

8    "Essex County and California Mining and Trading Company Meetings and Bylaws," Art. X, in Howe, *Argonauts of Forty-Nine*, 215.

9    *Around the Horn in '49; Journal of the Hartford Union Mining and Trading Company* (Wethersfied, CT: Rev. L.J. Hall, 1898), 28.

10   *Around the Horn*, 26.

11   George W. Allen, Diary (manuscript, Beinecke Library at WA MSS S-262), entry for September 6, 1850.

12   Woods, *Sixteen Months*, 181.

13   William W. Miller, "Voyage to California" (manuscript, Beinecke Library at WA MSS S-199), 101.

14   "Articles of Harts Bar Draining and Mining Company" in Woods, *Sixteen Months*, 146–147. See also Donald J. Pisani, *To Reclaim a Divided West: Water, Law, and Public Policy, 1848-1902* (Albuquerque: University of New Mexico Press, 1992), 16, discussing the Hart's Bar rules and the "healthy fear of outside capital" they displayed.

15   Ezra Bourne, "Journal . . . Typescript, and Related Material: 1850–1853" (manuscript, Bancroft Library at MSS C-F 142), 50.

16    Woods, *Sixteen Months*, 147–148.

17    Isaac Barker, Diary, September 18, 1849, to December 31, 1850 (manuscript, Huntington Library catalogued at HM 19366), entry for October 3, 1850.

18    E. A. Upton, Diaries (manuscript, Bancroft Library at MSS 78/48 C), entry for September 22, 1849. Buys a share in Union Canal Mining Dam for $70, "which he will work out." (Presumably that he would pay for his share in labor.)

19    Woods, *Sixteen Months*, 147.

20    Warren Sadler, Journal, September 1849–September 1850 (manuscript, Bancroft Library at MSS C F 73), July 27, 1850.

21    Letter Elias Lothrop to mother, September 13, 1850 (manuscript, Beinecke Library at WA MSS S-1677).

22    C. C. Mobley, "Diary of a miner at Oregon Bar, California etc. 1850–1851" (manuscript, Huntington Library catalogued at HM 26612) [67] entry June 25, 1850.

23    George W. Allen, Diary (manuscript, Beinecke Library at WA MSS S-262), entry for July 15.

24    Woods refers to his preaching throughout his narrative. "Death of Rev. Daniel B. Woods," *St. Louis Post-Dispatch*, May 30, 1892, page 2.

25    Woods, *Sixteen Months*, 159.

26    John David Borthwick, *Three Years in California [1851–1854]* (Edinburgh and London: William Blackwood and Sons, 1857), 369.

27    See e.g., Pascal Julliard & Co., who registered a river turning claim on the North Fork of the American River (Placer County Records, V. 1 Mining notices, 1850–1856, Banc MSS C A 293, 2 verso).

28    Placer County Records, vol. 1, Mining Notices, 1850–1856 (Banc MSS C A 293), 146.

29    Peter Decker, *The Diaries of Peter Decker Overland to California in 1849 and Life in the Mines, 1850–1851* (Georgetown, CA: Talisman Press, 1966), 225.

30    John Steele, *In Camp and Cabin* (Lodi, WI: J. Steele, c. 1901), 34–35.

31    Amos Batchelder regarding a miners' meeting on a branch of the Feather River (manuscript, Bancroft Library at MSS C-B 614, 167, entry for January 7, 1850). See also for the Mokelumne River, "Mining Laws," *Daily Alta California*, July 27, 1851 (regarding meeting on July 12, 1851). For the El Dorado Mining District, Placer County Records, vol. 1, "Record of Claims" (manuscript, Bancroft Library at MSS C A 293), 98.

32    "Convention of Miners," *Daily Alta California*, July 27, 1851. Mormon Island was at the junction of the North and South Forks of the American River, and miners came from ten miles up each fork and ten miles downstream.

33    "Convention of Miners," *Daily Alta California*, July 27, 1851.

34    "Miners' Convention," Sacramento Daily Union, August 1, 1851 (also reported in *Daily Alta California*, August 2, 1851).

35    Steele, *In Camp and Cabin*, 35.

36    Alonzo Delano, *California Correspondence* (Sacramento, CA: Sacramento Book Collectors Club, 1952), 40–41 (letter of March 2, 1850).

37    Delano, *California Correspondence*, 93–94 (letter, Independence, September 1, 1850).

38    George W. Allen, Diary (manuscript, Beinecke Library at WA MSS S-262) entry for June 14, 1850.

39    Placer County Records, vol. 1, Mining notices, 1850–1856 (manuscript, Bancroft Library at MSS C-A 293), 8 verso.

40    "Mining Laws," *Daily Alta California*, July 27, 1851 (Mokelumne River resolutions provide for trials before a jury of twelve miners).

41    Borthwick, *Three Years*, 154.

42    Decker, *Diaries*, 227 (entry for August 7, 1850).

43    Decker, *Diaries*, 227.

44    Judge Tod Robinson was judge of the Sixth Judicial District of California and sat at Sacramento. "The District Judgeship—Tod Robinson, Esq.," *Sacramento Transcript*, January 7, 1851; "Judge Robinson on the Bench," *Sacramento Transcript*, January 9, 1851.

45    "Canal Companies," *Sacramento Daily Union*, July 29, 1851.

46    "Excitement at Coloma," *Sacramento Daily Union*, July 30, 1851.

47    "The Park's Bar War," *Marysville Daily Herald*, July 17, 1851.

48    "The Park's Bar War," *Marysville Daily Herald*, July 17, 1851.

49    Felix Paul Wierzbicki, *California as It Is and as It May Be* (San Francisco: Grabhorn Press, 1933), 58–59.

50    "Regulations Regarding Claims, Passed in Convention, June 7, 1850," Art. 4 (manuscript, California State Library, catalogued at fc347-49). Amos Batchelder, Journal (manuscript, Bancroft Library at MSS C-B 614), 617 (entry for January 7, 1850). "Miners' Convention," *Sacramento Daily Union*, August 1, 1851.

51    It merely stated, "That upon the river we claim all the ground that is dried by damming or wing-damming" ("Mining Laws," *Daily Alta California*, July 27, 1851).

52    Steele, *In Camp and Cabin*, 35.

53    E. A. Upton, Diaries (manuscript, Bancroft Library at MSS 78/48 C), October 17, 1849. Five days earlier, on October 12, the company had voted "to expel a number of trespassers on the bar."

54    Pisani, *To Reclaim a Divided West*, 19.

55    William Shaw, *Golden Dreams and Waking Realities; Being the Adventures of a Gold-Seeker in California and the Pacific Islands* (London: Smith, Elder and Co., 1851), 85.

56    For example, a disaffected miner destroyed the water wheel of A. A. Enos's company. The company itself tried the man and found him guilty; it would have executed him had not Enos and one other man persuaded them to banish him instead. A.A. Enos, *Across the Plains in 1850* (Stanton, NE: A.F. Enos,1905), Eighteenth Letter (no page number).

57    Upton, Diaries, October 17, 1849.

58    Letter George Applegate to brother, California Correspondence, June 27, 1850 (manuscript, Beinecke Library at WA MSS 9).

59    Letter George Applegate to brother, California Correspondence, June 27, 1850.

60    Letter George Applegate to brother, California Correspondence, June 27, 1850. Also letter Applegate to brother, December 1, 1851.

61    William W. Miller, "Voyage to California" (manuscript, Beinecke Library at WA MSS S-199), October 21, 1849.

62    See Rudolph M. Lapp, *Blacks in Gold Rush California* (New Haven, NJ: Yale University Press, 1977), 55–64.

63    William W. Miller, "Voyage to California" (manuscript, Beinecke Library at WA MSS S-199), October 22 [1849].

64    Lapp, *Blacks in Gold Rush California*, 57.

### 7. Lynch Trials and Frontier Criminal Law

1    "Public Meeting-Law of the Mines," *Daily Alta California*, March 21, 1852, 2, col., 4 (regarding events of February 27 and 28).

2    Christopher Waldrep, *Lynching in America: A History in Documents* (New York and London: New York University Press, 2006), xvii.

3    William D. Carrigan, "The Strange Career of Judge Lynch: Why the Study of Lynching Needs to Be Refocused on the Mid-Nineteenth Century," *Journal of the Civil War Era* 7 (2017): 293–312. Ida B. Wells, *Southern Horrors: Lynch Law in All Its Phases* (New York: Age Printida, 1892); Ida B. Wells-Barnett, *The Red Record: Tabulated Statistics and Alleged Causes of Lynching in the United States, 1892-1893-1894* (Chicago: Donohue & Henneberry, 1895).

4    See also Monroe Nathan Work's statistics in the *Negro Year Book* (Tuskegee Institute, AL: Negro Year Book Pub. Co., 1912–1922). The 1885–1912 statistics appear in vol. 2 (1913), 237–239.

5    James Elbert Cutler, *Lynch-Law: An Investigation into the History of Lynching in the United States* (New York, London, and Bombay: Longmans,

Green and Co., 1905), 47–48, quoting letter by "Prudence Goodwife" published in the *New York Gazette*, December 31, 1753.

6       Cutler, *Lynch-Law*, 13–40, traces the term "Lynch's Law" back to Charles Lynch of Bedford, Virginia. Christopher Waldrep, *The Many Faces of Judge Lynch: Extralegal Violence and Punishment in America* (New York: Palgrave Macmillan, 2002), 15–19: Lynch himself used the term "Lynch's Law."

7       Cutler, *Lynch-Law*, 27.

8       Richard Maxwell Brown, *Strain of Violence: Historical Studies of American Violence and Vigilantism* (New York: Oxford University Press, 1975), 110; Manfred Berg, *Popular Justice: A History of Lynching in America* (Chicago: Ivan R. Dee, 2011), 46–47.

9       Brown, *Strain of Violence*, 97, 120–122.

10      Waldrep, *Many Faces of Judge Lynch*, 28–29.

11      *Niles' Weekly Register*, vol. 49, September 5, 1835, 1, col. 1 (article has no title).

12      "The Vicksburg Tragedy," *Niles' Weekly Register*, vol. 48, August 1, 1835, 381–382 (account dated July 9, 1835).

13      "A Tale of Terror," *Niles' Weekly Register*, vol. 50, June 4, 1836, 234.

14      Waldrep, *Many Faces of Judge Lynch*, 27, 33–35.

15      "Vicksburg Outrage," *Niles' Weekly Register*, vol. 48, August 1, 1835, 377.

16      Ashraf A. Rushdy, *American Lynching* (New Haven and London: Yale University Press, 2013), 33.

17      Waldrep, *Many Faces of Judge Lynch*, 33–35.

18      Waldrep, *Many Faces of Judge Lynch*, 35–37.

19      Waldrep, *Many Faces of Judge Lynch*, 38.

20      "General Synopsis of Events," *Alta California*, May 3, 1851. Reprinted in "Crime and Lynch Law in California," *Barre Patriot*, March 28, 1851, Barre, Massachusetts.

21      "The Mob Law in California," *Weekly National Intelligencer Washington* (DC), July 26, 1851, 6.

22      See also "California," *New Hampshire Sentinel* (Keene, New Hampshire), August 14, 1851, 2; "Lynch Law in California," *Hillsdale Standard* (Hillsdale, Michigan), February 10, 1852, 2, cols. 4–6; "California—An Indian War," *The Republic* (Washington, DC), May 3, 1853, 2, col. 3.

23      Enos Christman, *One Man's Gold*, ed. Florence Morrow Christman (New York: Whittlesey House, McGraw-Hill, 1930), 202–203 (entry for October 7, 1851).

24      John David Borthwick, *Three Years in California [1851-1854]* (Edinburgh and London: W. Blackwood and Sons, 1857), 223.

25    Theodore Taylor Johnson, *Sights in the Gold Region, and Scenes by the Way* (New York: Baker and Scribner, 1849), 185.

26    G. B. Stevens, Letter Journal (manuscript, Beinecke Library, at WA MSS S-12), entry for July 18, 1849, typescript 75.

27    "Memoirs of Daniel W. Kleinhans" (transcript, Bancroft Library at C-D 5056), 5.

28    William D. Carrigan and Clive Webb, *Forgotten Dead: Mob Violence against Mexicans in the United States, 1848–1928* (Oxford: Oxford University Press, 2013), 24. Waldrep, *Many Faces of Judge Lynch*, makes a slightly different point: Western, and specifically Californian, arguments in favor of lynch law undermined Northern arguments against lynchings of Blacks in the South (49–50).

29    John Phillip Reid, *Policing the Elephant: Crime, Punishment, and Social Behavior on the Overland Trail* (San Marino, CA: Huntington Library, 1997), 126–127.

30    Reid, *Policing the Elephant*, 233.

31    Reid, *Policing the Elephant*, 232.

32    Reid, *Policing the Elephant*, 230.

33    Reid, *Policing the Elephant*, 197.

34    Reid, *Policing the Elephant*, 197, quoting Godfrey C. Ingrim, "Starting Out for the Gold Mines" (transcript, Kansas State Historical Society, n.d.).

35    Reid, *Policing the Elephant*, 195.

36    Reid, *Policing the Elephant*, 132.

37    Stephen J. Leonard, *Lynching in Colorado, 1859–1919* (Boulder: University Press of Colorado, 2002), 15–29; Darlene A. Cypser, "Myth of the Wild West: Law and Justice Prior to the Organization of the Territory of Colorado" (MA thesis, University of Colorado, 2017), 81–83.

38    Leonard, *Lynching in Colorado*, 18.

39    Cypser, "Myth of the Wild West," 117–169.

40    Jesse Macy, *Institutional Beginnings in a Western State*, Johns Hopkins University Studies in Historical and Political Science, Ser. 2, vol. 7 (Baltimore: N. Murray: Johns Hopkins University, 1884), 6.

41    "The Law of Nature—or Self Preservation," *Niles' Register* 46 (1834), 352–353. *Niles' Register* reproduced the details of the incident and trial from an article, "Trial and Execution of Patrick O'Connor," from *The Galenian*, June 23, 1834.

42    "The Law of Nature—or Self Preservation," *Niles' Register* 46 (1834).

43    "The Law of Nature—or Self Preservation," *Niles' Register* 46 (1834).

44    Charles Augustus Murray, *Travels in North America during the Years 1834, 1835 & 1836*, vol. II (London: R. Bentley, 1841), 107.

45    R[ichard] H. Dana, *Two Years before the Mast* (New York: A. L. Burt Company, 1840), 160.

46    W. H. C. Folsom, *Fifty Years in the Northwest*, ed. E. E. Edwards (St. Paul, MN: Pioneer Press Co., 1888), 89; see also E. S. Seymour, *Sketches of Minnesota, the New England of the West* (New York: Harper & Bros. 1850), 206.

47    Mark C. Dillon, *The Montana Vigilantes 1863-1870: Gold, Guns and Gallows* (Logan: University Press of Colorado, 2013), 91-102.

48    Frederick Allen, *A Decent Orderly Lynching: The Montana Vigilantes* (Norman: University of Oklahoma Press, 2004), 195 (on the oath of secrecy).

49    William Kelly, *An Excursion to California over the Prairie, Rocky Mountains, and Great Sierra Nevada* (London: Chapman and Hall, 1851), 24. See also Malcolm J. Rohrbough, *Rush to Gold: The French and the California Gold Rush, 1848-1854* (New Haven and London: Yale University Press, 2013), 277 ff, quoting Patrice Dillon, the French consul, on the "California Moral Code" that permitted crimes to be settled by knife or gun.

50    Bayard Taylor, *Eldorado; or, Adventures in the Path of Empire* (New York: G. P. Putnam and Son, 1871), 92.

51    Helen S. Griffin, ed., *The Diaries of Peter Decker: Overland to California in 1849 and Life in the Mines, 1850-1851*, 2nd ed. (Georgetown, CA: Talisman Press, 1966), 27 (August 4 or 5, 1850). See also Joseph Henry Jackson, *Anybody's Gold: The Story of California's Mining Towns* (New York and London: D. Appleton-Century, 1941), 219.

52    Fariss and Smith, *Illustrated History of Plumas, Lassen & Sierra Counties* (San Francisco: Fariss and Smith, 1882), 449. The date was 1854.

53    "Lynching," *Daily Alta California*, February 3, 1851.

54    "Amador County Correspondence—Murder and Lynch Law," *Sacramento Daily Union*, January 1, 1855. At Volcano diggings; the victim's name was McAllister.

55    "Lynch Law at Georgetown," *Sacramento Transcript*, October 10, 1850.

56    "Lynching," *Sacramento Daily Union*, March 28, 1851.

57    "Lynch Law at Melones," *Daily Alta California*, June 20, 1851.

58    "Another Case of Lynching," *Sacramento Daily Union*, April 4, 1851. See also "Lynching," *Sacramento Daily Union*, March 28, 1851.

59    "Judge Lynch—From the Times," *Weekly Pacific News*, February 1, 1851, 3.

60    Alfred Peabody, "Early Days and Rapid Growth of California," in *Early Voyages to California. Essex Institute Historical Collections*, vol. XII, no. 2 (Salem, MA: Salem Press, 1874), 7.

61    William Taylor, *California Life Illustrated* (New York: Published for the author by Carlton & Porter, 1858), 294.

62    Mary Floyd Williams, *History of the San Francisco Committee of Vigilance of 1851: A Study of Social Control on the California Frontier in the Days of the Gold Rush* (Berkeley: University of California Press, 1921), provides the most complete account of the committees of 1849 and 1851.

63    Brown, *Strain of Violence*, 103.

64    Brown, *Strain of Violence*, 108–110.

65    Brown, *Strain of Violence*, 95–133.

66    Williams, *History of the San Francisco Committee of Vigilance*, 105–108.

67    Mary Floyd Williams, *Papers of the San Francisco Committee of Vigilance of 1851* (Berkeley: University of California Press, 1919).

68    Williams, *History of the San Francisco Committee of Vigilance*, 203–206. The register of more than seven hundred names is reproduced in Williams, *Papers of the San Francisco Committee of Vigilance of 1851*, 806–814.

69    "The V.C. Rooms," *Daily Alta Californian*, November 3, 1851,

70    Williams, *History of the San Francisco Committee of Vigilance*, 212–214 (Jenkins), 268–271 (Stuart).

71    Williams, *History of the San Francisco Committee of Vigilance*; other vigilance committees formed in Stockton (375), Marysville (376), Santa Clara and Sacramento (377), Sonora (378), and Nevada City (379). Christman, *One Man's Gold*, said of Sonora's Vigilance Committees that all suspects (unnamed) were tried to a jury, and the committee hanged at least one horse thief and whipped and banished another (203).

72    Mary Floyd Williams, *History of the San Francisco Committee of Vigilance*, 376, notes the similarity of the Marysville Committee's constitution to that of San Francisco's. The comments on the committee's decision to take no action in the case of the Mexican attackers appears in "Great Excitement! Two Men Arrested by the Vigilance Committee," *Marysville Daily Herald*, June 26, 1851.

73    Christman, *One Man's Gold*, 191. These resolutions were passed on June 29, 1851.

74    Christman, *One Man's Gold*, 190. See also Alonzo Delano, *California Correspondence* Irving McKee ed. (Sacramento: Sacramento Book Collector's Club, 1952), 126. See also Williams, *History of the San Francisco Committee of Vigilance*, 383n77 (references to vigilance committees in mining camps).

75    Williams, *History of the San Francisco Committee of Vigilance*, 383.

76    *The Shirley Letters from California Mines in 1851–52* (San Francisco: T. C. Russell, 1922), 268–269.

77    "The Outrages in the Mines," *Daily Alta California*, July 17, 1850.

78    Waldrep, *Many Faces of Judge Lynch*, 68.

79    Rodman Paul, *California Gold: The Beginning of Mining in the Far West* (Cambridge, MA: Harvard University Press, 1947), 206.

80    David A. Johnson, "Vigilance and the Law: The Moral Authority of Popular Justice in the Far West," *American Quarterly* 33 (1981): 558–586 at 564.

81    Johnson, "Vigilance and the Law," 572.

## 8. Trial by Judge Lynch

1    "EXCITING FROM THE NORTH. Two Men Whipped! And one Hung for Murder!!" *Sacramento Transcript*, March 26, 1851.

2    Joseph Warren Wood, "Diaries of Crossing the Plains in 1849 and Life in the Diggings from 1849 to 1853" (manuscript, Huntington Library at HM 318), entry for June 25, 1852.

3    Willian Binur, *Wooded Up in Log Town. A Letter from the Gold Fields* (Berkeley: Bancroft Library Press, 1851), 12 (letter to Sarah, March 8, 1851).

4    Jacksonville Code Article V, January 20, 1850, in Daniel B. Woods, *Sixteen Months at the Gold Diggings* (New York: Harper & Brothers, 1851), 126.

5    "A Lynch Trial in California," *Household Words*, vol. 3 (London: Bradbury & Evans, 1851), 611–612.

6    Dame Shirley (Louise Clappe), *The Shirley Letters from California Mines in 1851–52* (San Francisco: T. C. Russell, 1922), 123 (Indian Bar, October 29, 1851).

7    Daniel W. Kleinhans, Memoirs (transcript, Bancroft Library at BANC MSS C-D 5056), 5, 13.

8    "Confession of the Nevada Robbery," *Sacramento Transcript*, April 7, 1851. Discussed below at 196–197.

9    "Summary Execution of Five Mexicans," *Sacramento Transcript*, May 2, 1851.

10    "The Lynching Affair in El Dorado!" *Sacramento Transcript*, May 12, 1851. This is one of the cases Royce used to illustrate the miners' hubris.

11    Richard Brown Cowley, "Journal of a Voyage on the Barque 'Canton' from New York to San Francisco via the Horn; Life in the Mines on the Mokelumne River" (manuscript, Huntington Library at HM 26652), 80 vs—81 rt, entry for July 6, 1851.

12    "Diary of Vicente Pérez Rosales," in *We Were 49ers! Chilean Accounts of the California Gold Rush*, eds. Edwin A. Beilhzarz and Carlos U. López (Pasadena: Ward Ritchie Press, 1976), 78–79.

13    John Hovey, Journal of a Voyage from Newburypont. Mass. to San Francisco, Cal. in the Brig Charlott by a Passenger Commencing Jan. 23, 1849, and ending July 23, 1849 (manuscript, Huntington Library at HM 322, 74–90).

14    Hovey, Journal, 80–81; Navarro in Edwin A. Beilharz and Carlos U. López, eds., *We Were 49ers!*, 166–167, wrote that the Americans from the Mokelumne numbered four to six and that they got only the means of execution changed, from being thrown off a cliff to hanging.

15    Enos Christman, *One Man's Gold*, ed. Florence Morrow Christman (New York: Whittlesey House, McGraw-Hill, 1930), 174.

16    Kleinhans, Memoirs (transcript, Bancroft Library at BANC MSS C-D 5056), 5.

17    "EXCITING FROM THE NORTH. Two Men Whipped! And one Hung for Murder!!" *Sacramento Transcript*, March 26, 1851.

18    "Lynch Law in the Gold Diggings," *New-York Daily Tribune*, March 18, 1851, 6: "A correspondent of the *Journal of Commerce*, writing from Nevada City, California, January 24."

19    Dame Shirley, *Letters*, 121.

20    Dame Shirley, *Letters*, 114–115.

21    Dame Shirley, *Letters*, 123.

22    Dame Shirley, *Letters*, 115–116.

23    Joseph Warren Wood, Diaries, June 25, 1852.

24    "Indians Hung at Rough and Ready," *Daily Alta California*, June 11, 1852; "Lynching on the Cosumnes," *Sacramento Transcript*, January 21, 1851.

25    "From the Mines," *Weekly Alta California*, February 8, 1849.

26    "Forty-Niner Profile: Josiah Roop," *Library Chronicle*, vol. 24 (Philadelphia: Friends of the Library, University of Pennsylvania, 1947), 72–78. Reproduced at yesteryearsnews.wordpress.com/2009/12/11/forty-niner-profile-josiah -roop/.

27    "Confession of the Nevada Robbery," *Sacramento Transcript*, April 7, 1851.

28    "Correspondence of the Union," *Sacramento Daily Union*, July 26, 1854; letter dated Greenwood Valley, El Dorado County, July 24, 1854.

29    See also "Immense Excitement! LYNCH LAW AT LAST!!" *Sacramento Transcript*, February 26, 1851. F. C. Ewer, a juror, was excused at his request on the ground that he was an editor of the *Sacramento Transcript*. He could not write an impartial report of the trial if he was a juror.

30    "Later from Sonora," *Sacramento Transcript*, July 24, 1850.

31    "Lynch Law," *Alta California*, January 20, 1851. Trial at Double Springs on the Calaveras.

32    Theodore H. Hittell, *History of California*, vol. 3 (San Francisco: N. J. Stone & Company, 1897), 295.

33    Jacksonville Code Art XV and Art XVI in Woods, *Sixteen Months*, 129.

34    Kleinhans, Memoirs (transcript, Bancroft Library at BANC MSS C-D 5056), 5.

35    "Judge Lynch at Rich Bar," *Daily Alta California*, December 16, 1851.

36    "Serious Affray at Columbia—Great Excitement," *Daily Alta California*, November 17, 1853. (The paper's "Nobel" was a mistake for "Nicholas.")

37    Letter from Sam to Willie, February 27, 1851, Sacramento City (manuscript, Bancroft Library at BANC MSS C-B 547 Pt. I:53).

38    Woods, *Sixteen Months*, 129.

39    Stephen Johnson Field, *Personal Reminiscences of Early Days in California* (San Francisco: s.n., 1880), 31–32.

40    J. H. Carson, *Early Recollections of the Mines, and a Description of the Great Tulare Valley* (Tarrytown, NY: W. Abbatt, 1931), 35–36.

41    Letter to the Editors, Nevada City, July 22, *Sacramento Transcript*, July 26, 1850; Letter Ephraim Delano to wife (manuscript, Beinecke Library at WA MSS S-59 D374), January 19, 1852, Turnerville, California.

42    "Confession of the Nevada Robbery," *Sacramento Transcript*, April 7, 1851.

43    Ellis advertised as an attorney in *Nevada Journal*, September 3, 1851, 1, col. 1, and represented William Hayden, defendant in a murder trial court, "From Nevada," *Sacramento Daily Union*, May 28, 1851. He was elected to the California Assembly, "The State Election," *Daily Alta California*, October 9, 1851.

44    "Decided," *Sacramento Daily Union*, October 23, 1851, 2.

45    Stephen J. Field, *Personal Reminiscences*, 107. On the duel between Judges Field and Barbour, which was broken off at the last minute, see Oscar Tully Shuck, *History of the Bench and Bar of California: History, Anecdotes, Reminiscences*, vol. 2 (San Francisco: Occident Printing House, 1889), 154–156. Note that this is different from the 1901 edition of the same name.

46    "For the Marysville Herald Row at Park's Bar—Judge Bernard Stabbed," *Marysville Daily Herald*, May 31, 1851.

47    "District Court," *Marysville Daily Herald*, November 8, 1850.

48    "Nevada Items—The Election," *Sacramento Daily Union*, June 7, 1851.

49    Shuck, *History of the Bench and Bar*, 306–311. Coffroth later represented Tuolumne in the state assembly. Ibid., 311. E. F. Ellis, Coffroth, and one other advocated for the bill allowing married women to transact business in their own names. The bill passed by more than three to one. Ibid., 311.

50    Shuck, *History of the Bench and Bar*, 311.

51    Coffroth was the prosecuting attorney in the murder trial of John S. Barclay. The victim, John H. Smith, was a friend of Coffroth's and he whipped up the crowd against the accused. Shuck, *History of the Bench and Bar*, 272.

52    "Excitement at Colombia," *Sacramento Daily Union*, November 21, 1853.

53    This summary is based on Hittell, *History of California*, 295–296. Hittell dates the events to November 13, 1853.

54    "San Joaquin News," *Daily Alta California*, June 7, 1852: Thomas N. Cazneau advertised regularly in the *Daily Alta California* as an insurance adjuster and notary in San Francisco.

55    "Died," *Daily Alta California*, April 10, 1852, death announcement of the daughter of Eugene F. Gillespie, Esq.

56    Dame Shirley, *Letters*, 123.

57    Dame Shirley, *Letters*, 130–131.

58    William Shaw, *Golden Dreams and Waking Realities* (London: Smith, Elder & Co., 1851), 60–61.

59    Richard Brown Cowley, Journal (manuscript, Huntington Library at HM 26652), 88, entry for November 2, 1851.

60    "Immense Excitement! LYNCH LAW AT LAST!!" *Sacramento Transcript*, February 26, 1851.

61    It was suggested the jury should also have legal advice but—curiously—the two men approached for the job both refused it.

62    "The Late Col. E. J. C. Kewen," *Los Angeles Herald*, November 27, 1879, 3, quoting from *Universal Biography* (New York and Hartford Publishing Company).

63    Dame Shirley, *Letters*, 154–155; the jury were absent for only a few minutes.

64    "For the Marysville Herald Row at Park's Bar—Judge Bernard Stabbed," *Marysville Daily Herald*, May 31, 1851 (one hour); *A Frenchman in the Gold Rush; the Journal of Ernest de Massey, Argonaut of 1849*, trans. Marguerite Eyer Wilbur (San Francisco: California Historical Society, 1927), 172 (two hours).

65    Dame Shirley, *Letters*, 122.

66    David Augusts Shaw, *Eldorado; or, California as Seen by a Pioneer, 1850–1900* (Los Angeles: B. R. Baumgardt, 1900), 141.

67    "From the Mines," *Weekly Alta California*, May 31, 1849.

68    Dame Shirley, *Letters*, 119.

69    Stephen J. Field, *Personal Reminiscences of Early Days in California* (San Francisco?: s.n., 1880), 63.

70    *History of the Ojibway Nation* (Saint Paul: Minnesota Historical Society, 1897), 485.

71    Dame Shirley, *Letters*, 155.

72    Dame Shirley, *Letters*, 121.

73    "Fatal Affray," *Weekly Alta California,* May 3, 1849; Samuel McNeil, *McNeil's Travels in 1849, to, through, and from the Gold Regions in California* (Columbus: Scott & Bascom, 1850), 25.

74    "A Most Melancholy Death," *Placer Times,* November 10, 1849.

75    Christman, *One Man's Gold,* 190.

76    Christman, *One Man's Gold,* 192.

77    Kimball Webster, *The Gold Seekers of '49* (Manchester, NH: Standard Book, 1917), 177–178.

78    Kleinhans, Memoirs (transcript, Bancroft Library at BANC MSS C-D 5056), 5.

79    John Clark, "California Guide" (manuscript and transcript, Beinecke Library at WA MSS 83), entry for January 15, 1854.

80    Adolphus Windeler, *The California Gold Rush Diary of a German Sailor,* ed. W. Turrentine Jackson (Berkeley, CA: Howell-North Books, 1969), 121. Windeler was a friend of the German victims. Dame Shirley, *Letters,* 152, wrote that the sum was $1,800; "Judge Lynch at Rich Bar," *Daily Alta California,* 371, December 18, 1851, gave the figure as $16,000. The events were also described in "Lynch Law at Rich Bar," *Sacramento Daily Union,* December 18, 1851.

81    "Judge Lynch at Rich Bar," *Daily Alta California,* January 1, 1852.

82    Dame Shirley, *Letters,* 152.

83    Dame Shirley, *Letters,* 154–155.

84    "Nevada Items," *Sacramento Daily Union,* June 7, 1851: "Judge Lynch has been holding a short term of his Court at Grass Valley . . . The proof was positive and the jury unanimous."

85    Theodore Taylor Johnson, *Sights in the Gold Region,* 185.

86    "Tremendous Excitement in San Francisco," *Marysville Herald,* February 28, 1851, 2, col. 4.

87    Marco G. Thorne and Levi Stowell, "Bound for the Land of Canaan, Ho!: The Diary of Levi Stowell, 1849 (Continued)," *California Historical Quarterly* 27 (1948): 163n70.

88    "Lynching," *Pacific Weekly News,* April 1, 1851.

89    Shaw, *Eldorado,* 142.

90    "Sacramento Intelligence," *Daily Alta California,* February 19, 1851 (three-hour trial, sentence of one hundred lashes administered immediately); *A Frenchman in the Gold Rush; the Journal of Ernest de Massey, Argonaut of 1849,* trans. Marguerite Eyer Wilbur (San Francisco: California Historical Society, 1927), 172 (murder trial began at two o'clock, arguments concluded by six o'clock, jury delivered its verdict at eight o'clock, and prisoner was hanged that evening).

91    "Confession of the Nevada Robbery," *Sacramento Transcript,* April 7, 1851.

## 9. Whipping, Branding, and Hanging

1    For examples of the jury's sentence either confirmed or altered by the crowd, see "Serious Affray at Columbia—Great Excitement, Colombia, Nov. 14, 1853," *Daily Alta California*, November 17, 1853; The "Lynching Affair in El Dorado," *Sacramento Transcript*, May 12, 1851.

2    "Law of the Mines," *Daily Alta California*, March 21, 1852, 2.

3    Dame Shirley (Louise Clappe), *The Shirley Letters from California Mines in 1851–52* (San Francisco: T. C. Russell, 1922), 155.

4    Edouard Auger, *Voyage en Californie* (Paris: Hachette et Cie, 1854), 205–207. Auger witnessed a convicted Mexican at Hawkin's Bar being whipped in the morning and hung the same evening.

5    Skip Breyfogle, "Diary of Joshua D. Breyfogle, Sr.," *Sierran* 41 (Summer 2013): 1–3 (July 4, 1853).

6    "For the Marysville Herald Row at Park's Bar—Judge Barnard Stabbed," *Marysville Daily Herald*, May 31, 1851. Hiram C. Hodge, Esq., of Nevada City, atty. for the people; C. M. Lamison for defendants. (Hiram C. Hodge was elected county judge of Nevada City soon after the event; see "Nevada Items," *Sacramento Daily Union*, June 7, 1851.)

7    Letter Charles Henry Randall to father and mother, San Francisco, September 13, 1849 (manuscript, Bancroft Library at MSS 68/40 C).

8    Solemnity and decorum: "Summary Execution of Five Mexicans," *Sacramento Transcript*, May 2, 1851. Hungry mob: David Pierce Barstow, *Recollections of 1849–51 in California* (Inverness, CA: Press of Inverness, 1979), 23.

9    "The Sonora Murder," *Sacramento Daily Union*, June 18, 1851.

10    John Walton Caughey, *Their Majesties the Mob* (Chicago: University of Chicago Press, 1960), 36.

11    "EXCITING FROM THE NORTH. Two Men Whipped! And One Hung for Murder!!" *Sacramento Transcript*, March 26, 1851.

12    "Confession of the Nevada Robbery," *Sacramento Transcript*, April 7, 1851.

13    "The Lynching Affair in El Dorado!" *Sacramento Transcript*, May 12, 1851. The sheriff persuaded the crowd to hand over the prisoner before it carried out its punishment.

14    "Summary Execution of Five Mexicans," *Sacramento Transcript*, May 2, 1851.

15    See e.g., Fariss and Smith, *Illustrated History of Plumas, Lassen & Sierra Counties*, 442.

16    Dame Shirley, *Letters*, 270.

17    Stephen Johnson Field, *Personal Reminiscences of Early Days in California* (San Francisco?: s.n., 1880), 33; this case was also reported in "Sacramento and Placer Intelligence," *Alta Californian*, April 8, 1850, 2. Clark,

"California Guide" (manuscript and transcript, Beinecke Library at WA MSS 83), entry for April 30, 1854.

18    Rosales in Edwin A. Beilharz and Carlos U. Lopez, trans. and ed., *We Were 49ers! Chilean Accounts of the California Gold Rush* (Pasadena, CA: Ward Ritchie Press, 1976), 78–79.

19    G. B. Stevens, Letters (manuscript, Beinecke Library at WA MSS S-12), 75.

20    "Lynched," *Sacramento Transcript*, January 30, 1851.

21    William Shaw, *Golden Dreams and Waking Realities; Being the Adventures of a Gold-Seeker in California and the Pacific Islands* (London: Smith, Elder and Co., 1851), 59.

22    Katherine A. White, ed., *A Yankee Trader in the Gold Rush; the Letters of Franklin A. Buck* (Boston and New York: Houghton Mifflin, 1930), 110–111. Letter dated Weaverville, October 5, 1852.

23    William H. C. Folsom, *Fifty Years in the Northwest* (St. Paul: Pioneer Press Company, 1888), 89.

24    "Lynch Law," *Daily Alta California*, August 12, 1852.

25    "Public Meeting—Law of the Mines," *Daily Alta California*, March 21, 1852.

26    Dame Shirley, *Letters*, 156.

27    David Brown's execution was originally scheduled for one hour after he was sentenced, but some "more mildly disposed" got it extended to three. Ibid. See also "EXCITING FROM THE NORTH. Two Men Whipped! And one Hung for Murder!!" *Sacramento Transcript*, March 26, 1851 (hanged the same afternoon at four o'clock); "Hanging Affair on Weber Creek," *Sacramento Transcript*, April 7, 1851 (hanged the same afternoon); "The Sonora Murder. Lynch Law!— Three Mexicans Hung!" *Sacramento Daily Union*, June 18, 1851 (hanged the same evening).

28    "Summary Execution of Five Mexicans," *Sacramento Transcript*, May 2, 1851 (hanging the day after the trial).

29    Enos Christman, *One Man's Gold*, ed. Florence Morrow Christman (New York: Whittlesey House, McGraw-Hill, 1930), 192.

30    John Clark, "California Guide" (manuscript and transcript, Beinecke Library at WA MSS 83), entry for September 16, 1853.

31    Joseph Warren Wood, *Diaries of Crossing the Plains in 1849 and Life in the Diggings from 1849 to 1853* (manuscript, Huntington Library at HM 318), July 5, 1852.

32    "The Sonora Murder," *Sacramento Daily Union*, June 18, 1851.

33    Henry Sturdivant, Journal from Dec. 8th. 49 (manuscript, Huntington Library at HM 261), 47 (entry for April 29, 1851).

34    Edward Gould Buffum, *Six Months in the Gold Mines* (Philadelphia: Lea and Blanchard, 1850), 83.

35    Letter David G. Ferson to brother, Shaws Flats, July 10, 1851 (manuscript, Beinecke Library at WA MSS S-1315).

36    Execution of Jose Forni—His Confession," *Daily Alta California*, December 11, 1852 (parents take children to watch the spectacle). "The Romance of Hanging," *Daily Alta California*, January 12, 1852, 2.

37    "The Gold Fever Abroad," *Californian*, September 9, 1848. Oscar Wilde actually said, "The truth is rarely pure and never simple."

38    This seems to be the prevailing explanation for the name. See e.g., David Rohrer Leeper, *The Argonauts of 'Forty-nine, Some Recollections of the Plains and the Diggings* (South Bend, IN: J. B. Stoll, 1894), 99.

39    Buffum, *Six Months*, 83–85. Other accounts, with some variations, appear in Theodore H. Hittell, *History of California*, vol. 3 (San Francisco: N. J. Stone & Company, 1897), 272; J. M. Letts, *California Illustrated: Including a Description of the Panama and Nicaragua Routes* (New York: R. T. Young, 1853), 108–109; Mary Floyd Williams, *History of the San Francisco Committee of Vigilance of 1851* (1921), 78n33; "From the Mines," *Daily Alta California*, February 8, 1849, at 2.

40    On Buffum, see Doyce B. Nunis Jr., "Edward Gould Buffum: Early California Journalist," *California History*, vol. 73 (Berkeley: University of California Press, 1994), 114–129. Buffum's father was Arnold Buffum, a famous abolitionist; his sister, Elizabeth, also worked toward humane criminal punishment.

41    Buffum, *Six Months*, 84–85.

42    Buffum, *Six Months*, 84.

43    William Lewis Manly, *Death Valley in '49* (San Jose, CA: Pacific Tree and Vine, 1894), 448–449. On the Downieville trial and execution, see "Sacramento Intelligence," *Daily Alta California*, July 9, 1851; "The Hanging at Downieville," *Daily Alta California*, July 14, 1851; "The Downieville Tragedy," *Daily Alta California*, January 29, 1852; Fariss and Smith *Illustrated History of Plumas*, 445–447; Alexandre Jean Joachim Holinski, *La Californie et les Routes Interocéaniques* (Brussels: A. Labroue et Compagnie, 1853), 232; Borthwick, *Three Years*, 222–223.

44    "The Downieville Tragedy," *Daily Alta California*, January 29, 1852 (a letter decrying the supposed distortion of the facts by the *Picayune* and "the press of the whole country"); on the *London Times*, see Fariss and Smith, *Illustrated History of Plumas*, 447.

45    "A Woman Hung at Downieville," *Marysville Daily Herald*, July 8, 1851. Barstow, *Recollections of 1849–51 in California*, 21 (some drunken men pushed her door in during the night; Juanita jumped out of bed and stabbed one of them to death).

46    On Cannon's story, see Fariss and Smith, *Illustrated History of Plumas*, 445–446. John Boessenecker, *Gold Dust and Gunsmoke, Tales of Gold Rush Outlaws, Gunfighters, Lawmen, and Vigilantes* (New York: John Wiley & Sons,

1999), 145, submits that a white man who killed in response to an equivalent insult would have been acquitted, while William B. Secrest, *Juanita* (Fresno, CA: Saga-West, 1967), offers a different reading of the sources that is less sympathetic to the defendant.

47    "Sacramento Intelligence," *Daily Alta California,* July 9, 1851 (size of the crowd); Barstow, *Recollections of 1849–51 in California,* 23 (wild mob).

48    Boessenecker, *Gold Dust and Gunsmoke,* 142.

49    See e.g., Fariss and Smith, *Illustrated History of Plumas,* 149.

50    Fariss and Smith, *Illustrated History of Plumas,* 443.

51    *History of Alameda County, California* (Oakland, CA: M. W. Wood, 1883) mentions, "Judge A. M. Brocklebank, a well-known lawyer and brother-in-law to the late ex-Governor Weller" (685).

52    Boessenecker, *Gold Dust and Gunsmoke,* 143.

53    Fariss and Smith, *Illustrated History of Plumas,* 446, 424, 438.

54    Enos Christman, *One Man's Gold,* 174.

55    Hovey, "Journal," 82 (Calervarus, January 3, 1850).

56    Mahmoud Rayes et al., "Hangman's Fracture: A Historical and Biomedical Perspective," *Journal of Neurosurgery: Spine* 14 (2011): 198–208; published online December 24, 2010; DOI: 10.3171/2010.10.SPINE09805.

57    Clark, "California Guide" (manuscript and transcript, Beinecke Library at WA MSS 83), entry for August 5, 1853.

58    Clark, "California Guide."

59    *The Gold Rush Diary of Ramón Gil Navarro,* eds., María del Carmen Ferreyra and David S. Reher (Lincoln: University of Nebraska Press, 2000), 42 (August 22, 1849).

60    Juanita in the Downieville hanging jumped. Five Mexicans gave the signal for their own deaths. "Summary Execution of Five Mexicans," *Sacramento Transcript,* May 2, 1851.

61    Dame Shirley, *Letters,* 156.

62    Adolphus Windeler, *The California Gold Rush Diary of a German Sailor,* ed. W. Turrentine Jackson (Berkeley, CA: Howell-North Books, 1969), 127.

63    For a discussion of flogging as a harsh and degrading punishment, see James Q. Whitman, *Harsh Justice: Criminal Punishment and the Widening Divide between America and Europe* (New York: Oxford University Press, 2003), 175.

64    "Lynching at the North," *Sacramento Transcript,* May 27, 1851.

65    Dame Shirley, *Letters,* 269. This punishment was administered by a vigilance committee.

66    D. A. Shaw, *Eldorado,* 141–142.

67    Letter Kimball Dimmick to Sarah, October 23, 1848 (manuscript, Bancroft Library at C-B 847). For another description of a whipping, see "Lynch Law at San Jose," *Sacramento Daily Union*, March 19, 1851 (one hundred lashes, prisoner fainted twice).

68    "Nevada Items," *Sacramento Daily Union*, June 7, 1851.

69    Fariss and Smith, *Illustrated History of Plumas*, 443.

70    Letter Allen Varner to David Varner, March 5, 1850 (manuscript, Huntington Library at HM 39980).

71    Field, *Personal Reminiscences*, 33.

72    "Lynching on the Cosumnes," *Sacramento Transcript*, January 21, 1851.

73    See also Fariss and Smith, *Illustrated History of Plumas*, 450–451: the district court (not the miners) sentenced a young man to twenty-five lashes in 1854.

74    Buffum, *Six Months*, 83–84.

75    Dame Shirley, *Letters*, 125.

76    Letter Kimball Dimmick to Sarah, October 23, 1848 (manuscript, Bancroft Library at C-B 847): "The sentence was universally approved and my Sheriff carried it into execution on the spot"; letter Allen Varner to David Varner, March 5th, 1850 (manuscript, Huntington Library at HM 39980).

77    Fariss and Smith, *Illustrated History of Plumas*, 443.

78    "Lynching on the Cosumnes," *Sacramento Transcript*, January 21, 1851,

79    D. A. Shaw, *Eldorado*, 141 (said to be in 1854).

80    "Lynch Law," *Sacramento Transcript*, December 19, 1850.

81    "More Lynching al Nevada," *Sacramento Transcript*, May 24, 1851; also *Alta*, May 24, 1851.

82    "From Sonoma," *Sacramento Daily Union*, April 19, 1851.

83    "Warning to Sydney Birds," *Sacramento Daily Union*, June 3, 1851.

84    Farris and Smith, *Illustrated History of Plumas*, 449. The sheriff's name was William J. Ford; the events took place at Downieville and were reported on September 16, 1853.

85    D. A. Shaw, *Eldorado*, 141.

86    Dame Shirley, *Letters*, 269–270.

87    Whitman, *Harsh Justice*, 103–105.

88    "Another Case of Lynching," *Sacramento Transcript*, January 13, 1851.

89    Field, *Personal Reminiscences*, 34–35.

90    Dame Shirley, *Letters*, 130.

91    William Shaw, *Golden Dreams*, 114.

92    A. Warner and Company, *History of Allegheny County, Pennsylvania, Including its Early Settlement* (Chicago: A. Warner, 1889), 244, on branding, cropping, and cutting off ears in Pennsylvania in 1782 and 1783; Glenn McNair, *Criminal Injustice: Slaves and Free Blacks in Georgia's Criminal Justice System* (Charlottesville, VA: University of Virginia Press, 2009), 146–147 (branding and cropping as criminal punishment of slaves).

93    Bayard Taylor, *Eldorado, or, Adventures in the Path of Empire* (New York: G. P. Putnam, 1850), 92. I assume this is the sailor punished for stealing $5,000 in 1849 as described by Ryan, 62, because the dates are similar.

94    G. B. Stevens, Letters (manuscript, Beinecke at WA MSS S-12), 75.

95    William Kelly, *Excursion to California over the Prairie, Rocky Mountains, and Great Sierra Nevada. With a Stroll through the Diggings and Ranches of that Country*, vol. 2 (London: Chapman and Hall, 1851), 25.

96    "Lynching on the Cosumnes," *Sacramento Transcript*, January 21, 1851.

97    Samuel McNeil, *McNeil's Travels in 1849, to, through, and from the Gold Regions in California* (Columbus: Scott & Bascom, 1850), 26.

98    In 1826, only Rhode Island did not yet have a penitentiary and therefore still applied corporal punishment including cropping (a piece of each ear cut off) and branding. *Annual Report of the Board of Managers of the Prison Discipline Society* (Boston: T. R. Marvin Congress Street, 1826), 19.

99    "Lynched," *Sacramento Transcript*, January 30, 1851. Letter Jacob H. Engle to brother in Jane Bissell Grabhorn, *A California Gold Rush Miscellany* (San Francisco: Grabhorn Press, 1934), 35–36.

100    "Another Case of Lynching," *Sacramento Transcript*, January 13, 1851. "Lynching on the Cosumnes River—Two Men Hung!" *Sacramento Transcript*, March 10, 1851. "Horse Stealing and Lynching," *Daily Alta California*, January 16, 1851. "Horse Stealing and Lynching," *Daily Alta California*, January 16, 1851. "More Lynching," *Sacramento Transcript*, May 30, 1851. "Lynch Law on the Mokelumne," *Sacramento Transcript*, January 8, 1851. "Another Branding," *Sacramento Transcript*, February 7, 1851.

101    "Lynched," *Sacramento Transcript*, January 30, 1851. Letter Jacob H. Engle to brother in Jane Bissell Grabhorn, *A California Gold Rush Miscellany* (San Francisco: Grabhorn Press, 1934), 35–36.

102    "More Lynching," *Sacramento Transcript*, May 30, 1851.

103    Theodore Dwight Weld, *American Slavery, as It Is: Testimony of a Thousand Witnesses* (New York: American Anti-Slavery Society, 1839), 152. In July 1838, a Mr. Micajah Ricks of Raleigh, North Carolina, offered a reward for a runaway slave, Betty. In the course of his description, he said, "I burnt her with a hot iron on the left side of her face. I tried to make the letter M."

104    "San Joaquin Intelligence. Lynching at Sonora," *Daily Alta California*, July 11, 1851.

105    "San Joaquin Intelligence. Lynching at Sonora," *Daily Alta California*, July 11, 1851.

106    "The District Court," *Sacramento Daily Union*, May 31, 1851.

107    "The Fremont Excitement," *Sacramento Transcript*, April 14, 1851.

108    Dame Shirley, *Letters*, 286.

## 10. The End of the Hangtown Oak

1    Mary Floyd Williams, *History of the San Francisco Committee of Vigilance of 1851*, 151.

2    Theodore H. Hittell, *History of California*, vol. 3 (San Francisco: N. J. Stone & Company, 1897), 292, first session of the court for Tuolumne county held at Sonora in July 1850. Courts came later to more distant parts of the mines. The first district court session in Downieville was July 5, 1853. Fariss and Smith, *Illustrated History of Plumas, Lassen & Sierra Counties*, 427.

3    Williams, *San Francisco Committee of Vigilance*, 142–147; see also Peter H. Burnett, *Recollection and Opinions of an Old Pioneer* (New York: D. Appleton, 1880), 386.

4    Williams, *San Francisco Committee of Vigilance*, 146–147.

5    Stephen Johnson Field, *Personal Reminiscences of Early Days in California* (San Francisco?: s.n., 1880), 33.

6    "Expenses of Witnesses in Criminal Cases," *Daily Alta California*, October 15, 1851.

7    "The Court of Sessions," *Marysville Herald*, April 15, 1851; Judge Haun was away, so the court would be adjourned from day to day until his return.

8    "Expenses of Witnesses in Criminal Cases," *Daily Alta California*, October 15, 1851.

9    "A Belgian in the Gold Rush: A Memoir by Dr. J. J.F. Haine," *California Historical Society Quarterly* 37 (1958): 311–346 at 330.

10    Letter Riley to Major General Jones in DC, August 30, 1849, Ser. 573, 31st Cong., 1st Sess., H. Ex. Doc. 17, 92. On the lack of jails as one of the causes of lynching, see Gordon Bakken, "The Courts, the Legal Profession, and the Development of Law in Early California" in John F. Burns and Richard J. Orsi, *Taming the Elephant: Politics, Government, and Law in Pioneer California* (Berkeley and Los Angeles: University of California Press, 2003), 74–95 at 75.

11    "Murderers of Smith and Foster," *Daily Alta California*, September 14, 1850.

12    "Flogging Criminals," *Sacramento Transcript*, March 6, 1851.

13    *Evening Picayune,* August 1850, quoted in Hubert Howe Bancroft, *Popular Tribunals,* vol. 1 (San Francisco: History Company, 1887), 130–131.

14    "San Francisco Correspondence," *Marysville Herald,* August 9, 1850.

15    Letter Charles Henri Doriot to brother Victor Doriot, July 12, 1851 (manuscript, Bancroft Library at MSS 85/70 C).

16    "Flogging Criminals" *Sacramento Transcript,* March 6, 1851.

17    Enos Christman, *One Man's Gold,* ed. Florence Morrow Christman (New York: Whittlesey House, McGraw-Hill, 1930), 203.

18    "Daring Robbery in Nevada," *Sacramento Daily Union,* April 2, 1851; "The Robbery at Nevada—Arrests," *Sacramento Transcript,* April 3, 1851.

19    "The Excitement at Nevada," *Sacramento Transcript,* April 5, 1851.

20    "Confession of the Nevada Robbery," *Sacramento Transcript,* April 7, 1851.

21    "Confession of the Nevada Robbery," *Sacramento Transcript,* April 7, 1851.

22    John Clark, "California Guide" (manuscript and transcript, Beinecke Library at WA MSS 83), entry for August 9, 1853.

23    Henry Vere Huntley, *California: Its Gold and its Inhabitants* (London: T. C. Newby, 1856), 136, describing events at Marysville, March 20, 1852.

24    Shubael Stowell, Diary (transcript, Beinecke Library catalogued at WA MSS S-1728), 22, entry for October 25, 1850. See also letter Ephraim Delano to wife (manuscript, Beinecke Library at WA MSS S-59 D374), entry for January 19, 1852.

25    Ezra Bourne, Journal (typescript, Bancroft Library at BANC MSS C-F 142), 32–33.

26    Charles H. Chamberlain, Statement, 1877 (manuscript, Bancroft Library at BANC MSS C-D 56), 2.

27    Huntley, *California,* 190–192.

28    "Serious Affray at Columbia—Great Excitement," *Daily Alta California,* November 12, 1853, 3. See also "Correspondence of the Union," *Sacramento Daily Union,* November 29, 1852.

29    William Defensor Thomas, *The Enemies of the Constitution Discovered, or, an Inquiry into the Origin and Tendency of Popular Violence . . . together with a Concise Treatise on the Practice of the Court of His Honor Judge Lynch* (New York: Leavitt, Lord, & Co., 1835), 48–53.

30    "The Sonoran Troubles," *Daily Alta California,* July 19, 1850.

31    "The Sonoran Troubles," *Daily Alta California,* July 19, 1850.

32    Herbert O. Lang and B. F. Alley, *A History of Tuolumne County, California* (San Francisco: B. F. Alley, 1882), 41; "The Sonoran Troubles," *Daily Alta California,* July 19, 1850, names Mr. Wm. Ford as the man who threw himself into the crowd and saved the prisoners.

33    Lang, *History of Tuolumne County*, 43–44.

34    "The Sonoran Troubles," *Daily Alta California*, July 19, 1850; Lang, *History of Tuolumme County*, 40.

35    Christman, *One Man's Gold*, 192.

36    Letter David G. Ferson to brother, Shaws Flats, California, July 10, 1851 (manuscript, Beinecke Library at WA MSS S-1315).

37    Christman, *One Man's Gold*, 193.

38    Christman, *One Man's Gold*, 194.

39    Letter David G. Ferson to brother, Shaws Flats, California, July 10, 1851 (manuscript, Beinecke Library at WA MSS S-1315).

40    "Arrest of Franklin Sanford," *Sacramento Daily Union*, July 1, 1851.

41    "Murder and Summary Execution of the Murderer.—Mokelumne Hill, April 12, 1852," *Sacramento Daily Union*, April 15, 1852.

42    "San Joaquin Intelligence," *Daily Alta California*, February 28, 1851.

43    Letter to the Editor, *Marysville Herald*, September 12, 1850.

44    Michael J. Pfeifer, *The Roots of Rough Justice: Origins of American Lynching* (Urbana, IL: University of Illinois Press, 2014), 13.

45    Richard Maxwell Brown, *Strain of Violence: Historical Studies of American Violence and Vigilantism* (New York: Oxford University Press, 1975), 113.

46    Pfeiffer, *Roots of Rough Justice*, 12–23. James H. Carson, *Early Recollections of the Mines, and a Description of the Great Tulare Valley* (Tarrytown, NY: W. Abbatt, 1931), 36.

47    David Goodman, *Gold Seeking: Victoria and California in the 1850s* (Stanford: Stanford University Press, 1994), 69.

48    Geoffrey Serle, *The Golden Age: A History of the Colony of Victoria, 1851–1861* (Melbourne: Melbourne University Press, 1963), 83.

49    George Henry Wathen, *The Golden Colony, or, Victoria in 1854* (London: Longman, Brown, Green, and Longmans, 1855), 139.

50    "Melbourne," *Geelong Advertiser and Intelligencer*, February 14, 1852, 2; also reported in "Late from Australia. Lynch Law in the Gold Mines!" *Sacramento Daily Union*, May 29, 1852.

51    *Sydney Morning Herald*, February 25, 1852, 2. Justice A'Beckett made his charge two weeks after the hanging, so it is likely that the rumor he heard was a garbled account of the event.

52    Adelbert Norton, *Life and Adventures of Col. L. A. Norton* (Oakland, CA: Pacific Press Publishing House, 1887), 291.

53    Norton, *Life and Adventures*, 293.

## 11. Massacring Indians and Ejecting Spanish Speakers

1    Josiah Royce, *California, from the Conquest in 1846 to the Second Vigilance Committee in San Francisco [1856] A Study of American Character* (Boston and New York: Houghton, Mifflin and Company, 1886), 277.

2    William W. Miller, "Voyage to California" (manuscript, Beinecke Library at WA MSS S-199), 102 (entry for October 21, 1849).

3    Benjamin Madley, *An American Genocide: The United States and the California Indian Catastrophe, 1846-1873* (New Haven: Yale University Press, 2016).

4    Madley, *American Genocide*, 88.

5    Sherburne F. Cook, "Historical Demography" in *Handbook of North American Indians*, vol. 8, ed. Robert F. Feizer (Washington: Smithsonian Institution, 1978), 91–93.

6    Madley, *American Genocide*, 85–93.

7    Albert L. Hurtado, "Clouded Legacy: California Indians and the Gold Rush," in Kenneth N. Owen, *Riches for All: The California Gold Rush and the World* (Lincoln: University of Nebraska Press, 2002), 90-117, at 92.

8    Hurtado, "Clouded Legacy," 104.

9    Hurtado, "Clouded Legacy," 104.

10    Hurtado, "Clouded Legacy," 105.

11    California Statutes 1850, Chapter 133, Section 20, in Kimberly Johnston-Dodds, "Early California Laws and Policies Related to California Indians" (Sacramento: California Research Bureau, 2002), 30; Madley, *American Genocide*, 159.

12    California Statutes 1850, Chapter 133, Section 3, in Johnston-Dodds, "Early California Laws," 28. See Madley, *American Genocide*, 158–159.

13    "An Act Amendatory of an Act Entitled 'An Act for the Government and Protection of Indians passed April 22, 1850'"; Johnston-Dodds, "Early California Laws," 35.

14    Madley, *American Genocide*, 151–160.

15    Henry Sturdivant, Journal (manuscript, Huntington Library at HM 261), 50–51, entry for July 2, 1851.

16    William Kelly, *An Excursion to California* (London: Chapman and Hall, 1851), 253–254.

17    Madley, *American Genocide*, 67–102.

18    Madley, *American Genocide*, 74–75. The Cayuse Indians, blaming the whites for infecting them with smallpox, had attacked a mission near what is now Walla Walla, Washington, setting off the Cayuse War.

19    William S. M'Collum, *California as I Saw It: Pencillings by the Way of Its Gold and Gold Diggers* (Los Gatos, CA: Tallisman Press, 1960, reprint of 1850 edition), 147–148. G. B. Stevens, Letters, July 1849 (manuscript, Beinecke Library at WA MSS S-12), 57. James L. Tyson, *Diary of a Physician in California* (New York: D. Appleton & Co.: Philadelphia, G. S. Appleton, 1850), 63.

20    Warren Sadler, Journal, vol. 2 (manuscript, Bancroft Library at BANC MSS C-F 73), entry for June 7, 1850.

21    John David Borthwick, *Three Years in California [1851–1854]* (Edinburgh and London: William Blackwood and Sons, 1857), 134.

22    Heinrich Lienhard, *A Pioneer at Sutter's Fort, 1846–1850*, trans. and ed. Marguerite Eyer Wilbur (Los Angeles: Calafia Society,1941), 182.

23    Indian Difficulties," *Daily Alta California*, January 1, 1851.

24    Rosales in Edwin A. Beilharz & Carlos U. López ed., *We Were 49ers! Chilean Accounts of the California Gold Rush* (Pasadena: Ward Ritchie Press, 1976), 74 (March or April 1849).

25    Alonzo Delano, *Life on the Plain and among the Diggings* (New York: Miller, Orton & Co., 1857), 312.

26    Theodore Taylor Johnson, *Sights in the Gold Region*, 153; see also letter Thos. B. Eastland, Bear River, June 15, 1850, to Governor H. Burnett, *Journals of the Legislature of the State of California at its Second Session*, vol. 2 (n.p.: Eugene Casserly, 1851), 770.

27    Delano, *Life on the Plains*, 311.

28    "The Governor's Message," *Sacramento Transcript*, January 10, 1851 (Governor's Annual Message to the Legislature Tuesday, January 7).

29    "Latest from the Mines," *Weekly Alta California*, April 26, 1849.

30    "Governor's Annual Message to the Legislature, January 7, 1851," *Journals of the Legislature of the State of California, Second Session* (n.p.: Eugene Casserly, 1851), 15; Alonzo Delano, who liked and admired his Indian neighbors, quoted the governor's words and had to agree (Delano, *Life on the Plains*, 320).

31    "Our Indian Policy," *Daily Alta California*, May 29, 1850.

32    Silas Weston, *Four Months in the Mines of California: Or, Life in the Mountains* (Providence: Benjamin T. Albro, 1854), 11–14.

33    Weston, *Four Months*, 11–14.

34    Weston, *Four Months*, 13.

35    Weston, *Four Months*, 15.

36    William Kelly, *Excursion*, 143–144.

37    William Kelly, *Excursion*, 144.

38    Fariss and Smith, *Illustrated History of Plumas, Lassen & Sierra Counties*, 213–214.

39    William Tell Parker, "Notes by the Way" (manuscript, Huntington Library at HM 30873), entry for December 8, 1850.

40    "American Manners and Customs," *Daily Alta California*, October 4, 1851.

41    Parker, "Notes by the Way" (manuscript, Huntington Library at HM 30873), 167–171, entry for November 5, 1851.

42    "Murder on Feather River," *Sacramento Daily Union*, November 18, 1851.

43    Clark, *California Guide* (manuscript and transcript, Beinecke Library at WA MSS 83), entry for April 30, 1854.

44    Daniel B. Woods, *Sixteen Months at the Gold Diggings* (New York: Harper & Brothers, 1851), 138.

45    María del Carmen Ferreyra and David S. Reher, eds., *The Gold Rush Diary of Ramón Gil Navarro* (Lincoln: University of Nebraska Press, 2000), 35.

46    Shirley Ann Wilson Moore, "'We Feel the Want of Protection': The Politics of Law and Race in California, 1848–1878" in *Taming the Elephant: Politics, Government, and Law in Pioneer California,* ed. John F. Burns and Richard J. Orsi (Berkeley: University of California Press, 2003), 96–125, at 108.

47    Intro to William Perkins, *Three Years in California*, 20; also, Jay Monaghan, *Chile, Peru, and the California Gold Rush of 1849* (Berkeley: University of California Press, 1973), 136–137.

48    Malcolm J. Rohrbough, "We Will Make Our Fortunes—No Doubt of It! The Worldwide Rush to California" in Kenneth Owens, *Riches for All* (Lincoln: University of Nebraska Press, 2002), 55–56.

49    John Boessenecker, *Gold Dust and Gunsmoke, Tales of Gold Rush Outlaws, Gunfighters, Lawmen, and Vigilantes* (New York: John Wiley & Sons, 1999), 148, quoting J. Ross Browne.

50    Ferreyra and Reher, eds., *Gold Rush Diary*, xiii.

51    Rosales in Beilharz and López, *We Were 49ers!*, 31.

52    Letter miner (signed "Robert") to his wife, Julia, May 1850 (manuscript, Huntington Library at HM 4166).

53    Woods, *Sixteen Months*, 159.

54    Joseph Warren Wood, *Diaries,* Huntington entry for October 17, 1850.

55    "Southern Mines—Races," *Sacramento Transcript*, August 6, 1850.

56    Hovey, *Journal*, 66, Middle Bar, Mokelmne River, October 25.

57    Rosales in Beilharz and Lopez, *We Were Forty-Niners!*, 46 (entry of March 1, 1849).

58    Charles De Lambertie, *Voyage Pittoresque en Californie et au Chili* (Paris: the author, 1853), 262–263.

59    Navarro in *We Were 49ers!*, 123.

60     On the lynching of Mexicans in America, see Carrigan and Webb, *Forgotten Dead* (2013); William Carrigan and Clive Web, "Repression and Resistance: The Lynching of Persons of Mexican Origin in the United States, 1848–1928," in Jose A. Cobas, Jorge Duany, and Joe R. Feagin, *How the United States Racializes Latinos: White Hegemony and Its Consequences* (New York: Routledge, 2016), 68 ff. These do not focus on the period 1848–1852 or compare the number or kind of lynchings of Mexicans, Chileans, etc. with those of American citizens.

61     "San Joaquin Correspondence," *Daily Alta California*, June 18, 1851.

62     The exception is that of the three Indians and a Mexican almost hanged for burning bodies discussed in Chapter 10. "The Sonoran Troubles," *Daily Alta California*, July 19, 1850.

63     "From California. More Lynch Law." *Richmond Times*, June 6, 1851, col. 6.

64     Navarro in *We Were 49ers!*, 117.

65     Hovey, *Journal*, 113, entry for July 13, 1850.

66     Dame Shirley, *Letters*, 257.

67     Dame Shirley, *Letters*, 227–228.

68     Letter David C. Ferson to brother, Shaws Flats, California, April 20, 1851 (manuscript, Beinecke Library at WA MSS S-1315).

69     "The Alta California and the Sonorian Troubles," *Alta California*, August 19, 1850.

70     "The Placer," *Placer Times*, July 21, 1849; *Alta California* of August 2, 1849, stated that the "desire to expel foreign 'vagrants' is very general." For more examples of early expulsions, see Hubert Howe Bancroft, *History of California*, vol. 6 (San Francisco: History Co., 1888) 404–405.

71     William Redmond Ryan, *Personal Adventures in Upper and Lower California, in 1848–9*, vol. 2 (London: W. Shoberl, 1850), 298.

72     "Governor's Special Message," *Daily Alta California*, April 25, 1852.

73     "Miners' Meeting in Nevada County," *Sacramento Daily Union*, May 7, 1852.

74     Rosales in Beilharz and López, *We Were 49ers!*, 68.

75     Bayard Taylor, *Eldorado, or, Adventures in the Path of Empire* (New York: G. P. Putnam, 1850), 87.

76     Ryan, *Personal Adventures*, 299.

77     Friedrich Gerstäcker, *Gerstäcker's Travels*, trans. from German (London and Edinburgh: T. Nelson and Sons, 1854), 234–235.

78     "San Joaquin Intelligence," *Daily Alta California*, July 29, 1850. The same article reports similar resolutions passed at Mormon Gulch.

79     Gerstäcker, *Travels*, 236.

80    An exception: "Anarchy and Revolution. Expulsion of all Foreigners from the Mines!—Tremendous Excitement!" *Sacramento Transcript*, July 29, 1850: the miners of Mormon Camp resolved "that all Mexicans and South Americans be banished from this Township within one week."

81    Gerstäcker, *Travels*, 234.

82    Ryan, *Personal Adventures*, 296.

83    "The Sonora Troubles," *Alta California*, August 15, 1850.

84    Gerstäcker, *Travels*, 224.

85    Gerstäcker, *Travels*, 225.

86    Quoted in Perkins, *Three Years in California*, 31.

87    G. B. Stevens, Letters (manuscript, Beinecke Library at WA MSS S-12), typescript 57 (July 1849).

88    G. B. Stevens, Letters, typescript 57. See also "San Joaquin Intelligence," *Daily Alta California*, July 29, 1850.

89    Taylor, *El Dorado*, vol. I, 102.; William Redmond Ryan, *Personal Adventures*, 297.

90    William Ryan, *Personal Adventures*, vol. II, 396 ff.

91    "Order Reigns in Warsaw," *Daily Alta California*, August 15, 1850; "The Sonoran Troubles," *Daily Alta California*, August 9, 1850; "American Manners and Customs," *Daily Alta California*, October 4, 1851.

92    "The Overland Immigration—The Mormons," *Daily Alta California*, May 28, 1851.

93    "San Joaquin Intelligence," *Daily Alta California*, July 29, 1850.

94    "Miners' Meeting in Nevada County," *Sacramento Daily Union*, May 7, 1852.

95    De Lambertie, *Voyage Pittoresque*, 259–261.

96    Bancroft, *History of California*, vol. 6, 404, n65, notes a third instance of Americans overruling the decision to banish Mexicans, reported in the Marysville Directory, 1858, 25–26. I have not been able to find this volume.

97    "From Stockton," *Sacramento Transcript*, August 10, 1850; also reproduced in Upham, *Notes of a Voyage* (Philadelphia: the author, 1878), 328–329.

98    "Order Reigns in Warsaw," *Daily Alta California*, August 15, 1850.

99    Gerstäcker, *Travels*, 225.

100   Another example of opposition—too little and too late—followed the July 21, 1850, meeting at Sonora to expel foreigners. Heckendorn and Wilson, *Miners' and Business Men's Directory* (Columbia: Clipper Office, 1856), 43.

101   "The Alta California and the Sonorian Troubles," *Alta California*, August 19, 1850. Ryan, *Personal Adventures*, 297.

102    Ryan, *Personal Adventures*, 297.

103    *The Statutes of California Passed at the First Session of the Legislature* (San Jose: J. Winchester, State Printer, 1850), Chapter 97, 221–223.

104    Heckendorn and Wilson, *Miners' and Business Men's Directory*, 6.

105    Bancroft, *History of California*, vol. 6, 406 n73.

106    California Assembly Journal, 1849–1850, Session, 802.

107    "San Joaquin Intelligence," *Daily Alta California*, August 7, 1850.

108    "Latest from Stockton," *Daily Alta California*, June 4, 1850 (reprinted from an article in the *Stockton Times*, June 1, 1850).

109    "Repeal of the Foreign Miners' Tax Law," *Daily Alta California*, March 20, 1851. The repeal happened on March 14, 1851.

110    Bancroft, *History of California*, vol. 6, 406. The tax raised only $29, 991 in the fiscal year 1850–1851. Ibid., 406 n73.

111    "San Joaquin Intelligence: From Sonora," *Daily Alta California*, August 12, 1850.

112    Hovey, *Journal*, 122, Red Bluff Bar, Tuolemne River, September 30, 1850.

113    Heckendorn and Wilson, *Miners and Business Mens' Directory*, 43.

114    "Sonora—Disturbances in the Mines," *Daily Alta California*, May 27, 1850. This is reprinted in Perkins, *Three Years*, 397–400; for Leo as Perkin's alias see ibid., 395.

115    "Sonora—Disturbances in the Mines," *Daily Alta California*, May 27, 1850 (letter dated May 19).

116    "Sonora—Disturbances in the Mines," *Daily Alta California*, May 27, 1850.

117    "Sonora—Disturbances in the Mines," *Daily Alta California*, May 27, 1850.

118    Emmett P. Joy Mimeograph, February 14, 1962, Bancroft Library at F 869 M68 J6 (a compilation of historical documents), includes a copy of this letter, said to be in the library of the California Historical Society.

119    "Effects of the Tax on Foreign Miners—The Memorial from Stockton," *Daily Alta California*, June 4, 1850.

120    Hovey, *Historical Account*; James J. Ayers, *Gold and Sunshine* (Boston: R. G. Badger, c1922), 46–58.

121    Ramón Gil Navarro, *California in 1849* (1853), reprinted in Beilharz and López *We Were 49ers!*, 116–164. See also newspaper accounts: "The Disturbance at the Mines," *Daily Alta California*, January 2, 1850; "The Chilean Disturbance," *Daily Alta California*, January 7, 1850; "The Disturbance at the Mines," *Placer Times*, January 19, 1850.

122    Hovey, *Historical Account*, 6.

123    Hovey, *Historical Account*, 6.

124   Hovey, *Historical Account,* 5–6.

125   "San Joaquin Intelligence," *Daily Alta California,* July 29, 1850.

126   "San Joaquin Intelligence," *Daily Alta California,* March 21, 1851.

127   Bancroft, *History of California,* vol. 6, 404 n65.

128   Taylor, *Eldorado,* 87.

129   Woods, *Sixteen Months,* 159.


## 12. Outside Capital and the End of the Gold Rush

1   "Speech of Mr. Benton, of Missouri, "On the Adjudication of Land Titles, and Sale of Gold Mines in New Mexico and California, Delivered in the Senate of the United States, January 15, 1849," *Weekly Alta California,* September 6, 1849, 1.

2   Maureen A. Jung, "Capitalism Comes to the Diggings: From Gold-Rush Adventure to Corporate Enterprise" in *A Golden State: Mining and Economic Development in Gold Rush California,* eds. James J. Rawls and Richard J. Orsi (Berkeley, CA: University of California Press, 1999), 52–77 at 53.

3   John Bidwell, *Echoes of the Past about California,* and John Steel, *In Camp and Cabin* (Chicago: Lakeside Press, R.R. Donnelley & Sons Co., 1928), 203–204, writing in March 1851.

4   J. G. Player-Frowd, *Six Months in California* (London: Longmans, Green, and Co., 1872), 91.

5   Donald J. Pisani, *To Reclaim a Divided West: Water, Law, and Public Policy, 1848–1902* (Albuquerque: University of New Mexico Press, 1992), 16–17, n20.

6   Pisani, *To Reclaim a Divided West,* 16–17; Mark Kanazawa, *Golden Rules: The Origins of California Water Law in the Gold Rush* (Chicago: University of Chicago Press, 2015), 93.

7   Dame Shirley (Louise Clappe), *The Shirley Letters from California Mines in 1851–52* (San Francisco: T. C. Russell, 1922), 217. Letter, Indian Bar, April 10, 1852.

8   "From Marysville," *Sacramento Daily Union,* July 11, 1851.

9   Frank Marryat, *Mountains and Molehills; or, Recollections of a Burnt Journal* (New York: Harper & Brothers, 1855), 272.

10   Donald J. Pisani, *Water, Land, and Law in the West: The Limits of Public Policy, 1850–1920* (Lawrence, KS: University Press of Kansas, 1996), 7–12; Pisani, *To Reclaim a Divided West,* 11–32; Kanazawa, *Golden Rules,* 150–156, 183–216.

11   Tuolumne County Records, 1850–1927 (manuscripts, Bancroft Library at BANC MSS C-A 152), Folder 7. See also Placer County Records v. 1 Mining Notices, 1850–1856 (manuscript, Bancroft library BANC MSS C-A 293).

12    Placer County Records V. 1 Mining Notices, 1850–1856 (manuscript, Bancroft Library at MSS C-A 293), 136 (dated October 25, 1852).

13    See Pisani, *Water, Land, and Law,* 8–10, noting that rights based on prior appropriation appeared in New England in the early nineteenth century under different circumstances.

14    "Miners' Meeting at Ophir," *Sacramento Daily Union,* January 25, 1854.

15    But see David Schorr, *The Colorado Doctrine* (New Haven: Yale University Press, 2012), showing that, in Colorado, the doctrine of prior appropriation was used to spread the benefits of water diversion as widely as possible.

16    Gregory Yale, *Legal Titles to Mining Claims and Water Rights in California, Under the Mining Law of Congress, of July 1866* (San Francisco: A. Roman, 1867), 60.

17    See King, *United States Mining Laws,* 286 (Oregon Gulch Mining District, December 29, 1855).

18    King, *United States Mining Laws,* 277 (Yuba County Mining Laws Resolution 10, April 11, 1852). Upper Yuba: Snake Bar and all above, embracing the North and South Forks of Yuba River. Resolution 10. See also Laws of Little Humbug Creek, April 8, 1856, in King, *United States Mining Laws,* 291: "[t]hat no person or persons shall be allowed to divert the waters by a ditch or otherwise from Little Humbug to the prejudice of the miners working on the Stream." Pisani, *To Reclaim a Divided West,* 24 (miners' resolutions at Vallecito Camp and Diamond Springs prohibiting companies from diverting water to the detriment of miners downstream).

19    "Mining Intelligence," *Daily Alta California,* February 10, 1855.

20    Miners of Hoit's Divide, miles away from the nearest water source, passed their own resolutions asking the legislature to protect the water companies' interests—and by extension their own—by enacting a "law that shall establish and substantiate the right of priority of survey, occupancy and use." "Miner's Meeting—El Dorado County," *Sacramento Daily Union,* February 18, 1854.

21    Douglas R. Littlefield, "Water Rights during the California Gold Rush: Conflicts over Economic Points of View," *Western Historical Quarterly* 14 (1983): 415–434 at 425.

22    Littlefield, "Water Rights," 425.

23    Littlefield, "Water Rights," 425.

24    Siskiyou County: Little Humbug Creek Mining District, April 8, 1856, in King, *United States Mining Laws,* 291: Art 8th.

25    Perry Gee's Journal of Travels across the Plains to California: Directed to Sarah Ann Gee, Geneva, Ashtabula Co., Ohio, 1852–1853 (manuscript, Bancroft Library at WA MSS 213), entry for January 13, 1853.

26    Dame Shirley, *Letters,* 218, April 10, 1852.

27    Pisani, *To Reclaim a Divided West*, 25 on elected judges.

28    Littlefield, "Water Rights," 426.

29    Pisani, *Water, Land, and Law*, 30–35.

30    Shuck, *History of the Bench and Bar of California* (Los Angeles, CA: Commercial Printing House, 1901), 361.

31    John Carr, *Pioneer Days in California* (Eureka, CA: Times Publishing, 1891), 255.

32    John Carr, *Pioneer Days*, 255–257.

33    Miners Meeting, Trinity County, Weaverville Mining District, June 7, 1853, in King, *United States Mining Laws*, 276.

34    Pisani, *Water, Land, and Law*, 33.

35    Shuck, *History of the Bench and Bar*, 362.

36    John David Borthwick, *Three Years in California [1851-1854]* (Edinburgh and London: William Blackwood and Sons, 1857), 302.

37    Pisani, *Water, Land, and Law*, 25.

38    Herbert O. Lang, *History of Tuolumne County* (San Francisco: B. F. Alley, 1882), 100, notes that Tuolumne County Water Company was incorporated in 1851; "South Fork Canal Company," *Sacramento Daily Union*, September 14, 1852, reports the sums raised for that project.

39    "From the Interior," *Sacramento Daily Union*, November 29, 1852.

40    Franklin Buck, *Yankee Trader*, 127, letter of August 20, 1853.

41    Quoted in Pisani, *To Reclaim a Divided West*, 21.

42    "Meeting of Miners in Butte County," *Sacramento Daily Union*, December 11, 1857.

43    Pisani, *Water, Land, and Law*, 25.

44    "Valuable Stock," *Sacramento Daily Union*, September 12, 1853.

45    "Tuolumne County," *Sacramento Daily Union*, May 3, 1854. Pisani, *To Reclaim a Divided West*, 19, mentions a dividend of 42 percent per month.

46    Franklin Buck, *Yankee Trader*, 127, letter of August 20, 1853.

47    Littlefield, "Water Rights," 427–428.

48    Littlefield, "Water Rights," 428.

49    "Water Companies, Canals, Mining, the Cosumnes and Deer Creek Canal," *Sacramento Daily Union*, May 4, 1854.

50    Pisani, *Water, Land, and Law*, 24–31.

51    Barbara Eastman, "The Journal of John Jolly," *Chispa: The Quarterly of the Tuolumne County Historical Society* 5, no. 3 (1966): 161n142, quoting a letter

from John Wallace, superintendent of the Tuolumne County Eater Company, January 10, 1853, to relatives in England.

52      Littlefield, "Water Rights," 423.

53      "The Riot in Calaveras," *San Joaquin Republican*, August 9, 1856.

54      "The Miners on a Strike—Three Thousand Miners in Council," *Daily Alta California*, March 17, 1855. See Pisani, *Water, Land, and Law*, 26n12, on miners' strikes against private water companies.

55      The Miners on a Strike—Three Thousand Miners in Council," *Daily Alta California*, March 17, 1855.

56      Rich Gulch Butte County, Laws of May 22, 1852, in King, *United States Mining Laws*, Resolution 9.

57      "Laws of Ohio Flat District," Sect. IV; King, *United States Mining Laws*, 289.

58      "The Miners on a Strike—Three Thousand Miners in Council," *Daily Alta California*, March 17, 1855.

59      Pisani, *Water, Land, and Law*, 27.

60      Pisani, *Water, Land, and Law*, 28.

61      *Robert's Rules* (2000) (note 3), xxxv.

## Conclusion

1      King, *United States Mining Laws*, 279.

2      John David Borthwick, *Three Years in California [1851-1854]* (Edinburgh and London: William Blackwood and Sons, 1857), 369.

## ACKNOWLEDGMENTS

I have been working on law in the California gold rush for twenty years and am grateful to have had the help of many institutions and colleagues. The first and kindest of these was John Phillip Reid at New York University Law School, who allowed me to spend weeks consulting his copious notes for a book on gold rush law that he had abandoned.

Fortunately for me, the unpublished letters and journals from the gold rush are concentrated in three wonderful libraries with knowledgeable and helpful staff. An acquaintance once called the Beinecke Rare Book Library at Yale "a spa for academics," and it is indeed the most wonderful place for research. I was especially lucky that the Beinecke supported my work there with the Archibald Hanna, Jr. Visiting Fellowship. The beautiful Huntington Library in Pasadena is useful and enjoyable with its vibrant community of scholars. I thank Peter Blodgett, especially, for help and encouragement during my stay; and Morex Arai and Hector Acosta for supplying the images I needed. Finally, the Bancroft Library at the University of California, Berkeley, has unique ties to the gold rush and a tirelessly supportive staff. The most pleasant and helpful part of my stay there was time spent with Donald Pisani, who provided encouragement and guidance for my work.

I was extremely lucky, also, to spend my sabbatical year at the Vere Harmsworth Library in Oxford, UK, with its comprehensive collection of gold rush publications on open shelves. The Rothermere American Institute, which houses the Vere Harmsworth, generously made me a senior research fellow during my stay with dining rights at Somerville College. I am extremely grateful to Nigel Bowles, director at the time, for including me in the lively community at the Rothermere. The Rothermere has remained a home away from home ever since.

I was honored and grateful to be made a Guggenheim Fellow for 2016–2017, which enabled me to spend a second period of research at the Vere Harmsworth.

This project would not have gotten off the ground, let alone landed, without the generosity of multiple universities. The University of Wisconsin enabled me to spend two years of intensive research as the J. Willard Hurst Fellow. Arthur McEvoy was a good friend and guide during that time. A yearlong Irving S. Ribicoff Fellowship at Yale Law School provided the time and resources for more research. James Q. Whitman and Robert Gordon were great counselors and friends during that time.

I most especially thank the deans and my colleagues at Seton Hall Law School for support, moral and financial, in the long time it took me to complete this work. They have been both patient and appropriately pressing during that time.

Finally, I am deeply grateful to Elizabeth Knoll, who has given invaluable guidance, practical help with the manuscript, and encouragement throughout the project. I am also indebted to James Q. Whitman for providing feedback on the criminal law chapters. And I give sincere thanks to two anonymous reviewers whose slightly painful but accurate insights goaded me into making this a better book.

# INDEX

Alcaldes, 35–46; biased against
Spanish speakers, 43–45;
criminal trials, 45–46; elections
not taken seriously, 42–43;
outrageous verdicts, 43;
Spanish-speakers' opinion of,
44–45; storekeepers, 41–42;
towns, 36–40. *See also indi-*
*vidual alcaldes by name*
Anti-monopoly sentiment, 74–76
Australian gold rush, 47–49, 63, 144,
204–207

Bagley, Will, 23
Balsam Lake, MN, citizen trial, 135
Bardt, Dr., lynch trial, 123–124, 169,
175
Benin gold rush, 78
Bigler, Henry, 22, 23, 26
Black miners (free), 120–121
Bonner, Thomas D., Justice of the
Peace, Plumas, 45
Borthwick, John D.: Americans as
organizers, 259; French miners,
110; Indians, 212; lynch law, 129;
meetings, 9–11; miners' court,
115; mining rules, 65, 67; wage
labor, 80; water companies, 252
Brannan, Samuel, 23–28, 53, 142
Brazil gold rush, 77–78, 99
Brown, "Judge," alcalde, 41

Brown, Richard Maxwell, 126–127,
140, 204
Buffum, Edward Gould: early mining
claims, 30–33; Indian miners,
54–56, 58; no scope for capital,
81–82; punishments 176, 177,
178; sentencing 174
Burnett, Peter H.: as governor 3, 214,
235, 237; as miner, 32

Canada: suppressed miners' meet-
ings, 63–64
Capital investment: few opportuni-
ties, 81–82; hostility toward, 64,
74–76, 251–257
Carrigan, William, 125, 204; and
Clive Webb, 130
Carson, James H., 33, 44, 46, 95,
158
Chicken, roasted live, 139
Chileans, 87, 152, 221, 224
Chilean War. *See* Iowa Log Cabins
incident
Chinese mining company, 110
Claim clubs, 71
Claim disputes: arbitration, 89–90;
fighting, 85–87, 98
Claims: jumping, 66, 88, 92–94;
number, 70–71; one claim rule,
98; requirements, 65, 69–71;
rule bending, 95–100

**323**

www.ingramcontent.com/pod-product-compliance
Lightning Source LLC
Chambersburg PA
CBHW021830090426
42811CB00032B/2095/J